1

AUTOBIOGRAPHY OF ROBERT EVANS

TUCSON

"You'd better tell me the truth lady or I'll have to take you in and charge you. We'll find out what took place here so you might as well tell me right now what happened."

In my half sleep, drowsy condition, I thought I was dreaming because those words sounded like something I might have heard in a second rate crime movie. But I wasn't dreaming and now I was half awake. I looked through the curtain of the window facing our porch. Across our small lawn I saw an ambulance. The morning was still and quiet because it was early and then I remembered it was Sunday.

"What's going on?" My words joined me as I slid out of bed and started for the closed door. My sister JoAnn and my brother Art stopped me. My stomach turned cold.

"Don't go in there," commanded my brother who was five and a half years older than me.

"Keep Bobby in there," I heard my mother say from the other room. Her voice was tense.

"Just stay here and we'll tell you in a few minutes about what's happening," my sister said in a calming tone. She was seven years older. I listened to my older sister and brother but now I was frightened.

I returned to the window and saw a sheriff's car behind the ambulance in the long drive way. Our house was behind a larger home almost an afterthought in comparison to the bigger one in front of ours. The neighbors were out on the driveway behind the sheriff's car in bathrobes and speaking in hushed tones. One was pointing at our house.

I heard my mother crying softly and then a different man's voice with a comforting timbre was saying, "I'll take it from here deputy."

I turned back to my sister and she had her finger to her lips telling me to be quiet.

"I whispered urgently, "What happened?" My look was insistent and demanding.

My brother spoke, "Daddy Bob died."

3

A few, long minutes later I heard the creaking of the gurney leaving our porch and moving across the grass toward the ambulance. I ran to the window and saw a rounded form covered with a white sheet. It wasn't the first time I had seen a dead body but now I knew Daddy Bob was under it.

"I just felt him sneeze a couple of times at least that's what I thought it was. It was a kind of jerk. Then I thought he had just gone back to sleep. Then early this morning I rolled over and touched him and he was cool and rigid," my mother was explaining to the lawman in our living room. "I shook him and he didn't move. I was startled and jumped up and then I looked at him and knew he'd died.

Now I was hearing every word my mother said.

"Don't worry Mrs. Maxwell I believe you." This voice was comforting with understanding. We'll take him to the morgue and when you're ready, have a mortician contact us for further arrangements.

It was Easter Sunday, 1946 and I was one month shy of my eighth birthday.

IDAHO FALLS

The year before this happened I heard my mother say, "I do," in the living room on my Grandfather's house in Idaho Falls, Idaho. The ceremony was small with just my grandparents, my sister and brother, and a few of my mother's friends. It was April, 1945 and this was her second marriage. Bob Maxwell was marrying my mother. He had come home from World War II, a sailor with a heart condition. He had been mustered out and would later receive money from the G. I. Bill to retrain for a new skill that didn't require a lot of physical effort. He was tall, six feet two inches, slim, angular, with an olive complexion. His face looked like Eugene O'Neill's although it didn't register with me until I was an adult and learned who Eugene O'Neill was and what he looked like. His face was narrow, with low eyebrows, sunken eyes dark and hard, and a black moustache that was close to his nose, then sloped down to the corners of his mouth, and was close to his upper lip. He wore a dark suit on this his wedding day with a white shirt, and a blue necktie. When he said, "I do," he became my stepfather.

My mother was five feet four inches, with auburn hair mid-length, hazel eyes, nicely figured, freckled, had high cheek bones, a happy smile with a gap between her two front teeth, a joyful spirit, and she was 39 years old on this day of the uniting ceremony. Her wedding dress was off white, plain, with a red rose pinned above her left breast. She seemed pleased at the moment because her life was headed in a new direction and this day symbolized that change.

Bob Maxwell was to be the first father I would know since I had no memory of my biological father. Descriptions of him, Tom Evans, came from relatives and friends.

My mother and real father had met in Pocatello, Idaho. He was a reporter for a small newspaper and she was in a nurses training program. The romance was torrid and when they were married in 1930 my mother dropped out of the nursing program to become a good Mormon stay-at-home wife. My dad was a Mormon too, but of limited commitment, falling into the category of a "Jack Mormon," where drinking and limited church attendance was the regimen of ecclesiastical faithfulness. My sister was born eight and half months later in Pocatello and my brother followed 20 months after her in Hollister, California.

My father was the editor of the small Hollister newspaper and when prohibition was ended by the 21st Amendment he found smoking, drinking, and partying to be a delightful routine. He was well liked and my mother was contently happy to be his wife and companion. She had a wonderful openness to her and she laughed easily. They were happy together.

"It was the happiest time of my life," she would say later.

My father's career progressed to San Francisco where he was at various times a reporter, a public relations director for the Ice Capades and did public relations for the Golden Gate International Exposition on the newly formed Treasure Island in San Francisco Bay.

It was in San Francisco in May of 1938 that I was born during a stormy time in my parent's marriage. I'm told my father enjoyed long days and nights of work and partying where he met

5

interesting men and particularly fascinating women who found him charming. He had dark hair, big blue eyes, a deeply timbered voice, and a gift for compelling and entertaining conversation. He found beautiful women irresistibly indispensable.

"Take the baby, save the mother," my father emphatically instructed the doctors at St. Joseph's Hospital as he paced outside the delivery room. I was huge compared to other unborn infants and turned in an awkward position in my mother's birth canal. Forceps were used inside my mother and when I finally entered the outside world I was almost 10 pounds and destined to be a sickly child.

"Shut that damned kid up or I'm going to smack him," my Father shouted at my mom.

My father's frustration came as a result of my medical misery. I had allergies that caused asthma. My skin was ablaze with eczema. Pneumonia came twice calling. After 14 months of my existence, my father had had enough of married life. His job and partying was exciting and his home life was boring, irritable, and annoying.

Years later I asked my sister JoAnn what happened during the breakup of my parent's marriage.

"I overheard our mom and dad arguing and our father said that he wanted to take a break from the marriage. Mom was irritated and asked what he meant by that. He said he needed a quiet house to come home to, I can't concentrate. Mom was tense and sensed that things were falling apart and pleaded for them to work things out. I remember her saying that dad was rarely home because of his work and other activities and said that he didn't do anything with us, his children. He wanted us to go to Utah and live with his parents. He wanted time alone to think about where things were going between them. He kept saying that he would take care of us."

So that's what happened. He stayed in San Francisco but sent us packing to American Fork, Utah to stay with his parents where we lived and depended on them for our existence. He sent no money despite my mother's pleas for some "dough re me," a phrase I read in a letter my mother wrote to my father that somehow survived down through the years.

6

"We moving back to Idaho Falls to stay with my folks," finally pronounced my mother. I can't stay here if your son won't send us money and at least my folks will take care of us and we won't be a burden to you."

"I'm sorry Bernice that Tom isn't sending support for you. I've tried to call him and he promises to send money but it never comes," my grandmother told my mom. "We feel terrible about this and want to help but we are strapped for money as well. This damned depression is hard on everybody and we are no exception."

Mom shared this conversation with me many years later when I inquired as to why things didn't work out between them.

My father's family bought bus tickets for the journey and we arrived there with my Mother a single parent with three kids, no skills, and no money.

I was four years old then and World War II had begun. My father entered military service doing public relations work in the east bay near Oakland. He did not fight on any war front.

When I was an adult my brother Art related what happened when we arrived in Idaho Falls, Idaho.

"What are you going to do, Bernice?" Art explained. Grandma Harris was demandingly asking. I remembered her because I stayed with my grandparents for a while before starting first grade. She looked like a picture Grant Wood's American Gothic, puritanical, a face with no makeup, and unsympathetic.

Our mother began crying, "I don't know," Art stated empathetically.

"Well, you made your bed, now you'll have to lay in it," our grandmother's voice came with a tone of finality, my brother said as he described the situation.

What my mother did was pray and then reach down inside her inner core and made a decision. Idaho Falls was a Mormon community and my mom asked the parishioners in the church ward to help her find work. Since she had no real skills, only housework was offered. She got down on her hands and knees and scrubbed floors to make what little money she could. Her parents let us stay with them. Mom saved just enough money to go to cosmetology

7

school and became a beautician. However, it took months but she persevered and got through.

She got a job in a hair dressing salon and over the next two years became the manager. My brother and sister entered Eagle Rock Elementary school and I was a ward of my grandparents. My American Gothic grandmother made me pray before every meal and before every nap, I was too young to pronounce the word "religious" but I told her she was too "leerigious." My grandfather reminded me of Wallace Beery, a loveable old guy with a warm heart. He was Mormon but had a proclivity to take a drink and sometimes drank for two weeks, lost jobs, and endured the wrath of grandma American Gothic.

"Melvin, have you been drinking again," I would hear her say.

"No, I haven't so don't ask again," I could hear his unconvincing words in the air as he trailed away to another part of the house avoiding my grandmother.

Even I could tell he had been drinking because I could smell Sen Sen, the licorice tasting breath shield. In my grandfather's case, it was a tell-tale giveaway that he had a drink somewhere downtown.

Grandpa was a musician and had a musician's spirit. He could play piano, violin, drums, and the trumpet. He gave music lessons to supplement a meager family income. In Portage, Utah early in his marriage, he had a general store and taught Native Americans how to play music and created a band. They used to call him B Flat because that was the key in which he always played his music. It was also at that store where my mother, as a child, stole a tribesman's horse and rode away for a joy ride for a short time. She came back with the horse and all was forgiven after apologies and assurances were given that it wouldn't happen again.

"Grandpa, can I nap with you?" I would beg because I didn't want to snooze with grandma. I knew he would say yes and that I wouldn't have to pray before lying down. Also, grandpa always told me a story about his days as a farmer and sheep herder.

"It was winter and shhhhheeeewwww was it cold," he began most stories and went on to tell how hard life was when he was a boy or as a young man in the cold, unforgiving midwinter in Idaho.

8

Grandpa would also take me out to a garden plot and we would plant potatoes. He would open a hole in the ground and I would drop into it, part of a cut up Idaho Spud. I bragged that I only made one mistake by dropping in two pieces instead of one.

When I turned six I was enrolled in first grade in Miss Nick's class.

"If you behave properly I will give you a good card," she instructed the class. I did my best to be good most days and saved my "good cards" so I could trade them in for a prize.

"Tell the class Bobby what you want with your good cards and why you want it."

I was standing before 25 or so pair of eyes.

"I want that wooden piggy bank," I said. "I want it because I want to save my money and buy War Bond." However, at six years of age and my mom barely surviving financially, I never came close to saving enough for a war bond and I knew that when I said it.

It was 1944 and the World War II was raging in Europe and Asia and I began to follow the battles on the radio. Since I was now in school I was allowed to see movies on the weekend. My brother Art who was eleven years of age, sometimes worked in a bowling alley setting pins and he shared his earnings by buying movie tickets for me.

It seemed each time we went to the movies old Bill Pointer would come in. He had a disability and didn't work. I guessed his age to be in the thirties. He was tall, dark haired, wiry, wore glasses, "to see crooks better," and had a mental incapacity. He said he was a policeman and was a crime fighter. He wasn't of course, but everyone in town went along with his disillusion. He would walk up to the theatre ticket window and say he had to go inside to look for crooks. The owner of the theatre instructed his employees to allow him in and to play along. He would enter the darkened room and walk down the aisles and in front of the screen and then settle into seat in the back row and watch the movie and protect us from the "crooks.
He always saw movies in the day time.

Bill Pointer eternally wore blue clothing to emulate the color of a policeman's uniform. At least that was my guess. He had a fake badge anyone could have bought at a dime store and a fake pistol. He walked most places but sometimes rode a bicycle.

One day I was walking down a sidewalk and saw Bill riding his bike heading my way.

"Get out of the way, I'm looking for crooks," he shouted at he approached me. I guess I didn't move fast enough and he ran me over and left a knot the size of a pellet on the front of my hairline that I still carry even today.

Some of the kids in Idaho Falls used to tease and pester Bill Pointer about not being a policeman. He reacted verbally and emotionally saying he was going to arrest them. The taunting went on. Then Bill was given tips as to where to look for crooks in other parts of town. Often it was enough to have him leave the area and end the taunting.

I never teased Bill because I thought it was cruel and unfair that an impaired person should be treated so insensitively. I didn't know if Bill knew me or not or whether he ran me over because he thought I was one of the kids that tormented him. I didn't take his crashing into me personally but feeling the pain of the crash made me stay out of his way in the future, even in the movies.

The shows we saw were always war movies with a familiar plot. The Americans were the good guys and the Germans and "Japs" were the bad guys. There was always it seemed, a young soldier commonly called "the kid" whom the veterans tried to shelter before a battle. He always got wounded or killed, a sorrow felt by all of the viewing audience that called for a violent retribution from his fellow soldiers on the dreaded enemy and the screen writers patronizingly found hundreds of ways to deliver it.

Another popular scene would show an officer from the one of the branches of the military knocking on the door of a perfectly kept cottage type home with a white picket fence back in America. The knock would be answered by a middle aged matronly woman. The officer would ask if she was the Mother of William Smith and she would say yes and invite the officer in.

"I'm afraid I have bad news Mrs. Smith, on behalf of the President of the United States I regret to inform you that your son William was heroically killed in action defending his country in the Pacific Theatre."

Then from another room would enter a beautiful younger woman who would inquire as to what had happened. It would be Billy's sister. When she learned of her brother's death she would try to console her mother who was now uncontrollably sobbing.

After a few moments the officer would try to excuse himself and begin to leave whereupon the lovely sister would stop him and insist that he stay for dinner because, "Billy would have wanted you to stay."

After dinner the officer and the sister would take a walk and somehow make a romantic connection. But duty still called and the officer had to leave the next morning to go back to battle at the front. Somehow a promise was made by the sister to wait for his return and when he did finally come back from the war, whether wounded or in good health, was reunited with the Billy's sister who is now his promised fiancé and they marry and live happily ever after.

In these movies, everyone was called upon to make a sacrifice for the betterment of the war effort. Individual desires were subjugated by using the phrase, "Don't you know there's a war on?"

I once found a silver dollar and my friends wanted me to spend it on them. Root beer was a nickel then, so it would have been easy to spring for drinks all around. In our Mormon community caffeine intake was discouraged so root beer was the preferred soft drink. But I had other plans. I went down to the war surplus store and bought a Helmut that looked like the kind our soldiers were wearing. I hoped it would protect me from an attack by our enemies. As an adult looking back on that time, I realized that attack on Idaho Falls was about as remote as me a six-year old boy, attacking Tokyo. But as a child I had been indoctrinated by movies and other media to believe that I had made a wise purchase.

One of my friends was Jimmy Brown and we all loved Jimmy because he would always be the bad guy when we played out kid's games; the Indian in cowboys and Indians, the German when we played war, and the robber when we played cops and robbers. One day another friend Ned, was given a bow and arrow set for his birthday and we told Jimmy climb up a tree that was nearby and he would be the wild game while the new owner of the bow and arrow set would be the hunter. Jimmy dutifully climbed up the tree. We kids stepped back several yards, maybe 40 or so and Ned let an arrow fly toward the tree. Jimmy tumbled out of the tree screaming and hit the ground. We thought Jimmy had really outdone himself in fulfilling his role as wild game but then we saw he had an arrow stuck between his cheek bone and his eye socket. We ran up to Jimmy and pulled the arrow out of his head. But his scream brought Ned's dad out of the house and when he saw what had happened to Jimmy, he took the bow and arrows away from Ned and broke them over his knee. Thankfully Jimmy did not lose his eye and he continued to be our best bad guy friend when we played our games.

Food was rationed as was gasoline, tires, and most other things during the war. We didn't have a car but like everyone else, we had a ration book.

"Art, where's the ration book?" My mother desperately questioned my brother.

"I don't have it, I must have lost it."

"Come here, Art," my mother said as she took out a piece of wood from the wood pile next to our coal burning cooking stove. She hit him on his back side four or five times and he cried out.

"You are never to take a ration book again. Now we can't buy food. Damn you."

The next few days became another humiliating time for my mother because she had to go begging for ration stamps from relatives and friends until to get by until time elapsed and we could qualify for another ration book.

In addition to ration stamps she also had to ask for meat tokens. But living in a Mormon community with many relatives nearby she was able to borrow enough stamps so we could buy enough food until the next ration book was scheduled to be issued.

Ration books weren't an issue for my Aunt Wanda and Uncle Ed. They lived on a farm near Menan, Idaho. There they raised hogs, chickens, sheep, and cattle. They grew potatoes, hay, and corn. When we visited them there was plenty to eat and all of us must have looked like starved orphans as we dug into the bounty of a Sunday dinner. Since we didn't have a car we rarely got to go to the farm because we had to rely on the good graces of some relative who was invited to visit the same time as we were.

Our diet consisted of basic food back in Idaho Falls. Fried bologna was a favorite of mine but canned meats such as Spam or chipped beef were staples as were potatoes, carrots, and canned corn. An invitation to Uncle Ed and Aunt Wanda's farm was looked upon as being an honored guest at a Horn of Plenty banquet.

Uncle Ed was good looking thin-framed man who had been mildly successful. He was able to buy farm equipment and bought a 1941 Chevrolet sedan in 1944, a sign that war-time farm prices provided a fruitful income. My aunt Wanda was a plain woman who was a good farm wife. She worked hard on the farm, cooked, cleaned, and bore children. Her last child died when she was an infant.

"Don't touch it Bobby," the stern voice of my grandmother ordered. My curiosity had taken me to the side of the coffin in my grandparent's living room as I was reaching up.

A tiny white casket was sitting high on top of a dresser in my grandparent's living room. I stood there alone looking at it and wondered why the baby inside died. I was not allowed to attend the burial and stayed with a neighbor down the street while the family attended to the internment. It was the first time I had confronted real death outside of the movies. I had been told that we all die and that the little baby had been taken up to heaven. I was six years old and felt that something was very unfair because I was alive and the baby had done nothing wrong to die so young.

Another thing that struck me as unfair had to do with mom. She was looked upon as something of an irresponsible pariah in Idaho Falls because she was a divorced woman at a time when you were considered a social misfit because of an unsuccessful marriage. She was struggling financially and socially. Idaho Falls was a small town at the time and everyone knew what was happening to everyone. Further, the news in the church traveled fast so nothing escaped being known. It was my father who had made the decision to end the marriage yet he was living in an urbane setting, enjoying the life of a military officer and not sending money for alimony nor child support. Mom sought financial help from the military officials but she was told that because he was an officer, and that nothing could be done to aid her. That was the story I was told, however truthful it may have been, and it could be suspect as to its voracity.

My sister JoAnn was 14 years old and told wonderful stories about my father. She idolized him because he read the Sunday

13

newspaper to her and had occasionally taken her to functions and events when he was an editor in Hollister and San Francisco. She loved to read Rudyard Kipling and memorized passages about the water boy Gunga Din and Rikki-Tikki-Tavi, a story about a cobra and a mongoose. She was short, thin, blue-eyed, cute, and beginning to show in interest in boys, a desire my mother strongly recommended she control. She had a friend Thelma Daisy and they began to embrace the taboo of secretly smoking cigarettes. This was a most forbidden practice in Mormon Idaho Falls and my mom who already felt the indignation of the town's citizens was trying to be careful of not having additional wrath fall on our family.

Arthur my brother had a most unusual personality that he would carry all his life. He hated authority figures, was undisciplined, somewhat antisocial, given to adventurous hyperbole, but had a human side. He looked out for his sickly little brother. His red hair, blue eyes, freckled skin, and lanky frame gave him a distinctive appearance. He parted his hair right down the middle. His smile revealed he was his mother's son, because he also had a gap between his two front teeth like hers. His unconventional choices in life made him stand out from other kids his age such as saying how he was going to float down the Snake River in a washtub.

He was smart and followed his own path intellectually seeking adventure and challenges. He did his homework from school if he liked the subject but if he didn't he did nothing in spite of threats that he may fail if he didn't "do better" from his teachers. He was a reader of books and told compelling stories mostly made up in his head with little to back them up with facts. He wore bib overalls as many of us did but he'd always had one strap unfastened.

He was chastised by my mother for trying to have a sexual encounter with a girl down the street while her mother was out grocery shopping. The girl's mother came home and caught them playing "house" and discovered Art on top of her. He was only 11 years old when he made his advances at the girl who was 10. He said it was all his fault but that the girl had invited him in but he made the move to advance toward her. He also would get into fights at school and was my mother's most difficult child.

I looked up to both of my older siblings in spite of their sometimes unconventional traits because they were my family and I was but coming to the age of reason. And now on my mother's wedding day, we were all in my grandparent's living room viewing solemnly my mother's vows on this day in April, 1945. We were now going to have a new father, a stepfather named Robert Maxwell and we had been instructed to address him as "Daddy Bob." Because my mother had chosen this man, I decided that he must be an all right person because I trusted her unfailingly.

That night, the night of my mother and "Daddy Bob's" honeymoon, they stole away somewhere and my brother thought it would be a good idea to sleep in mom's bed. We often had to share a bed because of the cramped conditions in our $15.00 a month duplex mom rented. Mom's bed was bigger and softer. When got in we felt lumps of some kind. When we investigated we found mom's friends had stuck knives and spoons under the sheet as a practical joke.

"That boy will do better in a dry climate," the doctor was saying to my mother just after I had my tonsils out. "It'll help his asthma. Staying here in damp, cold weather will only cause a recurrence of his problems. A lot of people are finding better relief from asthma in Arizona where it's dry."

I had asthmatic reactions in California where I was born and in Idaho. My mom would cover my chest with Vicks or some other bad smelling ointment that proclaimed that its medicinal vapors would clear my nasal passages and lungs. All it did for me was burn the skin on my chest and gave no relief to my asthma.

My just married mother and "Daddy Bob" began to plan for a move after the school year was completed. It was decided that JoAnn and Art would stay with our biological father in Utah while the remaining three of us would take Greyhound buses to Arizona.

By now my real father was on his second marriage. Her name was Anise Louise and they had met when he was enrolled at Northwestern University. My father had rented a room from her family while attending the university. He was studying journalism and dabbled with the idea of being a dentist. When the depression struck America, money for my father's education dried up and he dropped out and began a career as a journalist. Now after World War II the acquaintanceship was renewed and a marriage followed.

Perhaps it was guilt that my father felt that caused him to agree to take JoAnn and Art for the summer while my mother and her new husband began a new life together. He had acted irresponsibly toward our family by not sending alimony or child support when my mother and he were divorced so possibly this was his way of trying to make amends.

"I'll be glad to be leaving Idaho Falls," I heard my mother say to "Daddy Bob." This town is too narrow-minded for me. I know we'll have to make a new life in Arizona but I'm ready for a change."

We left Idaho Falls on a Greyhound bus and we sat near the back. Along the way I began to feel sick to my stomach.

"Mom, I'm going to throw up." I did and the smell permeated all of the air in the bus. Other passengers were nice enough to offer tissues and handkerchiefs to help clean up the mess and the bus driver cleaned up the rest at the next stop.

"Would it be possible to sit in the front seat?" my mother asked the driver. "I think he'll feel better there."

I'll check with the other passengers to see if they'll be willing to change seats with you," the kindly bus driver said and he made the accommodation for me, mom and Daddy Bob.

The new location worked and I was able to keep food down.

"I'll have a roast beef sandwich," I told the waitress in the Greyhound Bus station somewhere along the way on our journey south. It was the first time I had tasted roast beef and I loved its flavor. There had been no roast beef in our house during the war so this was a real treat because now rationing was ending and beef was now becoming available in stores and restaurants.

We arrived in Tujunga, California, one of the many little cities that made up the larger Los Angeles metropolis. My Uncle Dee and Aunt Mary lived there with my two cousins Susan and Ed. I hadn't seen them for over a year and was shocked to see Ed, who was four years old now, harnessed up with a leash strapped to his back being led around like a dog. He'd wandered off so many times that this was his parent's solution to keeping him close and in check.

Sue, Ed and I played hide and seek that afternoon and had a wonderful time. Near the end of the game I began to feel tightness in my chest and an asthma attack coming on. I told my mom that I wasn't feeling well and she told me to rest. We had no medicine to deal with asthma. That night she rubbed by chest with Vicks and told me to try to relax. Again, it didn't help. Things got worse and I only got a few minutes of sleep by sitting up in bed that night.

The next morning I awoke tired and my lungs burning with short, wheezing gasps. We were scheduled to continue our journey to Arizona by getting on another bus. When we found our bus we requested a front seat and were granted permission to sit there. As the bus drove south and we crossed into the desert areas, I began to sneeze and cough up phlegm. I began to feel better. The discharge of asthmatically induced fluids continued for at least two hours and as we approached Phoenix my lungs were clear and I felt healthier than I had ever known. I breathed deeply into my lungs and it didn't hurt and the wheezing was gone. I couldn't believe it and neither could my mom who had agonized over my ill health most of my life. My new found good health validated by mother's decision to take me to the dry climate of Arizona. I was the most grateful because I began to perk up and ask questions about the plants I had never seen before.

"That's cactus and there's lots of different kinds," the bus driver told us and added that it thrived in the desert even though there was little rainfall in response to my loud 'What's that'." He stopped the bus in Phoenix and some people got off and new people got on.

"What's that they're saying," I whispered to my mother. People were saying words I had never heard before. Others understood what was being said but not us.

"They're speaking Spanish," my mother whispered back. That didn't explain anything to me. I didn't know there was a Mexico, a Spain, or any other Hispanic-speaking country.

"Does everyone speak Spanish in Arizona?" I asked wondering if I was in a foreign country and puzzled and fearful that we wouldn't be understood.

"No, but there is a large number of people who speak Spanish here but most people also speak English," my mother reassured me.

We got off the bus in Tucson and I was wearing a white sailor's outfit my mom had bought for me. My shoes were dusty and scruffy. There was a Hispanic boy about my age with a shoe shine kit and he asked if I needed a shine. I looked at my mom and Daddy Bob and they looked at the boy who was trying to earn a few cents and nodded yes. I put my foot on his wooden box where he kept his polish, brushes and shine rags and looked at his fingers. They were covered with dark shoe polish stains. He carefully tried to roll up my white bell-bottomed pant leg to uncover my shoe. The polish on his fingers began to stain the white cloth and I stopped him, bent down and rolled up the hem. I felt a profound sense of embarrassment for myself and the shoe shine boy. We had lived modestly in Idaho and I never had much money except for the silver dollar I had once found and now I was hiring a "servant" to shine my shoes. I was his age and never contemplated ever having any kind of employment at age seven, yet this contemporary was "working" for me.

After my shoes were polished my parents found a hotel. Daddy Bob went out to talk to a realtor and mom and I stayed in the lobby waiting for his return. He came back late that afternoon and said we would go looking at houses tomorrow.

The next day we went to the realty office and a fat man chewing a dark cigar was sitting behind a big desk and not terribly interested to deal with us.

"There's a housing shortage Mrs. Maxwell and I don't have much to show you in your price range," he grunted. "I'll show you what we have but you'll have to be ready to move quickly if we find anything at all."

I didn't like him or his rude, cynical attitude and he didn't care what I thought or how he was treating us.

By the end of the day we had found a small house on the south side of Tucson on Columbia Avenue. My parents bought it and within two weeks we were living there. Daddy Bob also bought a 1929 Studebaker coupe with a rumble seat where I sat and where my sister and brother sat when they returned from the summer they had spent with our real father. My sister was singing a new song she loved called "Sentimental Journey" a tune I found monotonous but was supposed to be the theme song for returning soldiers hoping to reclaim the memory of the America they left behind before they went to war. The Studebaker soon became problematic. It wouldn't start and replacement parts were hard to find. Daddy Bob sold it for a loss and we would now take public busses to town from a bus stop three-quarters of a mile walk up on South 6th Avenue.

Mom got a job in a hair salon and Daddy Bob received a military pension from the government due to suffering a heart condition in the Navy. He started a small business making jewelry, mainly silver and turquoise with his income. He also began to drink port wine and smelled of it when he came home. To his credit he taught me to tell time and occasionally took me horseback riding at a dude ranch stable where the horses were tame because they were more tired than a worn out battle-scarred jeep.

"Your son will be enrolled in the afternoon session Mrs. Maxwell. We have to have double sessions because there's a shortage of classroom space. I'm sure he'll be fine," said Principal Hollingshead at Government Heights Elementary School on Ajo road. It was an eight block walk from our house.

"Write your name at the top of the page and don't print," the teacher instructed.

19

"**Don't Print**!" I only knew how to print. I was not taught to write cursively. "My God, what if I print? Will they kick me out of school? I don't know anything but printing." My head was reeling and my stomach was feeling sick. I sat paralyzed and couldn't fill out the form in front of me.

I was in a new town and a new school with new teachers and I didn't want to fail. I had successfully passed first grade back in Idaho but Arizona was a new challenge I couldn't adjust to. My emotions and anxiety continued to build and when the teacher came by to check to see how I was doing she demanded, "Why aren't you filling out your paper?"

I looked up at her then turned my head and vomited. The other kids in second grade looked at me in shock and dismay. They were not as understanding as the nice adults had been on the bus. They were horrified and repulsed by the sight and smell of my breakfast being splattered all over the floor.

"I'll call the janitor and have him clean it up," the teacher said.

When he came with his pail of water and a mop I was again glaringly stared at by the other students who knew how to write their name cursively and not use block print.

I was humiliated and wanted to run away. But I stayed and hoped for supportive treatment from someone. Mustering all of the courage I had, I took my paper that had some bile on it, up to the teacher and told her I had gone to school last year in Idaho and we were not taught how to write our name, only print it. She was tired from teaching in the morning classes and in the afternoon heat was exhausted. She was sensitive enough to tell me that I could print my name for now until I learned to write. It was a bad way to start with the teacher and a horrible way to introduce myself to new classmates who now followed my every move with wary eyes.

The September sun seemed to grow hotter as the day wore on. It filled all of the classrooms with its heat especially in the afternoon session in which I was enrolled. There was no air conditioning so the windows were open. The air was still and the body heat from the students in the classroom increased the sweating that we all experienced. Concentration lagged as the lessons were presented. Above the chalkboard the alphabet was lettered in cursive writing. I studied that more than anything because I had to learn how to write the Arizona way. I would look up at the cursive capitals and lower case letters and try to carefully fill in answers using the curved letters to make words and sentences in our workbooks. It was slow to come but progress was made as I practiced at home rewriting printed words from books in a sloping style with the letters connected with attached lines.

As the school year went on, things at home got worse. Daddy Bob began to drink more and came home late with a bad smell of alcohol on his breath. His Eugene O'Neill look became more depressed, unresponsive, passive, and morose. His eyebrows seemed lower and the smile wrinkles around his mouth more deep. The only animation he showed was when he argued with my mom and when he imposed more strict rules on us kids. Then there would be quiet in the house and no one talked. There was heaviness, uneasiness, awkwardness and glances between my brother and sister were short and unhappy.

Christmas came and 1946 was supposed to be a better year but it wasn't in our home. Daddy Bob began to stay home more often "not feeling well." The smell of bad wine was everywhere when we came home from school. The jewelry shop produced little income because Daddy Bob wasn't there as often and mom earned most of the money in our family. Her cheerfulness was gone and a tired weariness set in. There were no more outings so radio broadcasts and music stations took the place of conversations.

This heavy mood stayed in our house as spring approached. Then on that Easter Sunday morning I learned that Daddy Bob had died. His death was a shock because he was a man in his 40's, just how deep in his forties, I never knew. His funeral was not well attended because we had few friends in Tucson. I don't remember much about his funeral but I did wonder what our life would bring now that he was gone.

"Mrs. Maxwell, you'll receive a pension from the Veterans Administration. If however, you remarry it will stop. There is good news for your children. Mr. Maxwell made arrangements with our services to provide for financial assistance if they enroll in college. Also, there are provisions to provide some aid for necessities such as clothing. You'll have to file a report accounting for such expenses. Again, these services are only available if you remarry. I repeat, if you marry your pension will stop."

My mother had taken me with her when she met with the official from the Veterans Administration. He was a kindly, balding man wearing a gray shirt and glasses with a wire frame. He was somewhat sympatric to my mother's sorrow, and smiled gently at me.

I never knew how much the pension was because mom never discussed specific financial details with us kids. However, I know it wasn't much because we still didn't have a car, took busses, and lived modestly.

After dinner on a warm spring evening my mother gathered us around.

"I've opened a credit account at the Victory Market. JoAnn and Art you can charge groceries, school needs such as paper and pencils, but don't buy silly things like candy or other things that are not necessities. Bobby, you are too young to be allowed to charge anything."

I didn't understand credit but trusted that my elders, mom and my siblings did and that they would do the right thing in providing for our needs.

The next month I was able to see how things worked.

"Give me six bananas and dozen pencils and charge it to my mom's bill," Art was saying to the Hispanic lady named Belinda, who owned the store. She tallied up the cost and posted it to mom's bill. I stood next to Art and wondered why he needed a dozen pencils. The next day I asked him what he did with them.

"I gave them away at school," he said matter-of-factly.

"Mom said you weren't supposed to run up her bill on foolish things," I protested.

"Shut up! Mom said we could buy pencils and stuff."

"Yeah, but not to give away! You should only buy pencils to use at school for yourself or give one to me," I lectured

I turned away in amazement. As time went by Art continued to charge crazy things and when mom saw the first bill she scolded him for being irresponsible but didn't take his name off the list of authorized chargers. A couple of months later I went with my mother to the market on a Saturday evening.

"I'd like to see my bill," my mom asked Belinda.

"Of course," she willingly said looking forward to mom settling up with her.

Mom studied the bill for some time and her hazel eyes were focused. Then she opened her purse, resigned to pay the bill.

"Do you have a pen?"

"Yes," Belinda said.

Mom signed her entire paycheck for a week's worth of work over to the market. I looked at the amount and it showed $40.00.

"What did you just do?" I said astonished and holding my fingers to my chin.

"I just paid our bill," my mom said dejectedly.

"You mean you worked a whole week and signed your entire check over to pay our bill?" I said loudly and incredulously.

"Yes, I did," mom said as she looked down at me and her shoulders sagged.

Without thinking I just blurted out, "That will never happen to me."

When the summer months came, mom's energy was taxed even more because of the hot weather and because she had to walk several blocks up Columbia Street to South 6th Avenue to catch her first bus. Once in downtown Tucson she transferred to another bus that took her close to her job in North Tucson where she walked the remaining distance to work in a hair salon. After working all day on her feet, she had to repeat the journey to get home. JoAnn wasn't much of a cook so mom made dinner, then rested. By now JoAnn was 15 and Art was approaching 14.

We didn't have a washing machine so all of us packed our dirty laundry to a laundry shop where we bought soap and bleach, washed our clothes, then ran them through a ringer, put them in a dryer, folded them and then walked home. It was a 16 block round trip.

JoAnn made friends with a girl named Betty Straw. She lived a block away and had older brothers named Raymond and Henry and both had cars. The brothers had friends and JoAnn and Betty went on double dates, danced, went to movies, and sneaked cigarettes to smoke.

I overheard JoAnn telling Art about one night when they were driving around with Betty Straw and some guys in the car.

"While we were driving at night we played a game. Whoever saw an oncoming car with only one headlight shining and said 'perdittle' first got to claim a kiss from anyone in the car. I was in the back seat but I kept my eye out for car's oncoming lights. Sure enough, I was the first to see a car with one headlight on and shouted out 'perdittle.' Everyone asked who I was going to ask to give me a kiss. I chose Mory and he gave me a long kiss. I've had my eye on him for some time and I hoped I would see one car light out first or if he did he'd choose me to give him a kiss."

"Did he give you an open-mouth kiss?" Art asked in a perky voice.

"I wouldn't let him but maybe next time," JoAnn said joyously.

"Henry wanted me to come up with some gas money and I was down to my last quarter and I wanted to save it for school but I gave it to him but told him not to expect me have a lot of money," continued JoAnn.

JoAnn told me when we were both adults, that money was so tight in our house that mom told her to use old rags folded up in place of Kotex when she had her periods. She said she was always worried that someone would look in her purse and find old cloth and ask why it was being carried around instead of being thrown away.

When school started JoAnn entered Wakefield Junior High School and dived into learning Spanish. She had a facility for language and scored high marks in foreign language but everything else was modest.

The summer before Art entered Wakefield, he sought out adventure.

"Mom, I think we should get a nannie goat. We can save money by milking it and Mr. Gray said the milk is better for you than cow's milk."

Mom who grew up around animals as a child wasn't put off by the idea but countered. "We don't have a place for it. We don't have a pen and even though we may save money on milk we still have to feed it and that costs money."

"I'll build a pen from scrap lumber and the goat can eat grass. Heck, they eat anything, potato peels, apple peels, banana peels, even paper. I'll take care of it and you won't have to worry one bit. Just let me have it."

"How much does it cost?" My money conscious mom asked.

"I can buy a goat for five dollars," Art proudly said. He thought he had accounted for everything and was arguing his case like a high priced lawyer.

"What about the smell and what happens if the neighbors object?"

"I can hose her down outside with water and goats don't make a lot of noise. Nobody will even know she's here. I'll build the pen out by the back alley."

We did have a fenced yard and grass was growing around our house, facts that buffered well for Art's point of view.

"On weekends I'll take the goat out into the desert and she can eat some of the plants out there," he continued to plead.

Mom began to weaken. "I'll think about it."

My mom began to save a little from her tips at work and set it aside. One day she came home and said, "You still want that goat, Art?"

"Yeah, can I have it mom? Oh please let me have it."

"How far away is it from here?"

It's about a mile away but Mr. Gray told me he'd let me have a rope to lead it here."

"How long will it take you to build a pen for it?"

"I can build it in a day, or even less."

"When you build the pen, then you and I will go up to Mr. Gray's place and talk about the goat."

"Thanks mom, I'll take care of it, you'll see," Art confidently spoke as if he had progressed through the rites of passage test.

So, within a week we had a goat munching on everything we could scrounge up to feed it. Art milked it and strained the milk through a flour sack. The milk tasted different than a cow's but tolerably good. The neighbors registered a few comments about the goat's bleating but no one asked us to get rid of it. We tried to pet it but "Nanny", her new name Art gave her, wasn't an animal to warm up to a human's touch.

Nanny was with us for a few months but Art's interest was transferred to another beast.

"Mom," Art began. "I want to get a donkey. I can sell Nanny back to Mr. Gray and he'd give us what we paid for her. For a few more dollars he said he'd sell me a donkey."

"The goat at least gave us some milk," mom said shocked that Art would want a donkey. "We can't keep it here. It won't give us any value and we'll have to buy feed for it. Not this time Art. No donkey."

Art had already told me how much fun it would be to have a donkey to ride so I was a coconspirator urging mom to relent.

"Mom, it would be fun to have a donkey," I urged. "We could all ride it and the kids in the neighborhood would pay a nickel to ride it. We can take it out in the desert and let it graze on weeds. We'd tie it to the fence when we weren't riding it and it can't get out of the yard so it'd be a good thing to have for Art and me."

JoAnn had no interest in a donkey so she stayed out of the conversation.

"Mr. Gray will throw in a bridle so we can ride it. It'll be good for Bobby to have part of the donkey as his pet," Art said continuing to lobby.

"I'll brush it mom and help Art take care of it," I said pleadingly hoping mom would yield.

"Nope, no deal," mom said with certainty.

Later that night Art came to me and said," Keep asking mom to get the donkey. You'll be able to ride it and we can take trips in the desert and go down to the Santa Rita River with it."

I was torn internally because my selfish side wanted the donkey to share with Art and to explore whatever adventures it would provide. But I also felt guilty because I knew mom didn't have a lot of money and we no doubt would have financial difficulties paying for feed. Mom seemed so firm in denying our request that I figured that she wouldn't change her mind.

"Okay Art, I'll ask her some more and maybe she'll give in."

Over the next month I asked mom several times for permission to have the donkey and the best response I got was, "we'll see."

In March of 1947 mom relented and said we could get the donkey and the deal was made. We traded in the goat Nanny, and brought home our new girl, "Nancy" the name

27

we gave her. Art got to know her first and led her around with the bridle. He had ridden her at Mr. Gray's and was able to ride her around our neighborhood. We tied her up to our fence and she spent the night quietly. That wasn't the case the next morning as she began to bray with the signature "HEE, HAW, HEE, HAW" that all donkeys have. It didn't take long for our neighbors to complain about the early morning "racket."

The next Saturday, I was anxious to get my turn riding Nancy. The neighborhood kids gathered around and we led Nancy out of our fenced yard and next to some Tamarac Pine trees. Art helped me on and handed me the reins. I moved the reins to the left and Nancy moved away from the trees and then I gently kicked my heels into her side. She took a few steps and then began to bolt forward running at top speed for about 30 yards. At that point she dug her front hooves into the ground and lowered her head. I came off her back and slid down her neck like a slippery slide and hit the ground. The reins were pulled out of my hands. Nancy now free of her rider took off running and was uncontrolled. Her speed was much faster than Art and me and the rest of the kids who had gathered to watch.

"We've got to run after her and catch her," Art declared with terror in his voice.

All of us tried to keep pace but couldn't keep up. She was pulling away as we followed. We could see her running a couple of blocks away from us so we followed on foot, jogging, sprinting, and walking. Some of the kids that were with us began to drop away from the chase and were laughing at us.

Nancy ran up to South 6th Avenue, a four lane road and headed south. She ran for about two miles dodging cars and finally ended up at the Tucson Rodeo Grounds and was resting when we finally caught up. The reins were hanging down to the ground and she was breathing heavily and we were too. Art slowly approached her and she let him come close. As he neared she turned her head forward from him and started to walk away. To his credit Art didn't rush up to her but slowly followed and guided her toward a fence. She slowed and he put his hand on her rump near her tail. Slowly he worked his hand forward until he was able to grab the reins. She was now captured.

We led her back home with the whole journey traversing four miles. All of the neighborhood kids had dropped out a long time ago and were spreading the word about our debacle. We were preparing ourselves to be teased and made fun of for the foreseeable future.

"Don't tell mom what happened," Art drilled into me.

We of course didn't tell mom but word spread so quickly that she soon found out and our ownership of Nancy was over. Nancy was taken back to Mr. Gray's and returned. No other animals were brought home to replace Nanny and Nancy. Our city/farm life was over for the moment.

Even through mom got her money back from Mr. Gray cash was always an issue in our home. I knew this because our lifestyle and that of our neighborhood. No one had a football to use in our sandlot games. We took an empty Quaker's Oats cardboard cylinder canister and stuffed it with rags to give it weight so we could throw it farther when plays called for a pass.

There were times when mom came home dead tired from work and our dinner consisted of milk, rice, sugar, and nutmeg. Other times we had only bread, milk, sugar, and nutmeg. I liked the meals, they tasted good, but everyone knew it wasn't a balanced dinner.

Because money was tight, I used to walk up to South 6th Avenue and thumb a ride into town, then ask people on the street for two to five cents for 'bus money' to get back home. When I had gathered ten cents I went to the "B" movies at the Star Theatre where I saw a lot of films starring Johnny Mack Brown, Hopalong Cassidy, and Lash LaRue. Then I would thumb a ride back home.

One Christmas season I bought my mother a box of candy on layaway by collecting soda bottles and turning them in. I got two cents for small bottles and three cents for tall ones. The candy cost $2.00. It took two months to raise the money to pay for the chocolates.

However nice a gesture that was, I am ashamed to tell that I stole Christmas presents for the rest of my family, a yoyo for Art and a bottle of perfume for JoAnn. I would enter a store and pick up two items such as yoyos. I'd look around to see if the clerk was watching. I'd focus my full attention on one yoyo pretending to examine it carefully while I would slowly lower the other yoyo below the counter and into my pocket. Then I would put the first yoyo back on the shelf and leave the store. It would be impossible to do the same thing today because of monitoring cameras, bar codes, and alarms on merchandise. In the 1940's stealing was much easier.

"Mom, can I join the Cub Scouts," I asked.

"I'm sorry Bobby, we don't have money for that," she said heavily.

One evening several weeks later I asked, "Mom there's a carnival in the neighborhood. Can we go?"

I was resigned to have mom say no but I thought I'd try to persuade her. To my surprise she said yes. I was astounded and energized with excitement. We had no car so we had to walk. Mom was wearing a red dress and looked more beautiful than ever because she said we could go. When we got there she bought tickets for a couple of rides and a chance at the ring toss, a skill I couldn't master nor could anyone else. No one took home a prize.

I noticed that men were glancing at my mother with inquiring eyes. She looked beautiful to more than me. Some followed us around but her demeanor said no to any advances.

I loved mom for taking me to that carnival because I knew she was giving up something in order to pay for that short evening of fun. I still tear up sometimes to this day knowing that she made the sacrifice.

My third grade started again in double sessions and again I was enrolled in afternoon classes. Miss Kindle was my teacher, a blond, blue-eyed woman, trim in figure, short, and catered to the "good" kids. I joined the safety patrol and wore a white belt and with strap over one shoulder. After school I would stand by a cross walk and watch for a break in traffic, then stand in the middle of the road and stop traffic so other students could walk across the road safely.

Art was attending Wakefield Junior High School that featured grades 7, 8, and 9. Part way through the school year he and other kids his age decided to cut school. I found out about it a week into the risky adventure.

"You better let me cut school too or I'll tell mom what you're doing," I declared with confidence. "You'll be in a lot of trouble if I can't go with you."

"Yeah, You can come along but don't tell anyone," Art said optimistically.

So, for the next two weeks I joined the pack of neighborhood kids who would pretend to head off to school but once out of sight we congregate and then be off on some escapade.

One of our excursions took us to the banks of the Santa Rita River where the girls in the group had packed a picnic lunch from scrounging food from home kitchens. While the girls were preparing the lunch we guys were throwing clods of dirt at targets in the river. When the lunch was ready one of the girls said, "Stop throwing those clods because the dust is getting in the food."

Art kept throwing clods and dust kept filtering down in the food.

"If you throw one more clod Art, we're going to pants you," Ray Straw yelled at Art.

Art, who hated authority of any kind, looked Ray in the face and picked up a clod and threw it. Immediately four guys jumped Art and they all fell to the ground. Art grabbed the first guy to reach him, Mike Pike and put him in a headlock. As the other teens struggled to pull off Art's jeans he kicked at them and didn't let go of Mike.

I tried to pull off the teenage guys but was easily pushed away because I was five or more year younger than any of them and because of my scrawny body.

31

"Let him go Art!" The three other guys shouted.

"I can't breathe," Mike grunted.

"Let him up Art,"

"I'm not lettin go until you promise to let me alone," bellowed Art.

"Don't pull on him, he's breaking my neck," Mike wept.

"Let him go Art, you're hurting him. Let him go. Everybody stand back and let Art go," Ray commanded.

There was a pause and the other guys got to their feet.

"All right Art, let him go," demanded Ray.

Art looked around and said, "Stand back and I'll turn him loose."

In one quick move Art let Mike go and jumped to his feet and faced his attackers ready to fight if they came after him. His eyes were wide and his skin was red. His hands were in fists.

Mike rubbed his neck as the others looked on. They were more concerned with Mike at the moment but within 15 seconds they're angry faces turned toward Art. Three of the guys charged Art. Mike was still recovering from his aches so he didn't join the assault. One dove at Art's ankles and grabbed them. The other two knocked Art to the ground and held his arms apart. Now Mike recovered his senses, and tore open the button fastening Art's pants. Then he began to pull at Art's pant legs. Art kicked hard but each time he did his pants began to expose his underwear. Finally, his shoes were off and so were the rest of his jeans.

"Take his pants down to the river and get them soaking wet," Ray told the others.

Mike came back with the jeans dripping wet and threw them at Art.

"Look, girls! Art wants to show you his underwear," Ray laughed at the girls.

The other guys laughed, jeered, and pointed at Art. He defiantly looked back at the group. The girls didn't bother to do more than glance at Art and went back to making lunch.

I watched Art's anger and humiliation and tried to approach him.

"Get away from me Bobby," he demanded.

"Why did you throw that clod, Art? You didn't need to do that," I lectured.

Art sulked away taking his wet jeans. He wrung them out and threw them over a limb to dry. He moved farther away from the group and began throwing clods in the river. An hour passed and Art put on his semi-wet jeans and came closer to the group.

"You want some of what's left," Ray asked Art.

"No!" came Art's rebellious answer.

Later that day, the food was packed up and loaded into Ray's car. The girls joined Ray in the car and they headed off back to town. The rest of us walked back towards home through the desert. Mike had a .22 rifle and a few bullets. A mile or so away from the river we came to a barbed wire fence. Before we climbed through it someone spotted a buzzard up in a tree about 150 yards away. Everyone wanted to take a shot at the bird. Everyone missed and surprisingly, the bird didn't move. Finally, someone mockingly asked if "pantless" Art wanted a shot.

"Damn right," he said.

"You can't hit anything. You're a piece of shit," Pete said, who was one of Art's attackers.

"If you let me have a shot, I'll hit it," Art said self-confidently.

Mike put a shell in the .22 and said, "Here you go asshole,"

The group was poised for another round of razing believing that since they hadn't hit the bird, neither could Art, especially after he stated so assuredly he could.

Art took the rifle and aimed it toward the buzzard. He rested his elbow on a fence post and steadied the weapon. He took perhaps as long as a minute, aiming. Everyone was looking in anticipation of hearing the shot. Then looks began to be traded indicating disbelief in Art's ability and getting ready to laugh.

I was saying to myself, "Shoot the damned gun, Art." and was prepared to take some of the verbal abuse directed toward Art.

Art continued to aim. Then he pulled the trigger and everyone's head snapped toward the tree. In an instant the bird toppled out of the tree and hit the ground. Everyone now looked at Art with newfound esteem.

"How did you do that?" Mike exclaimed.

"I read in a hunting magazine that when the target is above you, there is a tendency to aim above it. You have to aim below it to hit your target."

I along with everyone else was astounded Art had hit the bird. I was also glad to see that he had reclaimed some but not all, of what he had lost at the river.

"Grandpa is coming for a visit kids. He'll be here this Saturday," mom was telling us a few days later. "After grandma died grandpa has had a hard time adjusting to life without her. "He hopes that being away from Idaho will help him get over grandma's loss."

I was looking forward to seeing him because he was so good to me when I stayed with them during the day in Idaho Falls. However, I had a nagging thought in my head about our ditching school. We couldn't sneak away and be gone for a whole day with grandpa around.

When he arrived I was happier to see him than Art or JoAnn. They didn't know him as well as I did or so I thought, but maybe they knew him better than me because they were more familiar with his drinking spells.

We visited that weekend and on Sunday evening he was in a magnanimous spirit.

"Bernice," he said to mom, "I think I'll go to school with Bobby and see how he's doing,"

My heart sank. Grandpa hadn't been here but two days and he already had a plan to uncover my greatest crime. I began to plot. I figured that if I pretended to be sick on Monday I could delay the inevitable discovery of my cutting school, at least for a short time. However, I realized that I couldn't be sick for the entire time he was staying with us so I was resigned to being caught. However, I wasn't going to confess. I would let them discover on their own that I was absent.

In spite of my resolve, I entered Miss Kindle's class and decided to come clean. I approached her desk and she asked if I had a pass for being absent for two weeks.

"Miss Kindle, I've been ditching for the last two weeks."

She looked at me with utter disdain and I couldn't blame her because I knew I was guilty of doing something very wrong.

"Go to the Principal's office and tell Mr. Hollenbeck what you've done."

"Yes, ma'am," I said obediently.

"You've done what?" Mr. Hollenbeck said.

"I'm sorry, but I've been ditching school for the last two weeks,"

Just then my grandfather entered Mr. Hollenbeck's office and was introduced by his secretary.

"Is this your grandson Mr. Harris?"

"Yes, and I've come to see how he's doing in school here."

Mr. Hollenbeck said, "Have a seat. This grandson of yours has just told me that has been ditching school for the last two weeks. Did you know about this?"

"No, I didn't. I just came down here from Idaho Saturday and thought I'd come over and check on the boy," grandpa said, shocked.

"Well your timing couldn't be better." Mr. Hollenbeck said. "I'm going to have to punish him and you can watch me do it."

"What do you do in these kinds of cases?" grandpa asked.

"We normally give boys like Bobby swats with this," and he reached into his closet and pulled out a baseball bat with the barrel flattened with holes in it."

Grandpa said, "Go ahead and give it to him."

"Bobby, come over here next to the side of my desk and grab your knees," Mr. Hollenbeck demanded with a voice that touched on anger.

As I walked over to the side of the desk I knew what was about to happen but I thought I had a plan. I was going to begin crying with the first swat and scream louder with each successive blow. I didn't know how many swats I was going to get but I was prepared for ten.

"Aieee," I cried out after the first whack. I was trying to force tears to flow by the second strike and tried to rub my backside to show attentiveness to the pain. The third blow brought even louder shrieks from me and by number five I was in a state of howling. Then I heard the bat being returned to its place in the closet.

Grandpa was in complete agreement with Mr. Hollenbeck's method of discipline and I was glad that grandpa didn't call for more wallops. I was humiliated because I was wrong in the first place and felt ashamed because I felt I had disappointed grandpa.

"Now go back to class Bobby and don't ever ditch school again or I'll give you even more swats." Mr. Hollenbeck sternly told me.

When I went back to Miss Kindle's class my behind was still tingling with pain. She asked, "What did Mr. Hollenbeck say to you?

"He told me not to ditch class ever again and he gave me some swats."

Miss Kindle could see that I had been crying but didn't believe that Mr. Hollenbeck had meted out enough punishment.

"Go stand in the center of the room in front of the class," she instructed. Then she got up from behind her desk and said to all of the students in the room. "Class, Bobby has been ditching class for two weeks. This is what happens to boys who do this." She walked over next to me and slapped my right cheek and then the left. "Now, go sit down."

I walked to my desk and felt the sting on my cheeks and the disapproving glances of my classmates. Later that day I was told that I was no longer allowed to be on safety patrol.

That night when mom came home, grandpa explained what had happened at school. I didn't tell anyone what Miss Kindle did to me because I believed they would have approved because grandpa didn't protest Mr. Hollenbeck's swats. My mom blushed in embarrassment and said to me, "I'm very disappointed in you." That hurt me inside when she said it but I knew I had let her down.

As if that wasn't enough to be ashamed of, I then did something I'm still regretful of. I blurted out, "Art made me do it."

Mom wheeled toward my brother with a fierce look in her eyes. "What's going on Art?"

"I may as well tell you mom, I've been ditching school for three weeks."

"You damned kids. What they hell were you thinking?" She paused to gather her thoughts and then said, "You'll take whatever punishment the school gives you without complaint and I'm going to keep a close eye on all of you."

My sister was in the other room listening to our interrogation.

"JoAnn, get in here. Have you been ditching school too?"

"No she hasn't," Art said in a tone to defend JoAnn.

"You better not be ditching. I know you've been smoking and hanging out with boys so you better watch your step young lady or you won't be allowed out of this house," mom threatened.

I expected Art to beat the hell out of me later but he took the blame for both of us without so much as giving me a hard look. For that lack of a thrashing I was grateful.

"I'd better check on the boys at church as well to see if they've been attending service," grandpa said.

Art and I looked at each other and knew we'd been caught in another lie. On previous Sundays mom had given us bus money and fifty cents to put in the collection plate when it came around at the Mormon Church. While we were walking to the bus stop on the first Sunday, Art suggested and I agreed, that we should use the money intended for church to pay for a movie tickets when we got to town. On the way home Art instructed me in the melody and lyrics to sing, "Bringing in the sheaves, bringing in the sheaves, we will go rejoicing, bringing in the sheaves" a religious song sung at church. My performance was intended to convince mom that we were getting our share of religion at the Mormon house of worship.

After church services the next Sunday grandpa said, "Let me see the attendance records," to the Latter Day Saints' official.

Art and I were standing next to grandpa and knew our names wouldn't show up in the book of records. We looked at each other and waited for the lack of evidence to confirm our absence. The bus ride home was silent but a torrent from hell awaited us once we got home."

"What!" my mom screamed when the truth came out. "You kids are never going to get another dime for a show. I'm disgusted with you both and you especially, Art."

The flurry of words that came next washed over us like a tsunami and seemed never to end. My head dropped lower and lower while Art to his credit, took the verbal assault head on.

"I know mom, I'm sorry. It won't happen again. I'll do better," he said consolingly.

"You damned right you'll do better," mom shouted. Then she smacked him along the side of his head.

A couple of weeks went by and we were restricted to our neighborhood. Since we couldn't go outside of a couple of blocks, Mike Gomez and his younger brother Gilberto, two Hispanic friends who lived five houses down on Columbia Street, became my constant companions. We played cowboys and Indians and we would wrestle. My asthma was now contained by the warm Arizona dry air so physical activity was no longer a barrier to overcome. Mike and I were the same age and about the same size. Art had shown me how to get a wrestling opponent in a headlock and I could always get Mike in one and throw him to the ground. Gilberto usually jumped on me when I had Mike down on the ground and freed his brother.

One day Mike and I were alone and I got him in a headlock and threw him on the grass. He screamed that I was choking him so I let go of his neck but kept him on his back and began pushing his knees toward his chest. My hand slipped off his right knee just as he kicked and his knee smashed into my mouth. I felt pain and then part of my tooth on my tongue. I jumped up and reached into my mouth and pulled out half of one of my two front teeth that had been broken off. I ran home and showed my mom the half tooth I saved from the fight.

"Can this be put back on my tooth?" I asked.

Mom looked in my mouth and examined the damage. "No, and I don't have the money to get your tooth fixed.

Mike had told his mother what had happened and that he had broken off part of my tooth. Two days later I went to see Mike and Mrs. Gomez was in the front yard and she asked me to lift my swollen lip to see my broken tooth.

"Oh, it's not that bad," she declared. "It'll be fine. You won't need to see a dentist."

Mr. Gomez was a barber and made a modest living. No doubt Mike's parents had talked things over and decided that they weren't going to pay for a dentist. They were paying for Mike to take trumpet lessons and money was tight for them as it was for everyone in our neighborhood. It also was a time when injuries happened to kids who were growing up and those injured had to accept the outcome, unless it was a broken limb.

JoAnn was by now 16 and began to show signs of becoming a woman. She was five feet two inches, thin, had brown hair, and modestly filled out. She was wearing red lipstick, had pierced ears with earrings, costume bracelets, and a necklace. She earned looks by teenaged boys and some men.

Grandpa, who was still living with us, began to notice her as well. He began to drink heavily coming home drunk and smelling bad. One day he came home in the afternoon and JoAnn and I were alone with him. His pants were unzipped and his penis was showing. He said to JoAnn, "Why don't you come over here and sit by me?"

I stepped up to him and looked him in the eye and said, "Grandpa, your fly is open and you need to go to the bathroom and take care of yourself."

He slowly looked down and saw that I had discovered his intention and he staggered to the bathroom and took a long time before he came out.

Uncle Dee Grandpa's son, had moved to Tucson two months before and that night he and Aunt Mary came over for a visit to see us and grandpa. Grandpa had excused himself to go to sleep off his intoxication. When it came time for me to go to bed I went into the room where grandpa was sleeping and I was so disgusted with him that I hit him in the forehead with my fist. He bounded up and started chasing me. I ran into the living room where mom and my uncle and aunt were. Uncle Dee came to my rescue and stood in front of his father and prevented him from coming after me.

"That little shit hit me in the head," grandpa shouted, justifying why he had the right to chase and pound me.

Uncle Dee stood his ground and stopped grandpa's chase. "Now that'll do," he said.

I would never look at grandpa the same way as I had earlier in Idaho Falls. He was encouraging to me then, the caring Wallace Beery grandfather. Now he was a drunk, obnoxious, and out of control. Grandpa left Tucson and went back to Idaho Falls a week later. That spring he died of a heart attack and was found by a young boy who had come for a music lesson.

"Would you like to go to grandpa's funeral? It will be a way for you to say goodbye to him." mom asked.

"No, mom, I don't like grandpa now. He used to be good but he was bad the last time he was here," I said.

Mom understood. She had seen her father go on two week toots, lose jobs, and offend and embarrass her family. My grandmother had stayed by grandpa but knew the humiliation that came with his drinking.

"All right, you stay can here with Art and JoAnn but be a good boy."

The summer of 1947 saw mom working across town and we three siblings making our own way through the heat. We had swamp coolers that cooled things down somewhat but one cannot live inside all of the time.

Art would go out into the dessert or continue his friendship with the Gray
 family and another family the Greens, who lived in a huge war surplus tent. Mr. Green was the stepfather and was rumored to be having sex with the oldest of his stepdaughters. The Greens were making adobe bricks by stomping straw into wet caliche mud. They had made rectangular molds and would stuff the mud and straw into them and let the bricks dry in the sun. The Green family also was raising registered rabbits, animals that attracted Art. Because Art was in the doghouse with mom, he knew better than to ask her to buy other pets after our experience with the goat and donkey.

Art and I butted heads and he being five and half years older than me, had no trouble punching me out my nine year old scrawny body. It became a daily regimen.

"Mom, Art beat me up today," and I would show her red marks, bruises, or lumps.

"Art, come in here. Don't you beat up Bobby again," she sternly commanded.

The next day she would walk again to the bus stop, take two busses to work, be on her feet all day, and make the return trip tired. When she left in the morning Art would track me down.

"You told mom about yesterday," he would say in a menacing tone.

"Yes, and you better not beat me up today or I'll tell her again tonight," I tried to sound brave with a threatening air. It didn't work. Art pounded me again and again. I would tell mom who again tell Art not to beat me up.

"That's all you're going to do mom, just tell him not to beat me up? Aren't you going to do something to punish him?" I was imploring mom to take some action. She was my only protector and words didn't seem to dissuade Art from further attacks.

I came to realize that Art was taller than mom who was 5 feet 4 inches and now at 15, stronger than she was. Whipping him didn't appeal to mom as an option to control Art's violent behavior. So, as the hot, angry sun rose each morning, I came to expect some kind of an assault by Art without any recourse to stopping it by mom. I tried to avoid Art physically, and get along with him when I was around him so as to avoid another pummeling.

It was also that summer that I was exposed to another religion other than the Latter Day Saints'. At the market where we charged our groceries on credit, there was a poster advertising that there would be a revival meeting for three days beginning the next Thursday. I was curious as what a revival was and walked down by the market during the day on the advertised Thursday. A huge tent was being set up, one the size I had never seen before. That Thursday evening I wandered down to see if I could learn what a revival was.

When I arrived most of the seats were already taken so I wandered up and down the aisles looking for a single spot to sit down. There were none so I went to the back of the tent and stood.

"Hallelujah and Amen." I heard the man at the front of tent say. I got the message quickly that a revival was a religious service but not like the ones the Mormon's had. I was still curious to see how this was going to go.

I looked around and some of the people had Bibles in their hands and as the man raised his voice and seemed to shout, a murmur began to come over the crowd. After about

25 minutes voices from the audience got louder and shouts of, "Praise the Lord," rang out. Soon people began to stand up and go forward to the makeshift altar and stand in front of the loud-shouting man. He put his hand on some of the people's head and pushed them backward and they fell back and were caught by members of the religious group. I wondered if they were injured from the man's punching motion when he shoved them. Some writhed on the dirty canvas that was put down to make a floor.

"Arise, I say," said the man at the front. In time, all of the fallen picked themselves up from the floor and looked dazed but happy. More people were encouraged to come forward and be, "saved from damnation."

I didn't go forward. I just watched in amazement. I stayed for another 15 minutes and slipped out of the back of the tent. I didn't feel that I needed to be saved from damnation, although I knew I had done bad things. However, I wasn't quite sure what "saved from damnation" meant. But I was astonished that so many ordinary looking people felt they needed to go down front and atone for their sins by shouting, going into a trance, and having the man in front hit them on the forehead and fall to the ground.

Mom worked at the Catalina Hair Salon in north Tucson. The owner Mel Jorns and his wife had come to Arizona for the same reason mom had brought me, Mel's asthma. Mel had bought a trailer and pulled it from Wisconsin and had it parked at the Pepper Tree Trailer Park off of South Sixth Avenue.

Mel and his wife had been married for several years but had no children because she was barren. Over the time of their marriage, things had soured and she left Mel and moved to New York City and filed for divorce. Mel needed someone to manage the hair salon and he chose mom because she had been a manager of a shop in Idaho Falls. She was honest, got along well with the clients, and could deal well with the Prima Donna of the shop, a beautician named Mr. George who had an immense number of wealthy clients.

Mom made out deposit slips, logged in appointments, ordered materials for the shop, marketed beauty products, and assigned new clients to one of the other seven beauticians in the shop. Mel would ask her to stay late on Friday evening to go over the books with him. He was extremely focused on the financial records. When he found out that she didn't have a car and that we lived off of South Sixth Avenue, he offered to give her a ride home. As time went on, he offered her a ride to work and they chatted about the business.

"Kids, I'm inviting my boss for breakfast this Sunday, so be on your best behavior," mom informed us.

"What's he like?" JoAnn asked.

"He's nice but strict about the business," mom answered.

When he arrived that Sunday for breakfast, we guessed he was about five feet nine inches. He has receding black hair, large blue eyes, a prominent nose, and was tanned. His smile revealed that he'd seen a good dentist because his front teeth had gold U-shaped borders around them. He was burly but athletic and his demeanor was a man in command. He lit up cigarettes from a pack of Lucky Strikes.

Mom made pancakes and provided Karo syrup as a sweeter, served crisp bacon, and hot coffee. We kids drank milk. Mel revealed a habit of sucking air through the gaps in his teeth to clear food that had been lodged there.

When we asked him questions he opened up and told us a great deal about his life.

"What kind of car are you driving? We haven't seen many of those" one of us said.

"It's a Frazer with gunboat gray paint," he answered. "There was a shortage of new cars after the war but I went down to the dealer and offered to pay cash for it. There's a Kaiser and a Frazer. The Kaiser is named after Henry Kaiser who was a shipbuilder during the war. He built the Liberty ships that carried cargo to Europe to supply the war effort. The Frazer is named after Joseph Frazer who worked in the automobile business. The Frazer is the top of the line so I bought it."

All of this was news to me. "Can we take a ride in it sometime?" I asked and my mom shot me a look that said I had overstepped the bounds of showing my best behavior.

"How about after breakfast?" He answered and I looked at my mom happily with a look saying my question wasn't inappropriate.

All of us kids were excited to ride in Mel's new car because the only cars we rode in were the clunkers owned by the guys JoAnn knew. Mel's car had push button door openers on the inside. It had a radio and a heater and they both worked we were assured when we asked about them. It had a clock Mel said he paid extra money to have it installed. To the left of the steering wheel was the handle of a spot light Mel used at night when he went hunting. Our exuberance overflowed. This was too much to take in for a family without a car. I realized that a car gave people freedom to go wherever they wanted. They weren't limited to a bus route or a bus schedule. It was an astonishing thought to me.

Mel's trailer on South Sixth Avenue wasn't more than two miles from our house and he began to give mom a ride to and from work every day. They would discuss work issues on the way to work and business profits at the end of the day before returning to our home. His visits increased and we kids pumped him with questions about his life before he came to Tucson.

"I had a farm first, then a grocery store. I took some of my farm products into the store and sold them at a bigger profit than I would have received if I sent my crop the traditional way to a farm co-op," he proudly shared. "The government was buying up all farm produce so there was a ready market with good prices."

We were impressed.

45

With World War II still fresh in everyone's mind and because war movies were still being shown, I asked, "Were you ever in the war?"

"I went down to volunteer for the army and the doctors gave me my physical. They said that because of my asthma, I could not sign up. I was rejected and disappointed. So I went back to the farm and grocery store.

"When food was rationed I always had plenty to eat. I had cows and had one of them butchered when I wanted meat for myself. I used to keep butter under the counter and sell it to my good customers. I also would go in the back of the store where I had a small kitchen and melt some butter and fry a steak for myself."

Art said, "I've never tasted a steak."

"I made a lot of money," Mel continued. "When I was 28 years old, I had $28,000.00 in the bank."

I remembered mom signing over her week's pay to the Victory Market and that amounted to $40.00. When I heard $28,000.00 I was astounded at how much that was. It sounded as if he was a millionaire. I had scoured our neighborhood for soda bottles to trade in to buy my mom a box of chocolates and that took me a couple of months to achieve.

Mom had told us not to ask questions about his wife so we asked about how he grew up. "Were you raised on a farm?" JoAnn asked.

"Yes, my dad had a farm up in Door County. That's the peninsula in Wisconsin that juts into Lake Michigan. He grew hay and corn, and raised milk cows. I was the oldest of four so I worked on the farm early on and learned how to grow crops and raise animals," Mel said eagerly to his attentive audience.

Art said he knew the peninsula was on the eastern side of Wisconsin.

"I played football in high school. I was a quarterback in a single wing formation," Mel explained.

None of us knew what a single wing formation was. "What does a single wing look like," Art asked.

46

Mel drew it on a piece of paper and showed us some plays. He said he mainly ran the ball, rarely passing.

"One time we were back deep in our own territory and I took the ball and ran through the line. One guy jumped on my neck and I carried him for about 50 yards before I went down. My neck was almost broken but I wouldn't give up until I just couldn't go on," Mel bragged.

"Did you play college football?" JoAnn asked.

"No, I was on an All Star team and we were losing but the coach wouldn't put me in. I got mad and threw my helmet into the stands," Mel said unapologetically showing a new side to his personality.

"I took a trip with a friend of mine down to Texas and watched a football practice at Rice University. I knew I was as good as some of the players on that team and considered enrolling but instead I returned to Wisconsin and started farming. I played one season of semi-pro ball and a guy tackled me and bent my knee backwards and I heard a crunch. That ended my playing days," Mel related matter-of-factly.

It was clear he had moved on with his life by farming and owning a grocery store. He had sold those businesses to come to Arizona and now owned the hair salon. He seemed confident of himself and a man who could do things successfully.

"I also was the subject of a story that ended up in a hunting magazine." Mel proudly stated. I set the record for shooting the most raccoons in a single hunt, 14. I had hunting dogs and they found a bunch of raccoons and it was easy to bag that many. Next time I come over, I'll show you pictures of that hunt."

We were all captivated by Mel's stories about his life.

But we didn't see Mel for about ten days. Mom was back taking busses to and from work. When Mel returned we were all interested to hear what he had to say.

"I drove to New York in three days. I only stopped for gas and food. I slept very little in motels," he revealed with some pride and fatigue.

"How far is New York?" I asked.

"From here, it's over three thousand miles. He pronounced thousand a funny way. It sounded like 'tousand,' with no th sound at the front of the word. He also said other words unusually. Dare not came out as dasn't and pretty near as pertnear. He often said 'an so' for isn't it so. The state of Utah sounded like Uta. We figured out what he was saying after a while.

He looked at mom and said, "I've got to go back again. My lawyer said he would make sure the papers were ready when I return so as not to inconvenience me again."

Mel continued to take us all for drives in his car. We'd drive around on hot summer nights and the air flowing through the open windows cooled us. He drove through open fields with his spot light switched on looking for wild rabbits and he would chase them with his Frazer. His spot light reached farther into the night than the car's headlights and it found shiny reflections of the eyes of rabbits, coyotes, and an occasional deer. Mel would giggle in a high pitched voice as he got nearer with his tongue between his two front teeth. It sounded like, "thheee, hee, thheee, hee."

A month later mom introduced him to Uncle Dee and we went down to some faraway river and had a family picnic and Mel provided soft drinks he called pop. We had never had such luxury so I indulgingly drank lots of pop until Mel said that was enough. Mom didn't object to his mild reprimand so I obediently stopped drinking the pop.

Then Mel took out his hunting rifle and we all marveled at its beauty.

"What kind of gun is it?" We excitedly asked.

"It's a .348 Winchester," Mel explained in a confident voice as he loaded it with long, gold-colored shells with copper tips. Mel looked around and to make sure that no one was nearby and that it was safe to shoot, then picked out a target across the river and fired. A tin can on the other bank flew into the air as dirt exploded into a puffed cloud.

None of us had ever seen a rifle nor heard its shot in real life except for the .22 Art used to shoot the buzzard. The only shots we heard besides that had been in movies. We were all enthralled by what we considered a stupendous event.

"Do you want to shoot it Dee?" Mel asked.

"Yeah. Let me try it," said my uncle and he laughed after he made his shot that missed its target.

Mel's sharing of his car, rides, pop, and rifle blasts made him look like Diamond Jim Brady to us. He was something we had never experienced before and we enjoyed him being in our lives.

One late afternoon Mom and Mel were rocking in a swing set mom had bought and placed outside by the side of our yard. It was a hot summer evening about 8:30 and the sky was giving way from a hot orange to a light shade of lavender fading to purple. Mel had his back to me and because of the dusk, mom didn't see me. I overheard them talking.

"I'd follow you anywhere," mom said.

I looked at the expression on her face and it said apprehension like she almost wanted to take back what she had said. I caught the meaning of the moment. This was serious talk about the future between mom and Mel. I knew mom had wanted to have another relationship for companionship, for affection, for someone to help raise her three children, and for someone to complete our family. Mom's look made me wonder if she had overstepped herself. However, mom had a knack for reading people and now her mien changed and her confidence showed.

I was somewhat taken aback at what I was witnessing. Mom had just turned 40 and our inquiring questions of Mel revealed that he was 33. Would Mel want someone older than him for a wife? Mel hadn't said anything. He kept looking down at his hands. There was silence and the swing gently rocked back and forth slowly. Then mom did something I had never seen her do before to a man. She leaned over and kissed Mel on the cheek. He looked up and took her in his arms and then he kissed her on her lips.

I was transfixed to see what would happen next. They pulled back from one another and said a few words to each other, words I could not hear. They embraced once more and then Mel stood up and walked to his car. Mom followed him to the car's door and I went back into the house where the swamp cooler filled the living room with cool air and a whirring noise.

Mom came into the house five minutes later with a happy glow for an expression. She saw us sitting around trying to listen to the radio over the sound of the swamp cooler. I was the only one who knew what had just happened between mom and Mel. I saw mom try to return to her normal expression as if to conceal what she was feeling. I realized that she wasn't ready to reveal verbally, where things were between her and Mel.

Over the course of the next few weeks mom and Mel decided to date openly. One night Mel came to the house dressed in nice slacks, a starched shirt, sport coat, and a felt hat, a fashionable accessory for the 1940's and the kind we had seen in movies. While mom was getting ready Mel played cards with Art and they talked about animals, specifically registered rabbits. That was a Saturday night. Sunday Mel was again at our house to have breakfast.

"That guy at the supper club was smarting off. I should have clocked him," Mel said to mom as she made waffles.

"Yes, he was getting a little out of hand," mom agreed.

"What time did you get home last night, JoAnn?" Mom asked.

Art spoke before JoAnn, "It was after midnight."

JoAnn flushed because she was supposed to be home at eleven after she and Harry had gone to the movies.

"We double dated and Betty wanted to go up to "A" Mountain and look over the valley at the lights at night," JoAnn defended herself as if to say that she had no choice in the matter and was a victim of circumstance. "A" mountain rose above Tucson and was a place lovers went to see the night lights and of course, make out.

"I'll talk to him about getting her home on time," Mel stated authoritatively. We were all a little surprised that Mel was taking the lead as family protector. I looked at mom and she continued to make waffles but her demeanor was relief. JoAnn's face showed alarm because she had just started dating Harry and liked him and didn't want Mel or anyone else, to interfere with the development of an encouraging romance.

The next Wednesday Harry drove his car to our house and Mel was waiting to confront him. "What do you think you're doing getting JoAnn home late?" Mel's tone was hostile.

I was standing outside when the exchange took place and watched Harry recoil back.

"I didn't realize the time was that late," Harry said trying to recover.

"You'd better spend some money and buy a watch. Don't let this happen again," Mel said commandingly and his face was firm.

Harry wasn't expecting this reaction and especially not from Mel who wasn't JoAnn's father. He hesitated. He looked away and scratched his chin. He seemed to be searching for the right reaction.

"Who are you?" Harry warily asked.

"I'm Mel but it doesn't matter who I am. It matters that you didn't get JoAnn home on time and this conversation is about you and what you didn't do right." He stepped closer to Harry.

Harry didn't move away but looked Mel in the eye to study his face and it said conflict.

I liked Harry but I was nervous to see what was going to happen next. His body language indicated that he was a teenager, well built, and as tall at Mel. Nonetheless, he was in front of an aroused adult. He seemed to want to be respectful and was in an inferior position so he demurred and showed regret. He said one word.

"Sorry."

Mel had won the standoff and his attitude continued to be in control. With a stern look on his face, he turned away and walked toward the house.

We didn't see Mel for the next ten days or so but mom said he had to do something but would be back soon.

When he did return it was a Saturday afternoon. He looked tired but resolute.

"I drove to New York in three days. I only stopped for gas and took food with me to eat in the car and when I slept it was only for a few hours."

We had heard those same words from him when he had gone to New York the first time.

"When I got there I went up the office and she was there with her lawyer. I didn't even look at her. I said, 'where are the papers?' and signed them and walked out. I drove the same way coming back but stopped in Wisconsin to see my folks before coming back to Arizona.'

'My ex-wife never wanted to come to Arizona. She didn't like the beauty shop and she didn't like to hunt. All she wanted to do was live in a big city and shop for the latest fashions."

Mom offered to make him a sandwich but he said he wasn't hungry. Mom's looked at him in amazement and was sympathetic, caring, and relieved. Mel's tone was definitive, set, and intended to impress mom that his marriage was over and he was committed to mom and their life together.

One day during the next week, mom took me aside saying she had something to share with me.

"Mel likes you. He's never had children of his own and he thinks you and he have something in common. He came to Arizona to improve his health because he has asthma like you. I brought you here for the same reason. So he's taken a liking to you. Mel and I are going to be married sometime in the near future so he's going to be your new stepfather."

I liked Mel too. He seemed genuinely interested in our family and took us to places in his car. He seemed to like Uncle Dee, a man I looked up to for his wonderful humanity and happy nature.

As an adult I realized that I had a special place in mom's heart as well. She had conceived me during the stormy time she and my biological father were having difficulties. I was supposed to be the cement that held the marriage together. When the marriage failed, my mom instead of resenting me for not keeping things together, gave me her love because she realized that I was going to be her last child and therefore doted on me somewhat, especially after I became so ill.

However, mom was perhaps now reassessing my being the last of her children. Mel indicated that he wanted children of his own and mom was a proven bearer of children. I wanted a little brother or sister so I could be a mentor and protector as my two older siblings had been to me.

I was always scrawny looking, thin, and somewhat unhealthy. I was coordinated but small for my age.

"We're going to fatten you up," Mel declared as he urged me to eat more.

For the next month I ate more until my stomach was ready to burst. It didn't help. I stayed boney and disappointed Mel's efforts to make me whole.

Mel and Art bonded when talking about raising animals. Art's goat and donkey interested Mel but only in an amusing way. When Art talked about registered rabbits, Mel said he would buy the rabbits and Art said he would make hutches to hold them. I was told by Mel that I was to take care of the feeding and watering of the rodents. Art did build the hutches with wooden frames and chicken wire for walls.

"This is Buck Teddy," Art proudly told Mel as they toured Mr. Green's rabbits. "He's registered and his off spring are registered too," Art continued.

The next morning big, multi-colored, Buck Teddy was in our hutch along with three white females. Mel had bought them and expected me to take care of them. It was to be a money-making project. Buck Teddy didn't disappoint as a sire and soon the three does were expecting. The kits were born a month later and were tiny as small mice. I made sure there were plenty of pellets for all of the adults to eat and water for them to drink. However, within three days, the number of kittens decreased and we couldn't figure why there were fewer.

"The mother sometimes eats her young," Mr. Green told us. "Did you put a box in with the mothers with straw in it? Did you handle the kits?"

"No, we didn't put a special box for the does and yes, we did pick up the babies," Art answered.

"Well, there's the problem. Why didn't you come to me and ask about breeding the does?"

We had no answer. Mel was disappointed and so were we because the rest of the babies died. It was the first litter and a disaster. There were no further litters. A month later, Buck Teddy and the three other rabbits were sold back to Mr. Green, at a discount.

A few days later we were all in the living room of mom's small house. I said, "Daddy Bob used to like to take us horseback riding."

"He's no longer here and he is not your daddy anymore, so don't call him Daddy Bob anymore," Mel told me.

His tone was sharp and I didn't like it. I looked at mom, then at my brother and sister. No one said a word. It told me Mel was in control now and that he was the final authority in the house. I also got the feeling later verified, that access to my mother was going to be curtailed and it would be a loss for me and my siblings.

Mel came to our house every night now and by winter we hosted his brother from Wisconsin, Robert. He had been in the navy and had gotten out and became an accountant. He drove a new 1948 dark blue Chrysler Imperial with chrome squares in the grill. Mel offered to buy it from him and a price was agreed upon. After Robert left and returned to Wisconsin, Mel took mom for drives in the Chrysler and taught her how to operate the beautiful car with Fluid Drive shifting.

In March, Mel and mom got married. Our new stepfather was never addressed as "Daddy Mel" but only as Mel. Their reception was modest and held at the beauty salon with only a few friends and employees of the shop who served as well-wishers.

They honeymooned by going to California and driving down the Pacific coast. JoAnn and Art went to stay with our biological father in Utah and I stayed with Uncle Dee in Tucson.

Upon the return of the honeymooners, Mel described their trip along the California coast as slow, "wearing out my tires on a twisting and turning a road called Highway 1." He didn't seem joyous about their spree and shared no high points about sights or experiences. It was a little surprising to me that there wasn't more exuberance about something as life changing as a honeymoon.

Everyone was excited however, when Mel revealed plans to lease a 5200 acre ranch in Red Rock, Arizona about 40 miles north of Tucson. Dirt roads led to the ranch off of the main highway as Mel, mom and I journeyed to see our new home. Irrigation canals were bridged by sturdy, wooden boards wide enough for tires on each side of a car to pass over with a gap in the middle, a cost saving measure no doubt.

Five miles into the desert we came to our ranch. The first thing we saw was a large storage shed made of corrugated tin. Thirty yards away there was a building that housed a huge four cylinder diesel engine used to pump irrigation water. When we went inside to look at the engine, it filled the room, stood at least ten feet high and 25 feet long. None of us had ever seen a piece of machinery that big.

The road led around the engine dwelling to a modest wooden shack with two rooms, a kitchen and a combined living room-bedroom chamber. The most imposing part of the ranch was a dirt dam that held some rainwater from the spring rains. It served to store water for irrigation and had gates to release water into canals. It too, was a cost cutting measure to save pumping ground water to the parched dry land.

There was a spectacular view of Picacho Peak in front of us. We were on the South side of it and from that view it looked like a big saddle complete with a saddle horn. Moreover, the sunsets to the left of the Peak were astonishingly beautiful in the evenings. We were happy to be part of this new adventure.

Mel's plan was for him to farm the land while mom would manage the beauty shop. However, it would require her to drive the Chrysler to and from Tucson each day and provide a living income for us while crops were growing in the fields and waiting to be harvested, a bounty Mel hoped would increase our financial coffers.

Mel brought his hunting dogs out to the ranch. There were three red bone hounds named Whitey a brown, tall dog with a white streak on top of her head, Danny a male, brindle in color, and a shorter dog, and Little Red an all reddish brown male that was young. I loved those dogs. They would follow the tractor when Mel let me drive the tractor to plow some of the fields, even though I was only ten years old. They'd be next to the table when we ate and I would give them some of my food under the table. They'd lick my face when I played with them on the floor of the shack. They'd run alongside of me when I tried to race them. On cold nights they would sleep in the shed with me. They became my companions.

JoAnn and Art returned from Utah and moved out to the ranch. Mom fixed up the shack and made it livable. Art and I slept in the storage shed in single beds with the dogs while JoAnn dropped out of high school and got a job in Tucson as a soda jerk and lived with Uncle Dee. Art was enrolled in Eloy High School as a sophomore and I entered fifth grade in a school with four grades in one room. There were two of us in fifth grade, a girl named Phyllis and me.

The little school put on the play, "Johnny Appleseed" and I played the lead role. My sister came from Tucson to see the production which was modest to say the least, but enjoyable. There was polite applause at the end with feigned compliments for the cast and for the elderly woman teacher, whose name escapes me.

Mel took to the task of making a farm by buying three Case tractors, small, medium and large. He bought a land leveler to maximize irrigation water so it would flow evenly to reach the entire crop at the front and back of the field and not pool in low spots. He purchased a disc, a plow, a harrow, and a hay bailer, a planter for row crops, a combine, and irrigation tubes made of rubber and aluminum to transfer irrigation water from the ditch to the fields. He had the farm's gas tanks filled to fuel the tractors. He learned how to start the huge irrigation engine that took a half an hour to prime and start. He was astonished to learn that the giant engine consumed enough diesel to drink up $50.00 a day when running. Again, I remembered my mom's $40.00 paycheck for a week's work so that $50.00 a day for diesel seemed to be a huge expense. Mel set to work with energy clearing the land of tumble weeds, creosol plants, and dried grasses. He plowed, harrowed, seeded, and irrigated. Alfalfa, barley, and maize were planted in the fields. He seemed to know what he was doing and was committed to making a success of the farm.

However, one evening I heard mom say, "Mel, I think you better come into the shop and talk with Mr. George," she advised.

"What's the reason?" Mel asked.

"I think he wants a bigger percentage of his fees," mom revealed.

"I'll go in Saturday afternoon after the clients leave and talk to him," Mel declared. "I don't like that guy. He thinks he's a diva and the world revolves around him."

That Saturday was a turning point in our lives. Mel related the conversation to all of us later that evening.

"I started the conversation by saying Bernice tells me you want to talk to me. What do you want to talk about?"

"Yes, I want to talk to you about compensation. I'm getting a salary and a percentage of what I charge. I want a bigger salary or a bigger percentage. I'm the number one producer in this shop and deserve more."

"How much more?" I asked.

"He said he wanted $100.00 a week and a 50 % commission." He said it in a haughty tone. I dropped the Mr. in Mr. George out of contempt for him.

"I told him no one makes that kind of money and he said then he'd like to buy the shop and Bernice, could work for him. He said he'd pay you $50.00 a week and give you a 25% commission.

"I told him why not pay her what **you** want, and he said he couldn't because she didn't generate as much income as he did.

"Just to see what he was thinking, I asked him what he would give me for the shop and he asked what I paid for it. I didn't tell him I paid $8000.00 for the shop and was offered $14,000 for it six months ago. I just said what do you think it's worth. He said he'd give me $10,000.00 for it.

"I said the shop's not for sale. Then I told him that I'd raise his salary to $75.00 a week and give him a 35% commission. I said that with his tips he'd be making more than anyone in the shop. He said he was already making more than anyone in the shop but needed more or he was going to go to another shop on Speedway Avenue. When he said that I knew he had already accepted the other shop's offer and was trying to hold me up for an amount of money no one was getting. He was looking for a way to get out or buy the shop at a price below what it was worth. He was so arrogant that I wanted to smack him and trim him up.

"I told him to pack up his things and get out. Then he said he wanted to get the names of his clients and their phone numbers so he could tell them he was moving to another shop. I walked up close to his face and told him to get out now."

"What did he do then?" I asked.

"He tilted up his nose and spun away to get his things. It was good he did because I was going to clock him one." Mel said angrily.

After that conversation, we didn't like Mr. George and felt wronged by what he "tried to pull."

Things were forgotten for the moment and Mel went back to working the farm. But I overheard mom tell him that receipts were down so there was less coming in at the shop. Clients followed Mr. George to his new location and the person who replaced him didn't bring in anything close to the amount of money that he brought into the shop.

Even though less money was coming in there was a sense of wellbeing that pervaded the house. The crops were growing and expectations were high. Mel had planted 350 acres of alfalfa, barley, and maize. He expected to cultivate more acreage the next year as well as buy some cattle to graze on the open fields but he needed a good crop in order for the plans to come true. For now things looked good.

One night the dogs left as it got dark. The next morning when I fed them I saw blood on the muzzles of all three dogs.

"Mel, look at the dogs. They've got blood all over their mouths."

Mel called the dogs to him and he examined them.

"They've killed an animal and eaten some of its flesh," he declared. "Wash them up and get the blood off and we'll watch them."

I cleaned the blood off of their faces and wondered what they had gotten into. The next morning they were bloody again and I showed Mel. I washed them up again. Later that day a neighboring rancher came to our place in his pickup truck and said that some of his calves had been attacked and had flesh torn from them and eaten our dogs.

He said he tracked the dogs after he had run them off and he was certain that they were our dogs.

"How bad are they injured?" Mel asked.

"The skin on two calves is pulled away from the flesh and there's bare muscle showing. It looked like a scab is starting to form over the wound," the man said.

Mel offered, "Can I pay you for the damage?"

"Nah, but once dogs taste blood, they'll be back and they'll be like a pack of wolves. It gets into their system and they're never the same. If there's another attack, I'll expect something to be done."

"I understand," Mel said. "Let me try to correct the problem but let me know if there's more trouble."

The rancher drove his pickup truck away and Mel said to me, "hold the dogs."

He went into the kitchen and pulled out a sack and put some liver in it mom had brought home from Tucson and came back and held it up to the dog's noses. They smelled the meat and wanted to lick it Mel pulled back the liver and put it in the sack. He pulled off his belt and started beating Whitey as I held Danny and Little Red. Whitey yelped in pain. Mel turned to Danny as Whitey ran away. Danny was lashed next. Welts grew on his Danny's ribs and when Mel let go, he ran a short distance away and turned to look back. His eyes showed disbelief. Little Red was next and he bayed a howl as his eyes bulged out. His release saw him run away and when I called him to comfort him, he disregarded me.

"You better run damn ya," Mel yelled at the fleeing dogs.

I looked at Mel and his face was a mixture of anger and distain. I had never seen this side of Mel and it was significant that he would have such a hatred for his animals. He walked away and said nothing to me.

The next morning I got up early to examine the dogs. There was new blood on their faces. When Mel woke up he too was looking for the dogs. He found them by their feeding dishes where I had put out food. He grabbed Danny by his collar and walked him behind the shack and tied him to a fence post with a rope. He came back and took Whitey and Little Red and tied them up as well. He went back into the shack and brought his .348 Winchester rifle and loaded it. I couldn't look at what was about to happen. I went inside and then I heard three loud shots. I knew the dogs were dead. I couldn't believe he so cold bloodily spun bullets into his dogs with his high powered rifle that he had used to kill deer and the 14 raccoons that made him the featured story in a sports magazine.

When Mel came inside he said it me, "drag the dogs around to the dam and drop them away from the irrigation gates. I looked at mom and she nodded for me to do as I was told.

I went outside and around the back of the shack and looked down at Whitey. She had a hole in her head. So did Danny and Little Red. Whitey was about 50 pounds and the largest of the three. I untied the rope took her collar in my hand and reached for one of her front legs and pulled. Her dead weight was heavy and it strained my 80 pounds to pull her around the diesel shack, then in front of the storage shed where I slept, and up the steep mounded dirt of the dam. I left behind a trail with a mix of blood and dirt. I was breathing heavily as I laid her under a tree a hundred yards from the irrigation gate. I patted her brown hair, and said goodbye. The walk back to Danny allowed me to regain some of my diminished strength but had to steel myself to reach down to clutch him. I followed the same procedure and path that I took with Whitey and followed in the wake of the blood-stained ground. I put him next to Whitey but was too exhausted offer a farewell. Little Red was the smallest of the three but seemed as heavy because of my fatigue. When I put Little Red next to Whitey and Danny I paused to catch my breath. I looked down at the three dogs and began to cry. I knew I could not stay there too long because I had to get ready for school. I wiped my eyes to try to disguise my grief so that Mel wouldn't see it. He had been so unfeeling when he shot the dogs that I believed that I should project the same demeanor in spite of the hurt I was feeling.

Ten days later on a Saturday, Art was driving the mid-sized tractor. It had three wheels and whoever drove it had to be very careful to cross the canal bridge near the shack so that its one wheel in front didn't drop through the gap between the two boards. Art wasn't careful enough with steering the tractor nor was he going slow enough to make the necessary corrections to avoid trouble. The nose wheel dropped through the gap and the front of the tractor hit the bank on the other side of the canal. The front wheel broke off and fell to the bottom of the canal. Art put the tractor in reverse and tried to back the stuck tractor out of the canal. He only left black rubber tracks on the boards with the big back tires. Art shut down the tractor and went to find Mel. When Art arrived at Mel's side, I was with him.

"Mel, I broke off the front wheel of the tractor trying to cross the canal bridge," he said sheepishly.

"You what?" Mel roared. "Dammit, that's a cast iron housing. It will take a special welder to come out from Coolidge to weld it back on. That's going to cost a lot of money. Plus, we can't use the tractor until it's fixed.

"That's not all Mel," Art admitted. "The tractor's stuck and is blocking anyone from crossing the canal."

"Jesus Christ!" Mel screamed. "Get out of my sight."

Art slunk down and moved around behind Mel.

That afternoon Mel surveyed what had to be done to get the tractor off of the bridge. He got on the big tractor and drove behind the stranded one on the bridge. He laid down heavy boards across the irrigation ditch. He hooked a cable to the axel of the three-wheeled tractor on the bridge, then to the big tractor. The big tractor pulled and dug its wheels into the coarse dirt. It took three pulls for it to free the now two-wheeled tractor. Mel dragged it to the side of the road, unhooked the cable and drove the big tractor back across the bridge. One of the heavy boards was partially broken and Mel barely got across the bridge. Mel got a jack and pried the damaged plank out of the canal bank and then put in a heavy board to replace it. It took until sundown to finish the job.

That night mom called Art outside. We could hear what she was saying.

"You know how much that's going to cost to repair that wheel?" She berated.

"I know ma," Art tried to acknowledge. His words were weak by comparison.

"We can't afford to have these kinds of things happen. You've always been my wild kid and you damn sure did it this time."

"I know, I know," Art tried to appease mom by accepting the blame.

In fact, Art didn't know how much it cost to repair the tractor. He had no money and no sense of what had to be sacrificed to pay for a welder who was sought out by the Case tractor dealership in Coolidge, 35 miles away. It took the welder all day to come to the ranch, repair the tractor, and return. I never knew how much it cost but mom thought it was a lot of money and I'm sure it was.

That summer some of the first cutting of alfalfa was baled, put on a truck and was sent to a Tucson dairy. The driver had a wreck and the hay spilled over the highway and the hay was lost. The barley crop made it to market unscathed and a check found its way safely to Mel. It was too early to harvest the maize so we waited for fall to come.

"Looks like rain is on the way," Mel told mom. That'll be good because it'll fill up the dam then we won't have to pump so much water and we can cut down on fuel costs for that monster of a diesel."

"How much water does that thing pump when it's running?" mom asked.

"5200 gallons a minute," Mel said.

Mom almost jumped out of her seat, "Wow! That's a lot of water."

"It is, but the ditches soak up a lot of water and when we run water out to the far fields, we lose a lot through absorption and in to the hot sun through evaporation," Mel confided. "That's why we hope to fill up the dam with this rain."

As predicted the rains came but what was not forecast was how much. It was a torrential rain that caused flash flooding. Mom had a hard time getting through the dirt roads and on to the paved highway. School buses had to drive through high water in arroyos to get children to school. After the initial rain, more water from the sky followed and the dam began to fill up. Mel watched a pond become a lake, then a sea.

Around 5 P.M. on a November afternoon, the rain was still coming down. Mel examined the dam and water flowing down gopher holes dug deep near the top of the banks. They got bigger. He told Art to run to the irrigation ditch near the shack and bring a canvas to plug the growing cleft. Art ran to the shack where I was and told me to make sandwiches because we might be working all night to save the dam. By the time he returned with the canvas the gap had grown to a gulch and water was pouring through the other side of the dam. The flow was wider than the canvas, and growing. Mel had run to the storage shed for a shovel and tried to throw dirt into the breach but it was too little and cavity grew wider.

Within half an hour the dam gave way. The lake became a river of water. While I was making sandwiches water began to invade the shack and rose to the height of my knee. The water filled our irrigation ditches and washed over our cultivated fields. The maize crop was swamped and the stalks bent with the current and were almost laying on their side at ground level. We walked in the dark trying to survey the damage with each step causing a sloshing sound. The dam was lost and so was the maize crop.

That night we were all able to sleep in the dry storage shed because its floor was above the water level. Mom stayed in Tucson because she couldn't get back to the ranch because of flooding.

The next morning the water had subsided and the rains had stopped but muddy muck was everywhere. Mel hoped to relieve some of standing water around the shack by lowering the canvases in the irrigation ditch that ran west.

"Push down hard on that canvas," Mel snapped at Art and me who were down in the ditch. It was obvious that Mel was angry at losing the dam, the crop, and at Art because he thought the dam could have been saved if Art had come quickly with the canvas. In fact, there were too many gopher holes needing to be plugged to save it. The dam would burst no matter what.

I pushed as hard as I could but because I was shorter than Art, I could only lower the canvas as far as Art.

"Push harder Art," Mel yelled.

"I'm pushing as hard as I can," Art yelled back.

Mel reached down and grabbed Art's 145 pound body with his two hands around his neck and lifted him up out of the ditch as if he were a rag doll. He released one hand and slapped Art across the face then threw him into the wet, muddy field where his body sent up a splash in the standing water.

"Don't you talk back to me, goddamn ya. It's your fault all of this happened anyway. You're worthless and you'll never amount to anything. Now get down into that ditch and push the canvass lower."

Art got up from the muck, his clothes wet and muddy and got back into the ditch and pushed hard on the canvas. His anger was evident but he didn't challenge Mel. However, when he got back into the irrigation ditch his spirits were lower than any canvass.

In witnessing Mel's actions, I saw a new side of him. I knew he was angry about the dam and perhaps losing the crop. I understood that his wealth was also in jeopardy and maybe our future as well. But the extent of his violence and disregard for part of my family made me look at him differently.

Christmas break came from school and Mel had Art and me in the maize field.

"Cut the heads off the stalks and put them in the burlap sacks. Tie the bag through your belt so you can carry it down the rows."

As we proceeded to follow Mel's instructions we realized that we could only harvest a small amount of the crop and our efforts to salvage some of the maize was more about punishment than any expectation of making a financial gain from our efforts. As we continued our toil in the maize field we both incurred cuts on our hands and fingers from chopping and slicing off the heads that we had to lift from the slanted stalks. The flood and wind tilted the maize heads horizontally. The bags we filled were run through a combine to salvage what little we harvested from the 100 acre field. Even Mel realized that continuing the effort was pointless.

Near the end of the Christmas break, Mel and I ran across some of the other ranchers in a field of another farm. We stopped and as men of the land often do, the conversation came around to how the rains had affected their crops and what could be expected from the harvests. Mel listened to what the others had to say and when it was his turn to share his views I felt embarrassed at what he said.

"It looks like I'm done," he began. "All of my crops got washed out when the dam broke. I don't have enough cash flow to continue. In fact, I'm glad I ran into you guys. I'm selling my equipment. I paid 40% down and I'd like to get something out of the tractors and other machinery before the bank takes them back. Do any of you want to buy my equipment? It's only been used one season."

I looked at Mel and there was chagrin on his face and in his voice. He bravely admitted that all was done but he felt disgraced. I quickly looked at the faces of the other men and their heads were lowered and they spoke in respectful tones with empathy.

"It's a damned shame that you lost your crop that way," one said.

"No, I'm sorry but I can't take any of your equipment off your hands," another regretted.

The rest nodded sideways that they couldn't buy Mel's farm apparatus either. It was the first time I had seen Mel admit defeat. All of the other time our family had seen him dealing with the farm or life in general, he seemed confident and in control. He was trying to take losing the farm it like a man but it was punishing to see him like this.

As the days rolled on a grim reality set in. The only income we had was from the beauty shop and it was producing less now that Mr. George was gone.

We left the farm, moved back to Tucson and rented a small apartment on Grant Avenue. When Art tried to enter high school, it was learned that he had failed most of his subjects in the school in Utah when he stayed with our biological father. He had just turned 17 years old. He didn't want to continue in school and so it was decided that mom would give her permission for Art to join the United States Army. It was the spring of 1950.

Just after Art finished basic training in June, the Korean War broke out and he was sent to defend South Korea in a United Nations effort that was called a "police action."

It was also a time when the American government was subsidizing farmers to produce more cotton and gave money away to put in electric pumps that were much cheaper to run than the big diesel engine we used on the ranch in Red Rock. Had Mel been able to survive the flood we would have been able to plant cotton and make a success of the farm due to government sponsored funding.

WISCONSIN

"Bernice, I got this letter today from my brother Harvey," Mel said excitedly. There's a bar, restaurant, and dance hall back home that's come up for sale. Harvey and my brother Robert want to buy it and have me manage it. We'd be partners. It's called Fernwood Gardens. I'm going back there to look things over and if things look good, we'll buy it and I'll send for you."

Mom was supportive. Mel sold the 1947 Frazer and drove the Chrysler back to Wisconsin. We waited in Tucson to learn whether we would be moving to the Midwest.

JoAnn had saved money and gone to Cosmetology school in Phoenix and became a licensed beautician. She began working in Mel's beauty shop but didn't make a lot of money as she was new to the profession and was in the process of building up a cadre of clients. It was a slow process.

Mom called us together one evening. "JoAnn, you're going to manage the shop here in Tucson while Bobby and I are going back to Wisconsin to join Mel in the restaurant, bar, and dance hall. It will be a good opportunity for you JoAnn to run the shop and we hope to make a good life back in Wisconsin. You can stay in this apartment in our absence so you'll have a place to live. Mel and I hope we can get back on our feet after we lost the ranch."

JoAnn agreed to give it a try knowing she was the youngest beautician in the shop and had little experience in running a business. I had mixed feelings about leaving because my asthma had not returned since I came to Arizona and knew that Mel had left Wisconsin because he had difficulties with his asthma back there. But the thought of being in an environment where Mel had such success as a younger man was encouraging. His letters back to us seemed to indicate that his confidence had returned and he was sure things would work out well.

Mom and I boarded a train in Tucson headed for Wisconsin by way of Texas, Chicago, and Milwaukee. Mom and I played canasta on the train, ate in the dining car, slumbered in the sleeping car, and watched the miles roll by outside our window. When we got to Texas the train stopped and we got out for a short layover before boarding a train heading north. I went to the bathroom and came out looking for a water fountain to get a drink due to the hot weather.

There were two fountains, one labeled "White" and another identified as "Colored." I was confused and when I showed my mom the drinking fountains and asked why there were two she replied, "Don't ask questions here. I'll tell when we get back on the train."

When we got on our train and it began to move north, mom took me to our compartment and said there were states in America where "Negroes" were separated from the white population. I asked why. She said the "Negroes" were descendants of slaves and were looked upon as being inferior to whites in the south. White people passed laws keeping "Negroes" from associating with them.

"Are they inferior?" I asked.

"I don't think so but people in Texas and other places think so and have passed laws that keep the two groups separate."

It was the first time I had encountered racism and was puzzled by it. I had never thought about one group of people being that different from another enough to have laws separating them. It was incredulous to me but noteworthy to learning the ways of the world outside of my exposure to it in Idaho and Arizona.

The trip took three days and when we arrived in Door County, Mel was there to pick us up in the blue Chrysler. He drove us to Fernwood Gardens and it was about 9 in the morning. There were two gasoline pumps in front, a gravel driveway, and stairs leading to the entrance door. When we entered the first room it was darkened because the lights were off. We adjusted to the shadowy light and saw that the room was "L" shaped and that was the bar. It had a shuffle board, a Jukebox, tables with chairs, and booths. Behind the bar there were liquor bottles on shelves. Below were refrigerators for beer and soft drinks. There was a shelf at chest level that had jars with hard boiled eggs, and a rack for peanuts and beer nuts. Behind all of the shelves was a large mirror and we could barely see ourselves. Bar stools were evenly spaced in the front of the bar. Behind the barroom Mel showed us the kitchen where the meals were prepared.

Pots and pans hung from racks with hooks, cupboards were filled with dishes. Below the cupboards were drawers where tableware was stored and on the right wall was a large refrigerator that held meat and vegetables. To the left of the kitchen was a door that led to stairs and up on the second floor. This was where the living quarters were and our new residence.

The grounds outside had trees and under them a few picnic tables spaced far enough apart to provide privacy for guests. There was a creek and Mel said there were trout in it. I couldn't wait to try to catch a fish. I'd never been fishing before and it would be a new experience. Behind the building was another gravel space for us to park the Chrysler. Mel warned me not to go into the dense woods behind the building because it led to Lake Michigan and the wind and waves could be dangerous.

To the left of the bar-restaurant area was the dancehall. It was large and could hold close to 200 people who could drink and dance. The kind of bands booked was Lawrence Welk type musicians. They played polkas, schottisches, and waltzes. There was a large population of German decent so that kind of music and dancing appealed to them. There was a cover charge and people came from as far away as Sturgeon Bay and locally from Egg Harbor. Most of the dances were scheduled for Saturday night but the dance hall was available for special occasions such as weddings, birthdays, and anniversaries.

I was allowed to see the dance hall when it was empty and on our first Saturday night at Fernwood Gardens, I was permitted to enter and enjoy the music and watch the dancers until 9:30 P.M. Then I was to return across the way to bar-restaurant and go upstairs to my room and go to bed. I could hear the music when I went to bed and I could occasionally hear patrons down below in the bar.

Entire families came to the bar. The adults drank beer and hard liquor while their children were served sodas. The Juke Box was fed coins and songs like the "The Third Man's Theme" sounded out of it. Families enjoyed shuffle board games, drinking, dining and visiting. People were friendly and there was never a fight or argument. It was a nice experience for me to see how people lived in the Midwest.

On Sunday mornings I was instructed to sweep up and mop the bar-dining area while mom and Mel slept in. The day before in the afternoon, I was to get out the push mower and mow the lawn. I would start on Saturday afternoon and mow for a half an hour at a time, rest, then more for another half an hour. I would be able to finish by Sunday afternoon. It took about three hours to mow the entire grounds.

One Sunday afternoon after mowing I decided to try to catch the trout in the nearby stream. A tree grew near the bank of the brook and its limbs covered part of the water. I climbed up the branches and looked down and saw four fish. I used fishing line with a bobber because I didn't have a pole or reel. In spite of my efforts, no fish took the bait so I decided to bide my time and come back another day and one day I believed, I would catch a fish.

I was also directed to pump gas when cars wanted to refuel. It was hard for me to reach the windshields to wash them, so I got a short stepladder to aid in that task. One Friday night I was permitted to help serve drinks, mainly beer to customers. They rolled dice to see who would buy the round of drinks. I enjoyed talking with the patrons who were mainly farmers and tradesmen.

Early one Sunday morning about 4 A.M. the dance hall caught on fire. By the time the firemen came most of the building was blazing. When the fire was finally extinguished it was after 10 A.M. The building was a complete disaster. Nothing could be salvaged from it.

"When we see the lawyer, don't say anything, just listen," Mel instructed me. I rode with him to Sturgeon Bay and we were joined by Mel's brother Harvey and it was in the evening around seven.

71

The lawyer began, "I have some bad news for you tonight. I reviewed the insurance policy and it doesn't have a replacement clause in it. What that means is that you don't have enough insurance coverage to rebuild the dance hall. Your policy will help with some of the costs but won't cover all of expenses that you'll incur to reconstruct it. You'll have to borrow some additional money from a lender. I can recommend one to you and I have contacted the insurance company and increased your coverage, so that if another fire happens you'll be fine."

I didn't know all of the ins and outs of what was being said but I knew there was going be additional costs involved to get the dance hall back up and functioning again. Also, I knew that no money would come in while it was not open.

After an hour of questions and responses, the lawyer turned to me and complimented me for being attentive and involved even though I said nothing.

"You were listening carefully to what we talked about tonight. I could see that you were concentrating and were engaged. Do you have any questions you'd like to ask?"

"I was told not to say anything but to listen and not be a distraction."

The lawyer smiled and said, "You'll be a good businessman someday young man."

A month went by and meetings with insurance adjusters took place, checks were written and contactors interviewed. Finally, one builder was selected because he said he and his crew could lay 1800 blocks a day once things got underway. A loan was floated to rebuild the dance hall so that work could begin.

A bulldozer came and scraped the charred remains of the burned dance hall and trucks hauled away the debris. Then trenches were dug, pipes were connected near the ground, and a foundation was laid. Cement trucks dropped piles of gray concrete inside the new square and it was spread out and smoothed into a floor. The blocks began to be laid and grew each day into walls. A roof was put on and inside the new building, a bar was built. A new floor was laid, tables and chairs were delivered and set up, and decorations adorned and beautified the place.

An advertisement announced that the new dance hall was again ready to provide enjoyment to patrons. The first Saturday night it was opened the crowd was smaller than the one that had come to the old dance hall. I overheard Mel and his brother deciding what to do next.

"We'd better schedule a popular band to bring back the crowd," Mel said to Harvey.

"Popular bands cost more money and we don't have a lot right now. We may lose money even if the crowd is what it used to be," Harvey countered.

"We have to do something to get the people back," Mel implored.

"People are fickle. They went to other dance halls while we were rebuilding ours. It's hard to expect them to all come running back as soon as we open up. I'd like to take things slow and in time win back our customers. I don't want to lose too much money right away trying to get a big crowd." Harvey opined.

"Let's try to get a popular band right away and then taper off with less trendy bands later," Mel persisted.

"We'll lose money. A popular band wouldn't make us money in the old place so why would we think that we'll make money in the new one?" Harvey said. "We can't have a high cover charge nor can we jack up the price of drinks to pay for the added cost of an expensive band because people won't come to our place," Harvey said, as his voice rose in volume.

"You've got to trust me Harvey. I'm the businessman in the family. I know what works. We've got to do something dramatic even if we lose money to start."

Mel won the argument and a popular band was scheduled to perform. The crowd was larger than the opening night but money was lost because the band cost more than the money that was brought in.

The conflict between Mel and Harvey continued with each winning a concession from the other on this point or that point. However, money was lost no matter whose philosophy was in place. The torment wore on and there was an undertow festering between the two brothers.

One night it rained hard. Mom had gone to town with Nort who was married to Mel's cousin, Barbara. I went to bed at 9:30 but when I awoke the next morning mom was at my bedside.

"Bobby, wake up. We're leaving. Pack some clothes in my suitcase and meet me down stairs."

I looked at her through half-awake eyes and saw that she had been crying and her left eye was almost swollen shut.

"What happened?" I said astonished.

"I'll tell you later. Get dressed and come down. Harvey is going to take us to Sturgeon Bay and we are going to take a bus back to Tucson."

I dressed with great concern. I didn't concentrate on packing many of my clothes. When I came downstairs only Harvey and Mel were in the bar.

"You've taken this too far. You have messed this up and now your wife is leaving you. That's enough out of you," Harvey was pointing at Mel.

Mel was behind the bar but his eyes were bulging and he was angry.

"Don't you point your finger at me," he said to his brother.

Harvey didn't back down, "That's enough," he repeated and walked out the front door of the bar.

Mom was waiting for me outside on the porch. She was wearing dark glasses with green lenses now. She motioned for me to follow her and we walked down the steps. A minute later Harvey drove his car next to us. Mom got into the front seat and I got in the back. Harvey's car left the gravel driveway and got on the two lane highway heading south toward Sturgeon Bay.

74

"I'm sorry this happened. Are you badly hurt?" Harvey asked.

"I'll be all right. Thank you for taking us to the bus station," mom said in a hurt voice.

"Do you have enough money? I can stop by the bank and get some cash to carry you through to Arizona." Harvey said apologetically and with warmth in his voice.

"I have enough to get me there, thank you." Mom's voice was different. It said to me that she was thankful but didn't want any more from the Jorns family.

When we arrived at the bus station Harvey again apologized for Mel's actions. Mom thanked him again for the ride and turned away. I had said nothing the whole morning but had witnessed conversations that told me a lot of what had happened. Mom bought tickets to Milwaukee with transfers that would take us to Tucson. We didn't get on the bus until the afternoon but when we did I immediately began asking questions. Mom had purposefully located seats near the back of the bus where no one was near us. She sat by the window.

"Mom, tell me what happened," I insisted.

She began, "You know Nort who is married to Barbara?"

"Yes, of course."

"We went into Sturgeon Bay yesterday afternoon. He wanted to get some supplies for his bar you know, the one named the Ivanhoe."

I nodded yes.

"I was looking for some new tablecloths. It started to rain. We stopped along the way home at other bars. Bar owners often stop and spend money at other bars to stimulate business and then those owners stop and spend money at your bar on later occasions. We stopped at three bars and Nort had at drink at each."

When we arrived back at our place Nort continued to drink and Marv served him but was quiet and upset. You were already in bed when Nort left. There weren't but two customers left in our bar so Mel told them to drink up because he was going to close the bar early."

"What happened next?" I asked astonished.

"When the bar was closed Mel asked me to come to the back of the kitchen. When I went back there he grabbed me by the neck and dragged me down the stairs and to the woods. He began choking me and then he socked me in my eye and threw me to the ground."

"Why did he do that to you?" I said with anger in my voice.

"He thought Nort had done something to me," she said.

"Why didn't he punch Nort then, instead of you?" I probed.

"Marv thought I let Nort do something to me but I didn't. Nort didn't try to do anything to me but Mel got crazy and wouldn't believe anything I said."

I hugged my mom and said I was sorry she was beaten up. I realized as I embraced her that it was the first time I had been able to show my physical love by touching her since Marv came into our lives. He was not an affectionate man towards mom or any of us kids. As darkness came, mom was quietly crying wiping tears from her cheeks that had drained under her dark glasses. Some of those tears came from her injury and it was sad to know some came from the emotional degradation and humiliation that came from an utter loss of dignity and respect.

The Greyhound bus took us across the center of America and into its southwest. Mom avoided the other passengers and I tried to offer my sympathies by holding her hand much of the way. When we reached Tucson, we took a city bus to Grant Avenue and the apartment where JoAnn was living.

"What happened to you mom?" JoAnn said in a shocked tone.

Mom explained what happened in Wisconsin and Mel's battering of her. Her eye that was swollen when we left Sturgeon Bay was now a darkened patch under it. After an hour of conversation, mom tried to change the subject.

"How are things going at the shop?"

"I'm trying my best," JoAnn said. "Some of the other operators have been helpful and try to explain things to me but others are uncooperative and seem to resent me when I ask them to do the normal things like cleaning up their station."

"How are finances?" mom inquired.

"Not so good." JoAnn lamented. "My clientele is growing slowly but Sally left the shop to move to another shop on Speedway Boulevard. Her customers followed her and I didn't try to find a replacement so there's less money coming in now."

"Well, I'll be the replacement," mom said. "I'm going to call some of my old clients and try to bring them back."

Over the next month, mom got things under control at the shop. The remaining beauticians were glad to see her back and they responded to her guidance. Some of mom's customers came back to her and there was optimism that there was a slow recovery underway. Just when things seemed to be getting better, another devastating event happened.

"The sheriff said to me, I'm sorry lady but I have orders to take the equipment now," mom said.

"Can't you come back and the end of the day. I have customers with wet hair under hair dryers. You can't expect them to walk out of here in that condition," I asked the sheriff and I was pleading with him. "He was unsympathetic. He just told the movers to unplug everything and haul away everything."

"What did the customers say, mom," I asked.

"They were outraged and said they would never come back. I said to them that I'd call them and explain what happened and offer them a free service next time they needed one."

"Why did the sheriff and the movers take the dryers in the first place?" I said incredulously.

"Mel mortgaged everything when he got the ranch. He didn't tell me he had done that. I guess he believed he needed the money to buy farm equipment. I'm already mad at him because of what happened in Wisconsin but this is the ultimate disgrace."

An hour later a man showed up at our apartment and he and mom discussed getting some replacement equipment back into the shop.

"I think you'd be better off getting used dryers to start. I'll be cheaper and we can deliver them tomorrow morning before nine o'clock," he said.

"That'll be fine," mom said relieved. "I'll pay you something on the first of the month. Will you carry me until then?"

"Bernice we've done business with you for a long time and I know you're a responsible person. We'll work with you on this. I'm sorry this had to happen and I know it's not your fault."

"Thank you so much," mom gratefully responded.

The next day the used dryers were delivered as promised. A few clients came in for their scheduled appointments not knowing what had happened. They asked why the shop had changed and mom said it was a cost-cutting move. Mom also worked the phone later that day to call the clients who were so rudely removed from the shop the day before promising that things were settled now and offering free services if they would return.

Word spread quickly in the beauty shop world and clients began to drift away. Mom advertised special deals hoping to generate new business and keep some of her loyal clients in place. Things got worse. Some of the other beauticians left for other shops. Income declined and making payments for the used equipment became difficult. Mom persevered but things leveled off at a lower level.

Letters began to arrive from Wisconsin from Mel. He said he was sorry for what happened and he had confronted

Nort who said mom had done nothing wrong. Mel said things were not going well at Fernwood Gardens. Money from the dance hall was down but the bar business was stable. Restaurant income was lower as winter months set in but the holidays were forthcoming and he hoped for an increase in business. Mel said he was going to turn the business over to Harvey and wanted to come back to Arizona because his asthma was getting worse back there.

Mel still owned the beauty shop and wanted mom to stay on as manager. She wrote back a scathing letter to him, a letter she shared with JoAnn and me before she mailed it. She detailed how the shop's equipment had been seized and that business had fallen off in spite of her efforts to reclaim it. She said she was bitter about the way she had been treated by him and that he shouldn't expect her to take him back into her life.

More letters from Mel arrived and he was contrite. He said he was wrong and that he needed us as a family to be happy and that he would make us all happy too. He pledged to make things right and get back to making a financial recovery.

Over the next few months mom began to weaken. She felt Mel was sorry for what he did. She came to believe she needed him in her life to make things easier in terms of money and make her family complete.

Mel came back to Tucson two months later and lived with us. Now there were Mel, mom, JoAnn, and me living together. I was wary of Mael because this was the second time I had seen him exert physical violence in our family, first with Art and now with mom.

There wasn't a joyous celebration when Mel returned. A mode of family life was centered on not causing a problem for one another. There was no affection between Mel and us. There only sense of well-being occurred when Mel got his way. There was no encouragement from him for any of us. He didn't ask if I wanted to join the Boy Scouts and denied approval when I brought the subject up.

Mel however, decided to enroll in cosmetology school and he said that after he graduated, he, mom and JoAnn would make the shop a family operation. He registered and started classes. He had trouble learning the intricacies of cutting hair correctly, knowing the book work, and getting along with people.

One evening he slammed his books shut and said. "I don't get this stuff. I didn't do well on the last test."

He called me to the kitchen table and said, "Let's play canasta."

I could see he was upset. I purposefully lost at cards to him so as to not provoke him further.

"Maybe if you studied more instead of playing cards, you'd do better on tests," JoAnn admonished.

Mel jumped up from the table and went to the couch where JoAnn was sitting and pulled her up violently.

Mom yelled, "Don't you hit her."

It was enough of a reproach to stop him and he pushed her back on the couch. He returned to the kitchen table and looked at me with anger on his face.

"Deal!"

I did and continued to find a way to lose to him.

He dropped out of the beauty school two months into the nine month term.

Mel said he knew how to paint houses and got a job in a housing development that was mass producing homes to meet the housing shortage in Tucson. Painters were expected to cover so much space in an allotted time in order to keep pace with the other subcontractors to deliver a home at a promised date. Marv was paid $1.50 an hour or $12.00 a day for a $60.00 a week pay check.

I remembered that he had $28,000.00 in the bank when he was 28 years old and calculated that he would have to work almost nine years to make $28,000.00 again and that was if he saved every penny. Mel no doubt, did the same calculation in his mind as well and wasn't feeling he was getting ahead.

Mom and JoAnn continued to work in the beauty shop and slowly began to bring it back. Mom hired other beauticians who had a following to come to Mel's shop. She had to make concessions in the percentage she paid them to get them to come but things began to pick up.

"Don't you think it would be better if we bought a house rather than pay rent?" mom questioned Mel.

"Yes, but we don't have a lot of money for a down payment and the interest rate would drive up the cost higher than renting at the moment. I'll try to think of a way to try to get us into a home," he promised.

A month went by and then one day he said with optimism in his voice, "Get in the car Bernice, I'm going to show you a place that we might want to buy."

We all got in the Chrysler and drove to East Lee Street. When Mel stopped we were looking at dirt lot with no grass and 30 yards away from the street was a small shack.

"I got the key from the owner so let's go inside," Mel enthused.

We entered from the left side of the house. Inside there was a small kitchen with the sink facing the back side of the house. There was an older electric stove on the left side where we entered. To the right was a small living room. In back of that was a hallway that led to the one bedroom.

"Where's the bathroom?" mom said to no one as she explored the home.

"There's an outhouse out back," Mel answered. "Before you reject this house outright, let me tell you that it comes cheap and we can fix it up and make a profit. We can get started right away with some of the repairs and improvements."

Mom wasn't convinced that this was a good deal. She didn't see what Mel saw in its potential.

"We can start to dig a cesspool in back so we can put indoor plumbing and dig a hole in front to throw our garbage cans in the front of the house, then we can cover it over with dirt. I can do the painting. I know some guys that can lay

81

cinder blocks and will help me on weekends. It shouldn't take long to get it in shape."

Mom offered, "Let me think about it."

Darkness was setting in and it was cold so the house didn't seem livable at the moment. I looked around and there was no garage for the car or a carport. There was no lawn or shrubs in any direction, only a mesquite tree on the side of the house where we entered.

Mel always seemed to have a scheme to make money. He hated the thought of working for someone else. However, none of his plans had worked out since he joined our family.

Mel continued to lobby mom about buying the little house that needed a lot of fixing up. Over time she relented and a deal was made. The house cost $2000.00 and we could move in right away. Mel knew some men who were also painters and they agreed to help us move our household possessions to our new home. Mel had brought some whiskey from the bar a Fernwood Gardens and he paid our movers in Four Roses bourbon whisky. So we took residence in February. 1951. We, meaning Mel, mom, JoAnn, and me.

"Bobby, come over here. I've marked off the area where we need the cesspool dug," Mel explained. "Here's a shovel and a pick. I want you to start digging. It needs to be six feet deep. You can throw the dirt to the left side of the hole. That way it won't block our path to the outhouse."

The area that Mel staked out was eight feet long and five feet wide. I was instructed to dig after school each day. So I started in and the first layer of dirt was fairly easy to dig. However, below the surface hard caliche clay was difficult to penetrate. So I used the pick. I was still undersized for my eleven years and swinging the pick was challenging for me. However, I made progress, slowly. After going down two feet, I created a step by digging deeper a foot away from the back edge so it would be easier to climb out. At four feet, I made another step.

I was not given an allowance but my sister said that if I would do the dishes after each meal she would pay me a quarter a day. I gladly accepted and earned $1.75 a week. I saved every penny. I didn't buy comic books nor did I buy a soft drink to wash down my lunch at school.

Every Saturday I was assigned the duty of scrubbing the kitchen and living room on my hands and knees. I used Ajax cleanser then mopped up the watery slurry. When the floor dried I would wax it.

JoAnn met a young man Joe who was in the Air Force assigned to Davis-Monthan Air Force Base. He was in special services playing clarinet in the band. He was slight in stature and fit JoAnn's size perfectly. They dated and he began to teach her a few words and phrases in Italian. He took her to dances and it was clear that they were headed for a permanent relationship.

"I don't like most Italians," Mel defiantly told JoAnn. He said Italian pronouncing the first syllable to sound like "eye." "They don't work very hard and a musician can't find a lot of work unless they're in a big band like Tommy Dorsey's or Harry James'. If they do get that kind of job, they're always on the road. What kind of life is that if you want kids?" Mel asked.

It didn't matter what Mel said, JoAnn and Joe were in love and wanted to get married. They did and JoAnn happily moved out of our little house into an apartment with Joe.

Mel met other painters whom he coaxed into helping him fix up our house. Sometimes he paid them and other times they volunteered for a hot meal mom would make. One was named Frank but everyone called him "Frankaruskie" because of his Russian decent. Another was named Norm and he was an alcoholic. Norm had a wife and son. They liked Mel because he would try to keep Norm sober. Norm would sometimes leave for lunch, get drunk and not come back to work. He lost jobs because of his drinking so Mel would try to find him work and drive him home afterwards avoiding bars and liquor stores along the way. Frank and Norm helped with putting in rough plumbing, laying cement blocks, framing windows, pouring cement, and doing other jobs to add to our house and improve it.

JoAnn and Joe didn't find marital bliss once they were married. Shortly after their marriage they broke up. There were no children from this pairing so the divorce was fairly simple. JoAnn moved back into our home. A few months later, JoAnn met another Airman. His name was Robert and he was a sergeant working in security. He had been a policeman before joining the Air Force. He made an impression because he was tall, handsome, had dark hair, an olive complexion, was older than Joe and seemed more mature and manly. When he first came to pick JoAnn up for a date, he was wearing a white dinner jacket and he looked very impressive in contrast to our incomplete house.

Robert also began to help with the construction of our home. He was strong and energetic. Mom invited him to stay for dinner one evening. After dinner we were all sitting in the living room that was now passable to entertain guests. Mel was sitting on our couch and Robert was sitting in a lounge chair. Mel pulled one knee under his torso and bent his knee with his other leg. He purposely farted loudly and looked to see Robert's reaction.

"Thhee hee, Thhee hee," he laughed.

Robert, to his credit, maintained his composure and didn't react. Mel continued to express his unusual laughing pattern until mom said, "Melvin control yourself."

JoAnn was mortified and her look was hateful. I was embarrassed for JoAnn and for our family. I thought Robert was the hero of this little, uncomfortable drama.

Within three months JoAnn and Robert were married. He was reassigned to Colorado by the Air Force. They lived in Manitou Springs and JoAnn got a job in a curio shop and reported that she was very happy.

As the house began to show expansion and improvement living in it became more tolerable. There were two additional bedrooms, a bathroom complete with toilet now that I had dug a cesspool, and a shower and tub. The living room was plastered and painted by Mel. Plastic tile was laid over the bare cement floor. However, the carpentry for a roof over the new bedrooms was needed. It had to be spliced on to the existing structure. It required a professional and Frankaruskie was not skilled enough to do the job. Nor was Norm, even sober.

Mel contacted several workmen but settled on Bill Palmer who had a reputation for doing good work. He and his wife also had been written up in the Tucson Daily Star the newspaper as featured subjects for a newspaper article. They had done worthy charity work the article said.

Bill Palmer began to work on our home and was competently putting together a frame meshing the two parts of our house. He said that another job had come up and he had to leave our project for a short time but would return to finish the job. Mel was upset but said he would accept the delay. A week went by, then a month. Even in rain- scarce Arizona a bare roof exposes the interior to damage should a drizzle drop from the sky. Still no word from Palmer was forthcoming as to when he would return to our job so Mel sought him out to get a firm date.

Mel found Palmer, not on the job he said he was doing but on another he had taken in the interim after finishing the project for which he said he had to leave our house.

"What are you doing here on this job?" Mel related to us that night.

I looked at Mel who was dressed in his white painting overalls and saw a lump on his back.

"He said to me that he had taken our job over six weeks ago and that it was a little job and that he needed to work on bigger jobs when they came up and this job was a big job.

85

'I said that was not what we had agreed on. That's when he turned on me and swung a hammer at my head. I saw it coming and lunged forward and knocked him down like I used to tackle guys in football. The hammer hit me on my back. I pinned him to the ground and took the hammer out of his hand and raised it as I was going to hit him with it. He was scared shitless."

I was astonished as Mel told the story. That explained the lump on his back.

The hammer blow that missed Mel's head had struck him near his spine. I had seen Mel manhandle Art and I remembered mom's black eye so I could believe that he had won this confrontation because of his strength and aggressive nature.

"I shook the hammer in front of his face and told him he had better be back on my job this weekend and stay until it was finished. He said 'okay, okay' and was white in the face. I told him that if he didn't show up at my place that I would track him down again and beat the shit out of him."

Mel said to me, "Don't tell any of your friends about this."

I nodded that I wouldn't. However, I did tell one friend but swore him to secrecy.

I looked to the next weekend with anticipation to see if Bill Parmer would come to work on our roof. He was there at 8:30 A.M. and stayed all day. He told Mel he would come back tomorrow after he attended church. He did and the he continued to work on the roof for the next several days until it was finished.

When the house was structurally complete, Mel painted it and for the first time it looked like a house that other people lived in. It had taken months to complete because Mel and mom had to save up money to buy supplies and progress was start and stop. It was speeded up when a sober Norm convinced Mel to get a loan from the bank so things could go faster. Even with loan payments it was less than we were paying for rent.

The summer months were so hot in Tucson that people stayed inside with swamp coolers blowing moist air on them to relieve some of the oppressive heat. On some weekends Mel and mom would prepare a picnic lunch and we would drive in the Chrysler up to Mount Lemmon several thousand feet up. Its total height was over 9000 feet and the elevation provided cooler air and a break from the overbearing temperature. Mel and mom would lie on a blanket and recover their strength from a week's worth of work and I would hike the trails.

ALASKA

Mom would have been satisfied to live out life as we now knew it; Mel painting and she working in the beauty shop. However, Mel must have been born with the risk gene because he now felt the urge for another project that would earn more money for the family. He went to the public library and checked out books on Alaska and read them at night. He would read passages to us about how wonderful it was with its wildlife of moose, ptarmigans, salmon, huge brown bears, untamed rivers, and mineral wealth. He read about the construction of the Alcan Highway during World War II and how it was possible to now drive all the way to Fairbanks. He spoke glowingly about Mount McKinley, glaciers, Cook Inlet, and the Kenai Peninsula. He noted that Alaska was twice the size of Texas and equal to 20% of all the 48 states below Canada. We were informed by these books that in the Matanuska Valley, cabbages grew to weigh 60 pounds because of the long summer days of sunshine.

We had never taken a vacation together even though one was promised in Mexico and a stop at Guaymas for sport fishing. Now the conversation changed. It was proposed that we take a trip to Alaska and a search for new opportunities to homestead land, to fish commercially, or perhaps work on government projects that paid high wages.

It was exceedingly hot in July, 1952. Mel hated working for wages and wanted to find a way to make a "killing" in a project he controlled. Mom was willing to take a vacation to a cooler place and Alaska seemed like a welcome respite from Tucson's summer blaze.

Mel bought camping equipment, a green tent that would sleep the three of us and it had a coating that resisted rain. Mel also bought folding cots, sleeping bags, a camp stove that used white gas, a gas lantern, water canteens, and cooking pots to prepare us for our journey.

I had saved $40.00 from the money JoAnn had paid me to wash and dry the dishes. It was my nature to save for a rainy day.

"Bobby, give me your $40.00 and I'll buy fishing tackle with it. You can use the tackle box and the lures if we go fishing."

Mel didn't ask me for the money, he was demanding it. Fearing conflict and I truly mean fearing, I gave him my money but I hated him for insisting on it.

We only planned to be gone long enough to go up to Alaska, look around for opportunities and then return. Maybe three weeks to a month.

As the days approached for our departure Mel began practicing loading all of our baggage and camping gear into the car. When he believed he could get it all into the Chrysler he declared us ready to begin our journey. There was only a little space on the right hand side of the back seat for me to sit.

Money had been saved from my parent's two incomes and on a July evening we set a course north. Mel would drive for hours at a time. We'd stop for food and gas but then it was back on the road. About 5 or 6 in the afternoon he'd look for a motel to spend the night. The next morning we'd drive for an hour or two then have breakfast. When we reached Alberta, Canada we stopped for gas. Canadian money was worth 5% more than the U.S. dollar then and it was our first introduction to the Canadian imperial gallon which is almost 20% larger than the American. Another

American had stopped at the same gas station that we had and when he learned of the exchange rate and the cost of a gallon of Canadian gas (he thought was the same size of America's) he was so shocked that he turned his car around immediately and returned to the United States. We laughed at his witlessness and proceeded north. The weather was cooler than Arizona's and welcome.

North of Edmonton we entered British Columbia and left paved road to find the Alcan Highway. It was a dirt road with endless washboard ridges that slowed our pace to between 25 and 40 miles an hour. New cities or really small towns masquerading as cities came only after long hours on the road. We traveled to Whitehorse in the Yukon, Dawson, and Dawson Creek near the Klondike River, two towns almost on the same parallel as Fairbanks in Alaska, then southwest to Tok Junction, just inside Alaska. The roads got better and we entered Palmer in the Matanuska Valley. We stopped in Anchorage and spent a day there. Mel wanted to explore the Kenai Peninsula so we drove farther south. We again were on dirt roads and we stopped at Soldotna before turning off for another 11 miles to enter the village of Kenai. Now it didn't feel like summer at all but a late fall or early winter. It never seemed to get dark. Even after midnight the sky only appeared to be gray and you could see things move at a hundred yards.

Mel found a place to pitch the green tent and we set up "house." Mel went out to explore whatever opportunities there were. He had a knack for talking to people to tap into their local knowledge about what was happening in any given area. He learned that there was a fish cannery across the Kenai River. He discovered that there was a federal government project nearby and it was hiring laborers for $8.00 an hour, much better than the $1.50 he was making painting houses in Tucson. We all learned that there were seven churches and seven bars in Kenai and the bars had more attendees than the churches. One was a Russian Orthodox Church with an onion dome. Services were only sporadic there because a priest only came on special church holidays.

There was a grocery store that was still selling war surplus eggs that had been frozen. There was a movie theatre that was run down and showed older movies once every two weeks. All of the roads were dirt. There was a high school with a small enrollment. Kenai's population was about 1500 people and it was the largest town on the Kenai Peninsula.

Mel got a job on the government project as a laborer making the $8.00 an hour, the wage about which he had been told. His strong, physical, physique now worked to his advantage as he could not only keep up with the other laborers but could outwork them.

I met other young teens my age and one of them had devised a way to fish that guaranteed a catch. He had taken a wooden pole and attached a gill net to it. The net had a metal lead line at the bottom that lowered the net and made a big square. A rope had been tied to the end of the pole so when the whole apparatus was thrown into the Kenai River, the pole floated and the lead line dropped the net lower in the water. By holding the rope you could walk along the bank as the pole drifted with the current. Fish would hit the net and get tangled in its mesh causing a splash and signaling that a catch had been made. All you had to do was pull in the rope and bring the pole on to the bank. The flailing fish was easy to take out of the net so that in minutes you had a fish and the fish was always a nice salmon.

I asked if I could use his net when he wasn't fishing himself. He granted my request. I began by bringing back to our tent, freshly caught fish. We had so much salmon we soon tired of it. However, not everyone in Kenai was tired of salmon so when I next went fishing I caught four or five fish. The fish varied in weight from four to 15 pounds. I would string them on a rope and go door to door selling a whole fish for fifty cents. I could make two to three dollars daily.

While Mel worked at the government project and I fished and bummed around town, mom was trying her best to make our tent a home. She bought a tub and washboard to do laundry. She cooked on the Coleman camp stove. She dried extra salmon on a laundry line for later meals. Her spirits were good.

One day the union representative followed Mel back to our tent. Mel had come from the Midwest, an area of America that had a dislike for unions. He had never had to deal with them at his store nor at Fernwood Gardens.

"I'd like you to join our union," the man said in a firm but friendly way.

"I don't know if I should. I may not be here long. I'm thinking of going back to Arizona so if I pay money to join I wouldn't be here long enough to get a full year's benefit," Mel countered.

"Well, how about you only pay dues for the time you're here. A lot of workers are just here for the summer months so we make an allowance for seasonal laborers," the union rep offered in a compromising tone.

"What does the union really do, anyway?" Mel questioned in the hope there would be a way out of paying union dues.

"Well, we keep the wages high, we make sure there are safe working conditions, and we keep the niggers out."

I looked up at the man after his last comment. Mel had used the term "niggers often or other derogatory terms such as "coons" and "jigaboos," to refer to Negroes. Mel was a racist, which served as another reason for me to dislike him. My main cause for disliking him was my animosity toward him for his physical abuse of mom. However, I was surprised to hear the union representative use the term and I was especially taken aback that he would make it part of his duties to exclude Negroes from earning a living like everyone else. After becoming an adult I looked back on this moment as an example of my naivety.

Mel saw the reality of keeping his job, so he reluctantly joined the union. He sometimes worked overtime and made $12.00 an hour, an amount he would have to work a whole day if he were painting in Tucson. It served to keep us in Kenai through August and September.

School began so I enrolled in Kenai High School but didn't fill out the section asking for an address. I didn't have one.

"Robert Evans?" The voice of the teacher called out.

I raised my hand and said, "Here."

"Would you come up my desk please?"

When I arrived at the teacher's desk he said, "You didn't write down your address. We'll need that in case of an emergency."

I said I didn't have an address for a home because I was living in a tent five blocks away. The teacher looked at me strangely.

"Are you going to live there all winter?"

"I think we might go back to Arizona but for now that's where I live."

"How do you get your mail?" he asked.

"General delivery, Kenai, Alaska," I answered.

"Well, put that down on this form and then write down directions to your tent in case we have to contract your parents."

I did, and when I walked back to my seat some of the other students sitting near the teacher's desk looked at me with odd expressions.

One day after school while Mel was still at work, mom was lying down on her cot in the tent.

"Bobby, I need you to go to the store and buy me some Kotex. Here's some money to pay for it."

"I didn't understand exactly a how woman's biological menstrual cycle happened. No one had ever explained that to me. However, my sister had mentioned to me that mom had a heavy discharge and didn't feel well during that time. I had heard mom ask other women a couple of times for Kotex when she was in a public place and away from her supply at home. She would go to the bathroom with the women offering to help to give the needed item. To me the item was a mystery because I had never seen one.

I had never been asked to buy Kotex for my mom before so when I went to the store I was embarrassed to ask for sanitary napkins. When I entered the store there was an attractive young woman behind the counter and a few customers waiting to check out. I went to the magazine rack and studied the pages of several publications. I was killing time until the other customers left. Each time it appeared the coast was clear another customer would enter the store. This went on for half an hour. Finally, no one else was in the store and I gathered my courage to overcome my discomfort and went to the counter.

"I need to buy some Kotex," I blushingly said to the pretty girl.

She could see my discomfort and to her credit, picked up a box of Kotex and quickly put it in a brown bag. I handed her all of the money I had hoping I wouldn't get any change and could walk out quickly. She deposited some of the money in the cash register and returned the rest to me and said, "thank you," in a kind tone. I left as soon as I could and didn't make eye contract.

"What took you so long?" mom asked obviously needing the Kotex desperately.

"There were a lot of customers," I lied and left to go to the river.

One night mom and I went to bed on our cots in the tent. Mel hadn't come back yet. About 2:30 A.M. Mel came in and he had been drinking. I heard him tell mom that he had been at the bar down the street and some," guy had gotten smart," with him. Mel followed him into the bathroom and the two began to fight. Mel said he used his usual technique of grabbing the front of the man's shirt and pushing him against the wall, pinning him there. With his free hand, Mel who was left-handed, punched the man in the face.

"When I hit him in the mouth, his front tooth stuck in my fist. I left him there on the floor of the bathroom and came out and finished my drink. I didn't want to leave because if one his friends decided to fight I wasn't going to back away."

"Wash your hand before you go to bed," mom said. Her nurses training had taught her that infection can easily be contracted from broken skin being in contact with a person's mouth and missing tooth.

Mel rarely drank any alcohol but when he did he drank lots of it. His intoxication took the form of getting mean and wanting to fight. He would be confrontational to someone, anyone, until he was able to provoke an aggressive response. Then he would fight and because of his strength and knowledge of fighting, would win.

Near the end of September the weather began to cool more than usual. Cloudy days came and there was some rain.

"Melvin, if you're going to continue work out at the project, we're going to have to get out of this tent and into some kind of house," mom commanded.

Mel agreed. He didn't want to give up the good wages he was making just yet. He said he didn't want to spend the winter in Alaska but would ride it out until the first snow. That weekend Mel began to search for a place to rent.

"I've found a little place not far from here," Mel began in his sales pitch tone. "It was a sauna behind the house. It's the one with the robin egg blue paint. We've driven by it before. The owner lives in the big house and would take a steam bath in the winter and rather than try to return to the main house in the cold, he would stay in the bathhouse. He's willing to rent the sauna house to us."

"I'd like to see it before we decide," mom cautioned.

Mel took mom to see the place. It had one room with a coal stove, a table with four chairs, and a bed. One light cord hung from the ceiling to provide illumination. A side room served as the sauna. It was only wide enough for a sleeping cot and a 55 gallon barrel drum that was tipped upright at one end of the cot. The barrel was filled with rocks. Below the barrel was a gas stove to heat the rocks and when someone wanted a steam bath, they would pour water over the hot barrel and steam would fill the little room.

"Bobby can sleep in the steam room and we can have the other room," Mel joyfully lobbied. "We can rent this place for only $35.00 a month."

Next to the tent, this looked like a godsend. We moved in and mom made it look like a home. At night after dinner we would play cards and talk about the day's events at the government project.

"Some of the work is shut down in the winter because it's too cold. The inside work goes on but the plumbing and other outdoor construction is closed down. I'll be laid off if I stay that long but when the first storm comes, we'll leave and go back to Arizona," Mel stated.

One weekend night mom and Mel went out for a dinner where there was a bar attached. I was in bed in the steam room when they returned. I was awakened when I heard Mel accuse mom of having too much of a good time. I heard a thud and mom cry out. He had punched her again. Then next day I saw a bruise near her throat. I was working up a hatred for Mel. I felt powerless to do anything because if I confronted him, I would be knocked around and mom would try to intervene and then she would be pummeled even more.

The first storm came in early November. We packed up and left in the Chrysler for the long journey back to Arizona. The Alcan Highway was unforgiving to the rubber tires rolling over it. It was not uncommon to wear out one or more tires passing above it. We had our share of flats and Mel taught me how to apply hot patches to the holes in the inner tubes. We bought a tire pump at one of the gas stations so we could repair and pump up our tires out in the wilderness if we had a flat tire and of course, we did.

When we finally got back to our home on East Lee Street, JoAnn wrote from Manitou Springs that she would like to come back to Tucson and live with us. Her letter revealed that she was pregnant and that she had applied for spousal benefits with the Air Force but was informed that her application would have to be denied because Robert already had a wife drawing family benefits. It was a shock to us but was devastating to JoAnn

When JoAnn returned to Tucson she explained further what had happened.

"Robert was outraged when he learned that I had applied for dependent status with the Air Force because he said that he would be severely reprimanded if I informed his commander that he had married me. He claimed that he was in the process of getting a divorce and that he would take care of me with money. He said he would declare us his rightful dependents and we would make a life together."

"Did you believe him?" Mom asked then continued. "He's a bigamist. He didn't tell you about his former marriage until you received a rejection from the Air Force?"

"I want to believe him but I couldn't stay with him in Colorado until things were settled," lamented JoAnn. "I'm going to give him some time to sort things out but if nothing happens, I'm going to write his commanding officer and inform him of what has happened and let him do what has to do to reprimand Robert. I know he's a bigamist but I have a child on the way and I want this to work out if it can."

"How long do you think you should wait," mom warily asked.

"Well, I'm due in April with the baby. If nothing happens by then, I'll go forward. In the meantime he has promised to send money to carry us through. He gave me some money when I left and he gets paid the first of each month so I expect more then."

For two months afterward JoAnn's money came from Robert. However, the next month there was less money sent, then less again the next month. JoAnn wrote to him about the smaller amount and threatened to write his commander. The next month the full amount was restored.

One January night after 11 o'clock when our lights were out, there was a knock on the door. I opened door since I slept on the couch near the front door now that JoAnn was in the bedroom I had occupied. The person at the door was Betty Straw, a friend JoAnn knew when we lived on Columbia Street.

She whispered, "Is that you Bobby?"

"Yes," I quietly said, surprised she remembered my name.

Is JoAnn here?"

"Yes," I whispered back trying to be quiet so my parents wouldn't wake up.

"Can she come to the door, I want to talk to her," Betty said quietly.

I looked out of the door and saw a car parked some distance on the street with its parking lights on.

"She's asleep now. Can you come back tomorrow?"

"No, I have to work. I want her to come to a party. Come on Bobby, go wake her up."

I knew something was fishy about this visit. Somehow it seemed to Betty, more important that JoAnn be invited to a party at 11 P.M. than anything else. However, I thought JoAnn should make her own decision so I quietly said, "wait here."

I tiptoed back to the bedroom and woke JoAnn. She put on her bathrobe and came to the door, then stepped outside. She and Betty spoke for a minute or two. JoAnn came back inside and went to her bedroom and slipped into some clothes. She came back to the door and she and Betty headed for the car with the parking lights on.

Mel must have heard the door shut because he came out and said, "What's going on?"

I told him that Betty had come and invited JoAnn to a party and she agreed to go.

"I bet Robert is up to something," Mel said with apprehension.

The next morning mom confronted JoAnn and demanded to know what took place the night before.

"Did you meet Robert last night?"

JoAnn's head lowered and nodded yes.

"He gave me money and said the divorce was almost complete and asked me to give him some more time until things were resolved."

Mel, who had a suspicious nature about all people, stepped in.

"I knew it was him. If he's so honest, why didn't he come in the day time and explain things to you. Why did he have to come at night and have your friend come and get you out of bed?"

JoAnn replied. "He was sheepish about coming here and seeing all of you. He knows you are against him and disapprove of the situation."

"You're damn right. If I see him, I'll knock his block off," an angry attitude showed on Mel's face as he blasted out his words.

JoAnn's situation was left in limbo for the moment as we waited for Robert to live up to his promises.

As spring approached, Mel and mom began to plan to move to Alaska. They intended to sell our now completed home on East Lee Street and take up commercial fishing farther south on the Kenai Peninsula in Alaska. Mel had a capacity to meet people and convince them to enter into an enterprise with him as partners or at least as colleagues. He knew nothing about commercial fishing but George Davis did. He had met Mel while we were in Kenai and said he would show Mel how to fish if Mel would buy a skiff, an outboard motor, and nets.

Our dysfunctional family offered a new chapter. Art had mustered out of the army and had become an instructor for an Arthur Murray dance studio. He wrote that he had met a young woman and he planned to marry her in May.

JoAnn began to get bigger as her pregnancy showed. No more money was coming from Robert. She wrote his commanding officer and sent a copy of her marriage certificate to him. She received a letter back from the officer indicating that he had taken action against Robert and that he was no longer in the Air Force.

JoAnn wrote to Robert but her letter came back to her with a stamp stating that there was no one at that address and that there was no forwarding address either. She began to cry when she realized that the relationship was finished; that she was now alone and expecting a baby soon.

Mom said we would stand by her and perhaps she would like to join us in Alaska and make a life for herself up there. There were few alternatives. She had trouble making a living when she tried to go it alone before. Now with a child on the way she realized that she needed help. Perhaps she would meet someone in Alaska and could be happy. There was a preponderance of men to women there so at least the odds were in her favor. Moreover, wages were higher there as well so maybe she could save some money to get a start in life for her and her yet to be born child. JoAnn agreed to go with us and let a fate yet to be determined, carry the day.

Quite by chance, a neighbor a half a block away learned of our plans. He was renting the house he was living in and was interested in buying our home. A price was agreed upon and without a realtor, a transaction was done. One stipulation to the agreement was that we would stay in the home until May before the neighbor could move in. Money was exchanged when a loan was granted to the neighbor and Mel went down to the Ford dealer and traded in the Chrysler for a brand new 1953 Ford station wagon, tan in color with an all metal body. It had white wall tires and smelled wondrously fresh inside.

Mel sold the beauty shop for a measly $900.00. I remembered that he had paid $8000.00 for it and had been offered $14,000.00 when it was at its zenith. After the sheriff had repossessed the equipment while some of the client's hair was dripping wet, the clientele began to drift away. Mom was the mainstay but other beauticians took other jobs in shops and their clients followed them. Many of mom's clients remained loyal to her but going to Alaska the year before was the turning point for some to seek services at other shops.

"Mel, wake up. JoAnn has to go to the hospital. She's having labor pains," mom said as she shook Mel who was taking a nap on the couch that Sunday.

Mel sprung up and quickly gathered himself. It was mid-morning and Mel had napped after eating a big breakfast. Surprisingly, he showed concern for JoAnn and helped her to the new station wagon. He drove the short distance to the Tucson Medical Center quickly but safely. Once JoAnn was processed in, she was taken to the delivery room. At 6:14 that afternoon, April 12th, she delivered a little girl she named Caroline.

" Mother and baby doing fine," we were told by the attending doctor.

However, we were scheduled to begin our trip to Alaska on May 1st. That would be a short recovery time for JoAnn to undertake a long journey. In spite of that, a baby bed was bought and our trip was to go forward as planned.

Mom went with me to Catalina Junior High School to talk to the principal.

"We're moving to Alaska and we have to take Bobby with us. The school in Alaska ends before we can get there so it will be summer vacation when we arrive. Can he take his final exams early so he can get credit for his classes here?"

My mom thought it was a reasonable request.

"I'm sorry Mrs. Jorns, but I'm afraid that will be impossible. Our school year doesn't end until June 5th. To give final exams in April is too early for us to give credit to your son. Can you stay a little longer so Bobby can complete his school year? Perhaps he could stay with someone, finish his classes and join you afterward."

"No, we have to vacate our house by May 1st and he can't stay here and come later. We have to leave on that day. Isn't there something that can be done?"

My head was turning from my mom to the principal and back again. The look on the principal's face answered my mom's question before his words came out of his mouth.

"I'm terribly sorry, but there's nothing we can do. If he leaves before the end of the term and doesn't transfer to another school to finish out the year, he'll lose all of his credits. It's a serious decision you have to make Mrs. Jorns because it'll affect Bobby's years in the future and his graduation."

With finality in her voice, mom said, "We have to go when we planned. I'm disappointed that you couldn't do more to help us."

The principal set his jaw unsympathetically and declared, "I'm sorry too, but that's the way it is."

And so the die was cast. We began our journey as planned on May 1st. Little Caroline was only 16 days old but was tucked away as we set off.

Mel had bought a Jeep. Plywood was attached to the sides and back to create walls. The Jeep served as a trailer to carry our life's possessions as it was towed behind the Ford station wagon. Mel, JoAnn, and mom were in the front seat and I sat in the back seat. Caroline was in her bed that sat on the rest of the back seat. She was a marvelous traveler. She slept a good deal of the time and seemed to enjoy the gentle movement the road served up as we journeyed north.

Another part of the plan called for us to stop in Tacoma, Washington where we were to meet Art's fiancée Jane and attend his wedding. Three days later, we parked next to Art's soon to be in-laws' house in Tacoma. We entered and Art was waiting for us. It was a two story home and his Jane was upstairs. We were introduced to Jane's parents and a moment later we heard someone coming down the stairs and we looked with great anticipation to see what the new member of the family looked like.

I heard my brother say, "And this is Jane," and he held out his hand to her as she descended the last two stairs.

When I saw her, I was shocked. She wasn't attractive. She was tall and heavy. Her eyes were deeply set and had dark half-moon circles under them. Jane's nose was big with a point on the end, and when she smiled her mouth revealed teeth that were enormous. Her lower teeth stuck out in front of her upper. Her hair was brown but unkempt. The total effect was that she was not beautiful. In fact she was almost ugly. I couldn't believe Art would pick such a person. I was disappointed and embarrassed for my brother. Silently, I kept asking myself how Art, who was reasonably attractive, could end up with someone this unsightly. I tried to convince myself that there must be something special about her to make her acceptable. Maybe it was her personality, her humanity, or her kindness. Her loud and unpleasant laugh however, only contributed to her beastly appearance. Then I learned that she was still in high school. Another revelation shocked us when we were told she was pregnant but early enough not to show.

The wedding went forward two days later at a Methodist church and there was a modest reception in an adjoining room with punch, tea, coffee, cake, and nuts. Those attending were older and no one was attractive. It was my third wedding, two of my mom's to Daddy Bob and to Mel and now Art's which was the most formal and the most discouraging of all.

Art was also going to Alaska with us. It was Mel's way to rescue Art and JoAnn. Caroline's bed was relocated behind the back seat to make room for our added passenger, Art. Once in Alaska he was to get a job and Jane would join us later after she graduated from high school by flying to Anchorage where we would pick her up.

We left the United States and headed up the Alcan Highway with ruts, washboard bumps, and muddy washouts fresh from spring flooding. Permafrost made some of the road sag like warm, long taffy and misfortune was assured if ever a car broke through it and got stuck.

Art volunteered to help with the driving on the long, tedious ride. In order to break up the monotony, we riders would trade seats. One day Art was driving and I was in the middle of the front seat. Mel was sitting in the right passenger seat holding Caroline. Towing the Jeep loaded with our heavy belongings caused the Ford Station Wagon to sway if there was sharp turn. On the rough Alcan Highway drivers, any drivers would try to turn to avoid deep potholes or other obstacles to smooth out the ride.

"Art, you're getting too close to the shoulder, move back to the center," Mel sounded a warning.

"I've got it," Art yelled back.

Mel reached across in front of me and tried to turn the wheel to the left to move the car towards the center of the road. The station wagon's sudden turn caused the Jeep behind us to pull the back of the Ford to the right. Art turned the wheel back toward the right and overcorrected causing a more radical sway from the Jeep. Mom yelled from the back seat and within ten seconds the Ford headed for the left ditch. Hard braking by Art prevented us from crashing into the woods and we came to a stop.

We got out of the car and surveyed our predicament. Mel looked at Art with the same hate he had when he pulled him from the irrigation ditch in Red Rock."

"Damn ya, why didn't you listen to me when I said you were getting too close to the edge of the road?" Mel's voice was harsh.

Art said nothing but felt the wrath from Mel and the rest of us, as we too blamed him for not heeding Mel's warning. The Ford was in the ditch but the Jeep was still on the road.

We had to unload the Jeep of most of its contents in order for Mel to get in and start the motor. With its four-wheel drive in gear Mel was able to use the Jeep's power to pull the station wagon out of the ditch and back onto the road. Art was not allowed to drive the rest of the way which took a toll on Mel and his patience. At the end of each driving day, he was sullen and snapped at us all at when the smallest things upset him.

Days went by grindingly slow and miles of gravel passed under our cars interminably. It seemed as if we would never get to our destination. The mood was heavy inside the car. The trip became monotonous as the road passed through a path of spruce trees with no variation for days. It all added to the boredom of the trudging through Canada and into Alaska.

Paved roads finally appeared and the smooth pavement felt like we were riding on velvet after the dusty, rock throwing, noisy and rattling of the Alcan Highway. But south of Anchorage, a new dirt road was the only trail leading to our endpoint.

Once in Alaska, Mel found George Davis in Ninilchik, a small village of 200 people along the coast of Cook Inlet and he showed us a log home a mile away from the village that was for rent. It was off the main road about 40 yards. Upon entering we saw a kitchen with a table and chairs and a coal stove. The adjoining room served as a living room. The house had a second story with two bedrooms. There was no running water, indoor plumbing, or electricity. Outside there was another building that functioned as a storage shed. It was as large as a big living room and was empty. Compared to our little sauna home in Kenai this new place was big enough to accommodate all of us if we used the storage shed.

Mel rented it and it was decided that mom and Mel would take one of the two upstairs bedrooms and JoAnn and Caroline would occupy the other. I would sleep downstairs in the living room on a cot. Art would fix up the storage shed. It would be the bedroom for Art and Jane once she arrived from Washington. They would sleep there and we would all eat in the kitchen. The long sunny Alaskan days normally provided enough light even in the evening. However, on dark cloudy nights we used a Coleman gas lantern to brighten the room.

Water would have to be packed in but there was a stream about a third of a mile away. I was assigned that duty. Art and I rigged up a pack with shoulder straps and attached a five gallon gas can to it. I could take it to the stream and fill the can with water. With the pack, the can, and the weight of the water the load weighed over 45 pounds. To provide enough water for the whole family to drink, cook, launder, and bathe required several trips to the stream and miles on my legs.

That was especially true on laundry day. It was a physical drain on me to provide the water but also on mom who had to use a scrub board and a wash tub to clean our clothes. There was no wringer other than what our hands could extract the water out of our garments by twisting them. Clothes were hung outside on a line and with the mild Alaskan summer, they dried slowly. The washtub doubled as a bathtub for us. Several of us bathed in the same water to maximize this precious resource.

Mel and George Davis got in the station wagon and went to Kenai to buy nets, corks, lead line, ropes and buoy kegs that would be needed to fish. George suggested that a new 15 horsepower Evinrude outboard motor was needed for the skiff, so Mel bought one. Mel was spending the money from the sale of our home in Arizona to pay for all of the equipment.

Once back in Nanilchik, George showed how to "hang" net, which meant sewing the cork and lead lines to the top and bottom of the nylon mesh. Some of the nets were 50 yards long and there were several nets so it took a long time to get them ready for fishing. I learned how to "hang" net and it sped things up in anticipation of getting ready for the fishing season in June.

Mel had been told he could earn as much as $10,000.00 in the summer fishing, an amount three times as much as he was earning painting houses. Moreover, Mel could be his own boss and learning to fish was fairly simple.

Once the nets were ready, George had located a site on the beach of Cook Inlet to play out the nets. Buoy kegs were anchored in the water and the net was strung between them. When salmon caught their gills in the net, the mesh would hold them until they were removed and stored. When a fish tender came by from the cannery after each fishing session, the fish would be taken to it by the skiff and transferred to the larger boat. The number of fish was counted and a receipt was given to either George or Mel. The receipt would be presented and credit applied to Mel's and George's account for the fish. They could buy goods from the cannery and the cost would be subtracted from their account. At the end of the fishing season the profits would be split between Mel and George after expenses were deducted from the account. Now it was time to fish and start earning money.

"Bobby, the neighbor across the way is looking for some help to work his fish trap and I talked to him about hiring you. He'll show you what to do so I want you to go over and talk to him," Mel told me.

I walked the half mile to his house and knocked on his door. His name was Frank Van Horn. His wife answered the door.

"Mrs. Van Horn, I'm Bobby Evans and I was told by my stepdad that Mr. Van Horn was looking for help on his fish trap. Is he here now?"

She was a "native" a term applied to those in Alaska who were indigenous but had married into the "white" Russian settlers. Her skin was the color cinnamon, her hair black, and her eyes brown. Her look reminded me of the Mexican-Americans I had seen in Arizona.

"Yes, come in," she said.

"Oh yes! I talked to your dad and he said you'd work for me. We fish Tuesday and Thursday from 6 A.M. to 6 A.M. the next day. Once we set the pot, there's little to do until we raise the pot and take out the fish. You'll have be there at 5:30 in the morning on Tuesday, Wednesday, Thursday, and Friday. I'll show you what to do. I'll pay you $5.00 for each day and I'll keep track of what you earn and pay you at the end of the season."

I didn't know whether this was a fair or unfair wage but said, "That'll be fine with me."

"My fish trap is about half a mile from where your dad is fishing so you already know where it is."

I said I did.

"Be here at my house at 5:30 next Tuesday and help me set the pot. I'll drive you there with me."

"Yes sir, I'll be there on time."

A fish trap is a device that is a series of tall posts the height of telephone poles. A pile driver is brought in to drive metal stakes into the earth under the water to which the poles are attached when the tide is out. Because Cook Inlet has huge tides, some as big as 17 feet, it was easy to construct the fish trap. The poles are spaced 20 yards or so apart out into the sea. Chicken wire mesh is stapled to the poles. The poles stretch 300 yards out into the water and at that depth poles are fixed to metal stakes in a square. Guy wires connected to metal stakes helped to stabilize the poles.

A net with a small mesh about an inch square, is strung inside the four-sided pot from near the top of the pole all the way to the watery sand. The net had a bottom so fish can't swim under it to escape. The square net is called the 'pot." There was a small vertical opening that fish could find to enter.

Fish swimming near the shore would bump into the chicken wire and they would always seek deeper water. By swimming away from shore, the fish would be guided to the square and find their way into the "pot," where they could swim freely and feel safe. When the fishing period was over, the "pot" would be raised by pulling up the net to the top of the poles by hooking it to other horizontal log poles 30 feet up. There were two horizontal logs at the top around the square pot affixed parallel, one about waist high and a lower one for our feet to walk on that allowed fisherman to move around the square top. A dinghy or small row boat would then enter the pot and load the fish to take to the tender. "Setting the pot meant simply lowering the heavy mesh below the water line to the sand below and allowing for tides.

The first time I climbed the ladder to the top of square the tide was out and all I could see was guy wires fixed to rising metal stakes in the sand. When the 17 foot tides were out one could see only sand but from near the top of the poles the drop at low tide was more like 30 feet. Falling from that distance on those metal pickets meant that one would be impaled on them and certainly die. At low tide and looking down from the top of the poles I saw only sand, metal stakes, and guy wire. I wondered whether I could be careful enough not to fall off. It was a little unnerving to say the least. Wearing rubber hip boots on wet, slick and round walkway logs made for unsteady footing. I found that concentrating on the tasks of lowering the net helped me avoid vertigo. So did focusing on what was required to raise the pot help me avoid looking down at the perils below.

On the days I wasn't fishing, I packed water for the house and built up the supply so there would be plenty of water when I was away fishing. I also was told to walk through the forest to town to buy supplies. On more than one of those occasions I would see a cow moose with her calf. I was warned never to get too close to a mother moose or I could be trampled. I was very careful to give a wide space in a non-threatening manner when I saw those wild, magnificent creatures.

JoAnn found work as well in a cannery in Ninilchik. The work was demanding when a load of fish came in. The load was smelly, slimy, wet and cold from seawater. JoAnn had a slight build and only weighed about 100 pounds and was just five feet, two inches. She nevertheless worked as fast and as hard as the others who were bigger and stronger. Mom watched Caroline while JoAnn was at work.

Art, who was clever at times, made a bed frame from small logs he fashioned from trees. He wove ropes through holes he bored through the log frame to form a base. He gathered grass and sewed it inside of flannel blankets to serve as a mattress. When Jane came up to Alaska in June Art's invention became their bridal bed.

Art also found a job with an alcoholic fisherman named Harry Hamilton. He had a fish trap and a fishing boat he took out on Cook Inlet. Art served in many capacities but part of his assumed duties was making sure that Harry didn't drown or fall to his death from the fish trap.

George Davis taught Mel how to fish with gill nets but he also taught us how to clam. We would walk along the wet beach when the tide was out and look at the sand for a small indentation the size of a finger print. We were told to stomp with our hip boots next to recessed spot and if water filled in the hollow, that was a sign that a clam was underneath. By taking a shovel full of sand next to the watery spot one could expect to find a razorback clam. They were six to eight inches long and had a hard shell and sometimes the neck of the clam protruded outside. Cleaning the sand out of a clam was always a challenge and it seemed impossible to get all of it out. When we cooked them and bit into the flesh, invariably we would feel abrasive grit of beach sand while chewing.

One evening Mel looked at Jane and saw she was wearing a necklace with a Christian cross attached to it. Jane was explaining that her silver cross had a tiny piece of wood inside that supposedly was from the original cross on which Jesus was crucified.

"Let me see that," Mel said with curiosity.

Jane unlatched the necklace and handed it to Mel.

"I don't believe what's inside is from the original cross," Mel said with skepticism. "I'm going to open it up and look inside."

"It's bad luck if you open it," Jane protested.

"Don't open it Mel, respect Jane's wishes," mom insisted.

Mel looked back at the cross in his hands. He took out his pocket knife and pried open the religious symbol. There was a piece of wood inside.

"Don't tell me this is from the original cross. Wood that old would disintegrate after this much time," Mel bellowed defiantly.

I didn't believe the wood was from the cross of 2000 years before either but I would not have opened the cross to find out. Mel's ill-manner was an affront to Jane's religious beliefs. However, Mel had shown himself to be disrespectful of one's privacy and dignity before so I wasn't surprised that he unsealed the cross.

The summer wore on and it especially wore on mom. It became her summer of discontent. She was 47 years old and living like a pioneer woman existing in the 18th century. Cooking on a coal stove, laundering on a washboard, and surrounded by wilderness, took a heavy toll on her. Additionally, the income from fishing wasn't panning out like Mel had promised. He was also talking about spending the winter. The only school in Ninilchik was a K-8 with the nearest high school was 37 miles away in Homer. Mel wanted me to drop out of school and fish with him the next summer.

Mom wasn't the only one unhappy in Ninilchik. Jane wanted to return to the lower 48 states as well to have her baby. The nearest hospital was in Seward, 85 miles away. JoAnn similarly, was tired of the rugged life. A village of 200 people didn't appeal to her as a place to raise her baby Caroline.

———————————————————————————————

————————————————————

None of them verbalized their dissatisfaction to me. In fact, what was about to happen, was a well-kept secret of which I had no hint.

"Has Mr. Van Horn paid you your money yet, Bobby?" Mom asked.

It just so happened, that he had paid me the Thursday before and my earnings totaled $160.00 and it came in form of a personal check.

"Yes," I said. "We need to go to a bigger town to get it cashed."

"Well, maybe we can do that soon," mom postulated.

Mel and George Davis had gone to Kenai to collect their paychecks from the Libby, McNeil, & Libby Company on a Friday. They took the Jeep because they wanted to get some supplies for winter and it was better suited for some of rough roads.

"Go get us some water," mom said.

I put on the pack and went to the stream and filled the five gallon can and trudged back. When I returned to the house there were three suitcases standing at the door.

"Get in the car, we're going to Homer," mom ordered.

"Why are we taking suitcases?" I asked.

"Never mind," Art broke in.

Mom left a note on the kitchen table. There were still many of our possessions lying around.

We, meaning JoAnn and Caroline, Art and Jane, and mom and me, drove to a small airport in Homer and parked the Ford station wagon in the parking lot. Mom and Art went inside and bought tickets to fly to Anchorage. The flight would take off in an hour. Mom went back to the Ford and put a note on the dashboard.

There was a bank across the street and mom went with me to get my check cashed.

Shortly thereafter, the small plane taxied near the little terminal and we walked to it and climbed up its steps and sat down. It was the first airplane I had ever been in. The anticipation of being in the air was exciting. I must also admit that I too, was glad we were leaving Alaska.

I wasn't sad to leave Ninilchik and Mel. He had physically abused mom, exploited JoAnn, and intimidated everyone around him. I knew we would eventually end up in Arizona and hoped I would never see Mel again.

Once in Anchorage, we waited for another plane. This one had four engines with propellers and was much bigger. When we were strapped in and the engines roared for takeoff, I felt the tremendous acceleration generated by the long propellers. It was exhilarating and once in the air I looked out of the window. The roads below looked like threads and the homes same the size of Monopoly game houses. We went higher and higher until villages were barely visible.

Art sat next to Jane, JoAnn was with Caroline, and I sat next to mom.

"Bobby, when we get to Seattle, I'm going to need the money you made fishing in order to help pay for our bus ride to Arizona."

"I'll give it to you now mom. I know you wouldn't ask for it if you didn't need it."

When we got to Washington State, Jane's parents picked us up at the airport and took us to Tacoma where they lived. We stayed the night and the next day they drove JoAnn, Carline, mom, and me to the Greyhound bus station. We bought tickets and were heading south that morning. It took two days to get to Phoenix where we called Uncle Dee and Aunt Mary who picked us up and we stayed at their home for next several days.

"You'd better enroll in school here, Bobby. We don't know when we'll be going to Tucson but it might be a while," mom instructed me.

I entered East High School in Phoenix in the torrid heat of this Arizona September. I realized that mom was groping as to what to do and where to do it. She had said Tucson, so I expected that would be our destination. I decided that it was pointless to begin school and stay only a week or so before moving to Tucson. I went back to school, my second day there, and tried to check myself out.

"You can't check out unless your parent signs this form," the registrar said to me.

"If you give me the form, I'll have my mom sign it and bring it back to you," I said as politely as I could.

I was given the form and left the office. I went off campus and had lunch using the quarter mom had given me to take myself to lunch. I forged mom's signature on the form I had been given and returned about 1 P.M.

"I had my mom sign this at lunch time so I hope everything is in order for me to check out. We're moving to Tucson tomorrow," I said trying to sound as sincere as I could and pull off a successful ruse.

112

"Very well, have the high school in Tucson send for our records when you enroll."

"Yes, of course. I'll do that," and walked out the door having attended school a total of one day.

Mom wasn't happy I had done that but she was resigned to accept that not much was lost by my leaving school.

JoAnn decided that she and Caroline would stay at Uncle Dee and Aunt Mary's house until she could find a job as a beautician and find a place of her own. Mom and I were driven to Tucson that weekend by Uncle Dee and we found a trailer park where we could rent a furnished trailer.

I had to reenroll in Catalina Junior High School. At that time it was a school with grades 7, 8, and 9. I had to take the same courses I was enrolled in before I left last May when we left for Alaska, the same courses I from which I received no credit.

There was one exception however. I was given a class in World History. I was a modest student during my formative years. I had more time to study however, now that I didn't have to dig cesspools or work on the house on East Lee Street. I began to read the text thoroughly and I was particularly struck by those living in ancient civilizations. I was fascinated with Hammurabi's Code. I marveled about the achievements of the Hellenic Greeks. I saw a picture of the Parthenon in Athens and something burst out of me and I said out loud, "I'm going to go there some day."

I would be there for one semester, but couldn't transfer to Tucson High School until the next fall. So the spring semester was planned for me to take only two classes freeing up afternoons.

Mom got a job in another beauty shop and we lived in the trailer. To shower, mom and I had to go to a public shower facility at the trailer park, wash, dry off, change clothes, and then return to the trailer. We could walk to bus stops and mom got to work that way. I was able to walk to school and to food markets to shop.

One afternoon around six P.M., I was walking toward the market and a car slowed behind me and a voice said, "Hey!"

I ignored the voice but it sounded again, "Don't you walk away from me."

I turned around and saw the tan Ford station wagon and its driver. It was Mel.

"Why didn't you answer when I first called to you," he said forcefully.

I lied, "I didn't hear you."

"Get in the car,"

I did and asked, "When did you get to town?"

"Today, I came down from Phoenix."

I didn't say any more but I was angry but couldn't show it. The son of a bitch was back in our lives. When he said he had come from Phoenix, I knew how he had found us. He no doubt went to Uncle Dee who told Mel where we were. My logic was confirmed when he drove right to our trailer and stopped.

There was tension in mom's face when we walked inside. Mel was trying to be charming and upbeat but mom was wary. She couldn't afford to get a divorce and she was barely making a living being the sole provider. I would have gladly dropped out of school and donated whatever income I could earn to help with finances.

Mel started right in with his stories, "After you left, George and I caught some salmon to salt away to eat later. I've got them in barrels in the back of the car."

I had seen red barrels in the back of the station wagon when I was told to get in. I was steaming that Mel had found us. I had no curiosity about the barrels.

"On the way down in Canada, I picked up a hitchhiker. He was a student at Harvard University and had thumbed a ride all the way to Alaska during the summer and was working his way back," Mel's comments fell on uninterested ears.

"He had a pack and some canned meat. He offered me some and believe me, I cut thick slices for myself because

114

I was giving him a ride. When we came to the first gas station I went to the bathroom and watched to see if he would pay for the gas when to guy came to collect the money. He hesitated and I came out and said 'pay him.'"

"He did, but he didn't like to. I got some money out of him though because I told him that I expected him to buy some gas. He had more money than he let on."

Mel was sounding like he had gotten over on the intelligent student and had outsmarted him. If his story was meant to impress us, it didn't. It only showed how miserly and petty he was.

A month later Mel got a letter from Alfred, a man he had met while fishing in Ninilchik. Alfred checked out a fishing boat from Libby, McNeil, & Libby, the canning company. His contract called for him to accept less money per fish than fisherman who owned their own fishing boats. The benefit to Alfred was that he didn't have to buy a boat or maintain it. Alfred's boat was one of 35 the cannery checked out to fisherman. He had been successful in 1953 coming in as second boat, a term meaning that he had caught the second most fish in the cannery's fishing fleet.

Mel had made a connection with Alfred and the two of them planned to fish the next summer. Mel and Alfred would share the profits from their catch of fish, even though Mel was a beach fisherman and Alfred took his leased craft out on Cook Inlet.

Mel was still trying to get back in good graces with mom and didn't reveal his plans to her just yet. As a way to improve his standing with mom, Mel rented an apartment and we moved out of the trailer into better housing.

Art wrote from Seattle that he and Jane were doing fine. He had gotten a job at Boeing Aircraft as a riveter and Jane was preparing to deliver their child. JoAnn also sent word that she had gotten a job, moved into an apartment, and had a roommate, Peggy. She confessed that things were hard because child care for Carolone ate into her earnings from the beauty shop.

115

Since I only took two classes in the spring, I got a job as a box boy at a super market. It was near downtown and I walked to work after class. I was paid 50 cents an hour and on Saturdays I worked from 8 in the morning to 8 at night. I had a lunch and dinner hour. I used some of my earnings to take mom and Mel to movies and I put away $5.00 in my wallet.

"Let's go to Nogales," my friend Sam was saying. "We can drink and visit a whorehouse. Henry has a car and Joe and Bill will go with us."

Henry did have a car, a 1941 green Cadillac 4-door his father had bought him. Three months before, Henry had found a dynamite cap and lit the fuse with a cigarette. He didn't think the fuse was lit so he tried to relight it. However, it was lit and when Henry realized it, he tried to throw the dynamite cap away before it went off. Sadly for Henry, it exploded about a foot away from his hand and blew off his index and second finger, and half of his thumb on his right hand. When he recovered from his injuries, Henry's father tried to raise his spirits and bought Henry the Cadillac.

A date was set when all of us guys could be on hand for the 63 mile trip to Nogales, Mexico just across from the Arizona border. I told mom and Mel I was going to stay at Henry's after going hunting for coyotes in the desert. They were skeptical but allowed me to be away for the night.

We left about six P.M. that evening. We crossed into Nogales and drove immediately to the red light district. We entered the B-29 Club and thought we were in heaven. The floor had a line of Art Deco glass with blue lights illuminating the darken bar. It was something one would see in the movies. We sat on stools at the bar and ordered beer. Within two minutes we were approached by prostitutes. One asked me to buy her a beer which I did. She was older, maybe 35 and a little heavier than the other women. I didn't care. I was excited that I was about to enter the wonderful world of sex. I asked her how much it would cost me for her services and she told me it would be $3.00. A deal was

116

struck and after drinking my beer we adjourned to a sleazy back room with a corrugated tin roof. My $3.00 bought me access to my first sexual experience.

When I came out to the bar after I had finished, my friends had disappeared. I went into the street where the car had been parked and it was gone too. I began to walk up and down the streets in the red light district stopping in every bar to see if my friends were inside. At each stop, prostitutes waved me inside with the call, "Come on in, Shorty."

I must have walked in and out of bars for over an hour. Finally, at the last street there was a dead end. It was the last bar on the street and I almost didn't go in. Once inside I found it to be an unassuming bar. Happily, there were my friends sitting at a table having a beer.

"What happened to you guys?"

"When you went into the back room with that whore, we got in the car and Sam started throwing lit firecrackers out the window as we drove through town. The cops started chasing us so we crossed the border back into Arizona. We had to wait awhile until we could come back to Mexico."

"What have you been doing since you got back?"

"We didn't know where you were, so we drove around looking for you. We decided we better find a place that was out of the way and hide the car in case the cops were still looking for us."

I realized that I was lucky to have found my friends and was grateful.

"May I join you?"

It was a young prostitute, maybe 18 years old, named Carmen asking the question. She didn't proposition us but just talked to us about where we were from. I asked her what her fee was and she said, "$2.00."

I didn't have $2.00 left from the $5.00 I had tucked away in my wallet. I had spent money on beer for me and the first girl at the B-29 Club. The $3.00 I spent for sex cut into my reserves. I asked my friends to loan me enough for the $2.00 fee and they pooled their money to come up with it.

"You guys stay here and don't go driving around again. Wait for me."

Then I followed Carmen to a back room and enjoyed my second encounter of sexual bliss with her. After we came out to the bar Carmen continued to talk to us and ordered a tostada. She shared her food with me and after a while we left to cross back into Arizona. So far it had been a successful adventure.

Driving back to Tucson became an experience. Henry had been drinking and wound up the Cadillac to 90 miles an hour. Sam and Bill opened the windows and cold air blew in the car freezing us in the March night. We got back to town cold but happy. I stayed at Sam's house the rest of the night. The next morning I walked back home and tried to be excited about coyote hunting to suspicious ears. I guess I was convincing enough that my parents didn't pursue the matter further. That brought relief to my fear of being caught. I was tired from the night's activities and late hour of return.

The next few days also lead to another kind of relief. I did not contact any disease from my sexual escapades. I had a vague knowledge of venereal disease but didn't know how it manifested itself. By not having any symptoms of any kind told me that I had avoided not only a setback concerning my health but also escaped the embarrassment of having to tell my parents what I had actually done the night we went to Nogales. I also knew I would not face the humiliation of explaining my condition to a nurse or a physician.

By now I was enrolled at Tucson High School. My courses were of a general nature. The list of classes included English, health, welding, bookkeeping, history, and P.E. I was modestly interested in most of the classes but found a joy in welding. I was good at it and considered it as a possible career choice.

Mel was again turning the conversation to another trip to Alaska. Mom said she wouldn't live like an early American colonist in rough conditions.

"I'm tired of living in tents, shacks, and Abe Lincoln log cabins," she declared.

Mel went out of his way to assure her that wouldn't be the case this time. He said he had already talked with Alfred who said we could stay at his cabin. It had a well and running water. It had electricity to ease the burdens of life without it. Gradually mom began to be convinced that things would be different.

JoAnn wrote that she and Peggy were having a rough time getting by in Phoenix. She said that she had talked with Peggy about Alaska and she was interested in going there for the adventure and perhaps to find a good provider. Then JoAnn asked if the two of them could join us in returning to Alaska.

Mom said they could and Mel agreed as well because he believed that a family income with monies earned by each member could strengthen his pot. Peggy would be expected to contribute to the expenses of traveling to Alaska and that would cut down on what he would have to pay to get us there.

Mom insisted that I finish out the school year before we left. I realized too, that I was already behind in my credits and would have to make them up somehow. Mel and mom didn't seem to have a plan as to how that would happen however.

In June the long trek began on the usual bad Canadian roads with the expected flat tires, boring drives, and long monotonous views. Peggy was in her twenties like JoAnn and a good traveler. JoAnn's daughter Caroline was by now a seasoned passenger and a good rider.

When we finally got Alfred's cabin in Ninilchik he was there to greet us. He was about 40 years old, a native with a Hispanic complexion, quiet, kind and polite. He was five feet nine inches tall and 180 pounds. He dressed in work clothes and had rubber boots because of the mud. He had false teeth as so many of the people did in Ninilchik due to harmful elements in the water they drank that caused their teeth to fall out.

His cabin was elevated above the ground on stilts and under it he had stored barrels, boxes, and supplies to survive the winter. Because of its elevation snow could not rise to the doorstep. To the right of the cabin was a garbage pile with empty tin cans scattered around because there was no garbage service. To the left and back near the woods was the outhouse. The cabin may have had running water but no indoor plumbing. Four steps led to the front door on the left side of the cabin and upon entering there was a sink with a faucet. Four feet to the right of the sink was a black propane stove, a fact that relieved mom because she would not have to build a fire to cook. Upon further entry into the cabin was a kitchen table and around it cabinets. Behind the stove was a partition running half way across the room and behind the partition was a bed. Alfred had strung a rope with a curtain running from the partition to the end of the room. It would provide a little privacy.

Alfred had made almost $10,000.00 the year before. He had caught the second most fish in the cannery's fleet of fishing boats and had rewarded himself by buying a new 1953 green DeSoto sedan. It was parked to the left of the house and had recently been washed because there was no mud on it like other cars we had seen.

Mel's friendship with Alfred fell into Mel's concept of friendship. He made friends with those who could help him with his next project, adventure, or money-making scheme that would do something to benefit Mel. I had noticed this when he brought in Frankaruski and Norm the alcoholic. These two men helped him build our house on East Lee Street in Tucson. Mel had befriended George Davis who helped him learn how to fish the year before. Now Alfred was the next "friend" Mel was courting in order to live in his cabin and with whom he planned to share fishing incomes. We never seemed to have friends just because they were friends. There was always an ulterior motive for some economic gain attached to Mel's so-called friendship.

Once we were settled in at Alfred's cabin, JoAnn and Peggy planned to get jobs in Kenai at the Libby McNeil &

Libby cannery. It was 45 miles away but there were places to rent with reasonable rates right at the cannery. Mom would watch Caroline which eased JoAnn's mind because mom was good with Caroline and there would be no expense.

Mel planned to fish with gill nets on the beach again with George Davis. They met and began to prepare their nets and caulk the skiff to get it ready to go to sea.

Alfred was also getting ready to fish. He had made a list of the provisions he needed to be stocked in the boat he planned to check out. He was going into Kenai to talk to the leasing agent about checking out a fishing boat for the season. JoAnn and Caroline went with him because JoAnn needed to buy some warmer clothes and buy disposable diapers for Caroline. They came back late in the afternoon. Alfred had secured another boat and said it was easy to obtain one because he had done well last season. Alfred was nice enough to take JoAnn and Caroline to lunch at one of the cafés in Kenai. He had also bought Caroline a doll at the drug store where I had been so embarrassed two years before when I had to buy Kotex for mom. They had enjoyed a productive day.

I had turned 16 in May and Mel began to let me drive the Jeep when he was setting up his fishing camp on the beach. I was only allowed to drive supplies from the cabin to the beach site, usually with Mel sitting in the passenger seat to make sure that I was handling the Jeep properly. I didn't have a driver's license and there was no place to obtain one in tiny Ninilchik with its 200 people. Like most teenagers, driving was like a rite of passage and I looked forward to it.

Alfred, JoAnn, and I went to Kenai to again buy provisions. When we came out of the store a big box was of supplies was loaded into the front seat after the trunk was filled up.

"Would you like to drive?" Alfred said to me.

"Yes, if it's all right with you," I said, trying to sound competent and hold my excitement in check.

I got in the driver's seat and Alfred and JoAnn got in the back seat. I headed out of Kenai toward Soldotna about

10 miles away to join the Sterling Highway. All of the roads were dirt so I was careful to drive at an appropriate speed and avoid as many washboard bumps as possible. I concentrated so hard I was unaware of anything except steering the car and the road.

About 15 miles into the 45 mile trip I looked into the rearview mirror and saw Alfred and JoAnn kissing in the back seat. I had no idea they were becoming close and didn't know if mom and Mel knew either. I was surprised this was happening. For the next 30 miles I began to run some thoughts through my mind trying to understand why JoAnn and Alfred had found romance. Alfred had never married. Alaska had far more men than women so I could see why Alfred sought out JoAnn. But why was she willing to accept him? She had been married for a short time to Joe and illegally married to the bigamist Robert, the father of Caroline. She had difficulty making a living for herself and her daughter and had been living with us off and on for almost two years. Maybe she was lonely. Maybe she was tired of the tyranny of Mel. Maybe Alfred, who had done well in making a living, seemed like her best option at the moment. Did she love him, really? Was it because Alfred had been good to Caroline? Would she marry him? There was a 17 year age gap between them. Would there be more children born to this relationship? Would Alfred become my brother-in-law? There was much to be determined as I asked myself these questions. I continued to drive and tried not to show that I had seen them kissing.

A week later while Alfred was out of the cabin buying his Camel cigarettes, Mel said to me, "you're going to work on Alfred's fishing boat this summer."

"Bobby can't swim, how's he going to work on a fishing boat in Cook Inlet?" My mom countered. Her voice was above conversational but below strident in her protest. She knew as we all did, that the matter was settled once Mel decreed something, that there would be no argument that would convince him to change his mind.

I sat on my cot, and already accepted my fate with resignation.

Mel believed that this summer 1954, he would, "make-a-killing" fishing because he and George had more nets and he was going to share Alfred's earnings as well. He would stay as long as needed to finish out the season and then return to Arizona before the harsh Alaskan winter set in.

Ten days later Alfred and I drove to Kenai in the green DeSoto. He drove and I was a passenger this time. We ferried ourselves across the Kenai River in a dinghy, a small row boat. At the cannery Alfred's fishing vessel was docked. Alfred said it was 35 feet long and had a keel and a round bottom to make it more seaworthy. When Alfred took command of the vessel I was anxious to look around to see what the boat looked like. The side of the boat was painted black up to the gunnels. The cabin was the color of sea gray. Inside the cabin there was a control panel with switches to start the engine, an accelerator, toggles for lights, a horn, a wheel to steer the craft, glass windows to the front and side, and a door to close behind the wheel in case of bad weather.

The steps to the right led down to the galley. It had a couple of shelves with a wooden bar across it to keep dishes and cups from sliding out during stormy weather and the rocking motion of the waves. To the left were two sleeping bunks, one on top of the other. Near the floor was a six cylinder Chrysler engine with a crank to start it at sea in case the battery went dead. Alfred warned me to stay away from the crank fitting when the engine was running because if you got too close it would snag your pant leg and pull your led into it and chew up your flesh. There was a two-burner stove that had a small storage bin and was fueled by kerosene.

Back on top in the cabin's steering section one could step outside and look toward the stern. From this view there were three steps leading to a lower deck that was uncovered. Once on this deck leading to the stern, there was a square opening that was the "hold" where the fish catch was stored until it could be unloaded. The elongated fishing net, 900 feet long was stored between the hold and the stern. At the end of the stern was a black powered roller to aid in pulling in the net.

In front of the cabin was an anchor just behind the pointed bow. The area between the cabin and the gunnels was small, just enough room for two feet in rubber boots to pass.

Because the cannery leased the boat to Alfred and to other fishermen in the cannery's fleet, he and the others who checked out the cannery boats agreed to take less money per fish than fishermen who owned private boats.

I had a mix of emotions after examining Alfred's boat. I knew I had to be careful not to fall into the cold, unforgiving sea and certain death, because I could not swim. I felt additional anxiety when told the water was so cold that I could not survive more than four or five minutes because the freezing water would render me unable to move.

I also harbored worry that I would not know enough about the way the boat handled, and how to carry out my tasks as a fisherman. But on the positive side, I was excited about the adventure of being on the open sea with things I had never seen before. I would also be away from Mel's control and passing through that transitional time when a boy moves toward becoming a man, where there is a certain trust put in you. I knew I had to measure up to be accepted. I was impatient for my development to begin.

I didn't look like a man at five foot six and 120 pounds. However, I was determined that my physical limitations would not demonstrate a weakness of character or a show of fear in meeting the manly challenges adult fishermen faced.

Alfred explained that we would fish Tuesdays and Thursdays from six in the morning until six the next morning. He was patient while teaching me to be a fisherman. He showed me how to tie knots, how the net would be played out when we fished, and how to steer the boat.

After taking control of the boat, we set out the first Tuesday at 4 A.M.. We traveled for two hours before we came to the fishing area where Alfred had success the year before. Alfred told me to be careful not to snag my hip boots buckles as we played out the net. We set the net and waited. He especially told me to watch that the net didn't get caught in the "wheel" or the propeller of the boat. Things went fine the first day except I got seasick and threw up over the side. We only caught 56 fish. I wondered if that was the size of the catch we could expect each time we went out. I was told that the catch would vary but we did alright for the first time out.

"You'll probably get sick the first few times we go out because of the smells of the boat, the motion of the sea, and our irregular meals," Alfred counseled.

The next fishing day was a Thursday and Alfred's patience was lacking when I got the net caught in our propeller.

"If that net is really caught in the wheel it could break the drive shaft and we'll be stranded out here dead in the water," he shouted at me.

He was right to admonish me. My self-respect dropped to a new low because I stacked my own guilt on top of his reprimand. Alfred got in the dinghy and was able to free the net from the prop. I was careful from then on to make sure that never happened again.

The days we fished were mainly filled with boredom. The net would be set and we'd drift with the tide and current, hence the name "drifter" for the kind of fishing boat we had. Occasionally a fish would hit the net and there would be a splash as the fish tried to free itself by thrashing at the gill net. The mesh was about two inches square and the more the fish struggled the more likely it would get its gills caught deeper in the net. We would catch 50 to 75 fish each time out. During the long days I would swab the deck, clean the stove, coil rope, and listen to the radio and to other fishermen who had two-way radios and broadcasted messages to one another.

We had a radio that could receive reports by other fisherman who tried to disguise the kind of fish they were catching by changing the name. It was easy to figure out what fish they were reporting because the code was simple and everyone listening to their radios knew as well. Alfred's radio could receive information but he could not call out to others. He thought the cost of an upgraded radio was too much.

It was daylight most of the time. The long summer days lasted sometimes until midnight and even then the darkness that followed was more like a cloudy day than a truly dark night.

We had to have the net out of the water by 6 A.M. or risk getting caught by the fishing commission. A seaplane would fly over Cook Inlet enforcing the end of the fishing day. If the pilot saw your net in the water after the 6 A.M. deadline he would touch the seaplane down and issue a citation that could cost $900.00. Since a good fishing season netted the fisherman $10,000.00, a $900.00 fine was a significant penalty and served as a deterrent to breaking the law.

Once the net was on board we would look for a tender which was a 65 foot long boat with a wide beam to unload our fish. A tender could carry thousands of salmon. If one couldn't find a tender we went directly to the cannery to deliver our salmon. A man with a clicker would count each fish as we threw them onto a conveyer belt. We used a pew, a hoe handle with a hook on the end that looked like a pirate's hook at the end of his arm. We would stick the pew into the fish and pitch the fish and at the end of our thrust the fish would release and be on its way to the cannery. Inside the cannery the fish was gutted, scaled, butchered, packed into red labeled cans, boxed, and sent to the lower 48 states to be sold in stores.

Food on our boat was spotty. Neither of us was a good cook. Kerosene leaked into the compartment that was part of the stove. Our oatmeal stored in it had an oily taste so we decided to survive on canned food. Tuna, fruit cocktail, corned beef, and soup were the mainstays of our diet.

When we got back to the cannery we would clean the boat, dock it, and then drive back to Ninilchik in the green DeSoto. Sometimes JoAnn joined us on the ride home and I got used to driving while Alfred and my sister were in the back seat kissing.

The catch in the summer of 1954 was down because the year before some of the lazy fisherman realized late in the season that they hadn't caught many fish. To increase their catch, some had laid their nets near the mouth of streams to catch salmon swimming upstream to spawn. It meant that fewer salmon were able to complete their reproduction cycle so that this year there were fewer fish.

JoAnn learned that our boat was second to last and losing only to another fisherman in the fleet who drank a good deal of the time. Alfred confessed to her that the Libby McNeil & Libby fleet commander told Alfred he better pick up the pace or he may not get another boat next year. My sister told me of our standing but swore me to secrecy so that mom and Mel wouldn't know. I also knew to keep my mouth shut so that other fisherman wouldn't know either. I could see Alfred's strain as he seemed more focused on seeking out better fishing areas. He smoked more of his unfiltered Camel cigarettes. He listened more intently to the radio trying to learn where others were having success finding fish. He stayed up later at night hoping to see fish surface on the water, a sign that there might be others nearby.

Cook Inlet is about 120 miles long and our boat only traveled at about 8 to 10 knots an hour so getting to productive fishing grounds was a slow process and the fish swam from place to place and didn't remain in one area for any length of time. Since our fishing period was only 24 hours it was hard to get to the areas before the fish moved on. We were burning a lot of gas trying to locate schools of salmon and that ran up Alfred's fuel costs.

Upon our return to Alfred's cabin one Friday we all settled into bed late that night. Around 3 A.M. I was awakened by the sound of dishes tinkling in the cupboard. We had heard this sound before because Alaska has small earthquakes fairly often. I didn't pay much attention to it because the room was not swaying. Then there was a different sound. It came from Alfred. It was a high pitched voice. I looked over at his bunk and he had fallen out onto the floor. I jumped out of bed and saw him trembling involuntarily. Mom came over to see what was happening. His false teeth had fallen out of his mouth and were on the floor beside him. Mom quickly went to the kitchen and grabbed a dish towel. Alfred's jaws seemed to be gnashing. Mom reached for Alfred's chin and pulled down opening his mouth and inserted the dish towel inside. We watched over him for the next two minutes as he continued to twitch.

"Pick him up and put him back into his bed," mom directed me.

I reached behind his back and put my arms under his armpits and lifted. He was 180 pounds and I was only 120. He was taut and felt like cement. I lifted with all my strength to get his waist up to his bed. I laid him down and went to his feet to lift his feet on top of the blankets. He remained still for another few minutes. I looked at mom and she put her index finger to her lips to silence me.

After Alfred seemed to relax he barely seemed conscious. He fell into a deep sleep. I covered him up and looked at mom. She waved me to the porch outside. We were joined by JoAnn who heard Alfred's unusual sound.

"What happened mom?" I said astonished. "Should we take him to Kenai, there's a doctor there."

Mom whispered quietly, "He's had an epileptic seizure. He'll be all right in a while. He needs to rest. I've seen these attacks when I was in nurses training years ago."

Mom then turned to me and was serious. "If he has one of these convulsions while you're out fishing on the boat, take his teeth out of his mouth and put a cloth inside so he won't swallow his tongue. Make sure he is in a safe place so he won't hurt himself bumping into things. Keep him settled after his attack is over and let him rest. Do you understand?"

"Yes," I whispered back. My eyes were wide open and I was still astonished.

JoAnn looked at mom and said, "Will he be all right?"

"Yes, but these attacks will come again and you can't predict when. Bobby, you'll have to deal with them to make sure he is secure so he doesn't fall down and hurt himself and allow time for him to recover.

I looked at JoAnn and could see that she was aghast at what she had seen Alfred do and now what she was hearing from mom.

The next morning no one said anything to Alfred. We didn't want to confront him at what seemed like an embarrassing episode the night before. I however, was a lot more wary of Alfred and watched his behavior the next day closely to see how he responded after his attack. I also knew I had to be on guard when we were out on the boat fishing.

The next several times Alfred and I went fishing nothing happened to him. He continued to press, trying to find more fish and smoked more of his Camel cigarettes. Our catch was modest in spite of renewed efforts to locate more fish. I became more worried for him because the season was near the end and he was in peril of becoming low boat. That would lower his chances of securing a boat next year from the cannery. However, the "run" hadn't come yet and the "run" was when salmon made their move to their birth streams and the fishermen made their biggest catch.

In anticipation of our next fishing outing, Alfred drove the DeSoto into Ninilchik and talked with other fishermen who piloted their boats farther south on Cook Inlet. He came back encouraged and reported that some of the fishermen he talked to had witnessed sightings of salmon moving toward southern streams. That suggested that the fish had started their reproducing period and that we could expect to see more fish Thursday, our next assigned fishing day.

By now it was late July and at 3:30 in the morning we were under way to a fishing spot Alfred thought might be good. This would turn out to be a day like no other in my life. It was going to be warm day by Alaskan standards, maybe 80 degrees. The sky was beginning to turn from its dark gray to bright sunshine. Cook Inlet's water was smooth as a glassy mirror and a delight for fishermen who often had to deal with rough seas and of course, burn more gas plowing through it. It was easy sailing and we would get to our fishing spot in plenty of time to prepare to lay out our net by the 6 A.M. starting time. The engine's noise filled the cabin with its sound as we plied almost effortlessly through the blue-green water. An hour later, a school of porpoises swam alongside and playfully jumped above the surface of the water. They accompanied us for the next twenty minutes.

In spite of the ease of the moment, Alfred was smoking his unfiltered Camel cigarettes one after the other. I opened a can of peaches and we ate in silence. Alfred slowed the boat, and then we came to a stop. He checked his watch and when it read 6 A.M. he said, "It's time to fish. Throw the buoy keg over the stern and we'll play out the net."

I did as instructed and he started the engine and slowly piloted the boat forward and the net was pulled out behind it.

"We'll let the net soak and hope for the best," Alfred said.

Other boats were within a half a mile of ours and they were letting out their nets as well. Alfred's cousin Lou was nearby in his fishing boat. Not much was happening. There was an occasional hit by a fish, and we could see the cork line drop below the water for a short time before returning to the surface. The net would wiggle from side to side for a few seconds as the fish struggled to break free of the mesh. There would be a splash but then stillness would follow meaning a catch had been made and the fish had died.

Time passed slowly. The sea began to become more turbulent. Then around 11 o'clock I saw something that startled me. I had been using the binoculars to extend my vision but in a sudden flash salmon were breaking the water's surface and then plunging back into the sea. As far as the binoculars could take my sight, I could see thousands of fish flying above the water.

This was it, the run others had told me about. The salmon were compelled by nature to get back to their birthplace. The females would lay their eggs and the males would swim over them to fertilize them with their milky fluid in streams and rivers. New salmon would be born the following year and the cycle would be renewed. The run would last maybe two weeks. Fishermen counted on this moment to make their living. This was their harvest time. This was the day the fish surrendered their lives to give life to the fishermen.

A tidal wave of salmon struck our net as well as every other fisherman's around us, in an instant. The water seemed to boil as the thrashing fish caught their gills in the net's nylon squares. There was violence as the fish writhed in the net trying to save their lives and avoid death. Their death however, brought life to others.

Our net became bulky with fish within minutes and began to sink below the water's surface. Within an hour there was chaos among the fishing fleet. Most of the boats had two-way radios that signaled news of the run to other fishing boats that plowed their way into the channel of the run. Their nets were also strung out and became heavy with fish. The once open sea was now a crush of boats jockeying for the best advantage to set their nets.

I heard Alfred yell, "We're in a tide rip. I've got to get us out of here."

I looked over the side of the boat at the swirling water of the tide rip. The confluence of opposing currents caused water to spin and we were being pulled down like water draining from a funnel.

By now Alfred had jumped from the pit in the stern where we picking fish from the net and up to the wheelhouse and had the engine started. I could see that he pushed the throttle to three-quarters but the weight of the net dragged so heavily that the boat hardly moved. The whirling water of the tide rip made matters worse so full power was required to pull us out of the trough.

The spiraling water bought other boats together as well, including a wide-bodied tender whose captain had also applied full power to back away from our boat. The revolving water also sent a 15 foot water-logged tree floating on the sea into our net. It quickly got tangled and caught. All of the other boats labored to pull away from one another under the burden of heavy nets and turbulent water. Eventually they were able to move farther from one another. Our boat was unable to free itself from the tide rip. It took Alfred 45 minutes to slog our way to a safe distance from the other fishing vessels and calmer water.

"Pull the net in fish and all. We've got to that log on board to free it from the net. Then we can get out of here and get back to fishing," Alfred instructed.

Our crew of two, one a middle aged man hoping to salvage his pride and pad his fish count, and me who was new to fishing, were pulling hard on the net. The black roller at the stern was turned on to aid us. We had to lift the wet, heavy net over the stern by gathering the cork and lead line together laden with the heavy fish. Our hands and fingers strained under the weight of grabbing rope, mesh, fish and kelp. Slowly the net began to fill the stern of the boat. Before we could get to the log, the weight of the loaded net dropped the gunnels of our boat so low that seawater began to spill in over the side threatening to sink us.

"Throw the net out, we're going down," a panicked Alfred shouted.

I began to grab handfuls of the net fish and all, and cast them over the stern of the boat. Alfred was doing the same thing, using all of his might. Within minutes, the boat began to rise and water stopped sloshing over its sides. We floated higher and for the moment we had saved the boat, and very likely our lives. The bilge pump was now throwing water back into the sea but it would take a long time before all of the water we had taken on from Cook Inletto be pumped out. But the problem of the heavy fish and the log were still with us. Misfortune and anxiety loomed over us causing Alfred further worry. The situation was bad and it really was, but things were about to get worse.

By now all of the other boats were well over a mile away and their crews were focused on making a killing by catching the flying salmon churning in the water. We, however, sat in our boat stationary. Moreover, we were inactive in the water bobbing up and down, unable to do anything to improve our situation. Alfred now regretted not buying a two-way radio. There was no way for us to call out for a tender to come and take off our fish that we already had on board, so we could then release the log from the net. We continued to pick fish from the net keeping a keen eye on how low in the water we were. When we had cleaned the net as much as we could without risking being submerged, we stopped and looked around to assess our situation.

There was no help on the horizon. The fish continued to jump out of the water, but were moving away from us. The run of salmon swam from the great body of Cook Inlet toward streams where the fish had been hatched and lived in their infancy, and to the other fishing boats that were trying to move with them.

We, on the other hand, drifted with the tide and currents. We passed the time looking through binoculars trying to spot a tender, but the more we looked the more we realized that we were alone. We ate more canned meat and fruit cocktail, waiting, hoping, and despairing. The hours passed slowly and by midnight the Alaskan summer sun gave way to a dark, cloudy-gray sky. Visibility was cut to 40 yards. The cold waves slapped the sides of our boat marking time, causing us to roll from side to side.

I looked at Alfred and his face told a bleak story. His chance at a good yearly income was swimming away from him, breaking water that attracted other boats. I knew our catch assured that he would now drop to low boat in the fishing fleet with no chance of climbing out of that miserable rank. There weren't more than a handful of fishing days left in the season. Each time out would render fewer fish to be caught. We sat bouncing in the waves and couldn't do anything to get the fish from the net into the boat. The present moment held constant, but foretold Alfred's grim financial future.

Alfred was worried but his behavior didn't show it outwardly, yet the muscles around his mouth were tight, that told me he was churning inside. I didn't know how our situation was going to play out either. There was a chance that all of the boats would head for the cannery after the 6 A.M. Friday morning deadline signaled the end of the fishing day. They might not see us to render help.

I fell into my bunk after midnight and I could hear Alfred tossing in his. I knew what Alfred was feeling. If we couldn't hail a tender to unload our fish and we couldn't get the net out of the water by 6 A.M. a seaplane would spot us, splash down and issue a citation for perhaps as much as $900.00 for fishing beyond the 24 hour time limit. Alfred might be able to appeal the fine because the log had threatened to sink our boat, but that was uncertain when it came to the authorities enforcing the law. If he failed in his appeal, he would be further behind financially. If Alfred was low boat and he had to pay a $900.00 fine, his prime source of income would pretty much be killed for the year. There wasn't much work in Alaska in the winter, so he **had** to make his money fishing this summer, and things weren't going well now. Moreover, today was the heaviest day of the run. Alfred had fished long enough to know, and he told me that the next time out on Tuesday, we would see a smaller number of fish swimming up Cook Inlet to find spawning pools.

The boat rocked back and forth with the waves, and Alfred's turning in his bunk made sleep impossible. His nonstop smoking told me that his anguish was increasing. At 3 A.M. it started to become light again. Alfred hadn't undressed when he lay down, and his clothes were wrinkled from his tormented thrashing when he got up. I joined him and when we looked out of the cabin, there were no other boats to be seen.

I got up and made coffee on the kerosene stove and Alfred drank the strong blackened water from a dirty cup and had several refills. He chain-smoked his Camels, troubled. I felt sorry for him but couldn't think of anything to say that would relieve his misery. I looked out at the sloshing waves, and the weighted net with a tree trapped in it, and realized that the net made an agonizing loud statement about Alfred's future.

A half hour passed and Alfred was at the bow of the boat searching the water when he spotted a tender. He began shouting. I took a towel from the galley below and went up on deck to wave as furiously as I could. We screamed as loudly as we could, and our shouts made our throats hurt. Our efforts were rewarded two minutes later when we saw the tender turn its bow our way. It would be another 15 minutes before it was alongside.

"When we tie up, you get a pew and get ready to get the fish out of the hold as fast as you can. We won't have much time before the Air Patrol plane finds us," Alfred said frantically.

He didn't need to say we had a 6 A.M. deadline.

The tender caused white foamy water to rock our boat when it came close. We lashed the boats together and Alfred explained the situation to the tender's skipper and crew. They moved quickly to take on our catch.

I grabbed a pew and jumped into the hold among the fish with their slimy bodies and their blood that had been splashed with salt water that turned the seawater and blood into a brackish green. I was glad I was wearing my rubber hip boots. I tried to ignore the stench, but it took some doing. I pewed fish as quickly as I could and sent a steady stream of fish from our boat to the tender. A man with a clicker was counting the fish as they flew into the tender's hold.

"Hey, stick em in the head," said the clicker man. "We don't want fish with holes in the meat."

"We don't have time for that," Alfred shot back. "We've got to get these fish off the boat so we can take the net in before I get a ticket."

I tried to please both men by being quick about pewing fish with holes only in their head. Alfred joined me in pewing fish. It took us an hour to unload our catch.

As soon as the fish were transferred to the tender, I began to pull in the net, fish and all. Alfred went on board the tender to receive a receipt for his fish from the clicker man. When I reached the place in the net where the log was tangled, I tried to pull it inside the boat but it was too heavy. Alfred jumped down from the tender into the stern of our boat as did two men from the tender, and together the four of us, we were able to load the weighty log onto our boat without taking on any water over the side. Our efforts were intensified because we could hear the motors of a seaplane overhead. We freed the net of the log and threw it back into the water and it drifted away from our boat allowing us to focus on the net loaded with fish.

We continued to pull on the net until it was all in. We all breathed an exhausted but happy sign of accomplishment because we beat the 6 A.M. fishing deadline by ten minutes.

The tender's crew was washing down its decks as Alfred started the engine on our fishing boat. I was picking fish from the net when I turned to see Alfred step to the side of the door of the boat's cabin. He was looking back toward the stern when his body stiffened and he fell down the four steps into the galley and next to the turning engine and its dangerous crank fitting. This was the moment I dreaded. Alfred was having an epileptic seizure.

I jumped up from the stern to the deck level of the cabin and down the steps into the engine room. One of Alfred's arms was flailing near the crank fitting in front of the engine that was turning at 1200 revolutions a minute. If his sleeve got caught in it, Alfred's arm would be chewed up in seconds.

Alfred was upside down with his head near the galley floor and his legs and feet above twitching on the steps that led to the pilot's station. I pulled Alfred's stiff body forward and it was a struggle to turn his body around. It took all of my strength to pull Alfred's 180 pound taut body up the stairs to the pilot's level and out of danger. I turned off the engine and looked at Alfred. His face was pale. His jaws were thrashing. I grabbed a towel and pulled out his false teeth and stuffed the towel into his mouth like my mom had when he had an earlier seizure. I was glad mom had prepared me for this moment and hoped I could perform what was needed successfully.

I watched Alfred for the next 30 seconds and when I thought I had him stabilized, I yelled at the crew of the tender.

I shouted, "Alfred's having an epileptic fit and you need to call his cousin Lew on your radio. His call numbers are WC44-47, and his boat is named the Dolphin. Call him now and get him over here."

The tender's captain jumped down into our boat and looked at Alfred, who was still twitching and stiff. The captain leaned out of our boat's cabin and shouted.

"Call his cousin."

The radio man on the tender knew the call numbers, because he had heard them often over the summer, and he made the call. Within a half hour, Lew had tied up alongside our boat.

He looked down at Alfred's ashen face. He appeared to be in a deep sleep.

Lew screamed, "Alfred's having a heart attack. We need to get him to the doctor in Kenai right now."

I protested, saying that Alfred had an epileptic seizure, and the worst was over. The captain of the tender believed Lew because Lew was an adult and a relative and I was but a thin 16 year old youth. Within minutes, Alfred was taken from our fishing boat and onto the tender and was put in a bunk to rest further.

"Can you steer the boat?" The captain asked me.

I said I could. The captain told his crew to tie a line to our boat and it was done quickly. The captain returned to the tender and proceeded to pilot the tender and our trailing boat toward Kenai. We were twenty five miles away, and it would take at least three hours to get to a doctor.

An hour and a half later, I felt the tender slow and to my surprise, Alfred came out of the tender's superstructure and grabbed the line to our boat. When both boats were almost stopped, Alfred jumped onto the bow of our boat and released the line to the tender.

When he entered the cabin of our boat he said in a determined voice, "I don't want to be taken to Kenai on that tender. I don't want to appear to be an invalid."

I could see that Alfred was feeling the pressure of knowing he was low boat, and didn't want to be looked upon as a health risk as well to the Libby McNeil & Libby boat master. It might jeopardize his chance of getting another boat next year. He insisted on piloting his rented craft to the cannery.

"When we get to Kenai, we'll get the fish out of the net, pew them off, get our count, and go back to Ninilchik," Alfred said decidedly. "I've been smoking too many cigarettes lately, and that's why I passed out," he offered in words of denial.

I heard his words and said nothing. I knew it wasn't the truth, and he wouldn't seek the help of a doctor. He was refusing to declare that he had a problem, and I, certainly, was not going to argue with him in view of the pressure he was feeling.

Alfred started the engine and took control of the wheel. He set a course toward Kenai. The tender bid farewell and pulled away at a faster pace because of its bigger and more powerful engines. Its captain wanted to get the catch to the cannery as quickly as possible before the fish began to go bad.

I jumped down into the lower deck of the stern and again began picking fish from the wet and smelly net. My hands, like any other fisherman's hands when picking fish, began to bleed. The salmon's pointed and sharp teeth snagged the flesh on my fingers and palms as I freed their gills from the nylon mesh, causing deep scratches. The cold salt water felt good on my swollen fingers but the salt in the water stung the red nicks. I began to run out of space to store the net, so I stopped picking fish.

I had been concentrating so intently that I didn't notice the change in the weather. The sun was replaced by a heavy dark sky. But when the wind gusted to 35 miles an hour I was jolted by the rocking boat because of much bigger waves. I looked up and saw whitecaps on top of huge waves as tall as the cabin of the boat. I grabbed a railing to steady myself, and peed over the side. I went to the galley and opened two cans of tuna. I reached Alfred and gave him one. He was struggling at the wheel and could only take intermittent bites. We ate in silence as the boat was maneuvered to find the best angle to attack the waves.

There was no more work we could do now. We had to get out of this stormy weather and get back to Kenai and then do the heavy work still remaining. Blood rushed to my stomach to digest the food, and it was then that weariness struck. I had slept only two hours in the last day and a half, and my arms felt like ragged cloth sleeves hanging from my shoulders, while my legs felt like they were supported by flabby rubber bands. I realized that fatigue was controlling me, and I fell into my bunk below and was barely able to move. My eyes closed involuntarily and I welcomed the darkness and deep breathing. The gigantic waves that pounded the boat couldn't keep me from entering into a deep, exhaustive sleep.

The third time it happened, I woke up and later realized that I had slept only half an hour. The pounding of the dinghy that was tied to the bow seem to be part a dream until, I realized that the force of its hammering was just a few feet away from me. It was crashing into the outside of the boat. I got up forcing by body to call upon the reserve of energy it had gained from 30 minutes of sleep. I realized that my senses were slow and groggy but I needed to see if Alfred needed help.

I went up the cabin where Alfred was fighting the wheel to keep the boat from capsizing. The waves were now five stories high and three times the height of the boat. Alfred had wisely steered the boat to take on the waves at a three-quarter angle, which prevented the colossal surf from throwing the boat 180 degrees backward and upside down. The weight of the fish and the heavy net made the boat turn sluggishly and slowly.

I was shocked when I understood just how serious things were and that we could capsize in the heavy sea and be sent to the bottom. The round bottom of the boat made it more seaworthy as did the keel. But the short 35 feet put the boat in peril against these mammoth waves.

"Go up the bow, untie the dinghy and tow it back to the stern and lash it down," Alfred said hurriedly.

When I stepped outside the cabin the wind almost blew me backwards. I steadied myself, but was still bleary from a lack of sleep. I held on tightly to the railing on the side of the cabin and moved slowly along its side toward the bow. The boat rocked back and forth, taking on the waves. The sides of the boat dipped almost to the gunnels in the water. When the boat was at the top of a wave, I felt as if I was at the top of a Ferris wheel looking down several stories below. At the bottom of the trough, the waves were so high our boat looked like a toy. The jolts of the waves made it difficult to stand.

Slowly I got to the bow and untied the rope and began to lead the dinghy back to the stern. I had to walk over the narrow space of the deck between the cabin and the gunnels. It was just wide enough for the width of my hip boot. The dinghy pulled hard against my grip because of the force of the waves. I pulled equally hard with my right arm, but in order to move the small row boat forward, I reached across by chest with my left hand and gripped the rope. Just then a new wave hit the boat and rocked it hard to the port side where I was holding the rope. I felt my balance tip toward the water and I started to go over the side of the boat. I let the rope go with my left hand and made a blind, behind my back grasp at the railing at the side of the cabin. My first two fingers made contact and caught the railing and held against the pull of the rope of the dinghy that was trying to jerk me over the side. As the boat rocked back to the other side I was able to get a full grip of the railing. I stopped what I was doing and took a deep breath.

I had just faced a near death experience. Had I been pulled overboard there was no way I could have survived. My hip boots would have filled with water and pulled me to the bottom of the sea. An Olympic swimmer could not have overcome the force of the rough sea with water-laden hip boots. In my case, I couldn't even swim a stroke and would have had no chance of surviving. There was no lifejacket on board and even if I had been wearing one, it would not have been enough to save my life. Alfred could not have done anything to get me out of the water either. He would have had to stay at the wheel to prevent the boat from capsizing in order to save his fish catch and his life.

These thoughts passed quickly through my head in an instant. I took no longer than five seconds to think about my near drowning. I had to brace myself for the next wave, and to the tug of the dinghy's rope. I would have to pull hard again to drag it through the water to the stern and lash it in place. Even though the stern was no more than 20 feet from where I stood, it took me 10 minutes of careful movement to secure the rope and tie the dinghy to its proper place.

I cautiously made my way back to the cabin to focus on the battle Alfred was fighting. He was looking intently at the next menacing wave, and then the next one. I was hoping the stress of our peril wouldn't cause Alfred to have another seizure.

"I'm hoping the wind will die down or for a smaller wave so I can turn the boat around and head for the nearest port. We're using a lot of gas and just standing still against this sea," he said worriedly.

Another half an hour passed and nothing changed. Finally, Alfred said he was going to risk challenging a wave and turn in the other direction. I steadied myself knowing that if this attempt failed, we could be flipped over into the sea. I had just made it through one encounter with death and wasn't eager to face another. I braced myself and held on to the door handle to secure myself, and be ready to exit the cabin if that was needed.

Alfred picked his moment to give the engine full throttle, and he spun the wheel hard to the left as we went up the face of the wave. The boat climbed up the wall of the angry sea, and at the crest of the wave, it lifted out of the water. The stern that was turning seemed to almost come to a stop in midair, in what felt like a slow motion, weightless moment. The motor roared when the propeller was out of the water and then the boat smacked the water as it slammed back into the gray-green foamy fury like a raging whale. Alfred frantically spun the wheel back to the right as he cut back the power. The boat was still upright and Alfred let the force of the waves propel us for the next few seconds. Alfred positioned the boat to take waves from the right side of the stern. We survived at least for the moment and there was noticeable relief in Alfred's face. I too, felt a certain reprieve.

The boat was moving faster now as the sea propelled us closer to shore. The boat was still heaving, rising and falling, but at least we were making progress and not burning as much gas.

"I want to see if we can go into Kasilof. It's inside a river and the water will be calmer there and we can tie up until the storm passes." Alfred was talking out loud as much to himself as to me.

I wondered how our fish, still tangled in our net, would last if we had to stay overnight. We had no ice to preserve the fish and at some point the cannery would reject them if they were not delivered in a timely way. That would really put Alfred behind all of the other boats in the Libby fleet.

For the next hour, we rode Cook Inlet's furious elevator of marine torrent. But in the next 15 minutes our hopes brightened as the waves began to falter. The wind speed dropped and the sea became more manageable.

"I think we can make Kenai," Alfred said optimistically.

We hugged the shore at a depth just deep enough to float the boat. We found the Kenai River and flatter water. At 5 P.M. we were next to the dock and I jumped off our boat and tied a connecting rope to a cleat. The cannery's tall shadow shaded our boat and part of the river. It cast a tranquil feeling over us as well. It felt good to be on firm footing.

I began to stretch out the net on the dock. We untangled fish from the net for the next hour and a half. When the net was cleaned of fish and debris we stored it on board. I untied the boat and Alfred piloted it next to a fish dumpster where I secured it so we could unload the fish. I pewed salmon out of the hold, and another clicker man took count. After we had unloaded our fish, Alfred went inside to get a receipt for his count. The dumpster emptied the fish onto a conveyer belt that sent the salmon into the bowels of the building for gutting, slicing, and canning.

Alfred docked the boat back on the pier. I took bucketful's of river water and splashed it over the deck and into the hold. I scrubbed each with a stiff push broom and bailed the smelly, red blood and greenish sluice overboard into the river.

Alfred showed me the fish count from the tender and cannery and the total was 1273 salmon. That full amount was credited to Alfred's account. I knew after I saw the number that he was unquestionably low boat. We could have easily caught 2500 fish that day but the tide rip and the log in the net cost Alfred a chance to keep pace with the other fishermen.

The bulk of the fish had been processed by the cannery by the time we dropped off our last batch. JoAnn asked to leave her work station to join us on the ride back to Ninilchik. When we got across the river, she sat in the front seat and I drove. Alfred was so exhausted he slept in the back seat.

Something had changed in JoAnn. She was sympathetic to Alfred's plight but she was not close to him now, physically or romantically. When we got home I went to bed early while JoAnn went for a walk by herself.

Alfred and I went out again the next Tuesday and were greeted with calmer seas. The big run was over but there were still stragglers swimming towards spawning grounds in rivers and streams. We caught 614 fish that day, but it was the last of the big hauls for the season. From now on there would only be a few salmon dawdling their way to breeding grounds. If we caught 50 fish, that would be a good day now. Alfred's fishing season was essentially over.

Two weeks later Alfred turned in his boat to the cannery, he went inside to settle up his account. He was paid the difference between his catch minus food, gasoline, ropes, and other expenses. His payout was paltry compared to last year and other years. He estimated it was half of what he earned the year before, or about $5000.000.

Mel and George again, hadn't made as much as hoped for with their gill net operation on the beach. Since he was supposed to share profits with Alfred, our share was less than expected.

"Mom," JoAnn said, "Alfred has asked me to marry him. He asked me a month ago and I said I would let him know at the end of the fishing season. I hate to break his heart but I can't agree to be his wife. I don't want to live in this tiny village. I don't want my teeth to fall out like everyone else who lives here. This is no life for me and Caroline."

I listened to JoAnn and understood her mind. I also felt bad for Alfred as well but understood why she didn't want to stay with him.

Mom said, "You'd better tell him right away so he doesn't have any illusions about your intentions."

144

JoAnn didn't tell Alfred right away. She couldn't bring herself to break the news to him. Mom told Mel about her plight and he decided to get involved.

One evening we were all sitting around and Alfred stepped outside to cut some wood for our Ben Franklin stove.

"Go out there now and tell him, JoAnn." Mel said forcefully.

Intimidated, JoAnn stood and walked to the door.

"Alfred!" she said, calling to him.

The door closed behind her and we waited to see the reaction of the two of them when they returned. Apparently, the conversation went quickly because JoAnn was back inside within a minute. Alfred however, stayed outside a long time, then got in the DeSoto and drove away. He came back late and didn't say a word when he returned. He must have known we knew what had happened. He went to his bed and got in.

That night the cups rattled in the cupboard again. Alfred was having another seizure and mom and I attended to his teeth and mouth. Mel awoke and he and I put Alfred back into bed and covered him.

Days later as Mel and George Davis wound down their fishing operation, there was uneasiness in Alfred's cabin. He stayed away longer now even though it was his home. His eye contact was glancing and his conversation was polite but short.

We waited for Mel to declare when we would leave for Arizona and I was hoping it would be soon so as to break the heaviness that went unspoken in Alfred's home. The days in August were creeping toward September and the school year. It would take several days to drive the Alcan Highway to Arizona and enroll me in school, so a decision had to come shortly.

One evening when Alfred was away visiting a relative in Kasilof, Mel drew us together.

"I think we should spend the winter here," he said.

Mom almost exploded. "Where's Bobby going to go school? The school in Ninilchik only goes to the eighth grade. He's a junior in high school. He's already lost credit and I'm not going to have him lose more. We can't drive to Kenai from here and Homer's too far away on snowy and icy roads.

"I've talked to Alfred and George Davis about that," Mel said calmly and confidently. "There's a family in Homer that they know. Bobby can board with the family and there's a high school there he can attend. Alfred said we could stay here in his cabin. He and I will do some logging to make some money this winter."

JoAnn twisted in her seat. She didn't want to stay in Alfred's cabin after she broke off the relationship with him. Mom wasn't happy that I would not be living at home. No matter what the objections were, Mel wouldn't budge. The decision was made.

Three days later Alfred took me aside next to the pile of garbage cans outside his cabin.

"Here's your share," he said without emotion or appreciation.

He had handed me a check for $500.00. The amount said enough appreciation for me. We had never discussed my pay. It was clear Alfred and Mel had negotiated my wage. I thought it was most generous of Alfred and a great job of bargaining by Mel. I was looking forward to buying my mom something nice and a new toy for Caroline.

Saturday came two days later and Mel and I drove to the beach in the Jeep.

"Tomorrow we are going to Homer and you'll meet the family you'll be living with. They're the Dale family. There are two brothers living at home and two daughters. The older girl is out of school and the younger one is a senior in high school. When you live there, don't try to kiss them or anything. Also, there's a bank you can deposit the money Alfred gave you. At the first of the month you'll write a check for $50.00 and give it to Mr. Dale to pay for your keep."

I said nothing but did a quick calculation in my head. There are ten months in a school year and at $50.00 a month for my board with the Dale family, my $500.00 Alfred had paid me would be used up. Now I knew why Alfred had paid me exactly $500.00. I thought, thanks for nothing Mel, you've done it again.

"I guess that'll be fine," I said meekly, but didn't mean it.

HOMER, ALASKA

The next day Mel, mom, and I drove to Homer to meet the Dale family. They had a farm outside of Homer about seven miles. It overlooked Kachemak Bay and Kachemak Bay State Park. There was a large glacier looking back at us from the other side of the bay.

The Dale family greeted us with friendly smiles. They had a variety of skin tones. Jack was the patriarch and in his 60's and over six feet tall. Thin-faced, gray-bearded with a receding hair line, his perfect false teeth seemed out of character with his aging, craggy skin. He said he was from North Carolina which accounted for him being somewhat bigoted toward African Americans as I would later find out and extremely conservative. His skin was very white which made his blue eyes stand out. He was long and limber with a narrow frame. He was not completely upright but walked with a forward bending posture.

His wife was a native, with an olive complexion, short and plump. She had no upper teeth and was smoking a cigarette. When she took a drag from it her lips sunk inside her mouth cavity.

Butch Dale was the oldest son and six feet, two inches at least. He was 26 years old and drove a 1952 Buick. He too was lean like his father, nice looking, fair-skinned and spoke with a high pitched voice. Richard was a younger brother 23 years old and had suffered from polio. He was shorter, wore leg braces, eyeglasses, and a cap with a bill in front. His coloring was somewhere between white and that of an Alaskan native.

Diane was 19 years old and more native in her shading. She had dark hair, brown eyes, and was long and athletic looking. Nancy was 17, blue-eyed, fair-skinned, softer in physique, and nicely figured.

We exchanged pleasantries and Mel reviewed the negotiations he had made earlier without our knowledge.

"Show him you checkbook, Bobby," Mel instructed.

I reached in my back pocket and took out the new, red plastic-covered, folded checkbook and held it up for the Dale family to see.

"He'll write you a check the first of each month," Mel explained to Jack.

Jack nodded that he understood.

"Keep your checkbook in a safe place and don't lose it. You'll need to have it available to write your check each month," Mel was looking at me with authority.

I said, "I'll find a safe place for it."

We were shown around the two story house. Downstairs, there was a kitchen with a big coal stove. It had a large pot filled with soup. There was a sink with a faucet for running water by a window and there was a long table with chairs for dining. The next room was a living room with a Ben Franklin stove, a couch, a table with four chairs, one a soft chair. Next to this room were three bedrooms off to the side. Jack slept in one and Mrs. Dale slept in another, and the two girls shared the third. Upstairs was one large room with several beds and a metal chimney pipe. It was the only source of heat for the room. Butch and Richard slept there and it would my place to sleep as well.

The Dales even showed us the outhouse. It had two holes to sit on and accommodate the large number of people living there. I made a mental note to keep track of who was inside the house before I would use the outhouse so as not to infringe on anyone's privacy or encounter an embarrassing situation.

The home had a well so there was running water. It was wired for electricity as was the barn and workshop. There was no telephone.

We said our goodbyes and drove back to Ninilchik. The next week I was dropped off at the Dale farm and began my new life. I was sad to leave my mom, JoAnn, and little Caroline but was glad to be out of Mel's sight and control. I was apprehensively wondered how I would be accepted by the Dales but told myself to be polite, respectful, and be as helpful as possible.

The Dales were welcoming. Mrs. Dale told me to help myself to the pot of soup whenever I wanted. She made her own bread and it was brown and dense. Two slices required the appetite of a strong, hungry man. Butch showed me around the farm. It was 40 acres in size. The Dales raised chickens, cattle and milk cows, sheep, and geese. Jack had entered into a contract with an American oil company to provide horses to pack goods and equipment for geologists who were exploring for new oil reserves in the wild, back country nearby. The horse-buying plan was to send another son, Raymond, who was married and lived off the farm, down to the 48 states below Canada and buy horses and truck them up. Alaska was a United States territory in 1954. The trip to buy horses would be done this fall and have the horses up to Homer by October. Jack was also teaching himself about refrigeration because he wanted to create a cold storage business for Homer.

Butch became almost like an older brother to me. He included me in his activities and introduced me to people around town. We went to dances together, he danced and I didn't. I was in that awkward period when I wanted to get over with girls but had no social skills to apply to get them. Dancing would have helped me in the pursuit but I didn't know how and was too shy to try to learn.

Butch had me work with him on the farm. We pitched hay on a post to let it dry and then moved it inside the barnyard to a fenced off hay stack. He taught me to milk cows, herd sheep, gather eggs and candle them to eliminate eggs that had blood inside the shell. We went down to the beach and picked up low grade coal that washed up on the shore after a storm. This kind of coal was slow to ignite and

149

didn't give off as much heat as bituminous coal, but it was free for the taking. We hauled cargo from the Homer Spit, a man-made sand bar jutting out into Kachemak bay and into deeper water that allowed bigger ships to dock. In all of these activities Butch was encouraging and complementing.

His brother Richard who had polio was extremely intelligent. He knew a great deal about mechanics, engines, machinery, and animal husbandry. He couldn't do physical work but contributed with his knowledge.

The Dale two girls Diane and Nancy, were polite but standoffish. Diane was something of a tomboy. She would drive the tractor, work on other equipment and in the fields doing hard manual labor. Nancy was more feminine and helped with cooking and housework. I followed Mael's advice and kept my distance with both of them.

I was enrolled at Homer High School. The whole town of Homer was only 800 people at the time and the high school only had 40 students. Freshmen and sophomores were merged together as were juniors and seniors.

The teachers mainly came from somewhere in the lower 48 states. One teacher taught us English and typing. She had gone to Drake University in Des Moines, Iowa. She was older with gray hair, not married and perhaps looking for a husband in heavily male-populated Alaska. However, there were few men who were her peers in terms of her age, education, and interests. Other teachers followed a similar pattern in that they taught several courses and came to Alaska for a variety of reasons.

The Principal of the high school was Mr. Hatch. He was quite a gentleman. Formal in dress and demeanor, he was also something of a scholar, a cut above most of the other teachers. He came into our English class when it came time for the Shakespeare unit. He taught us Macbeth. He talked about the history of England, the intent of Shakespeare in the play, that of ambition, and the psychological nature of Lady Macbeth's cry of "Out, damned spot." His lesson was the third great educational encounter I had experienced. It left me with a new appreciation of Shakespeare and literature. The other two lessons that stood out to me involved music and history. My seventh grade teacher taught us Georges Bizet's Carmen with its seductive story and exciting, legendary music. The other great moment was the aforementioned lesson about ancient history and the Greeks Parthenon.

All of the students knew one another. Most came from blue collar, working families. All of the students worked outside of school on farms and businesses. Most of the students went to dances where the adults socialized along with the high school students.

There were no movie theatres in Homer so most of the students drank beer and liquor and I joined in. It wasn't hard to get an adult to buy alcohol for us teenagers. Surprisingly, no one got really stupid when they drank. There were a few couples who would neck in cars but there were no out of wedlock pregnancies during the eight months I spent in Homer. There were too few girls to go with the preponderance of boys so having a girlfriend made the others of us who didn't have one, envious.

Some had cars or knew someone who did. It was easy to hook a ride as there was sense of cooperation among the teens. No one got into fights. There was one adult bully who pushed his weight around with us teens but for some reason his tires went flat on Halloween night.

It was also in October that my parents moved from Ninilchik to Homer. They wanted to get out of Alfred's cabin for a number of reasons. Logging wasn't working out. There was an awkward standoff between Alfred and JoAnn after she pulled away from his affection, although mom said, he wanted to rekindle it.

Mel and mom rented a building in town that mom turned into a barber shop/beauty salon. JoAnn had a beautician's license as well so she worked in the shop too. Mel looked around for some kind of work but did not put himself out too much. Mom and JoAnn became the bread winners of the family.

When I learned that they had moved to the center of Homer, I decided to stay out on the Dale farm. They agreed to let me stay there. Had I moved back with my parents, I could have walked to school. Now I rode the school bus and helped with chores after I got back to the farm. I liked the way I was treated there better than living with Mel.

As the nights got colder, the days grew shorter. Deep into winter, I would walk through the snow-plowed drive way to the high snow banks along the road to wait for the school bus in the dark. The sun would come up around 9:30 to 10 and set at 2 to 2:30. I went to school in the dark and came home in the dark.

The cold weather had one advantage. There was a lake off of Lake Street. It was huge. An airplane with pontoons could fly in and out on it. In the winter it froze. Butch cut a hole into it and inserted an outboard motor with a stove pipe attached around the propeller that directed its churning water from the motor to the frozen surface. When the new water froze, it made a smooth surface on which to ice skate. Eventually the ice was thick enough for cars to drive on it and not break thorough. On winter evenings we would build a bonfire alongside the road and roast marshmallows.

The first time I was taken out to ice skate a bunch from the high school took me out a mile or so onto the lake. I was just learning to ice skate. They told me they would teach me how to skate. Once we were far away from the bonfire, they laughingly skated away and left me to find my way back. It wasn't difficult to know where to go but it was a trial to master the blades under my feet. It was all in good fun so I did not get upset.

Butch dropped me off at mom's shop in December so I could go shopping for presents. I asked mom if she would help me get a driver's license.

"Let's go next door. There's a trading post there and the owner is authorized to issue drivers licenses."

When we inquired inside the trading post, the owner asked mom, "Can he drive?'

Mom answered, "Yes."

"Okay, fill out this form and sign it," the man said to me.

I did as I was told. He folded up the form, reached in the drawer nearby and stamped the form, then tore off a section of it and handed it to me and said, "Keep this with you whenever you drive. You're now a licensed driver."

Mom and I looked at each other in surprise. There was no written or driving test. Mom's stating that I could drive was sufficient to be legally able to drive a car or a truck.

One of the presents I bought that day when I went Christmas shopping was a wallet for Butch. He needed one and he had been good to me so I was glad to be able to give him something he could use.

"Mel looked under the Christmas tree and was disappointed there weren't more gifts for him," my sister JoAnn told me as she took me aside from mom and Mel.

I had stopped by to drop off presents for my mom, JoAnn, and Caroline. I was going to buy Mel a carton of Lucky Strike cigarettes for his gift. Instead, I asked JoAnn to wrap the wallet I had bought for Butch up and put Mel's name on it. I left the beauty shop and went back into the cold weather to buy another wallet for Butch.

JoAnn attended one of the dances that were held during that Christmas season. I introduced her to Butch and they danced a good deal together that night. They seemed to enjoy each other's company.

"Would it be okay if I asked your sister out," Butch said to me as we were driving back to the farm that night after the dance.

"It would be fine with me. If she wants to go out with you I certainly have no objection." Of course I didn't have the authority to dictate to either JoAnn or Butch.

153

So the romance began. JoAnn acted in a small play and invited Butch to be in the audience. He came and liked the play. Butch was closer to JoAnn's age, just two years older. He was handsome, kind, more socially adroit, and attentive than Alfred. As a couple, JoAnn and Butch seemed to be getting on well.

My only concern was whether JoAnn wanted to stay in Alaska for the rest of her life. If Butch proposed, she had to make a good decision for herself and Caroline. She would have to move to the farm until Butch could build his own place. I wasn't sure there was enough money to go around from the farm's income. His brother Raymond was a trucker but only had one truck and not enough business for two or more. Butch had skills suited for the farm but not a skill to market in a labor setting. He was resourceful but was tied to Homer, the farm, and his family.

As the romance heated up, the weather cooled off. It got to be 14 degrees below zero. The upstairs bedroom where Butch, Richard, and I slept had no heat other than that generated by the stove pipe running up through the room. I piled six blankest on my bed and slept in my clothes. On several nights I was in the fetal position and breathed beneath the covers and shivered all night. In the morning I was groggy, cold, stiff, and not looking forward to the rest of the day.

"Bobby, we've got to get to the barn and milk the cows," Butch said to me.

It was a Saturday and the night before the cold wind had piled up snow drifts higher than the fence posts. I put on three pairs of socks, two undershirts, two outer shirts, a jacket and a parka. This was just before windbreakers were available to the general public. The Air Force had them and they had proven to be a much better fabric than any other on the open market.

Butch and I started out at eight that morning and when we entered the barnyard we sunk down to our waists in snow. We had shovels to try to pack the snow in front of us but when we took the next step we went down to our waists again. Our steps gained us only a couple of feet. We struggled in the snow until we finally got to the barn where the milk cows were. It was noon. The distance we had traveled was no more than 75 yards and it took the entire four hours to get there.

You've never seen happier cows than these when we began to milk them. Their milk bags were full and dripping. After we milked them, getting them outside so we could clean the barn was a challenge. When they returned from the cold outside, they were most happy to have a clean stall, fresh hay, and a warmer setting.

Jack, the patriarch of the Dale family, called me into the living room to help him candle eggs. An upside down coffee can with a light bulb under its open end served to shine light through the egg shell to sort out bloodied eggs from those that could be sold to the public. It was February first.

"Just a minute Jack, I'll be right back," I said hurriedly. I went upstairs and got my checkbook and hustled back down. I opened the check book and looked for a pen to write him a check for my board and room.

"You don't have to do that," Jack said. "You've done enough work around here to more than pay for your keep. Just help Butch with the chores and other stuff on the farm and you can stay for free."

I looked up shocked at what he said.

"You sure about that, I'm willing to pay you to stay here."

"No, that's not necessary. You're a good worker and good to get along with. Just keep helping out."

"Thank you, Jack. Just ask if you want something done that I can help with and I'll gladly do it."

I liked living with Jack, Mrs. Dale, Butch, and Richard. The girls were less warm but friendly. It was a stark contrast to living with Mel.

Diane invited a new boyfriend home for dinner one Sunday. When the man walked in I was surprised to see who it was.

"This is George Davis," Diane smiled as she introduced George to her family.

I had known George for two years since he was Mel's fishing partner. I nodded at him to acknowledge.

George had been married to a native woman and lived in Ninilchik. She had a drinking problem and didn't handle liquor well. She became confrontational with people and found obscure reasons to verbally attack others. I knew that if George filed for divorce, it couldn't be final so his dating Diane was a little surprising. So was the age difference. George was near 40 and Diane was 19.

The Dale family welcomed George warmly at dinner. George avoided eye contact with me for most of the evening. I thought it was because I had known his wife and perhaps he was feeling guilty about dating so soon after his breakup with her. Maybe he felt a little uncomfortable because of the age difference between him and Diane. I was taken aback a little but didn't exhibit any expression of my feelings to him or the Dale family.

One day at lunch time at school, I walked to my mom's shop and had lunch.

"You'll never guess who I ran into recently," I began. "George Davis came to dinner at the Dale's."

"He and Mel had a falling out." Mom explained. At the end of the fishing season, they went into Kenai to settle up with the cannery and crossed back across the river and went to a bar to celebrate the split of the money. I guess they drank quite a bit and they got into a fight and Mel beat the hell out of George,"

My mind quickly calculated what happened. Mel drank to the point of being mean and picked a fight with George. He swung over to his violent side and he usually won any fight he got into. The altercation ended any partnership Mel and George had. It also explained why

George wasn't particularly delighted to see me at the Dale's dinner.

George became a regular guest at the Dale's house. He and Diane eventually moved into a bungalow George bought and was fixing up. No one seemed to object and so it seemed to be a thriving relationship.

Over the next few weeks he and I were again on good terms. He didn't blame me for Mel's attacking him and he seemed to understand that I wasn't happy with Mel as well because I wasn't living at home with him.

George was a crafty with his hands and he had an engaging personality because he played the guitar and sang. He often entertained at dances. He always seemed to find a way to make a living.

I was enjoying my time with the Dales and George. However, I knew at some point that my time with them would end. It was mom who signaled a halt to my time away from home. "I want you to come back home. We may be leaving this spring to return to warmer weather and I don't want to leave you behind."

I couldn't refuse mom's request. I felt like defying Mel but couldn't say no to mom. I didn't want to return home but I had to. So I went to Jack and told him I'd have to leave.

"You've been good about paying us in a timely manner and we liked how you helped out on the farm. We'll miss you but I understand if you have to go back home," Jack said as he held out his hand to shake mine. Mrs. Dale gave me a hug. Butch said he'd see me again because he was dating JoAnn. Richard told me to stay in touch. Nancy said she would see me at school and wished me well. I saw George Davis and told him I was going back home and he looked at me seriously and said, "Good luck."

The beauty shop was open during the day and there was a back room with a small kitchen. There was an area for mom and Mel to have their bed. After closing hours we made beds in the space between the barber chairs for JoAnn, Caroline, and me. In the morning we would stack the beds in the back room stacking them up against the wall.

It wasn't long before I saw a new conflict involving Mel. JoAnn had seen a new hair style that was trimmed short. She had mom cut it in that fashion. When Mel leaned JoAnn had cut her hair, he blew up. She was wearing a scarf over her head when he confronted her.

"Did you cut your hair?" He demanded.

She said she did.

Mel pulled off the scarf covering JoAnn's head and said, "You stay in the back room when customers come in from now on. That looks terrible."

"How can I cut my customer's hair if I'm in the back room," JoAnn retorted.

"Then you better cover your head when you're out here," Mel said with hate in his voice.

Bud and JoAnn continued to date and I tagged along to dances. They were drawing closer and perhaps heading towards matrimony. Their closeness began to bother Mel.

He was itching for a confrontation and a new adventure. He had learned through an Anchorage newspaper that the government was buying uranium from private individuals who had found deposits around the four corners area of Arizona, New Mexico, Utah, and Colorado. It was a new wildcat type of exploration like gold strikes in the old west or the Yukon. Mel had been talking about trying his luck in this new bonanza. He planned to take us all somewhere near four corners and explore. That included JoAnn who would work along with mom to provide an income stream while he explored for the radioactive mineral.

"I'd like JoAnn to stay here and perhaps we can build a life together," Butch said disputing Mel's plan to leave Alaska.

"I don't see a ring on her finger. You don't have any claim to her," snorted Mel.

When Butch left, Mel unleased a harsh verbal assault on JoAnn.

158

"Do you want to live on that farm? The house is so small there's not enough room for you and Caroline. Here he is living at home and talking about making a life for you and him. That's hogwash. He can't even make a living for himself. He doesn't have enough money to get a place of his own. You can't be serious about staying up here. There's no work for you and even if you find something he can't provide for you. I won't allow you to stay here."

By late April, 1955 JoAnn was worn down by Mel and said she would not leave our family to stay in Homer and would join us when we left Alaska. It was a reluctant decision because she liked Butch.

Richard Dale, Butch's brother who had earlier contracted polio, now came down with a second bout. He was taken to a hospital in Anchorage and underwent treatment. He was there only two weeks when news came that he had died. He was only 24 years old. When I heard the news, I went outside as mom and Mel saw me leave. I began to cry to myself. I knew I could not show emotion in front of Mel because he would see that as a sign of weakness. I stayed out in the cool weather for some time before returning. When I returned my eyes were dry but I was silent. Later, JoAnn told me that mom saw I was upset and scolded Mel not to say anything to me about my emotions.

By now Mel had worn out his welcome in Alaska. George Davis and Alfred had nothing to do with him. The beauty shop didn't generate enough money to provide any kind of financial stability. The uranium bug had taken over Mel and was his new "get rich quick" adventure. Mom and JoAnn were also tired of the Alaskan winter. Mel tried to talk everyone into staying another summer in Alaska. However, there had been too many trials for everyone here, so his efforts failed.

One day a man came into mom's beauty shop looking for a haircut. Mom cut his hair and he liked how he looked after mom's trim. He struck up a conversation with Mel who began to spin tales of the virtues of Alaska even though we were leaving soon. The man introduced himself as Dan Parke. As the conversation developed Dan revealed he was part of the Parke family of Parke-Davis pharmaceuticals. Mel thought might be a possible "partner" in some scheme to make money with Dan. This was the hook Mel hoped to spring on us to win his way into staying longer in Alaska.

Dan Parke received royalties from his family's financial empire. He was in Alaska for the adventure of exploring its wilds. He sought out fishing and hunting rather than investing or getting involved in some money-making business. He had a camper shell on the back of his pickup truck and drove all over Alaska, settling for the moment in Homer. Since nothing was done to involve Mel in a business scheme, the friendship was ticketed to that of a friendship by mail.

Saying our final goodbyes to Butch Dale was hard for JoAnn and me. However, the decision was made to leave so we packed up our belongings in the tan Ford station wagon and began heading south and once again, down the Alcan Highway.

SALT LAKE CITY

It was May, 1955 and when we entered Utah, the warm weather felt wonderful. Mel's plan was to settle in Salt Lake City where there were more opportunities for mom and JoAnn to find work in beauty shops while he set about buying a Geiger counter and other equipment to explore for uranium. We rented an upstairs apartment and mom and JoAnn quickly found jobs.

I was enrolled in East High School. I arrived wearing jeans and a Pendleton shirt. All of the other male students at school were wearing suits and neckties. I thought it must be some kind of dress up day. However, every day the guys were wearing suits and sport coats. They looked at me as if I was a pauper. Some few came up to befriend me, trying to console me in what they considered my "impoverished"

160

condition. It was however, a little intimidating to see such a difference in our lifestyles.

Our family was joined by Art and Jane. They had grown tired of the rainy weather in Seattle. They rented an apartment just down the street from us. Art got a job as a carpenter and Jane stayed home with their new baby boy, Sammy.

The summer was hot and mom began to show signs of tiring. She continued to work but was almost exhausted when she returned in the evening. She was having exceedingly heavy flows in her periods, although we didn't know it until the day she collapsed. Mel happened to be home from exploring that day and he took her to a doctor.

"Take her to the hospital right away. Her blood level is low. She needs surgery right away. You need to plan to donate blood on her behalf. It'll save you money if you can give blood. Even if the blood type is different, each unit will be credited to her account," the doctor instructed.

Mom underwent a hysterectomy that evening. Mel, Art, and I donated blood but she still took five additional units before her bleeding was under control and she was stabilized. She stayed in the hospital for three days and was weak when she came home.

Mel was curious as to when she could return to work. He needed money he said, to live while he was near Moab, Utah exploring for uranium with his Geiger counter. Mom returned to work ten days later.

Mel came home from time to time to restock his wallet and tell us of his adventures. He brought rocks with him and some of them would make the Geiger counter click when it got near them. He said he was making progress exploring. He never asked me to come along and help him explore. I stayed in Salt Lake and began to mow lawns.

One visit later Mel came home and was excited.

"I've found uranium!"

We were excited too because maybe, just maybe, he would hit on this gambol and we all could cash in and stop chasing rainbows and have some stability in our home.

161

"I found it and went to file a claim. However, the land is on a school section and can't be claimed unless there is a zoning change. I'll have to get a lawyer to represent me and he'll have to apply to the federal government in order to get the change and then I can file a claim to take ownership."

"When will all of this happen and how much will it cost?" I asked.

"Well, there are other guys who found uranium on the same section. They'll want to claim it for themselves, so this could be expensive and take a long time." Mel said dashing our hopes.

Somehow, we knew this venture was doomed like all of the other ones. Mel had big ideas to strike it rich with his various plans in Arizona, Alaska, and now Utah but none of them ever worked out.

As the summer wore on, Mel became discouraged about finding uranium to claim for his own and sell to the government. In spite of his dispirited condition, one day he surprised us by bringing home our first television set. It had a metal case and when we'd watch programs for any length of time, the top of the metal became hot from the vacuum tubes inside it. It seemed almost hot enough to cook pancakes and eggs on it.

Two weeks later, he surprised us again when brought home a brand new blue and white Studebaker station wagon. Since I was never aware of the family's finances, I had no idea where the money came from for these purchases.

Mel began to scour the Salt Lake Tribune newspaper looking for another opportunity to present itself. This went on for a couple of weeks and then he proclaimed he had found one.

"They're looking for painters in Guam. They pay your way there and pay good money to paint government buildings. The boat leaves from San Francisco. I think I ought to look into that."

With that statement, the plan took form. We would drive to San Francisco and Mel would get on the boat for Guam. We would stay in the city with JoAnn and mom of course, working to pay for our stay until Mel would come home with a thick wallet full of the money he would make painting.

SAN FRANCISCO

We packed up the Studebaker and headed west toward the Bay Area. We arrived and were surprised by the weather. In August it was foggy in the morning and cool. By afternoon, the fog would sometimes burn off and the sun would come out for a few hours before the fog rolled back in around three or four o'clock in the afternoon.

Mel found and apartment on Baker Street between Fell and Hayes and at the end of Golden Gates Park's panhandle. Once we were settled in, Mel went to the address he had found in the Salt Lake Tribune to make arrangements to travel to Guam. He came home that evening and said, "The boat already left with the painters on it and they don't plan to send more. We're too late. The man at the office suggested that I contact the painter's union here and see if they can get me hired locally."

He hated unions and had been a reluctant member of the one in Alaska when he signed on to be a laborer. He hated paying dues and thought the unions were corrupt. However, he was pleasantly surprised when he learned how much union painters were paid in a strong union city like San Francisco. He found work right away and brought home good paychecks.

I was enrolled in Polytechnic High School across from Kezar Stadium. My high school classes had been a mishmash of varied subjects from Arizona, Alaska, Utah and now California. The counselor put me in basic math, machine shop, biology, English, P.E., and World History, even though I told him I had already had that class in Arizona. He said I would be enrolled in these classes until he got my transcripts from my other schools and adjustments could be made after that.

My asthma began to act up almost immediately in the cool weather and the growing plants in Golden Gate Park. My asthma had been under control since we first went to Tucson but now in the city of my birth, it decided to attack me again. I took over- the- counter medicine with modest success. I wheezed at night, coughed during the day, and any physical activity caused an attack of coughing and difficulty in breathing. My P.E. instructor thought I was faking my illness to get out of physical activity but when he saw my face turn red, then somewhat bluish when I ran, he relented and believed that my ill health was legitimate he relented and made me a towel boy. I was to hand out towels for those who showered at the end of P.E. and pick up the towels and count them and pack them away for laundering afterwards.

One morning in October, the counselor Mr. Ford, called me in. He asked me what I wanted to do after high school and I had a vague idea about going to college and perhaps becoming a pharmacist. He then reviewed my transcripts with me and said that I wasn't a Senior, nor a Junior, but a, "high Sophomore."

I said, "That's impossible. I know I lost credit in Arizona because I left school too soon to receive credit for one semester but to be that far behind my chronological class was incomprehensible."

You've traveled around so much that some of the schools you transferred into didn't have the classes you were taking at your old school. You've lost a lot of credit.

I sat silently for at least two minutes and then said, "Mr. Ford, please review your records carefully. I know I've lost some credit and I'm willing to take extra classes to make up some ground but I am serious when I say, that unless I can graduate with the Junior class, I will drop out of school and take up a trade. I'm going to come back tomorrow and see you. If you can't assure me that I can graduate with the Junior class, I will leave school as soon as we're finished talking and get a job."

"That's a radical decision, young man. Are you sure you want to do that?"

"I am not going to be in high school until I'm 20 years old. It's time for me either to get through school or drop out," I said resolutely.

I stood up and gripped the door handle to his office and said "I'll see you tomorrow," and walked out.

I came back the next morning before school started. I knocked on Mr. Ford's door and he looked up and waved me inside.

"Sit down Robert. I got on the phone yesterday after you left and called some of the schools you have attended. You were known as Robert Evans, Robert Maxwell, Robert Jorns, and then Robert Evans again."

He was right about all of the names I had used. I took the names of my stepfathers at various times because I didn't want to have a different name than the one my mom was using. It was a way of fitting in, I thought. At one point I just said to myself 'to hell with it." I'll take my biological father's name because that's who I am.

"What did you find when you called all of the schools?" I asked. "What's it going to be? I'll either stay in school or I'm going to walk out the door this morning and find a job."

"Well, I think I can say that you'll graduate with the Junior class but you'll have to take an additional English class."

"Enroll me now and I'll go to class. I want to get started."

I left Mr. Ford's office and headed for my first period class. The few minutes I had before class, saw an anger grow inside me. I was irate that Mel had been so cavalier to chase his "make money quick," schemes. None of them ever worked out and in the process, I was losing as well. It would mean I was behind my peers who would either get jobs or go to college and be ahead of me a full year for the rest of my life. I wanted to beat the shit out of Mel but I knew I was too cowardly and not physically able to.

I came home that evening and told my parents what had happened at school. I would be behind my classmates and graduate late. My mom was concerned but Mel only said, "You can live with us so you can finish school."

My asthma got worse as my grades got better. Mom saw me choking and coughing one afternoon. I almost passed out. She insisted that we move to warmer climate and Mel said he wasn't going back to Arizona. A compromise was reached and we planned to go down the peninsula south of San Francisco.

ATHERTON

Mel found a small place out of the way from the main part of Atherton, the affluent town just south of Redwood City. We were near the railroad tracks and therefore the rent was cheap by comparison to other housing. The dwelling we rented had a living room, a kitchen, one bedroom that Mel and mom claimed as theirs and a closed in porch where JoAnn and Carla slept. I slept on the couch in the living room.

I was enrolled in Sequoia High School in Redwood City and took two English classes along with my required subjects. Being on the peninsula and near Stanford University, the population of the area was more intelligent and educated than any other place we had lived. I began to blossom as a student. My grades moved up so that I was added to the Honor Roll.

JoAnn and mom got jobs in beauty salons and Mel went to work painting. Mel's asthma acted up now as mine went into remission. He had difficulty on the job and one day he came home early. He had been fired. The union representative came by that weekend and tried to console Mel and promised that he would find him another job and he did.

Mel's philosophy about work was to give his employer a full day's work the first day on the job. He would

166

not take breaks when the others did, take only a short lunch, and stay late finishing up as a way to win esteem from the boss. Afterwards he would work as the others did the rest of the time. Mel was a good painter preferring to do quality work rather than turn out a lot of production. Sometimes that got him in trouble with his employers who wanted more paint on the walls and cared less for quality.

Because everyone was working at physical labor in our house, I decided that I would help out by learning to iron clothes. This was before steam irons, so I had to take the clean laundry and sprinkle water on the garments to be ironed, roll them up, and finally do the finishing ironing when time allowed. Mom and JoAnn appreciated my efforts and paid me a little money for my work.

Mel must have appreciated it too because one day he came home and decided to buy me a car. It was a 1946 Chevrolet, four door, pea soup green in color. He paid $75.00 for it. It was ten years old and had about 75,000 miles on it and it burned oil. It was my first car. Mom took me down to the California Department of Motor Vehicles and I passed the written test with a perfect score and did well on the driving test. It was quite different from the requirements in Alaska where mom had only to attest verbally that I could drive.

Art and Jane had marital difficulties. They separated and Art came out to Atherton and got a job at a cabinet shop. He was good at learning this skill. He was working as an apprentice. He was encouraged to go forward with the requirements to become a cabinet maker but as would be his pattern, he didn't follow through to become a journeyman.

JoAnn applied for a job at Hewlett Packard, the electronics company that was started in a garage in Palo Alto in 1939. By 1955 it was a thriving enterprise and destined to grow into one of America's great companies. She was good with her hands and was trained as an electronic technician. Her pay was considerably more than she was making as a beautician. Moreover, she was given benefits which provided her for the first time, with a sense of security. Of course Mel expected her to pay more to the family pot since she was making more. She decided that as soon as she could build up some capital, she would move out of our home and into her own rental home and achieve independence from Mel.

As the new year approached, Mel began to have more difficulty with his asthma and employment. By January, 1956 he began to search around for better surroundings. He thought Sacramento would be a better place for our fortunes. Mom insisted that we stay until the school year was over.

When Mel was out of work because of bad weather, he turned his attention to going to the horse racing tracks. He bought racing forms and studied them hoping that some fortune-making revelation would show itself to him. He became a regular at the Tanforan and Bay Meadows race tracks. He began to track how many times the horse wearing the number one actually won a race. He did it for all of the numbered horses in the starting gate. He next moved to jockeys. How many times did Johnny Longden win or Willie Shoemaker or Ray Taniguchi. Next, it was how many times the favorite horse won, the next favorite, and so on. None of his analysis produced any rewarding returns. He studied the horses with the best times in their last three races but found that to be lacking because fast horses sometimes got blocked in a pack and couldn't break out. All of his efforts only taxed our already strained income.

SACRAMENTO

The summer of 1956 saw us once again on the move. Into the Sacramento Valley we came. Mel rented an upstairs apartment and found irregular work painting while mom as usual got a job in a beauty salon. She had become the bread winner due to her steady ability to find work in shops. Mom was now 50 years old and Mel seven years her junior. Mel wouldn't apply for a job at Aerojet when it was hiring, choosing instead to paint when work presented itself and when it didn't, play the horses with diminishing returns.

I was enrolled in Sacramento High School. By now I was insisting that I take college prep courses. I earned all A's and B's, and was on the honor roll.

In my chemistry class, I noticed that the teacher Mr. Scott was talking to a student who listened carefully. When Mr. Scott was finished talking the student wrote something on a note and gave it to him. Mr. Scott spoke again and the student wrote something back. I realized that the student either couldn't talk or wouldn't talk in response. I watched the student over the next few days and approached him. I asked if he knew how to write chemistry compounds. He wrote back to me that he did. I asked if he ever talked and he wrote back that he could but had a mental block so he didn't. He wrote that his name and it was Bill Lock.

I felt sorry for him. He was smart, disciplined, got good grades, and had a sense of humor that showed itself with a breathy laugh. We became one-way verbal friends. I would speak and he would write back. He wrote me a note one day asking me to be his laboratory partner. I said I would.

"If you haven't selected a lab partner, you need to do that today," Mr. Scott told the class.

At the end of the chemistry class that day, one of the most beautiful girls I had ever seen came up to me and asked, "Will you be my lab partner?"

Her name was Dana and she was so attractive I was intimidated to even strike up a conversation with her about chemistry or anything else. I had never had a date in high school. Perhaps this encounter with this lovely girl would be a way to enter into the wonderful world of knowing the opposite sex. However, just the day before I had promised Bill Lock that I would be his lab partner. I was torn by my desire to strike up a friendship with Dana by partnering with her and my empathy for Bill Lock. But I had made a commitment. I paused and finally said to Dana, "I'm sorry, but I already have a lab partner. I would have been glad to be your partner had I not already had one."

Bill turned out to be an excellent lab partner and we both did well. Dana found another guy to accept her invitation and he was entranced by her. She was not the best student so between her partner's infatuation with her and her average talent, they did not do well in labs.

I was invited and joined the Chemistry Honor Club. Another invitation was extended to me as well. It was for the Forum Honor Club, an organization at Sacramento High School for those excelling in history.

The rest of my courses were disjointed however. I had never been enrolled in algebra so I took that and did well. Others by now had already taken Geometry, Trigonometry, and some had Calculus. I was behind in higher math because of my checkered educational history.

Mel saw my report cards and my grades. He didn't offer a compliment but instead didn't have to punish me if had I received bad grades. Mel who prided himself in doing regular math and could actually add figures quickly, now tried to tap into what he called "my scholarly achievements." He wanted me to study the racing forms to see if I could find a magical system to win at the race track. I looked at it with little interest believing that if there was a winning system, it would have been discovered by now. I asked Mel about algebra. He said he never could understand it and transferred out of that class when he was in high school in Wisconsin.

As the year wore on, Mel continued to go to the race tracks and paint houses when work was unavailable. JoAnn and Caroline came up for Thanksgiving and Mel asked about JoAnn's work at Hewlett Packard.

"You know, you'll never get ahead by working for someone else," he said.

I had heard this this philosophical rant before from him. He had said the same thing to Uncle Dee in Arizona. My uncle worked as an aircraft mechanic and metal smith at an Air Force base in Goodyear, Arizona outside of Phoenix. He brought a home and made a good living. My aunt joined him at the base as a secretary when my cousins were grown. Together, they were doing quite well.

I compared my uncle's life with ours. We were in a rented apartment and they owned a house. We, through Mel's direction, were chasing dreams and not succeeding while they had a stable life with friends and healthy activities. Our income was sporadic, except for mom and JoAnn's, while my uncle had vacation pay and health benefits.

JoAnn stood up for herself and said, "You may be right Mel, but I have a company that pays me to take a vacation and my little girl can go to a doctor and a dentist when she needs to. My company is growing and we have profit sharing. I have never had it so good."

She could have added that for the last several years she had been part of the vagabond life Mel had taken her through and not provided any financial security.

I listened to the conversation and silently applauded JoAnn. I was silent because if I had said anything to support JoAnn I would have been reprimanded, scorned, and if I persisted, slapped. It wasn't the way I wanted to express my gratitude on this Thanksgiving weekend.

I always wondered why Mel, who believed that working for others was no way to get ahead, hadn't started a painting contracting business where he would find the jobs an hire others to do the work. Others had done it, but Mel didn't act on his own philosophy.

Irregular work plagued Mel's schedule. His trips to the race track however, were quite regular with predictable results, more losses than wins and a dwindling money supply. Christmas was modest for us. Spring came and Mel was making new plans.

"I think we need to sell your car," he told me.

I thought something like this might be coming because of his losing money at the race tracks. I hoped if he did sell the Chevrolet he would do something nice for mom. I knew I could walk to school it was only about a half hour

171

walk. He had bought the car in the first place so it was his money and he could dispose of the car anyway he chose.

"That's fine. When do you want to sell it?"

"Right away! If it rains maybe you can get a ride with friends or maybe I can take you."

Mom rode busses to her work downtown.

Within a week a buyer was found and the car was gone. The weather was good and walking to school didn't burden me.

"I think there's more work in San Jose," Mel declared.

He didn't have to say anything more. I knew our next move had been planned and it was only a matter of time before we loaded up the Studebaker and headed south.

I graduated in June and my mom was in the audience when I crossed the stage to receive my diploma. Mel was not. After the ceremony I was outside enjoying a moment with my fellow graduates and mom came up and hugged me.

"I'm proud of you. Art and JoAnn didn't graduate from high school so I'm happy you did. Because of your asthma, I want you to find a profession that doesn't require you to do hard labor."

It was the first hug mom had given me for many years. Demonstrative affection was not part of Mel's family regimen. I hugged her back. She was the one rock in my life and while I had difficulty showing my warmth for her, I felt it and I loved her.

She handed me a gift.

"Open it. I got it for you."

I stepped away from the other students and unwrapped the package she had given me. Inside was an electric shaving razor. I realized that she had to have saved money aside to buy me this gift. I looked up at her, hugged her and said, "Thanks mom, this means more to me than you know."

My graduation came with joy and regret. I was happy to finally finish school but now I was 19 years old, a year behind those with whom I was supposed to graduate with last year, and regretted the time I lost in school. My future was uncertain. Because I anticipated that we would move to San Jose, I hadn't applied to colleges. That was my fault not my parent's.

INVESTIGATING SHOPPER

My brother Art and Jane had reconciled and he was a crew chief of an investigative shopping group. He offered me a job for the summer and I jumped at the chance to get away from Mel and make some money for myself.

"When you go into a store to buy a product, buy two at the same price. A pound of coffee is a good buy in a super market," my brother explained to me. "If it costs $1.25 per pound, give the clerk two, one dollar bills and two quarters, not two dollars and fifty cent piece. That way a crooked clerk can ring one item up and keep the money for the second for himself if he's a dishonest."

I nodded that I understood.

"You'll stand in line and read the cash register's rings before you make your purchase. Memorize three or four rings before yours. You're going to include them in your written report. You'll have to make it a point to get a description of the clerk. Get height, weight, eye color, hair color, long or short, markings such as a tattoo, any jewelry to distinguish them from some other clerk. All of that will be in your report. You'll be expected to make 15 deals a day by driving from place to place. Your reports cannot have any strikeovers because it will look like you changed the report to try to catch a thief.'

'I'll pay you $50.00 a week. You'll be in a car with another person who will be doing the same thing as you, sometimes in the same store or in another nearby. Your report is going to describe how you paid money, the time, and where you paid it. We have to document what we do in

173

order to have firm facts when our interrogator comes in after we finished shopping an area. He'll look to see if the clerk stole any money and if our reports are good, he'll interrogate the clerk and try to get him to pay back the money he stole from his employer."

I took all of this in and within two days I was writing "good" reports according to Art. Employers hired our employer's agency to try to stop employees from stealing money from their businesses. Our shopping encounters also would identify efficient or inefficient service the employee was providing and comment one way or the other.

When I began my job we were working in Sacramento and Dixon. We would shop grocery stores, gas stations, dairies, department stores, tire shops, restaurants, and bars. I was too young to shop bars but Art made it his specialty. If we caught five employees a month stealing money, we would get a $25.00 bonus.

I did the job but thought it was a little insidious. The employer had a right to expect honesty from his employees and overwhelmingly, most were. However, some were truly corrupt and deserved to be caught and pay back the money they had stolen. However, I felt a little slimy being the undercover customer trying to "catch" them stealing.

Over that summer we traveled from Sacramento, down the San Joaquin Valley to Bakersfield, and all the way to Las Vegas, Nevada shopping businesses along the way. Making 15 deals a day and writing 15 reports in addition to driving many miles between the businesses we shopped filled up a day and then some. To make all of our deals we sometimes had to drive per100 miles a day.

Art was a good shopper in that he always made his bonus. Jane was one of the shoppers as well so together they were making decent money. Sammy, their son, was looked after by her parents for the summer.

We were working in the Bay Area near San Mateo when Art came to me and said, "How would you like to meet your real father?"

I had heard lots of stories about him. He had good jobs as a reporter, editor, and public relations man. He had been around famous people and events in his career so it seemed to me that he had an interesting life. I was curious about what he looked like and the kind of man he would be now that I was grown.

"Yes, I'd be curious to meet him," I said.

We often worked six or even sometimes seven days a week. But we had a rare Saturday free.

"Get in the car," Art said, "we're going to Gilroy. He's the editor there."

His home was out a few miles outside of Gilroy. He had married again and had a new family. When arrived around 2 P.M. he was taking a nap. We were greeted by his wife and his other children were outside playing. They were at least ten years younger than me. We were told to sit on the couch in the living room while my father was awakened. When he came in I saw that he wore glasses, was balding, about my height, and needed a shave.

"I was up late last night getting the paper out, so I was taking a nap," he said in a voice that was medium deep.

I stood up and we shook hands.

"It's a pleasure to meet you," I said feeling nothing inside since he had never been involved with my life. He may as well have been a total stranger, and in fact, he was.

He asked about my sport coat. I had bought it at a second hand store.

"The shoulder pads seem a little uncomfortable when I first put it on," I said.

"I wear them too, and they seem a little strange to me as well," he said, putting me at ease.

Art took over the conversation and shared with the editor where we were working and how little Sammy was doing. I listened and didn't say much. Art tried to brag on me a little bit by saying that I planned to go to college.

No questions were directed to me about what college I wanted to attend or what I wanted to study. The kids outside made a ruckus and took the editor's attention. They wanted to kill a chicken for dinner.

"Can I chop off his head?" one of them said.

"We'll see," Art's father counseled.

After an hour of small talk, it was determined that we would now be leaving. Nothing was said about coming back for a visit or staying in touch by mail, nor was a phone number given for me to call. Nothing was asked about mom or her life and where she was living.

"I've heard a lot about you," I said as I shook the hand of the stranger before me who was my father.

Art and I said nothing substantial about the visit on our ride home because there was nothing significant that took place.

The crew worked our way up northern California to Redding, Red Bluff, and east to McCloud. The lumber town was almost the classic case of a company town. Every commercial enterprise was owned by the company. There was the McCloud grocery store, hardware store, gas station, and pharmacy. Every dollar employees earned was mostly spent in McCloud.

It was there that I decided to leave the crew and help Mel and mom move to San Jose and continue my education. I earned enough to buy myself a 1951 Chevrolet sedan that I hoped to use for many years as I went to school.

SAN JOSE

"You grab the top of the washing machine and I'll take the bottom. We have to go up those stairs," Mel instructed. The apartment Mel rented was on North First Street, a two bedroom place in a nice section of town. Mom was downtown trying to find a job while Mal and I moved their belongings in.

176

"You can stay with us and go to school here in San Jose if you want," Mel offered. "You'll have to get a job, find a school that will take you, and pay some rent."

Having driven around the state while I worked on the crew gave me a chance to evaluate a good part of California. San Jose looked good when compared to other places.

"Thanks," I said.

It was too late for me to apply to San Jose State College so I went out to San Jose City College and got in the long lines of those trying to sign up for classes. It was hot and the process slow, especially when a coach took his football players to the front of the line and had them registered while we regular students waited.

"What do you want to major in?" the counselor asked me.

"Pre-med. I want to be a dentist."

I told her about my limited math background and knew I needed a course to advance my knowledge of math. I was enrolled in what was called "Survey of Math." It started with simple arithmetic and moved all the way to geometry. I also took Chemistry, English, U.S. History, Health, and a required P.E. class. The fees were reasonable, the text books not too much.

"Bobby, you may be eligible for some financial help from the Veteran's Administration," my mom said. "Daddy Bob set us up as his heirs so that if you qualify, the Veteran's Administration might pay for some of your college."

"What do we have to do?" I asked. I hadn't heard the term "Daddy Bob" since Mel outlawed the term.

"I have Monday off so we can go together to the local office here in San Jose and find out."

When we arrived, mom presented information to the advisor about Daddy Bob's will. He said he would check his records and mail his findings to us. Two weeks passed and then a letter came. It said that Bob Maxwell had indeed made us his heirs and that in order for me to receive any benefits I would have to go to San Francisco and take a test to see whether I was educationally prepared to be successful in college.

The test was scheduled and it took four hours. It consisted of math, grammar, reading comprehension, history, and constitutional questions. After I finished, I was told that my results would be mailed to me. I left not knowing whether I passed or not but I felt I had performed well.

While waiting for the results of the test to come in, I contracted to sell J. R. Watkins products door to door. My kit included spices, vitamins, vanilla extract, pain relieving liniment as well as many other products. Every afternoon after classes, I would walk around my neighborhood and try to hustle products from my kit. Some days resulted in nothing while others were a complete surprise. Vitamins netted me over $20.00 one afternoon and that was a big sales day.

A month had passed since I took the test for the Veteran's Administration. I wondered what was taking so long. At last a letter came and it indicated that I had passed the test and was qualified to receiver veteran's benefits. I was to receive $110.00 a month during the school year as long as I stayed in college and maintained a 2.0 grade average. It was not enough to live on but it would help with expenses at school and paying some of the bills to live.

My grades on my college tests were decent, a "B" average with a strong showing in math and history. The instructors generally were good. However, the student body was lacking. Many stayed in the cafeteria for long hours talking, drinking cokes, and not doing much. I found solace in the library when I was not in class. It was quiet and the other students there seemed more serious.

One of the students I met at college had worked in veterinary hospital. He would clean out the kennels, bring animals up to the doctor for treatment, and help in the grooming room. His name was Richard. He had an engaging personality and we struck up a casual friendship. He would later become a life changing acquaintance.

On Friday nights I went to dances at a youth hall in Santa Clara. It was for high school and college students. I forced myself to learn to dance, however badly. It was a way to meet young women. I began to date a few of them and developed a circle of friends. It was a welcome break from study and door to door sales.

Near the end of my first year at college, Mel had a new plan for his next adventure. Dan Parke, the man Mel had met in Homer Alaska and related to the Parke- Davis pharmaceutical company, contacted Mel.

He had stayed in Alaska after we had left. He had moved to Kenai and decided to stay the winter. One night he had gone to a bar and had an argument with one of the patrons, a native. When Dan left the bar, the man followed him to his rented cabin. Dan had gone inside and the man broke in and attacked him. Dave had a .22 pistol near his bed and as the fight moved in that direction, Dan reached for the pistol and fired at his assailant. The man fell back and Dan continued to fire. Dan reloaded and eventually put 20 bullets into the man. A constable was called and declared that it was self-defense. However, when the facts were presented to the district attorney in Anchorage, he decided to prosecute Dan because he had reloaded the pistol and continued firing. Had he stopped with the first clip the prosecution said, it would have been self-defense but because Dan reloaded, it moved beyond self-defense and constituted a crime. The jury believed the prosecutor and Dan was sentenced to jail for two years and he served 18 months.

During Dan's jail time, his dividends from the Parke-Davis kept rolling into his bank account. Upon his release Dan's bank account had $50,000.00 in it. He was looking to leave Alaska and contacted Mel about starting a new business that was catching on, an automated Laundromat. Dave wanted to build one in the state of Washington and wanted Mel to run it for him. Mel was excited about running a business again, being his own boss, and perhaps learning enough to start his own Laundromat.

"Bobby, I have this opportunity up in Washington," he explained after he detailed the events in Dan Parke's life. "You could come along. They have colleges up there and if college doesn't work out, you can work with me in the laundry."

I had experienced enough of Mel's plans for almost ten years of my formative life. I was 20 years old, a freshman in college, and decided to end being a part of Mel's adventures.

"I think I'd like to stay here and continue in college," I said with confidence.

Mom jumped into the conversation, "Where will you live, how will you make a living, and how will you be able to continue in college?" Her tone was almost pleading and said I'm worried about you.

I knew this was a turning point in my life. I had to rely on myself and not them. I had seen how JoAnn and Art had been pulled into Mel's life and had a hard time breaking away. I was determined to make it on my own.

I turned and looked both Mel and mom in the eye and said with resolve, "I'll find something. I don't know what but I'll find a place to live and go to school."

I didn't know what it would be but I was unwavering in my decision to get away from Mel and make a life for myself.

COLLEGE

I had lived at home my first year of college and when summer came I got a job with another company as an investigative shopper. I was able save a few hundred dollars because my room was provided for all of us as the crew traveled throughout California and Nevada and stayed in motels. I bought new tires for my 1951 Chevrolet four door and reenrolled at San Jose City College. That's when Mel and mom were heading out of California for their new adventure in the laundromat business.

I had met a fellow student at college who had worked in a veterinary hospital and was leaving and told me of an opening. It paid $1.25 an hour but being on call 10 nights a month provided free living accommodations. I now had to find a way to get away from Mel and start my life alone. I applied for the job and was hoping to be employed. A day later I stopped by and the Veterinarian said I was hired.

I moved into my new digs. The place was one small room that had bunk beds on one wall and a stove and sink on the opposite wall. Between the two walls was a table and two chairs. The fourth wall led to an outside door. A hallway led to the office and recreation area for the employees. It had a desk with a phone, a couch and another table. Between the living space and the office was a bathroom with a tub and shower.

Night duty only required that you be there to take emergency calls when animals were in distress from illness or had been hit by a car. Rarely did anyone call with a problem. If they did I would call the doctor who would come down and treat the animal.

This was a perfect set up for me because I had access to a telephone an electric typewriter, a desk to read and study. I also was hired to work between 4 and 6 in the afternoon and all day Saturday and half a day Sunday.

I fell in to a situation where I had a place to stay and had a job that paid enough to get by. In a short time I was given a raise to $1.50 an hour. I was working 20-22 hours a week and only had to buy my food and gas for the car and other small expenses and there was even a little money left over to spend or save.

In the afternoon I would clean up the hospital by mopping the floors, sterilizing the instruments, and assist with treatments when needed. On Saturday and Sunday I had to remove the animals one at a time from their kennel, remove the soiled newspaper and dispose of it, mop the kennel, dry it, and insert new clean newspaper into the kennel. It was dirty work and the animals weren't always good about being taken out of the kennels. I endured several scratches from cats, growls from dogs as well as bites from dogs and cats. I had been around animals when I lived on the farm in Alaska but this was a different kind of relating to pets.

Sometimes in the mornings I would bring animals up for treatment. I would tell the doctor which animal it was, dog or cat and he would give it shots, clean wounds, or apply ointments to needed areas.

In the afternoon, I would work in the grooming section combing out dogs or cats, giving medicated baths, or assist the groomer in drying the animal. When clients came in to see the doctor I would be in the room with him to hold the animal while injections were administered. When the clinic was closed late Saturday, I would clean up and be on call for emergencies. In the evenings I would read my textbooks, write book reports, and term papers. It was a workable situation.

When I was newly hired I was told to bring up a cat to be neutered. When I arrived in the exam room I saw a wooden box with no top. One end of the box had a half-moon cut out. I was told to lay the cat on its back with its hind legs protruding through the half-moon opening of the box with the opened top covering the rest of the cat's body.

"Hold the tail and one hind leg with one hand and the other hind leg with your other hand. Put your forearms on top of the box and push down," the doctor instructed.

I did as I was told and the doctor grabbed the cat's scrotum and pulled off the hair around it. He then took a scalpel and slit the scrotum twice; once for each gonad. He used his thumb and forefinger to reach inside and pull out the gonads. The cat understandably began to scream in pain. The doctor next took forceps and pullout the remaining tissue that connected the gonad to rest of the reproductive organ inside the scrotum.

I looked on in amazement. No anesthetic was used, just good old fashioned handling with a strong grip.

"Hold on to the tail and don't let go, I'm going to lift up the box," the doctor said.

I did with considerable trepidation. The cat flipped over on its feet and was hissing.

"You can take the cat back to the kennel now," the doctor commanded.

I looked at the cat that had just had his maleness taken away and wasn't happy about it and said, "You take him back. He's mad at me for holding him during this whole affair and he hasn't seen you so you are in a better position to return him to the kennel than I am."

The doctor laughed because he always wanted to see what reaction new kennel boys had when this procedure was performed.

"Now you can take him back to the kennel. He's okay."

Surprisingly, the cat settled down almost immediately and was docile when I picked him up to take him back to the kennel. It was my first exposure to assisting a surgical procedure and an eye-opener for me.

There were other unusual experiences as well. Late one Friday evening an officer from Animal Control called the hospital and said he needed me to open up so that he could drop off an animal. I turned on the lights inside the hospital and unlocked the door. I was waiting when I heard a truck roll up into the driveway on the side of the hospital. I heard the animal barking and expected to see a dog.

"I've got him in a choker and under control."

It was dark and the Animal Control vehicle's motor was still running. I opened the door and before me was a seal with a rope around its neck. The rope was threaded through a thin metal pipe so the seal could not move to attack the handler. Two other men were with him.

"Where do you want me to take him?" The man said.

I said, "Let's take him down the hall and put him in one of our enclosed runs to hold him.

We went down the hall, turned right into the grooming area, then left to another room, and left again into a run with cement block walls. The man guided the seal into the run then loosened the rope and slipped it over the seal's head as I closed the door to secure the animal inside.

"Is the seal injured?" I asked. "Shall I call the doctor to come down?"

"No, he's okay. We'll hold him here until we can arrange a way to take him back to Santa Cruz and release him into the ocean. That will be in a day or two."

"How did you guys get a seal from Santa Cruz here in San Jose?" I asked.

The man answered, "As close as we can tell, a couple of guys were at the beach in Santa Cruz and somehow captured the seal and put him in the trunk of their car. They drove to San Jose and were drinking in a bar and bragging about what they had done. People inside of the bar heard the seal barking and wanted to see it and giggle about the situation. Everyone came outside to the car and when the guys opened the trunk, the seal jumped out and went down the Alameda near Hedding Street. No one tried to recapture it. Apparently, everyone went back into the bar, had a good laugh and continued drinking."

I was aghast. "What happened next?"

"The seal began barking as it went down the Alameda and woke people up and when they saw the seal, they called us. When we arrived the seal had traveled six blocks and it took four of us to corner it to the point that we could get the choker on him and put him in the truck."

"Anything special I should do with him?" I asked.

"Nah! Just keep him here until we come to pick him up in a day or two."

It was near one in the morning when the Animal Control men left. It was too late to call the doctor so I closed the doors and turned off the lights. I made sure that I was up early when the doctor came in the next morning.

184

"Doctor, Animal Control dropped off a seal last night."

I told him the facts as they had been related to me and he laughed and shook his head.

"What do you want me to feed him?"

"Give him three cans of cat food and be sure to hose him down every hour or so. Don't get too close to him or he'll bite you. Their jaws are much like a dog's. And be sure he doesn't get out."

My second year of college was good. I changed my major from pre-med to Social Science. I had admired my teachers the last few years of high school. They were underpaid but were trying to give their students' knowledge to help them, not try to take something away. They were engaged and for the most part liked their students. I had always done well in history classes and liked knowing about the past, about economics and sociology, geography and political science.

However, one of the best courses I took that year was a course in European Literature. I was fascinated to learn about writings from ancient Greece and Rome, medieval poems, renaissance and enlightenment authors, German writers and of course the great Russian novelists. The instructor had read all of the works and could speak from firsthand knowledge of all works we studied.

It was during this year that I met Lauri. At a dance I spied her and she was beautiful. I asked her to dance and later after I got to know her better, I asked her out to a movie. We struck up a relationship and began going "steady." She had reddish-brown hair cut short, green eyes, freckles but could tan a deep brown that made her skin look perfectly inviting. She had nicely shaped breasts and a lovely waist and full hips. She had a knockout smile with perfect white teeth and an infectious laugh.

She had contracted polio as a child and one of her legs from the knee down, was smaller than the other and so was her foot on that leg. She had to buy two pairs of shoes in order to have the correct size for each foot. Her condition didn't bother me. I liked her for who she was and she was my first long-term girlfriend.

Her father was a machinist and very technologically skilled. Her mother worked in records at a firm that made tanks for the Sixth Army. She also was musical and had an organ in her home that she played. She worked occasionally at supper clubs playing music while customers dined. She was a strong-willed woman who had a good sense of humor.

Lauri had an older brother who was intelligent, engaging, well-spoken and talented in technology and music which pleased both parents. Lauri's younger sister was attractive and enjoyed a good laugh.

College required interesting academic work, employment provided a place to stay and money enough to get by, and Lauri gave me affection and companionship. Life was going reasonably well for this 21 year old independent man.

One evening when I was on night duty a woman called and wanted to visit her pet, a monkey named Jazz. Jazz had to be quarantined because he had bitten a neighbor. It was unusual to have a visit after hours so I called the doctor who said it was all right.

I unlocked the door and waited for the woman to arrive. When she did she was accompanied by her boyfriend. They made an attractive couple. Both were in their late 30's.

I escorted them into a treatment room and said, "Wait here and I'll bring Jazz up so you can visit."

Jazz was in a kennel and wore a leather collar that had a leash attached to it. That made handling him easier so that he wouldn't bite me. I took him out of the kennel and had a broom to keep him away from me. He walked passively up the hall and into the visiting room where his owner was waiting.

"Here he is, your little Jazz."

"Oh! Darling," the blond haired, full-figured woman said and Jazz immediately jumped into her arms. She began petting the monkey and cooing to it. Her breath revealed that she had been drinking.

Jazz unbuttoned the first two buttons of her white blouse and reached inside. When the opening was pulled partly away her black bra showed stunningly beautiful rounded breasts. She didn't mind the monkey reaching inside but it was a little embarrassing to me and it spurred the boyfriend into action. He reaching inside the blouse and tried to get Jazz's hairy arm out.

Jazz reacted aggressively toward him showing his teeth and began to screech. The boyfriend pulled back.

"It's okay Jazz," the lovely woman said trying to appease the affronted primate.

The boyfriend tried again to remove Jazz's arm from inside his girlfriend's blouse. Jazz lunged at him and only the leash I was holding stopped him from attacking the man's face.

The woman reached and grabbed Jazz and held him close to her. Jazz was now energized. I was afraid that if he monkey bit the man, Jazz would have to be quarantined for a longer period of time.

The man was angry and breathing harder and his breath revealed that he had been drinking also.

Jazz again reached inside the woman's blouse and slowly regained a calmer state as he was comforted by the woman.

I was looking for an opportunity to end the visit but the woman's affection for the monkey and the man's anger made for a dichotomy of emotions that was difficult to bring to a conclusion.

Finally I said, "Perhaps it would be wise to take Jazz back so that he won't have stay any longer than the Health Department requires for his quarantine. I can see that you really like Jazz and don't want to be away from him any longer that is necessary."

"But I love him so much, I just want to hold him a little longer," the lovely blond lady protested.

The boyfriend was looking to end the visit as well because he didn't like the monkey and he wanted to be back with his lady.

"Yeah, honey, let's give the monkey back so we can get going."

Within five minutes the visit was over. The woman thanked me and tried to give me $5.00 but I refused. I held Jazz until they were out the door, then locked it quickly so the woman couldn't change her mind and try to return. I took Jazz back to his kennel and put him in side. I quickly closed down the hospital and went to bed smiling about the visit I had just seen.

The next morning I told the doctor what had happened the night before and he and the rest of the staff got a good laugh. Jazz was released two days later when I was attending classes and the blond lady asked the doctor to thank the nice young man who brought Jazz up for her recent evening visit.

Two months later I received an emergency phone call on a Thursday night.

"My dog's been hit by a car and she's injured. Can I bring her in?"

"Yes," I said concerned. Give me your name and the dog's name and I'll call the doctor and have him come down to the hospital so he'll be here when you bring the dog in."

"Doctor, Mr. Andrew's Collie has been hit by a car and he wants to bring her in."

"I'll be right there," the doctor said.

While I was waiting for Mr. Andrews and the doctor to arrive, I opened up the side door and the front door. I turned on the lights in an exam room and laid out the sterile instruments. I then pulled Mr. Andrews file and had it ready so that the doctor could post the treatments he would be giving the dog.

Soon the front doorbell rang and I opened the door and saw Mr. Andrews. He had the injured Collie in his arms. Mr. Andrews had arrived before the doctor.

"Bring her in here," I directed and led them to the exam room. "The doctor will be here soon."

Doctor Smith was on call that night and he arrived within two minutes and began to examine the injured dog. My duties required me to hold the dog's muzzle to prevent it from biting the doctor.

After a short time the doctor declared," She's got broken ribs and had internal bleeding. I'll give her a shot to stop the bleeding and something to make her sleep. It will take a while to take effect but when it does, we'll get an X-ray to see how things look. She'll be in a lot of pain but she'll make it.

A relieved owner said, "Thank you doctor."

"I'll call you in the morning after I examine her to keep you updated," Dr. Smith said.

Further pleasantries were exchanged between Dr. Smith and Mr. Andrews and then each bid farewell.

When Mr. Andrews had left Dr. Smith said, "Open up one of the big kennels. Make sure it's on the top level and swing the door fully open."

I did as instructed and returned to the exam room. The doctor said, "I'll carry her back to the kennel."

He gently reached under front and back legs and lifted the Collie off the exam table. She was in a lot of pain and she began to try to bite at his head. I could see that her big teeth could bite off his ear so I sprang up with both hands and tried to grab her muzzle. The dog saw me move and her big jaws attacked my left hand and arm with crushing force and punctured my skin causing blood to spout. I pulled away and the dog again tried to bite Dr. Smith's head and neck. I jumped in again to try to close her mouth by gripping her muzzle. She was too quick for me and again bit my left hand and arm. More punctures and more blood shot out. However, this time I regrouped and was able to get control of the dog's mouth. When the dog was safely inside the kennel she settled down as the drugs began to take effect.

Dr. Smith looked at my wounds and saw that I was going into shock.

"Put your head between your legs," he shouted.

I did but my pale color was slow to return.

"Come up to the exam room and let's take a look at those bites," Dr. Smith said.

"Those are pretty deep. Can you move your hand up and down? Can you move your fingers?"

I could do both but the blood continued to run out of the wounds.

"I'm going to drive you down to emergency. You're going to need stitches."

"What about the dog and X-rays," I said.

"She'll be okay for tonight and we'll do the X-rays early tomorrow. Right now you need some attention."

He drove me down to San Jose General Hospital and a medical doctor was called into see me.

When he arrived he said, "Get me some suture material," the doctor directed to a nurse. He then turned to me. "When's the last time you had a tetanus shot?"

"I don't know if I've ever had one," I stated.

Over the next 45 minutes the doctor gave me tetanus shot, several stitches and bandaged my hand and arm.

"Don't do any physical work with your left hand for a while because the stitches will tear loose if you do."

I nodded and thanked the doctor. Dr. Smith drove me back to the veterinary hospital. My hand and arm were throbbing when I went to bed. I tried to keep my arm vertical so the blood would run down my veins and not toward my wounds. I didn't sleep much that night but was able to greet the staff when I woke up and was preparing to go to class.

Dr. Smith had told everyone at the veterinary hospital that I had performed heroically the night before and they all patted me on the back for what I had done.

Saturday morning came and two of the assistants called in sick.

"Can you work this morning?" Dr. Hanson asked me.

He was the owner of the veterinary hospital and was sympathetic to my condition.

"I wouldn't ask you to work if we had a full staff. You won't have to clean kennels, just bring up the animals for treatment. I'll put a rubber glove over your bandage to keep it clean."

I needed the job and living arrangements to continue so I said, "Sure, I can work."

I tried to use my right hand as much as possible to protect by throbbing left hand and arm. It was painful but I got through the morning.

At the end of the day Saturday Dr. Hanson said, "Thanks for helping out today but I need you tomorrow to clean kennels."

"I think I can do it." I said.

We started at six in the morning and I tried to use only my right hand. I could do the work but it was much slower than when I had the use of both hands. I got through the day and the days ahead as the hand's healing took hold.

In early June I asked Doctor Hanson who owned the clinic to give me more work in the summer.

"I need to make $300.00 a month. I need a newer car and I'd like to save some money to buy one."

"I'll give you the work but I am not going to give you a raise. You make $1.50 an hour and that means you'll have to work 200 hours a month. I'm paying you the top wage I give to kennel boys. Can you do that?" He asked.

"Yes, give me eight hours a day for six days and I'll work half a day Sunday," I declared.

"Okay, you can start the week after your school year is completed."

So I did. The hours combined with my ten nights a month of night duty made the job a grind. When things were slow, I would scrub down the surgery room, defrost the refrigerator, mop floors, assist in surgery, sterilize instruments, restock the medicine shelves, refill silver nitrate sticks, and do anything I was directed to do.

I had graduated from San Jose City College and applied to San Jose State College and was accepted. I continued through the summer to save money and planned to additionally save all of the money I was paid by the government for attending college. That amounted to $110.00 a month. I knew that coming from a family that scraped by that I could expect no money to come from them so capital accumulation was important if I wanted to get on with life. Over the course of my college years, I saved over $4000.00 and had no debt. I was able to buy a newer car, a nice brown suit and take Lauri out to movies, dinners, horseback riding, and a play.

Courses at San Jose State were more demanding. The reading was more expansive and complex, term papers longer, and book reports more thorough. The lectures were more structured and tests were more difficult. However, I liked the challenge and my grade point average actually went up. I enjoyed the lectures and liked going into the book stacks where it was quiet and sit among the great books and read.

At San Jose City College many students were unmotivated and the classic description of the school was a high school with a cigarette machine and juke box. The mood was more relaxed. There were good instructors at City College but many students didn't take advantage of them. At San Jose State students were more serious and focused. I liked the atmosphere a lot better even though the competition was stiffer.

I left the veterinary hospital when a fellow student offered to let me stay with him and his parents if I would drive him back and forth to San Jose State. I agreed to do it because it would give me more time to study without the work load I had been carrying. His family had a modest income and they lived in Saratoga off of Highway 9.

Lauri and I continued to date and drew closer and by my senior year I asked her to marry me and she accepted. I approached her parents and talked with them about marriage. They were somewhat reluctant because she would only be 19 and hadn't planned for any type of career or college. She was a solid student but not bound for college. Both her parents were concerned about her because she had suffered from polio as a child. They sheltered her more than her brother and sister. I promised them that I would work hard, provide for her and take care of her. I told them that my goal was to finish my senior year, graduate and enter graduate school to complete a teaching credential and then become a teacher. They knew Lauri wanted to marry me and they could see that I was working toward a career that was stable. Neither of them had gone to college and Lauri's father barely finished grade school. He was very good at his job as a machinist and Lauri's mother was very intelligent and worked in an important position handling documents for the Sixth Army at the company where she worked that dealt with government contracts. They agreed that we should marry and gave their blessing.

The wedding was set for March 18, 1961, the week before spring break. I had ordered a white dinner jacket and when I called that Saturday morning, the lady attendant said she couldn't locate my order. I said I was getting married that day and was there a way to find the proper clothing I had ordered. She panicked and dropped the phone. I could hear her scurrying around and moving objects and after five minutes, she came back on the phone.

"I found your order and you can pick up your outfit anytime."

I breathed easily and got in the car and raced to get my clothes. Everything was in order and I came back and changed and went to the church. My mom and brother were there as well as a few friends. I had asked three friends to be groomsmen and we were all decked out in the same outfits and they were waiting for me when I arrived.

We entered the church and I stood at the front and waited for Lauri's Father to walk her down the aisle. She looked beautiful in her white wedding gown. When I took her hand she was shaking slightly. I wanted to put her at ease so when we were asked to repeat after the minister's wedding vows, I made a point to speak loudly so that everyone in the church could hear. Lauri said later that it made her feel more at ease because I sounded confident.

After the ceremony, we drove around town with tin cans trailing after the car driven by her brother Charles. He honked the horn to alert everyone that the two of us in the back seat were married. Charles was very supportive and helpful.

We returned to Lauri's home and she insisted on opening gifts which we acknowledged with thanks to those guests at the wedding who came to the house. Around four in the afternoon we decided to drive to our honeymoon hotel in Oakland. Lauri's Father had booked a room for us. Lauri changed into a lovely black and white tight fitting dress and we left.

We got the hotel overlooking Lake Merritt and checked in. We had dinner and then went to the bar. Lauri was too young to order a drink but I was almost 23 and selected a Whiskey Sour and we shared it.

We went up to our room and I apologized to Lauri because I had to study my notes from the Roman Empire course I was taking because I had an exam the next week. I studied for an hour and then proceeded to enjoy the wonders of a wedding night.

When we returned to San Jose we moved into an apartment on Coleman Avenue near the San Jose airport. I got a job working at Lockheed Missiles and Space Division in Sunnyvale in the payroll department processing vacations. I worked on the swing shift. Lauri worked at Food Machinery Corporation or FMC as a clerk.

Soon after we were settled in our apartment Lauri began to feel sick one morning and then every morning. It was soon discovered that she was pregnant. I had good health benefits working for Lockheed and I found a highly respected doctor to care for Lauri during her pregnancy. She took her prenatal vitamins and we decided that we needed more room. We found a duplex on Yosemite Street and moved in. We had no furniture so I began scanning the newspaper for used table and chairs, beds, sofas and stuffed chairs. We moved in and Lauri made it look like a home. She was a good housekeeper and things were always neatly in place.

The Berlin Wall was built in 1961 and America still had the draft. I was now nearing the end of my college but wanted to finish.

"There's a letter from your draft board," Lauri said.

I opened the letter and it instructed me report to a downtown location to be bussed up to Oakland for a physical. At the appointed time I joined a busload of other men who were also called for their physicals. When we arrived at the location we went inside and were told to take off all of our clothing. Doctors listened to our hearts, took our blood pressure, checked for hernias and took blood for analysis.

We were then lined up along a wall for our hearing test. When we reached the end of the hall we were told to turn to our left and listen. A doctor in a white medical coat sat in a darkened space and whispered a number. We were told to repeat the number. When my turn came my bad right ear couldn't detect the number that was whispered to me.

"I'm sorry, I didn't hear you," I stammered.

The doctor pounded on the wall and shouted, "QUIET DOWN OUT THERE." Then in a loud voice he said, "**THIRTY SEVEN**."

I repeated the number and he said, "**NEXT**."

I thought to myself, that was some hearing test, precise in every way.

Next came the vision test. We were instructed to look through something that looked like a microscope that was tilted up so we could have our heads up looking forward.

"There's diamond shaped figure in the lens. Tell me where the checked box is. It will be at first, second, third base, or at home plate. You identify its location."

An Asian man who wore glasses was told to take them off and look through the lens.

"I won't be able to see anything if I do."

"Take off your glasses and look anyway. If you can't see the checked box, guess," a strident voice commanded.

The man peered into the lens and guessed.

"Second base?" His voice lilted up.

"**NEXT**." The medical examiner shouted.

Incredulously, the Asian man had passed the vision test because he had guessed correctly where the checked box was. I didn't want to be in a fox hole with him if the bullets began to fly.

Another doctor examined our feet. When it was my turn he noticed that the second toes on my feet had a raised knuckle.

"That hammer head toe ever bother you," he asked.

I spoke honestly, "No, I haven't had any problems with it."

"Curious," he said. "I just gave a guy a IV F for toes like that."

Days after I returned home, I got a letter saying I was IA and could expect to be drafted unless I volunteered for one of the branches of military service.

I went down to my draft board and told the official that I was a student in college and that my wife was in pregnant and wanted some kind of deferment.

"You're a student?" He asked. "That gets you a IIA deferment which means you can finish school. Your wife being pregnant doesn't make any difference."

"What about after my child is born, doesn't that give me another category of deferment?" I asked.

"Your child has to be 15 days old before you qualify for another kind of deferment."

After that meeting I knew I could complete my Bachelor's Degree and hopefully all of graduate school. However, I told myself that when my child was 15 days old I would take a birth certificate to the draft board and have it on file.

"I think it's time to call the doctor," Lauri declared. It was 3:30 A.M. I had gotten off work at Lockheed at 12:30 A.M. Lauri had called me earlier and said she was at her parent's house because she was beginning to feel labor pains. I drove to meet her and be ready to take her to the hospital if the pains became more frequent.

I called the doctor and he asked how often she was having contractions. I told him they were coming every 10 minutes.

"Take her to San Jose General Hospital and I'll come down," he ordered.

Everyone was awake as I assisted Lauri to the car and drove carefully on late-night empty streets. We arrived at the hospital and checked her in. A nurse came in and began to confirm the elapsed time of Lauri's contractions. The doctor arrived and along with the hospital staff, determined how much dilation Lauri had undergone.

"It's going to be awhile before the baby is born," the doctor declared.

"Why don't you go home and get some rest," a nurse said to me.

I wanted to be with Lauri through the whole experience. I was tired but said I would like to stay. Three hours went by and it was almost 7 A.M. I was getting tired. Yesterday morning I had attended classes, gone to work at 4 P.M. and it was now another morning.

"Go home. We'll call you when you need to come back," a morning shift nurse told me.

I went home and tried to fall asleep but only got snatches of sleep. At 2 P.M. I went back to the hospital. A nurse was with Lauri when I went in to see her and the nurse told me to support the small of Lauri's back when she felt her contractions. Lauri was looking tired. At 3 P.M. the doctor came in and said," take her into delivery."

I went to the waiting room and Lauri's mother was there. She had taken off work to be with us when our baby was born. I had always heard that some expectant fathers sometimes had some form of an emotional breakdown when their wives delivered. I didn't have a breakdown but I couldn't think of anything but Lauri and the baby. We didn't know whether the baby was a boy or a girl. I thought of all of the things that could go wrong. I stared at a newspaper not reading. I couldn't look at Lauri's mother.

"Mr. Evans, you can come in now and see your wife and your new baby girl," a nurse cheerily said.

When I saw my baby girl, she still had flecks of blood on her face. She was wrapped in a blanket and the nurse held her.

"Does she have any anomalies?" I asked.

"She has all of her fingers and toes," was the breezy answer.

I went to Lauri and hugged her and kissed her. She was worn out from trying to push hard to facilitate the birthing.

I went back to the waiting room after Lauri was taken to a hospital room and the baby was put at her side.

"We have a baby girl," I stammered and my teeth began to chatter. My breathing was labored. Some of my muscles contracted in my arms and legs. I was having an emotional reaction and Lauri's mom saw it. I tried to control myself but I couldn't. An hour went by and then I was allowed to see Lauri and the baby resting in bed together. We had decided to name her Katherine Ann Evans. I thought of Catherine the Great of Russia when we were thinking of names if we had a girl and Lauri agreed to the choice. We chose a "K" for Kathy instead of "C" in Catherine the Great because the "K" seemed more American than Russian.

When the baby was taken to the infirmary and Lauri fell asleep I left the hospital and bought cigars and candy. I went to Lauri's parent's house and gave her father a cigar and her mother and sister boxes of candy.

Fifteen days later I was at my draft board office and presented Kathy's birth certificate. I was told that I would be given a deferment and a forthcoming letter would confirm it. It was a relief because now I could finish my Bachelor's Degree and enter graduate school to do another year to earn a teaching credential. That Spring I finished my course work and earned my degree. I didn't attend graduation because money was tight and renting a cap and gown I thought, was unnecessary.

I applied to graduate school and was accepted. I began taking the required courses and prepared for the second semester when I would be doing student teaching. I decided that I could student teach and keep my job at Lockheed Missiles and Space Division. The course work wasn't that difficult but student teaching was a challenge. I worked under good master teachers but the college supervisors demanded additional research that had no relationship to instruction. I finished all my requirements by the middle of the school year and began to substitute teach. Additionally, I began to look at the local school districts to apply for a teaching position. I still worked at Lockheed as well.

"Good afternoon," the professor greeted us pleasantly.

One of the courses I enrolled in graduate school was history class that fulfilled one of my requirements.

"When I see you next week I want you to have compiled a bibliography of 100 books in the twentieth century and hand it in," the professor instructed.

Many of the 14 students enrolled in the class gulped at the task that lay ahead. I hit the book stacks as soon as I could and wrote down the key information to compile my

199

bibliography. I used onion skin typing paper because it was easier to erase errors when I made them. When we met the next week we all turned in our bibliographies. The professor glanced at them to make sure everyone had completed the assignment. He then handed the bibliographies back and looked at us.

"Now select 25 of the books you are going to read this semester from your bibliographies. Also, when I see you next week, have a written book report of five to seven pages and be prepared to give an oral report to the rest of the class as well. You will do this every week till the end of the semester."

Over the period of the class I had to read 100 pages a day every day for that one three-unit class. I had to write a book report and organize my thoughts to give an oral presentation.

It was a good class however because the other graduate students were serious with many working for an advanced degree. Their presentations made it possible for me to learn about the great books of the twentieth century. I became a scholarly student in that class. I had been before but this was beyond anything I had done before.

I did make one mistake. One of the books I selected was Alan Nevins, The History of the Ford Motor Company, and it had 900 pages. Each of the two volumes had 900 pages. I read the first volume and hoped that the professor would accept the fact that reading one of the volumes qualified as a reasonable effort for my required book reports. He did.

I was taking another graduate history course as well. My health began to suffer. I began to pass blood in my stools. My weight began to drop. I weighed 126 pounds. As the days passed I began to pass more blood. I finally realized that I had a serious problem when I was taking notes one day and my concentration began to fail and my notetaking wasn't keeping up with what being given in the lecture.

"I'm going to introduce you the silver cigar," the proctologist said.

He inserted it in to my rectum and probed to diagnose my problem.

"Tell me what's going on with you," he stated.

I told him of the demands the courses required and that I was working nights.

"No wonder you've got a bleeding ulcer in your colon. I'm going to put you in the hospital so we can get control of this and then get you medicated so you can function."

I entered the hospital and was given a heavy dose of steroids. Lauri got me settled in and then left to go home. I began to respond and told Lauri I was doing better the next evening when she arrived to visit me. She looked shaken and was holding back. I thought it odd that she was withdrawn but thought perhaps our baby was taxing her energy.

Our neighbors in the duplex we lived in consisted of a husband and wife. He worked in some kind of detective work and his wife stayed home. Some of the things he described in his work seemed mean spirited and slimy. His boss overheard me say something negative to my neighbor and confronted me. I stood my ground with the point I was making and he took offense. Things remained a little tilted between us and our neighbors. All of this took place before I entered the hospital.

I let things stand and began to apply for teaching positions in the San Jose area. There was a glut of candidates for the jobs and competition was stiff in Social Studies, History, and Geography.

I interviewed with the administrative staff from the East Side School District.

"The superintendent liked your interview and you seem well qualified for a history position here at our high school. It's yours if you want it. You'll be teaching five classes of United States history and coaching track," the principal said as he offered me a job.

"I don't know anything about track and have no coaching experience," I stammered. "I went to college to be a teacher and took demanding graduate courses and consider myself more of a scholarly person, not a coach. I didn't go to college to be a coach. I have not prepared for any kind of coaching and would not do justice to the athletes who come out for track."

I was hoping he would relent and assign me to classroom teaching.

"The teaching job is connected to the track assignment." He wasn't offering anything but teaching and coaching together.

"Thank you for offering me an assignment but I want to be a teacher and not coach," I said firmly and left the interview without a job.

I went to San Jose State's job placement service and saw an opening in Merced in the San Joaquin Valley. It was a team-teaching assignment and I had training in team-teaching in my graduate classes. I thought I would apply for the job while I had other applications out in Santa Clara, Saratoga, and Los Gatos.

Our phone rang and when I answered the Superintendent of the Merced Union High School District was on the other end of the call.

"I want to interview you for the team-teaching position we have listed," he said in a kind and almost pleading way.

I didn't want to travel to Merced for the interview so I said I was unable to travel during the week.

"I'll come to your house," Mr. Hopkins said who was the Superintendent.

I thought that was unheard of but said I would be happy to host him for the interview. A time was set up and he arrived at the exact moment he said he would be coming. He was tall and trim, well-spoken, kindly, and genuinely interested in me as a teacher and not a coach.

I had put on a dress shirt and tie and Lauri was wonderful in offering refreshments while the interview took place.

After a half hour he said, "I'm prepared to offer you a contract right now."

"May I notify you in a few days from now?"

I didn't know if that would be a deal breaker or not. I wanted to see if I had a better offer in the San Jose area before I took the job in Merced.

Mr. Hopkins intuitively knew what I was thinking and understood that I may have other offers.

"Of course you can take some time to think about my offer. Call me collect at my office when you've made up your mind."

When Mr. Hopkins left Lauri and I both thought he was a great leader and the job would be perfect for me. However, it was 110 miles from San Jose and away from our friends and family which was a barrier to Lauri.

I had not applied for teaching positions in Sunnyvale, Mountain View, Gilroy, and Santa Cruz or other surrounding communities. I had limited my search to the San Jose area which was my mistake if I wanted to stay in the Bay Area. I had turned down a position and none of the other of my applications resulted in job offers. Lauri and I agreed that I should take the position in Merced for a year or two and gain some experience and then try to come back to the Bay Area.

"Mr. Hopkins, this if Bob Evans calling to accept the teaching position at Merced High School," I said into the phone.

"I'm delighted you have accepted my offer. I was impressed with your background when I reviewed your file and was equally impressed with you when I met you at your home in San Jose. I'll send you a contract in the mail today. Your salary will be $5500.00 a year and I hope to offer a little more when our budget is finalized."

I went to a car lot and bought a 1957 Buick to pull a U-Haul trailer with all of our belongings. I was still working at Lockheed Missiles and Space Division at night and wanted to work as long as possible so I would have a little extra money before I moved.

"Hello," I spoke into our phone at home one afternoon.
"Is this Bob?"
"Yes."
"This is Burt the employer of your neighbor who lives in the duplex next to you. I have a recording I want you to hear. I think you'll find it informative."
I was bewildered by his offer and said I would try to schedule a time to listen to the recording.
"Who was that?" Lauri asked.
"It was our neighbor's boss. He says he has a recording that I should listen to. I don't know what it's about but I think I'll try to follow up on it. That's the guy I had an argument with some time ago, so I'm curious as to what he has."
Lauri looked shocked.
"If you listen to his recording you might as well take Kathy with you when you move to Merced."
She didn't say when **WE** move to Merced.
"What do you mean Lauri? What's going on?"
"I have had an affair with our neighbor. Remember when you were in the hospital? That night the neighbor and his wife came over and brought some wine. We started to play strip poker. It got late and we all went to bed in our bedroom. His wife went to sleep and he had sex with me. Since, he's been calling and we have spoken in very specific sexual terms. So you might as well take Kathy and move to Merced."
My heart sank and my stomach gripped me so hard I almost doubled over. I couldn't believe what I was hearing. Lauri's words explained why she was so standoffish the first night I was in the hospital when she visited me. My head was reeling. I had just finished all of my requirements to

start a new profession and a new life and now everything was collapsing around me.

I was stunned. I didn't know what to do or say. I was so hurt. Why had she had sex the first night I was in the hospital? Why did she continue to have phone sex? What did she want to do now? Did she want a divorce? Did I? Had I failed her somehow? Was she morally deficient? Did I want her to come to Merced with me after all of this? I was emotionally paralyzed at the moment and didn't know what to do.

I walked outside of our duplex and gasped for air. I looked at the other unit. It was around 5:30 in the afternoon. I went to the door and pounded on it. The door opened and it was answered by Hank, Lauri's lover. I grabbed him by the collar and pulled him out of the doorway and threw him the ground and stood over him.

"If you get up, I'm going to take your head off." I screamed.

He stayed down and looked up at me, his eyes wide open. I could see he was guilty and scared.

"If you ever come close to my wife again you're going to get the beating of your life. Do you understand me?"

He nodded.

I hated him and wanted to kick the shit out of him right then. However, I had enough presence of mind to realize that if I did and he called the cops I could be arrested and that could end any hope of a teaching career; something I had sacrificed for and worked hard for over the last five years.

"Get out of my sight," I yelled "and don't let me see you prowling around my place again."

He crawled past me, got to his feet and sheepishly went inside the door. I went back inside to confront Lauri. By now my shock had turned to anger.

"Why did you do this to me? And where was Kathy when all of this happened?

"Kathy was asleep in her bedroom. I don't know why it happened, it just did."

"IT JUST DID." I yelled. 'THAT'S YOUR EXPLANATION FOR PUTTING OUR MARRIAGE AT STAKE. AND YOU DID IT WITH KATHY IN THE NEXT BEDROOM?"

Lauri began to cry. I stood and watched her. She wasn't saying she was sorry or that she wanted to make things right with me. She was just crying. My emotions pulled back and I wondered what was happening. I took stock of the situation. I didn't want my world that I had come to know and love to end. I turned introspective. Had I done something to bring this on? I knew I had been away working nights, going to school days, doing heavy reading and studying, trying to make a life for all of us. In order to do that I had to sacrifice time, effort, energy, and some family time. My commitment to my goal I thought was shared by Lauri. Perhaps it was not. Whatever made Lauri do what she did would be mystery for the moment.

The immediate hurt overpowered both of us. We became emotionally spent. The future seemed far away. Merced and the teaching job may as well have been on Mars. I slept on the couch that night. I was in and out of deep sleep and periods of wide awake despair.

The next week required some resolution to the situation. What were we going to do? I had to face reality. I had made a commitment to go to Merced and begin a teaching career. I didn't want to be a single parent to Kathy. I wanted the wife I married. I didn't want the wife she had become. How was this going to be resolved?

After a week of torment I came to Lauri and said, "You are never going to see or talk to Hank again. If you want to be my wife and mother to Kathy, you've got to take a vow to get back into this marriage and make it work. I'm going to take the job in Merced and if you decide to come with me, you can take solace in knowing we'll be starting a new life in a new town where no one will know us and our

206

past. I will look the other way about what happened with Hank. I don't want you to answer now but I want you to think long and hard about your decision before you give it and then stick to what you've decided."

"I'll answer now. I want to continue the marriage. I'm not happy that we have to go to Merced but under the circumstances, it is best we leave." She said with tears in her eyes.

The next weekend we drove over to Merced and began to look for an apartment. We were surprised that the rents were as high as in San Jose. We found another duplex where the owner lived in the other side. The next weekend we loaded up a U-Haul trailer and moved to Merced. I wanted to work an additional week at Lockheed to earn another paycheck. Lauri and Kathy stayed in Merced that week. I slept on the couch of a friend and finished the week at work. I left at 2 A.M. and drove the two hours to Merced almost falling asleep on the way. I arrived at 4 and Lauri got up to greet me.

She had stayed in Merced without a car. She didn't know how to drive at that time but could walk two blocks to a good market. She seemed to be glad for the moment, to leave San Jose.

"We want to welcome 23 new teachers," the Principal of Merced High School said.

I was one of those teachers. I was introduced to my team-teaching partner.

"This is Mr. Lewis. He'll guide you through the curriculum and show you where the book room is." The Principal said.

"Hello, just call me Joe," and the tall, 6'4" man in a deep voice put out his hand to shake.

"Your name is Joe Lewis?" I asked.

He smiled a gracious smile allowing me to enjoy the joke everyone teased him about since his name was the same as the one time great heavyweight boxing champion.

Being welcomed in Merced was a monumental change from the employment life I had at Lockheed. It was also a dramatically different tone coming from the Bay Area schools where there were thousands of teachers and you were just one of the multitudes with no individuality. In Merced everyone was glad you came. The Superintendent, the Principal, fellow teachers, the community, and the students all were grateful that you were part of the school community.

School began and we shared lecturing to 80 students for four periods and I had a single class where I was the only teacher. There was no air conditioning and Merced is hot in the fall, sometimes over 100 degrees. Moreover, Castle Air Force Base was just seven miles away and B-52's and KC 135's were constantly in the air and the noise from their jet engines made talking above the loudness, difficult.

I learned that in order to be effective as a teacher you had to be prepared with good lessons that had interesting information, and present it in an entertaining way. I found I was good at it and the students responded enthusiastically. Our program was demanding because most of them were college prep classes so there was lots of homework and tough tests. There were oral reports, book reports, and something I put into the regimen, a term paper. The Principal complimented me for adding the additional requirement.

When I got my first paycheck that came at the end of the first month I was shocked. It was less that I was making at Lockheed as a payroll clerk and I had five years of college. I wondered if I had done the right thing.

Within a short time Lauri found a lady friend two doors away from our duplex. Apparently they talked a lot about sex and the various ways sexual gratification could be attained. I knew this because Lauri would ask me questions about the subject and focus on the subject inordinately.

A few months later the owner of the duplex sold it and told us we had to move unless we were prepared to pay 20% more in rent. We weren't so we moved to another duplex next to the railroad tracks.

. Merced College was founded in 1962 and began offering classes in 1963, my first year of teaching. During my second year of teaching Joe Lewis was told to call a dean at Merced College. He was teaching part time in the evening program. He made the call from the faculty lounge.

"Yes, I know someone who might be interested in teaching. He's an outstanding instructor and he's sitting right here. I'll ask him," Joe said into the phone.

Joe turned and looked at me. "Would you be interested in teaching part time at the college?"

"Yes, I would," I said.

Joe spoke into the phone, "yes, he's interested. I'll tell him you'd like to talk to him."

Joe hung up the phone and told me who to contact and where to apply for a college teaching position.

I made an appointment with the Dean of Instruction, filled out an application, and began an interview.

"Do you have any doubt about being able to teach at the college level?"

I knew why he asked that question. I only weighed 140 pounds, had my hair cut short, and almost looked like a high school student. This was a critical question I was being asked.

Gathering up as much confidence as I could I said, "No, I'm sure I can handle the assignment."

I was hired, given a curriculum guide and told I would be teaching United States History 17B in the spring semester. That was two weeks away. I began going through my college text books, pulled books from the college library, and began to put together my first lecture. The class would meet for three hours once a week so I needed a lot of information to present to the students.

I met the class which consisted of young students just out of high school, working adults, housewives, retired people, and Air Force personnel both officers and enlisted men and women. The ability range of the students was varied from those who barely got out of high school to others having a college education and who were taking the class to fulfill a requirement by the state of California.

The first lecture went well but I was only one week ahead of the students. I had to research, organize, and write a new lecture every week in addition to teaching my regular high school classes. It was a challenge so I was doing a lot of reading and writing in the afternoons, evenings, and weekends.

Meanwhile, Lauri was introduced to a man who was selling a lower middle class home and convinced us that we should buy it. He would require only a small amount for a down payment and he pay for the closing costs. He said he would paint the three bedrooms for us and he did. We moved in at the Lilac street location that had a large back yard for Kathy to play in.

I finished the school year and sold the old Buick and bought a new 1964 Volkswagen. It was my first new car. It got good gas mileage and we could afford the payments, barely.

Lauri began to work for the man who sold us the house. He had various incomes from rentals, selling carpet, and a budding log splitting business, etc. Lauri was doing clerical work and it became clear that things were moving toward more than an employee-employer relationship. I was taking classes as Fresno State that could be applied to the salary scale which would move to a higher income bracket.

Things between Lauri and me began to deteriorate. She began to disrespect me and her interests were being channeled toward her employer. I confronted her about her behavior. She called her parents and they came and took her and Kathy away. We were now separated.

"Bob, I've applied and received a teaching position at Merced College and I'm going to take it. It's been a good two years with you but I feel I have to pursue this opportunity," Joe Lewis declared.

210

Joe had graduated from Stanford University and had been accepted to law school but chose instead a career in education. He was very intelligent and read widely. He was married to an elementary school teacher and had started a family. He was now in his late 30's and wanted a new challenge. I completely understood his reasoning and motivation. However, there were unanswered questions affecting me. Would Merced High School continue to support team-teaching and who would be brought in to teach with me?

The answers came from the Principal who wanted teach-teaching to go forward and the person the district hired was Harlan Dake. He was from San Francisco and graduated from San Francisco State College. He was Jewish, intelligent, read widely, and unmarried. I was to meet with him and go over what our program had been and could become. When we began teaching together he made many contributions to our class. He was very organized and suggested new information to extend our history class to what was happening in the world.

That new way became the World Game. We assigned committees of three students to research an assigned country in the library. Since we had 75 students in our team-teaching classes that meant 25 countries would be studied. Then we would give a hypothetical problem and have the students try to solve it.

One problem we assigned was an American space capsule had its retrorockets misfire and the astronauts landed in Communist China instead of an area where the United States could retrieve the space travelers. The Chinese accused the astronauts of being spies. Your task student diplomats, was to get the astronauts back.

We took the students to the library to do their research. Word got out about our project and the Superintendent Mr. Hopkins, wanted to see firsthand whether the students were really working at research or just going through the motions. He came to the library and watched the students.

211

"I know the students are a little noisy but they are doing research and negotiating with one another to solve the problems we assigned them." I was a little concerned that Mr. Hopkins might take offense at increased noise in a library.

"They seem to be engaged and are actually working on their project," was Mr. Hopkins' reassuring reply. He had seen what we had seen, that the students were actively working engrossed in their work.

"This is an outstanding assignment you have created. Keep up the good work," Mr. Hopkins said as he left after an hour of observation.

I credit Harlan Dake for his contribution to the program and together we implemented it. After the research had been done, we would move the chairs in the classroom into a circle. The students bonded to the activity and began to costume out in the style of the country they represented. They created posters detailing the positions of their government. Once in place, we would have a little United Nations and have the students state their positions and try to solve the problems we gave them. Often debates got heated trying to win over other nations to one side or another. However, the emotions never were personal. Often things ended in a declaration of war. This was somewhat ironic since the late 1960's was the time of the peace generation.

Lauri had decided to come back and return to our marriage. She had learned to drive now and was more independent. I had sold the house and rented a house to live in. Lauri had made some men friends when she lived with her parents by going to some local bars but reassured me that she wanted to make another attempt to get back together.

"I have to chaperone the football game Friday night and the early game starts at 6 P.M. Why don't you come by the 18th Street parking lot right after school and we can get something to eat and then all go to the game. You can sit in the stands with Kathy and I'll do my chaperone duty." I suggested.

212

Lauri agreed. I was looking forward to being able to have them at the game because I could walk by and visit with them from time to time while doing my duty. The weather was warm and the evenings most pleasant.

When I locked up my classroom and walked to the parking lot I saw our Volkswagen in the parking lot. There was a white paper under the windshield wipers. As I approached I didn't see Lauri or Kathy. Perhaps they left me a note saying they would be back shortly so we could then proceed to a restaurant.

When I read the note on the windshield I was stunned. Lauri had set me up. She had one of the men she had met on the coast come over and take her and Kathy back to Aptos and was leaving me again. She had completely fooled me. I had no idea this was coming. I had been blindsided.

I still had to perform my chaperone duty and I didn't want to tell anyone what had happened to me. I put on a happy face and went to the game. That night was one of the loneliest of my life. Not only had Lauri left the marriage again but had betrayed me in the process. My daughter Kathy was taken from me. All I had was myself and my job.

The next week I asked Harland Dake who was living in an apartment, if he would be willing to move into the house I rented. I needed financial help and having a roommate would stretch my dollars further. I knew I would need to pay for a lawyer, make child support payments, and alimony. Harlan agreed he would move in at the end of the month. It would be cheaper for him too. He was from San Francisco and wanted to spend a lot weekends in the city and having a little extra cash would pay for gas and trolling for urbane women to date.

The months that followed produced a see-saw relationship with Lauri. She wanted to get back together and I didn't and then I wanted her back in the marriage and she didn't. We visited one another over the span of the next several months. Along the way, Lauri became pregnant. I might have suspected that the pregnancy could have been caused by other men and not me. But I didn't. The timing was right when we were trying to get back together so that her pregnancy was caused by me.

"I might have to leave my class early. Can you cover for me?" I was asking a colleague for help in case I had to leave. I was teaching a night class for Merced College
"Sure, what's going on?"
"My estranged wife is delivering a baby and I might have to go to Santa Cruz."
It was Thursday evening in late April, 1966 and I was teaching a night class in United States History. I called at break time to see how things were progressing and talked to Lauri's mother. She reassured me that things were progressing well and this birth was going to be an easy delivery. I told her that if I was needed, I would drop everything and drive to Santa Cruz that night.
"Hold the phone," Lauri's mother said. "A nurse wants to talk to me."
I could hear a conversation taking place but couldn't make out what was being said.
Lauri's mom came back on the phone, "She just gave birth to a baby boy."
"If there's any complications please let me know and I'll come over right way." I said and she stated she would.
I got Lauri's room number in the hospital and its phone number.

When I called Lauri's hospital room the next day I heard her say, "I named him Jon spelled JON and Robert after you," Lauri said into the phone.
I'll be over this weekend to visit you. Do you need anything?"
"Just be here," Lauri insisted.

"Will you come over and stay with me for the weekend. I've rented a bungalow for Saturday and Sunday and the kids will be there with us," Lauri was pleading for another try at marriage. Jon was now six months old.

"Yes, I'll come over this weekend to be with you," I said with some trepidation. I had been burned by Lauri before and was somewhat skeptical about her motives in this latest go around.

I arrived around noon and Lauri had a nice lunch prepared and told me she planned to make dinner that night.

"I want us to be a family again," Lauri began.

She seemed sincere.

"I plan to get a job after Jon is old enough and help with our family finances."

"How are you getting by now?" I asked.

"My family is helping me and the money you send is invaluable to just making it."

Our conversation went on back and forth the rest of the day. It became exhausting. Lauri made a steak dinner. I wondered how much was provided by her parents. When Kathy and Jon were put to bed an awkward moment was upon us. Where would she and I sleep? There was a second floor with a bedroom and a couch on the ground floor level.

"You can sleep with me," Lauri said.

She knew that I was always attracted to her because of her natural beauty and her offer would be hard to resist. I paused thinking that if I slept with her it would almost be as binding as a contract, to continue the marriage.

"I'm a little uncomfortable about sleeping with you tonight. What will that mean if I decide not to get back with you? What will you expect of me if I do?"

"You can do whatever you want about the marriage. I want to be close with you tonight," she said convincingly.

We slept together that night and made love. I felt guilty because I wasn't in the space of totally committing to the marriage. I felt as if I was taking advantage of Lauri. The next morning we got the kids breakfast and I helped pack things up. Nothing was said about how things would work out between us. I drove Lauri and kids back to her parent's house and sheepishly entered their home. Everyone was expecting me to say one way or another, what I intended to do. I wasn't sure myself and that made things very uncomfortable.

I returned to Merced and mulled things over for the next few days. I came to the conclusion that Lauri was in a desperate situation. She was living with her parents, had no job, was recovering from the birth of Jon, and didn't have an alternative other than to get back in the marriage with me. Her desperation kept jumping into my mind. Of course I was sympathetic to her situation and there were children to consider. However, I didn't feel that if she was independent that she would want to resume the marriage. Desperation wasn't a good reason to get back together. I had been burned by her at least three times by affairs and betrayals so there was a trust issue that was locked into the back of my mind.

"Lauri, I'm sorry but I don't think my mind is in the same place as yours. I don't want to bring up the past but it is an issue for me. I want to do what's right for both of us and I don't think I can resume our marriage with confidence."

She began to cry into the phone. I felt helpless and guilty for not helping her when she was down. Her crying went on for several minutes and I couldn't hang up with her in that condition. I waited for an opportune moment when she had recovered her emotions and we said goodbye by saying we loved each other.

"She needs a car and has no money to buy one. It would be wise for you to get her a car," Lauri's lawyer said to me over the phone.

"I'll consent to buying a car for her," I concurred. "She'll need one to get to work and care for the kids."

Her father, who was very knowledgeable about mechanical issues, found a 1957 Ford for $600.00 and I sent a check to pay for it. Lauri had found a job in a chiropractor's office, rented a small duplex, and moved out of her parent's house.

Once legal issues were settled, I had to pay child support and alimony but could have visitation rights. Lauri was good about letting me take Kathy for visits but Jon was too young to join us.

Over time, Lauri met a man who would become her new husband. He had a house in Watsonville and Lauri and the kids moved in. When our divorce was final, they married. This was a turning point for Lauri and the kids but also for me. I was the one who wanted to get back together and now, that was out of the question.

As devastated as I was, I had to find a way to provide child care, alimony, and build a life for myself. I buried myself in work, continued to teach in Merced College's evening program, and develop my skills as a full time teacher.

EUROPE

Since college I desperately wanted to go to Europe. After taking so many college courses involving the history of Europe, I set a goal to travel to Europe and visit historical sites, see the great museums, and sample the culture. That would require additional money and time to do it. I met an Art instructor at Merced High School who moved to a teaching position at Merced College. He indicated that he too wanted to go to Europe for the same reasons that I did.

I had traveled a lot growing up. I was born in San Francisco but moved to Idaho when my parents divorced, moved to Arizona for my asthma, traveled to Wisconsin, Alaska, Utah, and back to California. All of these moves were done for practical reasons not for cultural enjoyment. If we gained anything cultural it was by accident. My European trip would be done for cultural growth and fulfilling my dream of seeing Europe's enriching sites. My excitement began to build as I planned for the adventure of my life up to that point. It was a vacation that I had prepared for both in terms of paying for it and seeing the sights I had read about and studied for years beginning in junior high school, high school and college. I had scrimped to save money, taught at Merced College, and cut back on my expenses to pay alimony, child support, have money for the trip. I was animated in anticipation of visiting historical places, museums, battle fields, ancient relics and burial sites. I was expecting a cultural orgasism.

I researched a charter air travel service and found a flight leaving Los Angeles on July 4th, 1967. The Art instructor said he wanted to go with me. The fare was $418.00 for a round trip ticket. Our return flight would leave Amsterdam on September 4th so we would spend two months touring Europe. I sold my 1964 Volkswagen to another teacher and bought a new 1967 Volkswagen to be picked up in Dusseldorf, Germany. The cost of the new car was $1516.00, less than a new car would cost in American because I didn't have to pay shipping. I planned to drive the car as we traveled around Europe and then have it shipped back to America before we left.

I bought an old 1956 Dodge sedan in May to get around in and take us to Los Angeles where we would leave for Europe. I paid $125.00 for the less than perfect Dodge. The firewall was leaky and the motor burned oil so that smells from combustion permeated the inside of the car. I nicknamed the Dodge, "Gas Chamber."

On July 3rd we traveled to Los Angeles, killed time until the flight left in early morning on July 4th. I parked Gas Chamber in a lot and didn't care if someone stole it.

The plane was scheduled to fly nonstop to Amsterdam but fuel ran low and we had to stop in Scotland for a short time to take on additional fuel. We arrived at midnight and were bussed into a terminal in Amsterdam away from the airport. It was an inauspicious beginning. We were told our baggage would be brought to us on another bus. My traveler's checks were in my suitcase. When the baggage arrived, my suitcase was not there. I should have panicked but remained composed. I asked around if anyone of authority spoke English and one did. He said that another bus would arrive and perhaps my suitcase would be on it. A second bus came and yes, my suitcase was on it. I had not locked the suitcase so someone could have opened it and taken it contents and I would have lost my traveler checks. Being an inexperienced traveler, I got lucky. Everything was there inside the suitcase to my relief. With that mini-crisis gone, we checked into a hotel about 1 A.M. The next morning we could walk to the train station and buy tickets to Dusseldorf so that I could pick up the car I had ordered from the United States.

Once we had train tickets for the next day, Dick (my travel companion) and I began to take in the wonders of Europe. We visited Anna Franc's hideout residence and saw she was like other teenagers; having a picture of then Princess Elizabeth on her wall. With so much to offer the world, before she could ever really date, attend a university, marry, have her own family, and continue to contribute to literature, the dreaded Nazis discovered the Franc family's hiding place and sent the family along with other Jewish people from the Netherlands to concentration camps and death. Anna Franc's fate was the fate of six million other Jews and six million other people. Indeed over 60 million died in World War II, such a waste. Perhaps it pleased Malthusian devotees who viewed war as one way to control population but the loss of so much life was a horrible desecration of humanity. How many doctors, mathematicians, philosophers, scientists, and worthy people were among those lost, and for what purpose? To satisfy the false belief that Jews were the scourge of European problems and political dissent had no place in Nazi Germany? What a horrible time in human history.

After Amsterdam we took a train to pick up my new Volkswagen in Dusseldorf. Once on the road we drove to Heidelberg.

"I'm sorry," the hotel manager said in British English, "we are full up tonight."

219

I turned to Dick and said, "We've got to find a place to stay."

It was almost 7 P.M.

We roamed around and found a tourist center that remained open in the still sunny German evening. There on the wall was a notice to rent a single room in a home. The family offered their daughter's bedroom for a small sum and we got directions and found the place and were delighted to have a place to sleep.

This pattern of waiting until late in the afternoon or early evening to find a place to stay for the night continued throughout the trip. We had no advanced plans for lodgings so we fumbled our way along seeking refuge from the night air in frustration day after day.

Heidelberg had its charm highlighted by a beautiful university up on a hill with lights that illuminated its most striking features.

From Heidelberg we drove to Mainz and Worms, the place where Martin Luther was condemned for challenging the Catholic Church with his 95 Thesis on Halloween in 1517. From here we moved on the Munich.

"Dick, the gates are opening so let's go in."

The gates I spoke of were to the Dachau Museum, once a Nazi concentration camp. As we walked around the grounds I overheard someone point out the "blood ditch." It was behind the ovens and ran perhaps 150 yards. So many prisoners were shot that the ditch was "necessary" to carry away the volume of blood that flowed from the open wounds of the dead bodies.

Nearby was the gas chamber, a large room with one light bulb and an inverted funnel-looking spout in the ceiling. This was for the gas that was pumped into the room where unsuspecting prisoners thought they were going to have a hot shower before they were to be assigned to a work detail. New information suggests that few if any were gassed to death but what is crystal clear is that 31,000 were killed and many more died from malnutrition. Jews, Czechs, Poles,

Hungarians, homosexuals, communists and gypsies were among the dead.

The barracks built to hold 400 people were overcrowded and in time 1600 people were assigned to these barracks creating unhealthy, cramped quarters. This led to increased disease, dysentery, filthy conditions that contributed to early deaths.

"Medical experiments" were performed by doctors to see how quickly someone could be revived after being exposed in freezing water. Blankets, warm water, and some men were positioned between two naked women as a means to resuscitate those taken from icy water. The Nazis measured revival time to see how long Luftwaffe pilots could survive if they went down in the North Sea.

When I walked out through the main gates, I looked back inside the concentration camp and said to myself. "I marvel at how easy it is for me to walk out of this diabolical place and know that thousands of others in an earlier time would have given anything to be able to do what I was doing so effortlessly now without anyone trying to block my way.

After Germany, Dick and I drove to Austria and Vienna. It was such a charming city that was once the home of the Holy Roman Empire ruled by the Hapsburgs. We saw the building where the Congress of Vienna was held in 1815, where a gathering of European leaders tried to restore the old monarchies after the fall of Napoleon Bonaparte. It was a congress that was doomed to fail because a new era had been ushered in and the old order would never be the same. Reform movements would chip away at the old ways and the final destruction of the former regimes would come crashing down in the onslaught of World War I. That war ended the dynasties of the Hohenzollerns of Germany, the Hapsburgs of the Austro-Hungarian Empire, and the Romanovs of Russia.

On a Sunday we found our way out of Vienna and traveled across the entire width of the country in an afternoon. We stopped at Berchtesgaden in Germany. There

221

is a mountain there and an elevator shaft that takes visitor up to the top where there was Hitler's Eagles Nest, a gift to Hitler by the Nazi Party for his 50th birthday. It was a modest mountain retreat almost in the clouds. He would live only another six years and commit suicide as the Russian army was closing in on Berlin in May of 1945. But in his lifetime he had brought the greatest destructive war in the world's history.

We both now turned our eyes toward Greece. But to get here we had to travel through what was then Yugoslavia (which means southern Slavs). It was a communist country ruled by Marshal Tito then. We were careful to be on our best behavior to get through the country without any complications. We entered reasonably easily and began heading south. Along the way we saw a backward country, almost medieval. People were living in thatched huts and using hand tools in the fields. The roads were bad rarely able to let us drive at a good speed. The standard of living was very poor.

We stayed one night in Belgrade and noticed that there was a concession to western tourism as the word "Motel" appeared to advertise a place to stay. Since the country used the Cyrillic alphabet, it was a clear sign that westerners were welcome.

We passed into northern Greece and immediately noticed a different driving style by motorists. On a two lane road cars would pass other cars or trucks by honking and pulling out into the next lane to get by. If oncoming traffic was coming drivers would move to the shoulder of each lane and let the passing car through.

We approached Athens in the late afternoon. Late day shadows were elongated. As I looked to my left there standing in quiet majesty was the Parthenon atop the Acropolis. I couldn't wait to get to a hotel, park the car and race up to this wonderful relic of ancient Greece. It was the building I saw in a textbook when I was junior high school and promised myself that one day I would visit. My vow was coming true. My excitement was at a high pitch when I approached the gate where a guard stopped me from entering.

"Close at sundown." The guard said in the little English he knew which was much more than I knew of Greek.

My heart sank. My fulfillment would have to wait for another day.

The next morning I was up early and would be among the first to enter the gates on top of the Acropolis. Dick explained to me that the ancient Greeks knew to taper their columns so as to avoid an optical illusion of the building seeming to be leading out.

We spent the day visiting other sites as well, the Agora and the Temple of Dionysus. In the days ahead we went to a museum in Athens and learned of the four periods of Greek art: the Geometric period, Archaic, Classical, and Hellenistic.

A day later we flew to Crete and visited sites from the Mycenaean civilization. We toured Knossos and its temple, some of which was restored while other parts had been excavated and left as researchers found it.

We were now feeling more of the true treasures of Europe. Upon returning to Athens we drove to Marathon, the site of the Greek defeat of the Persians giving a lasting name to long distance races due to Phidippides running from the battle field to bring news to Athenians of victory, or "Nike." We drove to Sparta where in ancient times the tough-minded, militaristic citizens drilled themselves in rigid discipline to be warriors of renowned courage.

On one of our drives we got behind a wedding motorcade that stopped at each village where a priest would bestow a blessing on the newlyweds and then send them on their way to the next stop. We had to wait at each hamlet while the ceremonies took place and only took perhaps 5-10 minutes. Cars and trucks would pile up on each side of the road and even on sidewalks in an attempt to get a jump on traffic once things began to move again. If I passed a car on the way to the next township, the driver would feel an affront and jockey to get an advantageous position for the next round mad driving. This went on for at least seven villages but was fun to be part of.

We were ready to move on to Italy so we made our way through the Grecian countryside on our way to Patras, the port where we would load the car and take the ferry to Brindisi, Italy. We boarded late in the afternoon and it would be an overnight journey across the Straights of Otronto, where Marc Antony and Cleopatra lost to Octavius during Rome's civil war at the battle of Actium.

We explored the ferry and met Sue and Jane, two nurses from Australia who were exploring Italy on their own. We also met Charlie who was from South Africa but had just returned from fighting with the Israelis in the Six Day War, a smashing victory for the Jewish state and a crushing defeat for the surrounding Moslem world.

We bought over-the-counter food at the ferry's snack bar, visited, then settled into our seats to sleep through the crossing. We arrived in the morning, got the car off the ship, and started towards Rome. About ten miles into our drive, we saw Sue, Jane, and Charlie thumbing a ride. We stopped and picked them up and our little Volkswagen bug was packed full. We stopped in Pompeii and toured the excavated city that was buried in the volcanic eruption of Mount Vesuvius in 79 A.D. Excavation began in 1738 and has been ongoing since. We all slept in an orchard that night and continued on to Rome the next day.

In Rome the nurses and Charlie were going to stay in a hostel and Dick and I in a hotel. They encouraged us to join them at the hostel because it was very cheap and included a breakfast and an evening meal. I paid to park the car at a hotel garage and we took public transportation to the hostel.

Dick and I started the next day at the Roman Coliseum and were allowed along with all of the other tourists, to walk around inside and through the labyrinth of rooms at the lower level where wild animals and gladiators waited to entertain the crowd of 50,000 people who would attend the spectacles of ancient Rome. We crossed the street and toured the Roman Forum, the burial site of Julius Caesar, the Roman Senate, the Temple of Vesta attended to by the Vestal Virgins. We crossed the Palatine Hill and viewed the Circus Maximus a site that could accommodate 150,000 spectators. We visited the Baths of Caracalla, and the Baths of Diocletian both in disrepair but enough of the buildings were still standing to impress us with the size and grandeur.

"Susan, would you like to tour with me tomorrow?"

The attractive blond said in an upward lilt, "Yes, that would be nice. We can thumb a ride into the inner city and began our tour without having to walk and use up our energy and we can avoid public transportation."

The next morning we walked to the nearby road and Susan raised her hand and tilted her thumb upward. Cars began almost crash into one another to be the first to offer us a ride. The winning car was driven by an Alitalia airline pilot who not only gave us a ride to our sites but began to be a tour guide by explaining highlights of the things we were seeing. He bought us lunch before leaving us at Vatican City.

We saw the Sistine Chapel where we heard an American lady ask, "Are there any paintings here that were done by Michelangelo?"

Later we climbed the stairs to the dome where tiny mosaic pieces were formed to make dramatic religious figures. On the way down the stairs a woman was accosted by an Italian man trying to impose himself on her. She was holding an ice cream cone and pushed into his face to resist his advances.

We heard another American man ask, "How old was Moses when he posed for Michelangelo?"

Susan and I stared at each other and controlled ourselves until we were far enough away to burst out laughing.

We visited the Vatican Museum and saw paintings of some of the great renaissance masters, Rafael, Michelangelo, Da Vinci, Titian, and Caravaggio. It was a productive day with major sites revealing themselves to us.

Back at the hostel Charlie, the slightly built soldier of fortune, offered to get me a better exchange rate on my traveler's checks.

"I can take them to Istanbul and improve your take substantially."

"I'd like to go to Istanbul and see the great mosques."

"I'd better go alone." Charlie declared.

That sent up a red flag to me. I could have used the gain from a better exchange rate but I wasn't going to trust Charlie to leave with my traveler's checks with me staying behind in Rome.

"Thank you Charlie for your offer but I'll live with whatever exchange rates I get as I travel around Europe."

After several more days of seeing Rome, Dick and I started north toward Italy's northern attractions. Dick began to feel weaker and had little energy. When we got to Ravenna I took him to a hospital and after a short examination the doctor told me to go to a hotel and stay because Dick needed an appendectomy.

"He doesn't need surgery; he has low blood sugar and needs something to boost his energy." I protested.

The doctor did some blood work and indicated that Dick was suffering from drinking bad water.

"Have him drink beer." I was instructed.

We drove to Pisa and I climbed up the leaning tower. The cylindrical building made for interested climbing of it stairs. At times you felt as if you were rising at a steep pitch, then on a flat surface, and finally almost as if you were walking downhill. This was the building where Galileo proved the law of falling bodies, undoing Aristotle's belief that heavier object would fall faster than lighter ones. Galileo proved they fall at the same speed.

We traveled on toward Venice. I parked the car on a bridge leading to the city of canals and said I would go into the main part of Venice and look for a hotel.

"You stay in the car and rest. I bought some beer the last time we got gas, so drink that while I get us lodging."

It was a hot afternoon and I sweated trying to rush into the city and find a place to stay. I tried several hotels before I found one in our price range. I hustled back to get Dick. He was still very weak.

"I found a place that's right on the Grand Canal at a reasonable price. How are you feeling?"

"I still feel tired but I think I can make it to the hotel."

"I'll carry the baggage and we'll go slow and stop if you get too tired. We'll take our time. I'll get you there." I said.

We got to the hotel and Dick fell into his bed to rest and sleep. I walked around the area to find a restaurant where we could have dinner later that evening. When Dick woke up it was near 7 P.M. He felt better and a little stronger. We ate dinner and lingered afterward. We watched on the Grand Canal as three gondolas were lashed together and musicians and singers were aboard serenading a couple who looked like they were on their honeymoon. The evening was warm and romantic. We drank another beer to take in the moment. Dick was away from his wife and I had no relationship at the time so we vicariously shared the night with those who did have relationships.

We toured St. Mark's square in Venice and visited the Doges Palace. We walked along the canals and took a water taxi to an area where we could walk to see Marco Polo's house. Dick was still recovering his health so his touring was limited.

We drove next to Florence and toured the Uffizi Museum where many of the great Renaissance master's paintings were shown. Michelangelo, Titian, Da Vinci, Rafael and others. We were able to stay in a hostel which was easy on our wallets. Dick was still having some health issues but was slowly improving.

The next day we visited the Baptistery where the Doors of Ghiberti were in full display. They are three dimensional and are the work of a great master. During World War II an American captain had molds made from the doors and later bronze was poured into the mold and exact replicas were made. The doors that had been molded by an American captain were sent back to the United States and were hung in San Francisco's Grace Cathedral. More recently they have been taken down to preserve them.

A copy of Michelangelo's "David" is near the Uffizi standing outside for all to see. Nearby is the Pont de Vecchio over the Arno River and a site where vendors sell gold and jewelry by weight.

Dick was very knowledgeable about the museums we were seeing and what was inside. This was the benefit of traveling with an art instructor.

We said goodbye to Italy and drove towards France. We came to an intersection just outside of Vichy where there was a stop sign. I made a "Hollywood "stop by shifting into second gear without coming to a complete stop. I turned left on a two-lane road and in about100 yards there was a Gendarme who was wearing a white and black helmet and black boots that came up to his knee.

"STOP!" he shouted at me and I pulled over behind a Mercedes Benz sedan that had German license plates. I was driving a German car with German license plates as well. I have blue eyes and at the time, reddish-blond hair. He thought I was German and he was going to impose French hatred on what he thought was a German citizen. The French has lost the Franco-Prussian War, suffered horrible losses in World War I, and lost to the Germans in World War II. The French hated the Germans because of their losses in these wars. The policeman's antipathy was dripping when he approached my car.

He opened my door and motioned for me to get out. He took my arm and began walking back to the stop sign at the intersection.

I understood what he was doing and I tried to acknowledge that I had made a mistake. I said, "Oui, Oui, Monsieur."

He turned to me and shouted at me, "**Oui, Oui, Oui.**" His tone raged with sarcasm and loathing.

I said nothing more and when we got to the intersection, he shouted "STOP."

I nodded agreement fearful of saying anything that might further enrage him. We walked back to my car in silence, and then he said in a demanding and loud voice, "Passport."

I pulled out my American passport and when he saw the American Eagle on it, his manner immediately changed. The French were extremely grateful to the Americans who landed on the Normandy beaches and drove the hated Germans out of France and back to Germany.

I had expected a citation but he Gendarme only looked at my passport and handed it back to me. He walked to the Mercedes sedan in front of me and began writing a ticket. When he was finished he walked back to my car and waved for me to drive on. I assumed the driver of the Mercedes was a German citizen and was going to bear the wrath of the French policeman.

We drove on to Tours, the site where Charles Martel in 732 defeated the Moslems in France and stopped any further advance by them into Europe. We drove on to La Havre and I made arrangements to ship the Volkswagen back to San Francisco. However, the agent said the car would not be arriving until October 20th. That meant that "Gas Chamber" my old 1956 Dodge would have to be my transportation until then.

We booked passage on a train to Paris and when we arrived we got a "Metro" map and found to our wonder that this was a transportational blessing. We could go anywhere in Paris and not get lost.

We found a hotel on the West Bank of the Seine River. The greatness of Paris immediately showed itself. It is cosmopolitan with high fashion and beautiful people, it is multi-racial without obvious discrimination, people are reading good books, and the people exhibit the tactile nature of French culture by shaking hands and greeting one another with kisses on both cheeks. If there was any rudeness by the French, it might be from service people such as waiters, ticket takers, and hotel clerks. However, our experience has been met with genuine friendliness. Some of the other people we talked to had complained about French rudeness. That was not our experience.

"Dick I can't believe all of the treasures I'm seeing!" I gleefully said to my traveling partner when we entered the Louvre Museum. The antiquities section was the most thorough I had ever seen and that was only the beginning. The eras of Greek, Roman, medieval, renaissance, and beyond provided so many cultural gems that my mouth was aghast in amazement. There was the Mona Lisa, the Winged Victory of Samothrace, and Venus de Milo.

We spent the entire day in the museum and decided we would go back a second time to try to take in more of what it had to offer. It was culturally enthralling and couldn't ever be mastered but would provide days of enriching joy.

That evening we decided we had to go to the Moulin Rouge to see the Can Can. We took the Metro to an area close to the famous site. Ladies of the night were walking the sidewalks trolling for clients.

"Come this way," the head waiter said to us and walked us down to the front of the room and sat us in a large booth. Immediately, two ladies were at our side and another waiter brought a chilled bottle of champagne in a silver ice bucket and put it on our table.

I looked at Dick with a stunned look on my face. If we didn't act fast we were going to be charged with overpriced champagne and be propositioned by our new "companions."

I turned to the lady seated by my side and said. "Do you speak English?"

She nodded that she did.

"We are just here to see the show and are not seeking companionship or champagne. We would like a glass of wine to enjoy the show and nothing more."

The lady I was speaking to raised her right arm and snapped her fingers. Almost instantaneously, the waiter who brought the champagne was back at our table and whisked away the silver ice bucket and the bottle of champagne. The ladies smiled as they slid out of the booth and waved goodbye as they surveyed the room for other new arrivals to share their companionship with. We enjoyed the show and got back to the west bank near our hotel and treated ourselves to a sausage slathered with hot mustard.

The next day found us walking around the catwalk of the Eiffel Tower.

"Hi, Mr. Evans!"

I looked around to see who was speaking to me because I knew no one in France. It was one of my former students. In some ways I should not been surprised because we had met two of my former students in Florence, Italy at a hostel there.

We chatted about the sites we were seeing in Paris while a sweeping breeze blew past us. Seeing students at various places around the world would be a fairly common experience.

After several days in Paris our plans called for us to cross the English Channel by plane and see what the British had to offer. Our propeller driven plane landed on a dirt air strip outside London. I went inside and bought a meat pie from the snack counter. It was greasy and bad tasting. After enjoying French cuisine the last few days, this was a gastronomic come down.

We bussed 80 minutes into London drove by Big Ben and the Parliament buildings. By now it was August 12th and tourists made for stiff competition when we tried to find a hotel since August is the month many Europeans take their vacations. We were rejected several times but finally found one for about $25.00 which was expensive for us on our limited budget. We planned to be in the United Kingdom for 12 days.

The next day we bussed out to Stonehenge, the ancient site that research has shown that it was an astronomical instrument that lines up with a solstice. We were allowed to walk around the grounds freely and marvel at the large stones that were somehow dragged to this location and raised upright in a circle with lintels on top.

It was August 14th and our plan was to visit the Tate Museum and Parliament. The Tate was a treasure with Turner, Hogarth, Butler, Sargent, and Gilman. Its modern art collection was great with Picassos, Dali, Bellmer, Braque, Diego Rivera, and Paul Klee. Our stay consumed most of the morning.

At Parliament we missed a tour but were informed that we could visit both the House of Commons and the House of Lords. The tradition of the Black Lord was grounded in historical tradition. He knocks has the door of the House of Commons and it is slammed in his face, he knocks three times again on the House of Commons door and states his business (requesting that some members join the Lords and the Queen). Twenty-four Commoners cross to the Lords and stand to hear the Queen's speech. The Commoners return to their house and stay in session for perhaps three hours and can discuss any issue except the Queen's speech.

We next went to Westminster Abbey and its famous grave yard where Winston Churchill, Shelley, Keats, Browning, Darwin, William Pitt, Gladstone, and Disraeli are buried along with many other famous Englishmen.

We traveled to 10 Downing Street where the British Prime Minister's residence and office are. We could easily stand outside without any officials keeping us back. It is fairly unassuming but behind the door, world shaking decisions have been made.

Steeped in ceremony the British turn out for the changing of the Guard at Buckingham Palace. So do tourists and we were among them. It was most traditional and precise in execution.

We visited the National Gallery with it marvelous collection of art by many of the Dutch masters. Next we went to the British Museum that houses letters from historical leaders to famous people. From the hands of Gibbon, Rousseau, Descartes, Frederick the Great, Napoleon, Bernard Shaw, Anne Boleyn, etc. they are kept for posterity. It has historical documents such as the Magna Carta and Shakespeare's signature on a deed. It also has two Greek Bibles the Codex Sinaiticus and the Codex Alexandrinus as well as a Gutenberg Bible.

In the afternoon we saw "Hello Dolly" the musical play about a Jewish matchmaker complete with delightful acting, lively melodies, and colorful costumes.

After the play we visited the Drury Theatre where its famous director David Garrick made performances popular and were well attended.

Our next stop was the Tower of London where the "Beefeaters" greeted us and regaled us with stories behind the famous uniform they wore, red and blue with cutouts on the sides for mounting horses. They were also the king's tasters at one time.

Later in the day we visited the Imperial War Museum that was fascinating due to a collection of unusual weapons. V-1 and V-2 rockets, a miniature submarine, a German Jet fighter, were prominent among the collections.

After London we returned to Amsterdam to await our flight home. It was a time of reflection. This had been a trip of a lifetime with so many cultural attractions that broadened my perspective and added to my education. Dick and I were exhausted but had deeply benefitted from our two months in Europe.

Our return flight landed in Los Angeles late at night. To my surprise old "Gas Chamber," the 1956 Dodge was still in the parking lot. However, it wouldn't start. I waved down a taxi and asked the driver if he could jump start the car with battery cables.

"For five bucks." He said.

"Deal," I gratefully agreed to his fee.

With car started I thought we were on our way back to Merced and a return to our normal lives deeply enriched from our time on the Continent. However, the gas gauge showed we were running on drops. We were lucky to find a gas station that was still open because it was 4 A.M. Once fueled up we headed north and toward home.

Back in the classroom

When I returned from Europe I again felt the loss of my children. However, I was anxious to apply what I had seen in Europe to my classroom presentations. I had taken over 400 slides of the places I'd seen and wanted to implement them into my classroom presentations. Additionally, I planned detailed lessons, read all of the student's work, engaged with my department colleagues to a greater extent because I was now department chairman. I did extra duties for the school as well. I also enrolled in a Master's Degree program and began taking classes at night and weekends through Chapman University. The classes were not difficult but in order to earn my degree, I had to take the Graduate Record Exam and score high enough to stay in the program. I also had to take written exams beyond what the classes required in Education and Social Science. I wrote a Master's Thesis and had to take an oral exam.

Ironically, the oral exam was to be in Los Angeles at 1 P.M. on the day of graduation scheduled for that evening. I drove down with another teacher who also enrolled in the Master's program. We got caught in heavy Los Angeles traffic and I got to the Chapman University campus in Orange, California 15 minutes before 1 P.M. I ran to the room where a professor was waiting and was out of breath.

He asked the first question and my answer was, "I have no idea."

I had been given a reading list of books to prepare for the oral exam. The answer to the first question didn't find its way into my brain. It wasn't a good start. However, I had read all of the books and studied them for hours. As the oral exam continued, I was able to answer every question and in considerable depth. I knew so much in fact, that the professor began to ask me to evaluate the books on the book list. He then began a philosophical discussion about whether humankind was capable to being socialized to the extent that wars would no longer be fought. The oral exam went on until 4 P.M. The professor passed with me with flying colors and offered glowing compliments. I would graduate that night.

"We want to hold up the procession of advanced degree graduates to recognize someone special. The person in front of me was handicapped and I was the next person behind him as we waited to receive our degrees. The recognition was for the man in front of me. After going through the oral exam that afternoon, I was one person away from receiving my degree. However, I would have to wait another ten minutes before I was allowed to cross the stage, shake hands with the chancellor, and finally receive my Master's degree.

Armed with European experiences and now a Masters Degree, I was free of taking additional classes so that I could concentrate on my students more intently. My team teaching partner and I put together a program we called the "World Game." We had a double class consisting of 75-80 students. Now we assigned students to a committee to research, write, cast, costume and act out a 10 minute play in front of the class we called a "Histriodrama."

Again, like our World Game before, most students really got into the spirit of putting on their play. There were so many good ones.

One stood out in my mind. The topic was the Battle of Tours where Charles "The Hammer" Martel defeated the Moslem advance into France and the event became a turning point in stopping a Moslem takeover of a major country in Europe. The students created a character they named "Mohammed Ramadan Ali." They set up a ring where Mohammed Ramadan Ali and Charles the "Hammer" Martel would be boxers and the winner would take control of France. Ali was pummeling Martel and an announcer who sounded like Howard Cosell said, "Ali has control of this fight and frankly, the Christians don't have a prayer."

Somewhere in the fight Charles "the Hammer" Martel lands a haymaker of a punch on Mohammed Ramadan Ali and knocks him out to win the fight and save France from a Moslem conquest.

This was such a clever and inventive presentation of a key event in history that it proved that the students had done a good job of understanding the issues related to this battle and presented it in a creative way that communicated the essence of the result to all who watched.

The "World Game" and "Histrio-dramas" were very successful assignments.

Many of our classes had college-preparatory students so we had to provide a firm scholastic grounding to get them ready for higher learning after high school. We lectured and made students take notes. They had to keep a notebook with lecture notes, film notes, homework, and special projects. They had to write a term paper the second semester so we had to provide instruction in footnotes (when to insert them and how to make an entry) as well as a bibliography. We assigned specific assignments the students had to complete in order to accomplish a successful term paper.

"Who typed your term paper Gene?" I asked of a bright student whose father was a lawyer.

A blank look was the reply.

"Are you sure that your father's secretary didn't type it for you?"

Gene looked at me astonished, "How did you know she did?"

I didn't answer but it was clear that it had been done by a professional who had superior equipment and a high quality of paper. We both smiled at each other and the matter was closed.

Our team teaching classes became very popular with the students and with parents in the community. Often, parents would come to registration at the high school and request that their son or daughter be enrolled in our classes.

San Francisco 49ers

When my family left Alaska for the last time we journeyed to Salt Lake City for the summer of 1955. Mel unsuccessfully chased quick money exploring for uranium. Our next move was to San Francisco where Mel became a union painter and mom worked in a hair salon. We lived on Baker Street next to the panhandle of Golden Gate Park. I was enrolled in Polytechnic High School that was located across the street from Kezar Stadium. Our high school football team the Poly Parrots, used Kezar when it played its games.

I saw my first San Francisco 49er game that fall in Kezar Stadium. The team boasted having the "million dollar backfield" which featured Y. A Tittle at quarterback, Joe Perry at fullback, Hugh McElhenny at halfback and John Henry Johnson at the other halfback position. The 49ers had fired head coach Buck Shaw at the end of 1954 and hired "Red" Strater to replace him. McElhenny had injured his foot and saw limited action that year.

I saw the 49ers beat the Detroit Lions and lose to the Chicago Bears. At that time, fans could walk down to the sidelines in the last few minutes of the game so I got close to the action, close enough to see the blue eyes of George Conner, the fierce Chicago defender. After that I was hooked on professional football.

Because of my asthma, we moved down the peninsula to Atherton near Redwood City. The 49ers had a training facility in Redwood City and the next summer I visited the camp and watched the team practice. The coach now was Frankie Albert and the first round draft choice was Earl Morrall, a quarterback from Michigan State.

We moved to Sacramento due to Mel's asthma and I enrolled in Sacramento High School and graduated in 1957. We moved again to San Jose because work was too irregular for Mel. I began college and when the family moved to Washington State, I stayed behind and finished college. After graduate school I got a teaching job in Merced. The television networks showed all of the 49ers' games there so my initial interest was reinforced now by being able to view all of the 49ers' games.

After I earned my Master's degree I continued to follow the 49ers through television and the sports pages. In the summer of 1970 I took a 12,000 mile trip around the United States and Canada with another teacher. When I got back to Merced it was July.

"If you will get me a press pass, I'll send you an article about the 49ers and you can print it or throw it away. I just want to watch them practice down in Goleta. I don't want any money, just a press pass." That's how I approached the sports editor of the Merced Sun-Star, our local paper.

I told them my background and about my advanced degree. The sports editor seemed interested and got permission from the managing editor to seek a press pass for me.

The 49ers' public relations department wasn't responsive. After all the team had coverage from the San Francisco Chronicle, the San Francisco Examiner, the San Jose Mercury-News and other smaller newspapers in the bay area.

After two weeks I told the sports editor that I was going down to Goleta on my own and planned to camp out with my pup tent on the beach or somewhere nearby. The sports editor said he would call the 49ers and tell them I was on my way.

I drove my Volkswagen to Goleta and arrived around 5:30 in the afternoon. I found where the 49ers were staying and asked for the public relations office and George McFadden came out to greet me.

"You must be the reporter that Modesto called us about."

"Actually, I'm from Merced, 40 miles south of Modesto. I'd like to get some statistical information about the 49ers from you if that's possible."

McFadden said, "We can provide you with a media guide."

I had no idea what a media guide was and was embarrassed to show my inexperience.

"Will you be staying with us?" McFadden asked.

"No, my newspaper has a small expense account so I will be staying outside of training camp."

"There's no expense for you or your newspaper. Why don't you get your belongings and we'll get you set up in an apartment. After you get settled come down and have dinner with the team."

I was flabbergasted but kept my compose long enough to say, "Well how can I turn down your generous offer."

Within 15 minutes, I was in a furnished apartment and shaking my head in amazement about how easy I had gotten into the 49ers inner circle. I had never written an article before, yet here I was inside an NFL press corps with access to coaches and players. I had an idea for an article about former 49ers and asking, where are they now.

In another ten minutes I was in the dining hall. I looked around and saw the head coach, Dick Nolan. I walked up to him like I had done this a hundred times before.

"I'd like to introduce myself. I'm Bob Evans from the Merced Sun-Star."

Nolan looked up from his plate and greeted me by putting out his hand to shake.

239

"Did you get set up okay in an apartment and get settled?" He asked.

"Yes, and thank you for letting me into your training camp," I managed to stumble out.

"Good, go and get some dinner and I'll see you at practice tomorrow morning." Nolan said.

I looked around the room and there was John Brodie, Gene Washington, Dave Wilcox, and the rest of the team. I couldn't believe how fortunate I was. I got a tray and went through the line with the players and at the end serving line I had a plate full of steak, green beans, potatoes, bread, iced tea, and a slice of apple pie.

The 49ers were extremely generous with the press and radio and television media in 1970.

"You can eat with the team or in the evening, you can go to the Blue Ox Restaurant and have drinks and dinner and just sign for it." This offer was extended to all of the media including me. I however, didn't feel I was positioned well enough to indulge myself at the restaurant. I ate with the team which was more than ample and free.

I went back to my apartment and wrote my first article. I had been instructed to call collect and dictate my story over the phone to an awaiting reporter. This was before facsimiles, email, and texting. Early the next morning I called my story in and the sports editor liked what I had written. He made some suggestions as to how to write for a newspaper.

"Open with a catchy angle, write short sentences and paragraphs, try to inform the reader of something he or she did not know, and close with a connecting paragraph to the catchy opening."

I went to my first practice and saw the defense wearing the red home jersey while the offense wore white. Like all football teams, there was exercising, drills, breakdowns by unit such as offensive line, linebackers, wide receivers, etc. before actual non-contact scrimmages between the offensive and defensive units took place. What I wasn't allowed to see was weight room workouts, film study, and meetings with coaches.

For the next ten days I asked and was given access to players and coaches for interviews that became the substance of my articles that I called in to the newspaper. The team left to play an exhibition game and I left to return to Merced. The newspaper wanted to take my picture so it could be posted above my articles.

When the 49ers returned to Goleta, I also returned and continued writing articles on the team and its coaches. The NFL required that each team play six exhibition games in 1970. The 49ers always began each game with its starting lineup and then substituted liberally as the game went on. At the end of training camp the 49ers played the last game of the preseason in their home stadium, Kezar Stadium, across the street from Polytechnic High School where I had once attended.

I was given a press pass and took my seat in the press box next to other reporters. At the end of each quarter a sheet was distributed to all of the reporters listing every play each team had run. At the end of the half, a stats sheet was passed out covering all of the categories of the game: yards gained rushing, passing, time of possession, etc.

At the end of the game my press pass allowed me to enter the locker room of both the home team and the visitor. Once inside I could interview players and coaches. The head coach would generally make a statement about the game and many reporters would listen and ask questions. The players were showering and getting dressed but would answer questions while they put on their clothes.

I had to hustle like all of the other reporters did if I wanted to get questions answered by coaches and players from both teams. At times it bordered on frantic and you couldn't get all of your questions answered at times.

When I finished in the locker room, I returned to the press box to write my article. There are two types of articles about games. One is the actual game article about the actual plays that took place and the other is called a "Side Bar" where some aspect of the game is featured, perhaps the winning touchdown or the key defensive stop that turned the game around. I was told to write side bars so I focused my interviews with the players involved in the key plays and got coach's comments on turning point plays.

When the season began I was assigned by the sports editor to cover the 49ers. The public relations department of the 49ers issued press passes and two sets of season tickets to me to give my newspaper. The sports editor said I could have the season tickets because I wasn't being paid anything to cover the team.

"You can scalp the tickets or give them to friends, it's up to you."

I did some of both with the tickets and looked forward to each home game because these were real NFL games and the intensity was increased.

At one game I sat next to a scout for the Green Bay Packers. He was wearing a championship ring from one of the team's Super Bowl victories. He removed the ring and let me examine it. It was huge with diamonds implanted for each victory the team had won that season.

This was also an exciting time for the 49ers. The team had never won a championship and the year before in 1969 had a record of 4-8-2. But now the 49ers were 5-1-1 after the first half of the season. The crowds were larger as the season went on. The second half of the season saw a 4-2 record going into the last game of the season where the 49ers would play the Oakland Raiders across the Bay. The Raiders were a good team and already had won eight games.

I found a way to cover the game by contacting the Raiders' public relations director who issued a press credential to me and that got me in the press box . The day was rainy and the field was in bad shape. The 49ers needed a win to advance to the playoffs. The 49ers were motivated and outplayed the Raiders. At the final gun the score was 49ers 38, Raiders 7.

The 49ers had to travel to Minnesota to play the Vikings on a cold snowy day the next week and the first game of the playoffs. The Vikings had a very good team and most expected a Minnesota win. However, the warm-weather California team won 17-14 and would move on to take on the Dallas Cowboys in the Championship game that would be played in Kezar Stadium.

The 49ers head coach Dick Nolan had coached under Tom Landry in Dallas and ran the same flex defense as the Cowboys. This was Nolan's third year as head coach with the 49ers so it was the master versus the student. Dallas was a stronger team and won in a close match 17-10.

The management of the Merced Sun-Star thought I had performed well enough to ask me to continue the next season. I was only too happy to oblige. I was also given a whopping total of $50.00 for my articles even though I had asked for no money. I had written about 25 to 30 articles.

I also brought my published articles to the public relations person for the 49ers.

"Here's some light reading for you." I said as I handed a thick packet of my articles to him.

"Thanks," he said "I'll read them lightly."

It was the idea of the sports editor and it was a good one because it showed that the Merced Sun-Star was featuring a column on the 49ers. It also was good for me in the future because it provided more privileges for me with the 49ers.

After the 1971 regular school year ended I applied and was hired to teach United States History in summer school. The summer session ended at the end of July and as soon as it was over I was in my car driving down to Goleta to cover the San Francisco 49ers' training camp. However, this time I knew my way around the coaches, many of the players, and other members of the press. The public relations director welcomed me back to cover the team. He also included me on some preseason trips to games. One was in Miami against the Dolphins.

"Would you have liked to play on Astroturf?" I asked Stan Musial.

The 49ers and its press corps were staying at the baseball's legend's hotel, the "Ivanhoe" in Miami Beach. We asked for and were granted an interview with "Stan the Man."

"Yes, I would have liked to play on Astroturf. The ball zipped through the infield faster and I'm sure I would have had more hits."

After the interview, the press was invited to take a cruise on Musial's yacht. The cruise included drinks and lunch.

We interviewed Don Shula after the game that was played in the Orange Bowl and he was generous with his time answering question. The preseason game ended in a 17-17 tie.

The 49ers had a successful season but not as good as the year before finishing 9-5 clinching a playoff berth on the final game, at 31-27 victory over the Detroit Lions. This was the first season the 49ers played in Candlestick Park. The first playoff game was with the Washington Redskins and the 49ers won 24-20 and qualified for the NFC Championship game.

The game was played in Dallas and I was invited to travel and cover the game. The dreaded Dallas Cowboys won 14-3 but the 49ers' players and coaches thought they played a better game than the year before.

The next year I again taught summer school and as soon as it was over, I drove down to Goleta to resume covering the 49ers. My articles were becoming easier to write as I knew more about the players and learned how to portray sports stories with greater ease.

When I returned to Merced for meetings to prepare for the 1972 school year, I was approached by one of the French teachers. She had recently gotten divorced and complimented me on the articles I written about the 49ers. At first I thought she was just being kind but as the conversation went on I realized that she was making herself available for dates and it was clear that she was interested in going out with me.

I had been divorced since 1966 but hadn't dated much. I had created a set of criteria as to what I wanted in a person in my next relationship. Merced was a small town and had a small number of women who were college educated, had a marketable skill, and were stable. The French teacher was beautiful, had an incredible figure, and met all of my criteria. The only caveat was that she was new to the dating scene in Merced and had many suitors. Castle Air Force Base was a training base for pilots flying B-52's and KC135's so there were lots of young men eager to meet women in our area to date.

The French teacher's name was Donna and we went out a few times but I realized that I was one of many seeking her affection. I asked her if she would like to go skiing and she said she would but didn't know much about the sport. I said I would take her up to the slopes and get her set up with a set of rental skis and take her to the bunny hill. I said I would get her a lesson as well.

The next Saturday we got up early, had breakfast rolls and headed for the mountains. We wanted to get there about 9 A.M., rent skis for Donna, get a lift ticket and get to the slopes. The day was perfect up at Badger Pass Ski Resort. It was cold in the morning but warmed to a pleasant temperature by 10 A.M. It was a wonderful change from the heavy fog in the San Joaquin Valley. Once Donna was set up with her skis and finished with her lesson she tried the bunny hill. She had learned to snowplow and turn and insisted that she wanted to continue on her own while I skied on my more difficult hills.

After lunch, Donna wanted to go back to the bunny hill and said she would be fine and that I should continue to ski with my friends. I agreed with her plan but about 2 P.M. I heard my name called on the loud speaker and was told to go to the first aid station.

I knew something had happened to Donna so I raced down the hill and when I arrived at the first aid station, I saw her with her leg on a chair and her ankle wrapped.

"She needs an X-ray but we don't have that equipment here."

"I'll take her back to Merced and to emergency." I said.

After I returned her rental skis I helped her to the car I drove down the hill which took over two hours and to the emergency room at the hospital in Merced.

"She has a broken ankle." The doctor told me. "We put her in a cast and have given her some crutches. Can you drive her home?"

"Of course," I answered.

I felt terribly guilty about Donna's injury. I thought I should have stayed with her on the bunny hill and helped her develop her skills.

"I'll drive you to and from school every day," I said trying to provide some level of support and assuage my guilt.

Over that winter and spring Donna and I became closer. She no longer was dating a doctor she had been seeing. A pilot she had dated was reassigned to another air force base. I was moved up on her roster.

At the faculty Christmas Party there was a band with one of the faculty playing trumpet. There was finger food and drinks. At one point in the evening, I decided to get up and sing with the band. I sang, "I left my heart in San Francisco." Donna seemed impressed and after the party we had a wonderful rest of the night together and crossed over to a new level of affection due to making love that night.

The 49ers in 1972 struggled to make the playoffs with a record of 8-5-1. Quarterback John Brodie was injured and Steve Spurrier came in won a few games to keep the playoffs alive. But Brodie came off the bench in the final game to beat the Minnesota Vikings and assure the 49ers a playoff berth. Again the 49ers would meet the Dallas Cowboys in Candlestick Park.

The 49ers ran the opening kickoff back for a touchdown and were ahead 21-6 in the second quarter and had a 28-13 lead in the fourth quarter. Roger Staubach came in and broke all of the hearts in San Francisco by leading a voracious comeback and a win by a score of 30-28.

The 49ers' locker room after the game was like a morgue. Players turned their backs to the press and no one wanted to talk about the devastating loss. After being ahead for most of the game, the 49ers thought that this was the year they would beat Dallas. Three years in a row, the 49ers had lost to the Cowboys in the playoffs. Each year the 49ers record had gotten worse. One of the 49ers who had fumbled an onside kick giving Dallas possession had nightmares and suffered depression years after his bobble.

In 1973 the 49ers were scheduled to play in the Hall of Fame game in Canton, Ohio. The press was allowed to view the Hall of Fame induction speeches. One of the inductees was Jim Parker, the outstanding guard and tackle for the Baltimore Colts. He had graduated from Ohio State and his brother lived in Merced and suggested I interview Jim. I did and he was most accommodating in sharing information about his career.

The 49ers played the New England Patriots in the Hall of Fame game and won 20-7. After the game the 49ers stayed in Kent, Ohio for a week preparing to play the Cleveland Browns the next week.

"Would you guys like to go to Pittsburgh and see a Steelers" preseason game against the Baltimore Colts. I'll rent a car for you if you want to go." The public relations director was offering the press corps. We eagerly said yes and three of us drove to Pittsburgh and went to the Three Rivers Stadium arriving about 3 P.M. We entered the stadium and met the owner of the Pittsburgh Steelers Art Rooney who showed us around the stadium with its weight rooms, classrooms, and training facilities. He was an engaging, warmhearted character who chewed and smoked a cigar the whole time we were together. We met Terry Bradshaw and talked about horse racing.

That evening when the Steelers took the field and we focused on "Mean" Joe Greene. He had played his college football at North

247

Texas State and one of his teammates there was Cedrick Hardman who was the 49ers' first round pick in 1970. We wanted to see how "Mean" Joe played against Elmer Collett and offensive guard who had been traded by the 49ers to the Baltimore Colts the year before.

During the game "Mean" Joe Greene thought Collett had held him while pass protecting. "Mean" Joe spit in his face the next play and once offensive linemen are in their stance, they can't move without being ticketed with a penalty. Collett had a fierce competitive side to him and while "Mean" Joe's spit was dripping from his face mask he held his position until the ball was snapped but during the play he attacked "Mean" Joe and a scuffle broke out.

After the game we went down to the Pittsburgh locker room and met with "Mean" Joe Greene. He was anything but mean. He was engaging, smiling, and interested to know how Cedrick Hardman was doing with the 49ers.

The 1973 season was not a good one for the 49ers as their record was 5-9 and out of the playoffs. Draft choices the 49ers made for the last two years were not panning out and the talent level declined.

As bad a year as it was for the 49ers it was a devastating year at Merced High School.

Riots

The 1950's and 1960's provided a setting for conflicts involving civil rights. A number of civil rights organizations entered the fray to try bring about greater equality between the races. The Congress of Racial Equality or CORE was one. Other groups had sit-ins in North Carolina and tried to desegregate lunch counters. Sit-in volunteers were met with beatings even though the people sitting in, used non-violent tactics. Freedom riders in the south who tried to desegregate public transportation, were beaten while the police looked on. The killing of civil rights workers in Mississippi made national headlines. The founding of the Students for Nonviolent Coordinating Committee or SNCC, an organization that was anything but non-violent challenged Dr. Martin Luther King Junior's non-violent approach. The creation of the Black Panthers organization in the bay area had the effect of raising the public consciousness about the treatment of African-Americans. Emotions were polarized around the country.

In Merced the African-American population was much like the national average, about 10%. Many lived on the other side of the freeway. Sport teams at the high school were the beneficiaries of some outstanding African-American athletes. Additionally, Merced High School would graduate a person who was a nationally recognized scholar. He was the first African-American to serve as the school's Student Body President, he was Stanford's first Student Body President, and who would graduate from Harvard Law School. Later he would become a law professor at Harvard. He would author several books and instruct both Michelle Obama and Barack Obama at Harvard's Law School. His name is Charles Ogletree.

Merced High School also had a big agricultural population and its Agriculture Mechanics program was large. Many of its students wore big belt buckles, jeans, cowboy boots, and sported baseball type caps and wore large brimmed hats. Many drove pickup trucks with a gun rack inside the back window. Often rifles and shotguns were in the rack.

There were also a large percentage of Hispanic students attending Merced High School, maybe 20% of the student body.

Near the cafeteria there was a smoking area for students. A group of Hispanics threatened a group of African-American students. The black students didn't take the bait but there was enough of a disturbance that administrators came to the area and began taking Hispanics and blacks to the office for discipline. The blacks believed they were wronged and decided to boycott classes the next day. There were perhaps 10-15 students.

Soon thereafter tensions rose when the football coach was accused of not playing African-American players who were perceived as being better athletes than white and Hispanic players who started in front of them. Issues of practice habits of some players surfaced.

Some of the African-American players complained to a local insurance agent who was Caucasian. He agreed to watch a game and speak out if he saw any discrimination. During the game a backup African-American player was put in the game to return a punt and he ran it back for a touchdown. This same player would later play professional football. The insurance agent began to rail at the coach from the stands and strained relations grew from there.

During the game a backup African-American running back approached the coach and asked to be put in the game. The game was still competitive and the coach didn't think the backup player would help. An argument broke out and some believed that the coach pushed the player back toward the bench.

Many of the African-American students were aroused by the above mentioned movements in America. The next Monday some of the backup running back's friends began to rag on him saying that he shouldn't let the white man push him around. He felt belittled by his peers and decided to act.

The coach's house was firebombed one evening and the evidence led to the backup running back and he was arrested. He was convicted of his crime and was sent to a California Youth Authority or CYA facility. He was an angry young black man. Over time he and others were convicted of killing another inmate at the CYA camp and sent to a California prison in Tracy, California. There he and others were convicted of killing a prison guard and he was sent to death row at San Quentin Prison.

Things turned worse back at school when a fight broke out between an African-American and an Ag student. Because the African-American student population was in a minority, young males banded together and confronted other white Ag students. Many fights broke out in the days that followed.

The blacks began wearing "cake cutters" in their hair. It helped to comb their hair in to an "Afro" style but it also could be used as a weapon as the pointed ends were sharp and could puncture skin if struck hard enough.

One black student told me, "We saw the Aggie students with guns in their pickup and we said to ourselves that if we got into a fight with them we couldn't let them get to the parking lot because they could get into their pickup trucks and get their guns and shoot us."

One white student was cornered in a classroom by a black group and his life was only saved when the Principal and other faculty members stood between him and his attackers. Later a white instructor was attacked by a black student. Students ran out of classes and chaos broke out. Parents of all races and ethnic groups heard of the situation and raced to school to collect their young-adult children and protect them from the "other bad groups of students." The school was shut down when police were called in.

Another instructor and I got on the public address system and called for an emergency faculty meeting to be held in my team-teaching room that was bigger than other classrooms. Most of the faculty came to the meeting. We tried to present the most recent news we had about what was going on and urged that we stand together to restore peace at school. We agreed on a plan that called for doors to be locked at all times and only opened during passing time. If someone tried to break in to a classroom the students were to stay behind locked doors. If an instructor had to leave to assist in breaking up a fight, the students were to remain inside the locked classroom. If the instructor was injured trying to break up a fight, no student was to come to his aid. Students had to stay behind locked doors for their safety.

We also wanted to try to be a buffer between the warring groups and bring civility back to the school setting. We wanted to extend friendship to all students and try to break down barriers.

251

The other instructor and I met with the Principal at his home that evening and told him of our plan to protect students. He concurred that it was the right thing to do and said he would have police on campus in the days ahead. He thanked us for stepping up and being leaders during this troubled time.

When school opened again, things were tense. There was fear among parents for the safety of their children and attendance was down. Teachers were on edge. African-American students continued to cluster in groups when not in class. Hard looks were exchanged between white and black students but having police on campus kept the lid on for the moment.

Strident times continued for the rest of the school year. In fact, things would not be normal for two more years.

In the years before the riots I often paid for tickets for students who liked track and took them to the Modesto relays where nationally known athletes competed. I took one African-American student to the track meet. He was enrolled in my history class. We had a friendship outside of class and often talked about track events. After the riots this same student was a senior and would walk by me without saying a word even when I approached and spoke to him. Whites and blacks were now truly separate. It was an uneasy time and a small spark could set off a time bomb.

DONNA

On a positive note, Donna and I became closer and were committed to one another. She took me to a wedding of one of her relatives. I met her Mother in Walnut Creek and her sister and brother-in-law in San Jose. We went to the wine country and enjoyed good food.

Donna was a special person. She was very intelligent and well educated. She had studied in France for a year when she was in college. She loved to read books, good books, not romance novels. She was politically astute and was a child of the 1960's when civil rights called for reforms.

She was vehemently opposed to the Viet Nam war. She was environmentally conscious and supported issues relating to clean air and water.

She taught herself to become a gourmet cook. She joined the American Association of University Women's gourmet group and became a star. She took Bon Appetit Magazine and cooked many of its recipes. Her mother had done all of the cooking when she grew up while her father was a pastry chef. Donna however, didn't seek out his skills and knowledge so she entered adulthood with a bare minimum of cooking ability. Now she was making up for lost time and showed amazing skill, discipline, and tenacity in teaching herself to cook.

One day we were in a book store looking at cooking magazines. There was a picture on the front cover of one publication that showed a beautiful cake. I commented on it. We went about our business separately the rest of the day but when I came home the cake we had seen on the magazine cover was on the table.

In 1973 we had a itinerate live-in situation. She rented a house and I had bought a house and was living in it. We would get together for dinners and stay over at each other's residence. In the summer when I was teaching summer school and covering the 49ers, Donna would stay with her mother in Walnut Creek, work on her piano skills, visit museums, read books, and soak up the culture of the bay area.

In 1974 she moved into my house. I had used my college salary to pay my child support and used my summer school money as well as money I saved from my salary at Merced High School to pay down my loan on my house. By 1974 I had paid off the mortgage. Donna bought food and cooked but between the two of us, we had plenty of money.

During Spring break in 1975 we visited the Buena Vista Winery in Sonoma. It was a beautiful day and we were enjoying the moment.

"Wouldn't this be a nice place to get married?" Donna smiled at me as she asked the question.

I had not proposed to Donna but we were headed toward matrimony. We had not officially spoken to one another in specific terms about it.

"Are you proposing to me?" I inquired.

She didn't answer but I said, "Yes, this would be a good place to get married."

The grounds were beautiful with trees shading picnic tables. The winery was in a cave and it was a picturesque and charming setting.

We hugged, she smiled, and we agreed that we would get married at the winery.

It was August 3rd. I had just finished teaching summer school and would be leaving for Goleta to cover the San Francisco 49ers for the Merced Sun-Star. The day was hot. Our wedding was scheduled for 6 P.M. and family and friends had gathered to celebrate the moment. However, the judge who was to perform the ceremony hadn't arrived. At 6:10 he slowly walked up the hill where we were waiting.

"Where have you been?" one of my friends confronted the judge.

I took my friend aside and said, "Don't anger the judge, I want to get married today."

The judge mildly admonished us stating that we both had been married before and that we had to have been part of reason our marriages had failed. He then went on with the ceremony. Neither of us liked the tone of the Judge. Both Donna and I had been wronged by our former spouses and were the victims of their bad behavior. The judge didn't know that but he should not have assumed we had been contributors to our former marriages.

After the ceremony Donna called for champagne to be served. We toasted one another for a short time then we all drove to a French restaurant where a meal and reception would be consumed and enjoyed.

"Give everyone whatever they want. If anyone wants after dinner drinks or cigars, give it to them and give me the bill afterward," I told the owner.

254

We enjoyed the evening and about 11 P.M. Donna and I left for Walnut Creek and her Mother's house. Donna's Mother, her sister and our brother-in-law all stayed the night.

I had planned to leave early the next morning to drive to Goleta to begin covering the 49ers. I had pleaded with Donna to allow me to go for a week or so in order to write several articles in advance of our leaving for Hawaii and a honeymoon. However, she protested that I should not start covering the 49ers right away and try to catch up later with my sports articles. However, I did leave the next morning and Donna wasn't happy. She was probably right but I didn't want to jeopardize my newspaper job.

While in Goleta I called in the evening to talk to Donna and she was cool toward me to say the least. After a week I had written several articles that would run in the newspaper while we would be on our honeymoon. When I returned we flew to Hawaii but she still hadn't simmered down. Our Hawaiian honeymoon was off to a rocky start. We traveled to other islands and on the big island of Hawaii I went down to jewelry store and bought Donna an onyx ring and gave it to her as a peace offering. The next morning she said she had lost it. We looked thoroughly through the room but it didn't turn up. She apologized for losing it and we made up.

We returned from our "honeymoon" and resumed our teaching careers. Donna taught French and had her French Club to which she devoted a great deal of time to because she taught an elective course where students could choose to take French but also Spanish or German. In order to encourage and excite students about learning French, Donna took students to San Francisco to see French plays, attend museums, and enjoy French food. To pay for such activities she raised money through candy sales, fashion shows, selling crepes, and hosting dinners. She also gave scholarships with money that was left over. Over the course of her career she literally raised tens of thousands of dollars with every penny accounted for and spent it on students. I was very proud of her.

She worked countless hours with her club but she also was a perfectionist in preparing her lessons. She would work until 11 P.M. at night and most of Saturday researching, writing, and planning for her classes.

When time permitted Donna would apply her culinary skills to make incredible dinners when we invited people for dinner. However, she was kitchen dictator. Her desire to create the perfect dinner made for stressful times. She would go to great lengths to find the right recipe, shop for the food, and attack the kitchen's pots and pans to prepare an exacting meal. I literally stayed out of her way as she spent hours and sometimes days working on the dinner. The setting had to be perfect too. The proper napkins arranged just so, a color coordinated table cloth had to be in place. The wine glasses had to be just so. Hors d oeuvres were properly in sync with the dinner. Soup, salad, the main course, dessert and after dinner drinks rested in perfect continuity and made her dinners legendary. Guests commented that they rarely had a dinner this good and if they did, it was often at expensive restaurants. Some were even intimidated to host us back for a return dinner because they believed that they couldn't measure up. It didn't matter to Donna that meals weren't as extravagant as she made, she was happy to be out with our friends to enjoy whatever meal was served.

I continued to teach my classes with my team-teaching partner Harlan Dake and our program was well received at school and in the community. I also taught night classes at Merced College. I started teaching for the college in 1965 and would continue until 2007. Additionally, I continued to cover the San Francisco 49ers for the Merced Sun-Star.

Head coach Dick Nolan's teams after the 1972 season saw a losing record for the next three years. After the 1975 season Nolan was fired. I sent him a letter saying I thought the 49ers would give him another year to turn things around. He wrote back to me saying that winning was the nature of the NFL and that he hoped to get back into coaching for another team at some point. In fact, he would. He would eventually be the head coach of the New Orleans Saints and an assistant to the Dallas Cowboys under Jimmy Johnson.

In 1976 Monte Clark was hired to coach the 49ers and he posted a winning 8-6 record. However, the Morabito family sold the 49ers after the 1976 season to Edward DeBartolo who fired Monty Clark and made Joe Thomas general manager. Thomas hired Ken Meyer and the team had a losing season with a 5-9 record and Meyer was fired and Pete McCulley was hired at the new coach.

Joe Thomas then engineered a trade for O.J. Simpson with the Buffalo Bills. At Buffalo, O. J. was only interviewed on Tuesday at lunch due to so many reporters wanting to talk to him. However, the new public relations director for the 49ers had come from the Dallas Cowboys who had Tony Dorsett the prolific running back, and he did one on one interviews. The new 49ers public relations director said that O.J. Simpson would now do one on one interviews with reporters. However, many interviews were rushed and had to be given as O.J. was trotting off the field after practice.

The team continued to get worse with a 2-14 record. McCulley was fired and Joe Thomas got into confrontations with one reporter on a disco dance floor in Washington D.C. during that horrible season. At Candlestick Park Thomas also called for security to remove signs from fans that called for him to be fired. Things sunk to a new low and Thomas was fired to the joy of the team and the press.

Bill Walsh was hired. He had been the head coach at Stanford and had winning teams. Before that he had served under Paul Brown with the Cincinnati Bengals. When he didn't get the head coaching job with the Bengals when Brown retired, he joined the San Diego Chargers before moving on to Stanford. Now with San Francisco he moved the 49ers training camp to Santa Clara University.

Drawing upon Brown's philosophy of offense and broadening it out further to create what became known as the "West Coast" offense. It called for short passes to running

257

backs and receivers with a quick delivery from the quarterback. The goal was to get first downs and 25 of them was considered the magic number. Over time the defense would wear down. Walsh was a master at finding beneficial matchups for his offense against opposing defenses.

O. J. Simpson had an argument with a writer from one of the San Francisco daily newspapers. The reporter had a reputation for being a jerk. I happened to witness the confrontation and after the reporter walked away I said to O.J. "Don't pay any attention to that guy. He's a bad actor. None of us in the press corps like him."

Since I learned that O.J. Simpson would now be doing sit-down, one-on-one interviews, I asked the public relations director for an interview with the star running back. We met just after lunch in a lounge and we were the only people in the room.

Simpson was at the height of his popularity nationally. He was not the same explosive running back that he had been at Buffalo where he was the first to rush for 2000 yards. He was however the spokesman for Hertz rent a car, Dingo boots, an orange juice company and had made movies. He was a walking conglomerate.

I studied all of the media sources I could to maximize my time with him in the interview. When he sat down he recognized me as the person who had supported him against the argumentative reporter.

"O.J., I have just six questions for you because I know you have a great number of demands for your time." I began.

I asked about his being recruited out of San Francisco City College's football team. He told me that all of the big schools sought him out and that he had told some of the coaches that he always wanted a pair of alligator shoes.

"When the recruiting season was over, I had 75 pairs of alligator shoes." He smiled.

We talked about his winning the Heisman Trophy his senior year. The year before which O. J. should have won, the trophy was awarded to Gary Beban, the quarterback from UCLA who did not do well as a professional football player.

He said that when he was the first choice of the Buffalo Bills, he wanted to project a low profile so he bought a Chevrolet not a Cadillac. We talked about his 2000 yard season and whether he thought he could break Jim Brown's rushing record. He thought he could because there were now 16 regular season games instead of the 12 that Brown had played in during an earlier time in the NFL.

He mentioned that he was looking forward to an acting career and that politically, he voted for the qualifications of the candidate rather than any political party.

He was well spoken and at times almost seemed humble. This was a dramatic contrast to his later difficulties where he faced murder charges in California and burglary and kidnapping charges in Nevada.

We talked for over an hour, a long time for an interview that normally would conclude in 20 minutes. I had so much information that I wrote two columns about O.J.

When O. J. Simpson came to the 49ers via a trade, he was no longer the talented running back the nation had come to revere. His legs were damaged and he was no longer able to run at the breakaway speed that had made him an exceptional running back. He often didn't practice during the week because his legs would cause him pain and because the 49ers were a bad team, he didn't have the success fans expected.

Bill Walsh praised O. J. before he took the head coaching job with the 49ers but when he saw him practice and realized that O. J. was no longer the dominant runner he had been, Walsh began to play Paul Hofer as his starting running back. The press, especially the reporters from other cities began to challenge Walsh about his decision. Walsh was exasperated with the withering questioning and began to play up the talent of Hofer.

I remember Walsh saying with some sarcasm, "What do you want me to do, make sure O. J. gets a hundred yards."

Walsh put in special plays for O.J. and Simpson had some success in limited action. Walsh never said to the public that O.J. was diminished but not playing him full time brought a wrath of derisive questions from the media.

The team finished 2-14 but Walsh's offense began to show life. Often while losing, the 49ers piled up 400 yards of offense. The defense however, was another story. It could not stop opposing offenses as leads faded away and the losses mounted.

The next training camp in 1980 I asked for a one-on-one interview with Walsh and he and I sat outside on a bench.

I began by saying that I had covered the 49ers since 1970 and saw the good teams of the early 70's fade away to a disastrous won-loss record and a traumatic climate under Joe Thomas. I said further that Walsh's offense began to take hold and that he was able to provide hope in the future. I also noted that the mood of the team had changed. There was less conflict now and that the team seemed to be pulling together. Then I asked this question.

"Can you do with the defense this year what you did with the offense last year?"

He appreciated my remarks about the improvement in the offense and the new tone of unity the team was exhibiting. Then he answered my question.

"No, I can't bring about a big change in the defense this year. The offense dictates to the defense but we have to have better personnel in order to stop opposing teams."

It was candid of Walsh to share his thoughts. He didn't single out defensive players who were not good enough to make the team better but made a blanket statement about the defense as a group and indicated that until the defense got better, a winning record was out of the question.

But Walsh had claimed Dwayne Board off the Pittsburgh Steelers' roster when he was cut and he showed that he was a player that would be part of a winning team. Walsh drafted defensive end Jim Stuckey and Earl Cooper,

Joe Montana, and Dwight Clark on offense. All of these players would be contributors to the championship teams to come. Montana would be enshrined into the Pro Football Hall of Fame and become one of the legendary quarterbacks of all time.

The team would improve from 2-14 to 6-10 and Montana and Clark became starters and would be mainstays in the 49ers' offense for years to come. The 49ers were showing signs of improvement and with their record, the team would draft fairly high in the 1981 NFL player draft.

As it turned out this was a draft that landed impact players. 1981 was also the year that the 49ers claimed good players from other teams and made a significant trade that led to the most successful 49ers season in team history up to that point in time.

Defensive backs Ronnie Lott, Eric Wright, and Carlton Williamson were drafted and joined Dwight Hicks in the defensive backfield. All four became the starters in the Pro Bowl in 1984 season. Three rookies patrolled the defensive backfield, an unheard of proposition at the time. But Walsh showed he had an eye for talent.

The 49ers claimed linebacker Jack "Hacksaw" Reynolds off the Los Angeles Rams' roster and made a midseason trade with San Diego for Fred Dean, a devastating pass rusher.

The team jelled under Walsh's coaching staff. A blend of solid veterans and enthusiastic rookies put a champion defense on the field. At first it didn't look like a winning team as the 49ers lost two of their first three games. But then the 49ers won the next seven games.

The most dramatic win during that run came against the Dallas Cowboys. The 49ers lost to the Cowboys the year before by a score of 59-14 in a humiliating defeat. Dallas went on to have a 12-4 record in 1980 but was beaten out by the Philadelphia Eagles who lost the Oakland Raiders in the Super Bowl. .

On October 11, 1981 Dallas came to San Francisco and was confident of a victory over the upstart 49ers. San

Francisco had lost three playoff games to the Cowboys in the 1970's and didn't appear to be able to compete well against Dallas again. However, things had changed. The 49ers scored 21 points in the first quarter and went on to win convincingly 45-14 to avenge the defeat the team suffered the year before.

Fred Dean had just been traded to the 49ers and he terrorized the Dallas offensive line and quarterback Danny White. The 49ers also poured it on the Cowboys because of the loss from the year before.

Only one other loss was encountered by the 49ers the rest of the regular season, a three point defeat to the Cleveland Browns. San Francisco closed out its regular season with a 13-3 record. In just three years Walsh had taken the 49ers from 2-14 to 13-3 and the playoffs.

The 49ers met the New York Giants in Candlestick Park and defeated them 38-24. That win would set up a rematch with the Dallas Cowboys in San Francisco. The winner would go to the Super Bowl.

Dallas sent out the message that the "Real Dallas Cowboys" would show up for this game. As the game was played out the lead changed from quarter to quarter but Dallas was ahead 27-21 with 4:54 left in the game when the 49ers got the ball on their own 11yard line. The 49ers had become famous for throwing short passes for first downs so Dallas sent out five and six defensive backs to prevent pass completions. However, the 49ers began to run the ball with plays called 18 Bob and 19 Bob, end runs that called for the tight end to seal off the edge of the Dallas defense while the two 49ers' guards led running backs outside of the defensive line. The tight end was Charle Young who was picked off waivers from the Los Angeles Rams the year before. On one side of the Dallas defensive line was Ed "Too Tall" Jones and on the other side was Harvey Martin. Somehow Young was able to make those blocks and the 49ers made significant gains. Then the 49ers ran a reverse with Freddie Solomon that put the 49ers into Dallas territory. Passes to Dwight Clark kept the drive alive. With seconds left in the game Joe

Montana rolled out to his right from the Dallas six yard line, pumped faked throwing the ball as the Dallas defense began to close in on him. At the last second Montana threw a high pass in the end zone and Dwight Clark jumped as high as he could and caught the ball on his finger tips for a touchdown. The extra point made the score 49ers 28, Dallas 27. Clark's reception has been dubbed "The Catch" the greatest moment in 49ers' history to that point

Dallas got the ball and threw a long pass to a wide receiver Drew Pearson who looked like he was going to go all the way for a touchdown but Eric Wright grabbed the back of his jersey and brought him down in the muddy turf. Two plays later Dallas quarterback Danny White faded back to pass and was hit by Lawrence Pillers. The ball fell to the ground and Jim Stuckey recovered it to give possession back to the 49ers. Pillers, like others had been claimed off waivers by Walsh and he was now paying dividends. Joe Montana was able to run out the clock and the 49ers were now the National Football Conference champions and would play in the Super Bowl.

SUPER BOWL

When NFL teams make the playoffs, the press corps covering those teams no longer can receive press credentials from the local public relations director of the team. Reporters must call the league office in New York and be validated to secure press credentials.

When the 49ers made the playoffs I called New York and explained that was a reporter from a small newspaper in California and that I had covered the 49ers for 11 years and requested a credential to cover the San Francisco, New York Giants game. I secured a press credential but when I arrived in the Candlestick press box and found where I my a seat assignment was, I was shocked. My regular seat was moved to the back of the press box. There was just a tiny work place. I was disturbed but there was nothing I could do, it was too late to ask for another seat. The rest of the press box was full of other reporters from all over the nation. The 49ers defeated the Giants by 14 points 38-24.

I watched the game and did interviews in the locker room. I filed my story and knew I had to call NFL headquarters for the Dallas game. I was upset with the whole experience. I was resolved to have a better seat when the 49ers played the Cowboys.

I called the NFL headquarters on Monday after the Giants' game and complained that I couldn't possibly be expected to cover the NFC Championship game under the conditions I had received in Candlestick Park.

"I'll get you a good seat for the next game," the voice said from New York.

I was relieved to hear those remarks. However, when I arrived at the press box, my seat was worse. I was assigned to a stool at the back of the room. It had no backrest and there was no workspace to write my story. I called my sports editor and he said he would use a wire service game story for the Dallas game.

I was hopping mad when I called the NFL office the next week.

"I expect to have a better working situation at the Super Bowl because my seat at Candlestick Park was unworkable."

"I promise you that you'll have a good seat and working space at the Pontiac Silver Dome outside of Detroit," the public relations man said.

I felt somewhat relieved but was skeptical. There was another problem. How was I going to be able to go to Detroit and get to the game?

When the Morabito family owned the 49ers, the team was very generous with the press. Reporters were allowed to fly with the team or be assigned to a press plane. Hotel rooms would be provided and often meals and drinks would be included, all at the team's expense. For a small newspaper like the Merced Sun-Star it was a major perk for its reporter. However, when the DeBartolo family bought the 49ers the team was not good and had a losing record and received understandably, bad press. The DeBartolo family protested about the coverage and said it had continued to follow the Morabito pattern of paying for flights, hotels and other perks and expected better press coverage. The San Francisco Chronicle replied to the DeBartolos that their reporters would continue to write stories that reflected truthfully the quality of play of the 49ers whether it was good or bad. It offered further that the newspaper would pay for its reporter's flights and hotels and not be beholden to the San Francisco 49ers.

All of that was fine for a major, big-city newspaper that had lots of money from its advertisers. However, it wasn't good news for the Merced Sun-Star. There was no way my paper was going to pay for airfare, hotels, and meals for me if I was going to cover the Super Bowl. I had to figure out a way to get there on my own and have it paid for somehow.

My wife Donna said I should go even if I had to pay for all of my expenses. She said that it was an experience I should not miss.

I checked with my newspaper and was told they would pay my mileage to and from the airport. The 49ers chartered a plane for the press and other dignitaries such as sponsors, political figures, and Bill Walsh's wife. I was told I would have a seat on the plane. I could stay at the same hotel where the 49ers were lodged but the cost would have to come out of my pocket. I said to all of the parties that this would be a satisfactory arrangement for me.

When I arrived in Detroit the snow was everywhere and piled high from snowplows. The temperature was freezing. When I got to the hotel it was buzzing with on lookers who wanted to see some 49ers' players. O. J. Simpson now retired, arrived wearing a fur coat made from the pelt of a wolf. While he was no longer a player he was a celebrity with a national following. Joe Montana's wife arrived and people were trying to get a look at her. She was Montana's second wife and they would divorce later in a nasty, angst-filled, emotional confrontation.

I had to get to the NFL headquarters at another hotel in order to pick up my credential for the game and receive a gift package the NFL provides to sportswriters.

"Do you want a car? One will be provided to you at no expense. They are provided by General Motors to the media." I was told by a NFL public relations man.

I knew I would be on the press bus to the game two days from now and would only need to use a car one time to go to and from my hotel to NFL headquarters. I also knew other writers at the hotel would have a car so I declined the offer.

However, I had to get the NFL headquarters and there was no bus to take me. I looked around the lobby of the hotel and spotted a fan that looked eager to be part of the pre-game Super Bowl experience. I approached him and struck up a conversation with him. His name was Jim.

After a few minutes I asked, "Do you have a car and do you know where the NFL headquarters are, Jim?"

"Yeah, I have a car and know where the NFL is staying."

"If you give me a ride over and back, I'll see if I can get you some NFL paraphernalia."

He agreed and drove us to the hotel. There I found the 49ers' public relations man and got what I needed to get into the Pontiac Silver Dome.

"This will be one of the easiest games you'll cover." The PR man said. "Stringers will send up quotes after the game if you don't want to go to the locker room."

I had been in the locker room after the 49ers' win over Dallas and it was madhouse. National press as well as local coverage made for a mob scene. It was so crowded that it was almost impossible to move let alone get close enough to interview a player or coach. I decided to avoid the Super Bowl locker room right there because there were even more writers and media people that had appeared in San Francisco.

I looked around for some souvenirs to give to my driver who would take me back to my hotel. There were some magazines and an NFL pin available to I grabbed some and gave them to Jim. He seemed happy.

After arriving back at the hotel I found some other writers and one Tom Fitzgerald said he had a car and was going to the Renaissance Mall and asked if I would like to tag along. I said I would. It was mobbed with shoppers and Super Bowl fans. I bought one of the official Super Bowl posters, arranged for it to framed and mailed to my home in California.

Once settled in back at the hotel, I made arrangements to attend the NFL party that is hosted by the league. Fitzgerald said he would drive so we headed out in the cold of night to try to find the festivities. We got lost for a time but eventually found the facility that was the size of a warehouse.

Once inside the event was spectacular. Every NFL team had a table where owners, front office staff, and coaches sat. There was live entertainment. When we arrived Lionel Hampton was performing and when he finished, a curtain next to the stage where he played opened and there was Bob Crosby's band that immediately began playing.

There were three or four men on stilts walking around handing out balloons. Food and drinks were unlimited and it was top of the line. Ice sculptures had been chiseled out with big "NFL" letters and footballs the size of file cabinet.

This was a spectacle rivaling the size and scope of those of the Roman Empire. Many former NFL players were there as well as celebrities from the national media.

Two young girls asked Roger Staubach for an autograph. He had no pen so I let him use mine and he wrote his name on a paper napkin for the young ladies.

Fitzgerald and I stayed rather late but found our way back to our hotel in good order. I went straight to bed because tomorrow was game day.

SUPER BOWL XVI, The Game

I had breakfast in the hotel coffee shop and waited for the press bus to take us to the stadium. The game was scheduled to start at 4 P.M. central time. We arrived around 1 P.M. and I found my seat which was next to Fitzgerald's. My seat was much better than the one I had at Candlestick Park. The Pontiac Silver Dome was covered and the press box had no glass in front so it was a good venue to watch the game.

I decided to cross to another section of the press box to get a hamburger. Food is always provided in NFL press boxes. As I approached the next section a man in a dark suit wearing an ear bud with a white coiled wire stopped me.

"Nobody crosses into this section now," he commanded.

"What's happening? I just want to get a hamburger."

"The Vice-President of the United States is being directed to his seat so nobody moves. Everyone stays in place until he's seated." This was the instruction from the Secret Service operative.

I waited 15 minutes until George Herbert Walker Bush, Ronald Reagan's Vice President, was securely in place and then the man said.

"Okay, you can now cross over to the food section."

When I returned to my seat it was 40 minutes to game time. Some of the Cincinnati Bengal players were on the field warming up but there were no 49ers which seemed strange. Finally, at 30 minutes to kickoff Dwight Clark and Freddie Solomon, the two wide receivers came onto the field and began playing catch. They were the only 49ers' players on the field. With 15 minutes before kickoff the rest of the team came out on the field. But it was a mystery as to why most of the team arrived so late.

In the press box we were informed that the 49ers' bus had been held up by bad weather and heavy traffic which explained their late arrival on the field. If no players had not been on the field 30 minutes before kickoff, the 49ers would have been assessed a 15 yard penalty at kickoff.

268

The game started badly for the 49ers. Amos Lawrence fumbled the opening kickoff and the Bengals recovered and moved the ball inside the 10 yard line. However, Dwight Hicks intercepted a pass for the 49ers and brought the ball out to the 32 yard line. The 49ers then marched 68 yards to a touchdown with Joe Montana scoring on a quarterback sneak.

Good fortune continued for the 49ers as they ran up the score to 20-0 by the end of the first half. San Francisco fans were delirious with joy. However, Bill Walsh told the 49ers at halftime that they would have to score two more times and not let the Bengal offense on the field for long periods of time.

The Bengals roared back in the second half and looked like they were going to break the game open when they were at the 49ers goal line. However, the 49ers put up a great goal line stand and stopped the Bengals on a fourth down play.

However, the 49ers had bad field position for most of the third quarter and surrendered 14 points before putting the game away with field goals. The Bengals scored a late touchdown but failed to recover an onside kick and the 49ers held on to win its first championship ever in its 35 year existence.

I wrote my game story featuring the goal line stand the 49ers made to stop the Bengals' momentum. Tom Fitzgerald said he was going to write another side bar story before driving back to the hotel.

"If you want to wait, I'll give you a ride back to the hotel afterward."

"I'll try to get a ride back now so that I can call in my story. Thanks anyway Tom."

When I left the Silver Dome, it was cold and dark. There were busses parked along the roadway.

"Are any of these busses going back to the 49ers' hotel?" I asked.

"Get in this bus." I was told.

As I entered I asked how soon the bus would leave.

"I have no idea."

I got inside the bus and it was a warm relief from the freezing cold outside. However, I sat there for 20 minutes before a man came on the bus and called me outside.

"Get in that car over there." He instructed.

I did happily because I thought I would get a direct ride to the hotel. Surprisingly, the car drove a short distance toward what looked like a warehouse and stopped.

"Go inside and wait. I'll try to get you a ride back to your hotel." The driver told me.

"How long before I can get a ride?" I inquired.

"I have no idea."

I was discouraged as I got out of the car. My early departure from the stadium wasn't going well and I kicked myself for not waiting for Fitzgerald to finish his second story and getting a ride with him.

When I entered the warehouse I was carrying my typewriter that had a San Francisco 49ers sticker on it. As soon as I walked through the front door I saw about a hundred Cincinnati Bengals fans. They took one look at my typewriter and began to boo. I didn't know whether things were going to get worse but I put on a brave face and got inside. It was warm and the heat from the seething Cincinnati fans made for a hot reception.

I waited for another half hour. Finally, a man entered the building and waved for me to follow him. I did.

"Get in that car and the driver will take you to your hotel."

I gladly got in the front seat. In the back seat were two men who spoke Spanish. They had done a radio broadcast back to Mexico of the Super Bowl. The ride took another half an hour but finally I was back at the hotel and could file my story.

The lobby was mobbed with 49er fans and I had to wait for another 15 minutes to get into the elevator and up to my room. When I entered the red light on the telephone was blinking. I called down to the front desk and was told I had a message from home. I called Donna immediately to find out if there was an emergency.

She was ecstatic and wanted to talk about the game. I too, was happy for the 49ers and their fans but had to call in my story so I cut the conversation short.

I next got on the telephone line with another writer at the <u>Merced Sun-Star</u> back in Merced who would type my dictated story to him. If I were covering the game today, I would have a laptop computer and would simply email my story back to the newspaper. However, in January, 1982 I filed my story the old fashion way by dictating word for word over the phone to the other writer back in Merced who typed my dictation and made sure it got into the newspaper.

It was almost midnight when I finished and hung up the phone. I had been given an invitation to the 49ers post-game party. I once again had to get in line to get on the elevator and up to the level where the party was taking place. When I arrived at the door I was stopped by a security guard.

"You can't go in."

"But I have an invitation." I protested.

"The fire Marshall stopped any more people from coming in because there are too many and there's a fire hazard."

I accepted my fate and got in line for the elevator and when my turn came I went down to the lobby. I looked around the gift shop but most of it was junk so I didn't buy anything. About 1 A.M. I again got in line at the elevator and went up to the room where the 49ers' party was being held. This time I was allowed to enter.

The first person I saw was Chris Berman of ESPN. I had talked earlier in the week with him. He was considering leaving ESPN and I told him there might be an opening at Channel 7 in San Francisco for a sports broadcaster. Berman is a tall 6' 4" and stood out in the crowd. We chatted for a couple of minutes and I excused myself because I wanted to get a celebratory drink and share in the excited moment of the party.

I looked around, got a drink, and saw running back
Bill Rink on the drums playing with the band. Many of the
players were all enjoying the party and I was able to
fraternize with them. It was fun but by 2 A.M. the party was
shut down.

I got on the elevator with a couple of the players and
saw a woman who was wearing a sash with words that
spelled out "Miss Super Bowl." To my knowledge there was
no official Miss Super Bowl. When she got off at one of the
floors, I smiled at the players who winked back at me and
one said, "One of our linebackers fucked her earlier this
evening." Perhaps she was seeking additional attention.

My room was on the same floor with a friend Dave
Newhouse who wrote for the Oakland Tribune. I knocked on
his door and he invited me in. Inside there were other writers
from various Bay Area newspapers. There was some beer so
we continued to celebrate.

After a while I heard Dave say, "I think we're out of
booze."

I took this to mean that the party was over. But no, it
meant that Dave was going to call down for room service and
order champagne. The bar was closed but we could still get
drinks by calling room service. When the champagne arrived
we all shared it and enjoyed the fellowship. The next time I
looked at my watch it read 4 A.M. I excused myself from the
fun and went to my room.

"I need a wakeup call at 5:30," I said into the phone
to the person at the front desk. "What time do you get off of
your shift?" I asked because I had to be in the lobby at six to
get on a bus soon afterward to ride to the airport to fly back
to San Francisco.

"I get off at 6 A.M." the voice said.

"Please don't forget to call me at 5:30. I have to
make connections to get back to California."

"I won't sir." The voice assured me.

I took a shower and went to bed and fell into a deep
sleep. At 5:30 the phone rang for my wakeup call. I jumped
out of bed and dressed, packed, and went down to the coffee

shop where a few of the other writers were assembled. Things were dramatically quieter now but the quiet was broken when Frankie Albert, the original quarterback for the 49ers came into the room. He had been drinking all night celebrating. He was still cheering the 49ers victory.

He went to the back of the kitchen and came out with a tray of thirty glasses filled with orange juice and asked, "Anybody want a screwdriver?"

Everyone declined but most of us drank a glass of orange juice. Albert regaled us with stories from his playing days at Stanford and with the 49ers. He had also been the 49ers head coach at one time and shared some of his experiences with us. I had seen him at the Redwood City training camp when he was the coach and when I was in high school. I told him I remembered him driving a new 1956 Buick. He laughed and said he remembered that car too.

Shortly afterward busses arrived to take us to the airport. Many were feeling the effects of the late night we had just experienced. I was looking forward to getting into my seat on the plane and getting some needed sleep on the way back to San Francisco. I was delighted to see that my seat was by a bulkhead which provided me with additional leg room. However, many of the other passengers were still celebrating. There were auto dealers, politicians, and other reporters. And of course, there was Frankie Albert who was wound up.

When the plane took off everyone was seated but as soon as the plane climbed to cruising level, it seemed that everybody got out of their seat and began drinking and carrying on. Because I was by a bulkhead there was a little more space which was soon invaded by partiers who stepped on my feet. Sleeping was out of the question.

On board were Governor Jerry Brown, Assemblyman Willy Brown, and the columnist Herb Caen. Governor Brown was contemplating running for President of the United States. Some of the car dealers confronted the Governor over some of his policies. He tried to hold his ground but some of the drinking celebrants made for antagonizing scene.

"Do you know the words to Leroy Brown?" Frankie Albert asked me.

I mumbled some of the lyrics and he tried to remember them. He somehow got on the public address system of the airplane and began singing.

"Bad, bad Governor Brown, baddest Governor in the whole damned town."

There was a roar of approval from most of the crowd on board.

Later in the flight the crowd began chanting for Herb Caen to get on the microphone. In time he did.

"Governor Brown is contemplating going to Washington," Caen began. "We'd like to send him," then paused, "to Washington State."

Laughter filled the plane.

Caen continued, "Governor, can you appoint Frankie Albert to the Alcohol, Beverage, and Commission?"

Everyone howled their approval.

This mood continued all the way to San Francisco. I got no sleep and was groggy when I got off of the plane.

"Can you give me a ride home?" Dave Newhouse asked.

I had parked my car in long term parking at the airport and said I would be happy to give Dave a ride to his home in the Oakland Hills.

"Can you give Hildy a ride to Jack London Square as well?"

I didn't know who Hildy was but said, "of course."

I had a little Volkswagen bug so Hildy got in the back seat and 6' 4" Dave got in the front seat.

"After you drop us off, are you going to the victory parade in San Francisco?" Dave asked.

"No, I'm going home as soon as I drop you guys off. I need some sleep."

Hildy did most of the talking on the ride over to Oakland. She said she knew Conrad Hilton and stayed in

274

many of his hotels. She would call him directly if she wasn't satisfied with her room or the service she received. Dave later told me that Hildy had lots of money and knew many wealthy and well known people. Her stories seemed to confirm that.

I dropped off Hildy first then Dave. I drove down Highway 13 to Interstate 580 and headed for U.S Highway 99 and home. When I got there Donna was waiting for me and wanted to know all about my experience. I shared everything that had occurred. She had prepared a one of her amazing dinners to celebrate the 49ers' victory. I ate it happily and enjoyed the moment.

"Sweetheart, I've got to go to bed early. I'm beat."

Donna understood and said, "Go to bed whenever you feel like it. You musts be tired after all you've been through."

I went to bed around 8 P.M. I had just dropped into deep sleep when the phone rang. The ringing jarred me awake. I grabbed the phone and said, "Hello."

"Were you at the game?" the voice said.

"Yes, who is this?"

"This is Bobby Monds, do you remember me?'

Bobby had been one of my students and I did remember him.

"Of course, Bobby, what do you want?"

"Can you get us some 49ers players to play in a fundraiser basketball game?"

"Yes, when is your game?"

"In May."

"Bobby, this is January, call me in April," I said and hung up and went back to sleep in what seemed like 30 seconds.

HIGHLIGHTS OF COVERING THE SAN FRANCISCO 49ERS

During the eleven years of covering the 49ers I had the opportunity to meet most of the famous players in the

NFL. Postgame interviews made for easy access to the players and coaches.

One coach stood out for me and that was Don Shula. He looked you in the eye and listened to your question with respect and provided thoughtful answers. Obviously, Bill Walsh stood out as well because of his superior ability to evaluate talent, make trades, draft well, and game plan. All of this led the 49ers from being a team on life support to winning a super bowl in just three years.

Dick Butkus was a surprise because of his reputation as being one of the meanest linebackers in the NFL. The Chicago Bears came to Candlestick Park to play the 49ers. The 49ers won the game but I wanted to talk to Butkus because he already had five interceptions in seven games. Three interceptions for the season would be a fantastic accomplishment for a linebacker but five in half a season was phenomenal.

I approached Butkus in the locker room after the game and introduced myself.

"Good afternoon, I'm Bob Evans from the Merced Sun-Star," I stuck out my hand to shake his and expected him to almost crush my hand when he shook it. Instead he took my hand with the softest handshake I've ever had. I don't know if he had hurt it but it was a surprise.

He was in no mood to talk.

"What do you credit your five interceptions to, which is a feat quite exceptional?"

As he continued walking out of the locker room, he said, "I give all the credit to Don Shinnick's defense," and walked out of the locker room to the awaiting bus that would take the team to the airport.

Joe Namath was something of another surprise. He was a good football player but an even greater celebrity. I talked to Namath in Tampa and in San Francisco. He had an even tempered personality and was patient with reporters asking questions. In Tampa he put on jeans but no underwear. As he walked out of the locker room he was

276

surrounded by four security guards who shielded him from adoring fans. He was escorted to the New York Jets' bus but there was quite a buzz as he walked by the assembled people outside the stadium.

Football sometimes provides powerful stories within the context of a game. The Atlanta Falcons had a coach named Norm Van Brocklin who taught his players to play dirty, that is, take cheap shots at opposing players, hit late, and pile on players who were down on the ground.

Charlie Krueger a defensive tackles for the 49ers, who normally said little about opponents and their style of play, called out the coach and the Falcons. His comments made national news and called attention to himself. The game was in Atlanta but there would be another game later in the season in San Francisco with the Falcons.

Krueger's wife admitted to me that he was terrified about playing the Falcons when Atlanta came to town.

When the game began Atlanta got the opening kickoff and its offense took the field. The first four plays were directed at Krueger who only wore a single bar for a face mask. He was doubled and triple teamed and the Falcons got a first down.

One of the Falcons poked Krueger in the eye and it began to swell shut. However, Krueger had played for Bear Bryant who was known as a tough coach and if you could survive his practices you were considered a he-man. Krueger once told me that when he was at Texas A&M Bear Bryant sometimes had three practices a day. When Charlie played in college all of the players had to play offense and defense and he lived up to the challenge.

When the 49ers defense came off the field after the first series, the Krueger was asked if he wanted to come out of the game.

He refused and as the game wore on his eye was completely closed. When the 49ers' defense broke their huddle, the Krueger would reach under his crossbar and pull his eyelid open so he could see the player had had to line up against. The Falcons would have to kill Krueger before he would come out of the game.

The game itself was close. The 49ers were leading but the Falcons late in the game, put together s drive and were inside the 49ers five yard line. Krueger pulled his eyelid up to find his man and took on the offensive guard. The 49ers defense held and the team won the game.

In the locker room reporters gathered around the 49ers' defensive tackle. Everyone was asking the same question.

"Was it a dirty play that closed your eye?"

"No, the guard pulled and we were all wrapped up in a pile and someone accidentally poked me in the eye. I don't consider it a dirty play."

The defensive tackle was talking rapidly and effusively, unusual for him. One of the radio reporters who had been a former 49er seemed to be aware that the defensive tackle in question had taken some prescription, probably Benzedrine, to get ready for the game.

The radio reporter said, "I'll talk to you next week about this game.'

The defensive tackle said, "You can talk to me now," in rapid fire conversation. But the radio reporter backed off of asking further questions.

Krueger to this day still swears that being poked in the eye was an accident but the drama surrounding the play of that game will always be locked in my memory.

Social movements sometimes impact the NFL. For a long time there were no African-American quarterbacks or middle linebackers. The Kansas City Chiefs changed that by posting Willie Lanier in the middle of their linebacking corps. He was responsible for calling defenses and controlling what the defense did to stop opposing offenses. He did it with Hall of Fame competence while making a social statement with his play. Since then many teams field African-American middle linebackers.

Quarterbacking was similarly changed as several African-Americans began running offenses. Doug Williams was the first black quarterback to win a Super Bowl with the Washington Redskins.

Sports reporting changed too. Women began to cover sports teams. In the case of the San Francisco 49ers a woman reporter from Sacramento was assigned to cover the 49ers team. That included locker room interviews. Bill Walsh was opposed to letting her into the locker room after games for privacy reasons when players are showering, drying off, and dressing into street clothes.

A compromise was put in place where reporters both male and female, would request players to come out of the locker room whether in uniform or in regular attire and answer questions from the press corps.

It delayed gathering information because players would appear one at a time. Before the new policy was instituted, reporters could enter locker rooms and rush to get player's reactions to the game. Depending on the angle of the sports story whether a side bar or a game story, different players would be sought out. Sending out one player at a time delayed getting to talk with the player each reporter wanted. There are deadlines in newspaper reporting whether news or sports, so this was a constraint on getting the information one needed in a timely way in order to file a story.

The NFL is very media conscious because exposure to sports writers widens the fan base which means more revenue for it and its teams when people get motivated to attend games and buy tickets, parking space, food and drink, programs, etc. The league wants to cooperate with reporters whether written, radio, and television. If the team had to buy newspaper space or media time it could not afford to pay for what it was getting free with media sports coverage.

After one game the new system's protocol was observed right after the game. However, some of the male reporters, including me, violated the policy by going into the locker room and began talking with Ronnie Lott, the amazing rookie cornerback and later Hall of Famer. The female reporter observed the policy to the letter but found out we got additional information that found its way into newspaper stories.

Her editors and the ownership of her newspaper also learned that we had got information but she couldn't by observing the stated policy of having players come out of the locker room to speak with reporters. The paper filed a lawsuit claiming discrimination based on gender.

She was an accredited sports reporter, had been given a press credential and therefore should have been given equal access to players and coaches just as the male reporters had. She did not choose her assignments but was told by her newspaper that she was to cover the 49er game.

The 49ers now had to make a decision. Would the team insist that every reporter observe the policy of waiting for players to come out of the locker room or would it fight the lawsuit in court? There was another possibility. The team could allow all reporters into the locker room after games even though players would be showering and dressing and everyone would be exposed to nudity.

The male reporters had been in lots of locker rooms after games and were not affected by the showering and dressing of players. However, it would be new for female reporters and would uncomfortable for players and perhaps for her as well.

But that's the decision the team made. Everyone was allowed into the locker room after the game. Many players grumbled about the invasion of their privacy. Many wore a towel after showering that covered their pelvic area front and back. However, at some point the towel had to be removed so players could dress at their cubical and that caused a problem for the players. Many players turned their backs to the aisles and faced forward into their assigned areas. Often the towel was dropped and quickly replaced by underwear.

The female reporter was completely professional in that she tried to get her interviews when players were covered by a towel or after they had dressed. She made it a point to look the players in the eye and didn't allow herself to look lower. She was there to gather information for her sports article and do her job.

Since that time female reporters have been allowed into locker rooms in almost every sport. However, they had to overcome a lot of resistance from teams and players who were opposed to dressing in front of women.

THE END OF MY SPORTS WRITING CAREER

In spring of 1982 Al Davis owner of the Oakland Raiders, made the decision to move his team from Oakland to Los Angeles. Other teams in other leagues had moved from city to city. The Boston Braves became the Milwaukee Braves and later, the Atlanta Braves. Davis believed he had the right to move his football team just as the Braves had done in baseball.

Davis was unhappy with the Oakland Coliseum, a stadium built in 1966, and Oakland in general. However, the Raiders drew well and had a strong fan base. The NFL Commissioner, Pete Roselle believed that Davis should keep the Raiders in Oakland because it drew well. Los Angeles already had the Rams. In the 1960's the Los Angeles Chargers moved to San Diego because it could not compete with the established NFL Rams. Ironically today, the Rams and Chargers will be sharing the same stadium in Los Angeles.

The Raiders made the move and litigation began in the courts to determine who had the power to make the decision to move, Davis or the National Football League.

"I'm going to take over coverage of the San Francisco 49ers." My sports editor said. He had been covering the Raiders and would have continued had the team remained in Oakland and I could have remained the 49ers reporter for the Merced Sun-Star. I had been something of a pioneer in that I was the first to cover a major sporting team back in 1970.

281

A Merced College instructor following my lead began covering the San Francisco Giants. Later the sports editor started to cover the Oakland Raiders. But Al Davis' decision to move his team to Los Angeles thus ended my sports writing career.

When I first began covering the 49ers the Merced Sun-Star paid me $50.00 at the end of the season. I had told the paper that I didn't want any money when I was given a press pass to cover the 49ers. Over the course of eleven years the paper increased my "salary" to about $500.00 for the season and by paying me mileage to and from Candlestick Park, I pocketed about $1000.00.

I was happy with the arrangement because I got some trips, meals, hotels, and a press box pass so I saw every home game and some of the away games. Further, when I covered the team's training camp, I was allowed to have free lodging and training table food. The perks were worth it to me. I had traveled to Seattle, San Diego, Kansas City, Miami, Dallas, New Orleans, Tampa, and Cleveland with the team. I covered a Hall of Fame game in Canton, Ohio. I had covered playoff games and a Super Bowl. I had met most of the "star" players along the way. I made friends with some of the 49ers. I had learned how the NFL and one of its teams functioned. I made lasting friends with some of the other sports writers. I was invited to speak at service clubs about the 49ers and the NFL. Overall, it was a good experience and one I still treasure.

Having covered the 49ers for over a decade reminded me of the length of a starting NFL player. Some lasted longer and some shorter but 11 years was about what would have been a good NFL career.

LOCAL POLITICS

When I first began teaching in 1963 I was fortunate to be hired by a wonderful Superintendent, Clair Hopkins. He had taken over the Merced Union High School District when it was a fly by the seat of your pants organization. He brought structure with his policies, such as the first Salary Scale, sound financial stratagems, and integrity to purchasing equipment throughout the district. He hired qualified professionals to lead the several high schools. He was available if you wanted to talk to him at the district office. He was fair in dealing with all of the certified and classified staff. His word was gold. When he said the district could only afford a 3% raise, his credibility was so believable that no one complained and accepted his recommendation.

In 1974 Mr. Hopkins retired and a new Superintendent was selected by the Board of Trustees. He was not as strong a leader. He began to allow parents to dictate curriculum in some cases. Relations with the faculty deteriorated. Salary negotiations became contentious. He let some of the new trustees get involved with operational matters, instead of staying in their defined role of policy setters. Things got so bad that the board of trustees fired the Superintendent but with the salary of a Principal even though he had no duties. This is a mid-year decision. The fired Superintendent used his time off and his salary to go back to college and become an accountant.

One of the trustees had a brother who owned a stationary store in Nebraska and prevailed on the Business Director to buy pencils from his store. Local vendors rightfully, were upset because they could have provided supplies for less money and kept profits in the community. The Business Director should have stood up to the trustee but didn't.

What had been a professionally run school district with honor and admiration was now is shambles. Many of the staff who had served under the earlier, outstanding regime were aroused and angry. I was one of them.

The California Teachers Association supports educational legislation, candidates for office, and local school districts. Each school district has an organization called the District Teachers Association or DTA. Within the DTA is a political arm that endorses candidates for Board of

Trustee elections. I volunteered to be on DTA's political committee.

However, I had no idea how to campaign or run a campaign. Others happily did. I contacted Herb Cruickshank who taught in the Merced City School District and a board of trustee member who served on Merced County School's board. Both had been involved with local political campaigns for school boards. In a crash course, both men gave me valuable information as to how campaign.

Since I was given a leadership role on DTA political committee, I began interviewing board of trustee candidates for our school board. I also sought out individuals whom I thought would be good candidates. I called a meeting to interview candidates and our committee settled on our choice for trustee. He was an astronomy instructor at Merced College.

I then called another meeting to create a political action committee or a PAC. Surprisingly, we argued for a considerable amount of time trying to select a name for our PAC but finally settled on one. It was the called "Committee for Educational Excellence."

In order to raise funds to support our candidate we held a wine and cheese tasting and sold tickets to teachers but also to businesses, doctors, and other concerned citizens. We garnered a few hundred dollars. To raise more money I appealed to the political arm of CTA and wrote up a proposal justifying our need for its support. There was a meeting going on in Los Angeles and we had members of our DTA in attendance. I sent our proposal in an "overnight" delivery service and our members presented it to the CTA board. Happily, we were awarded $700.00 from the parent organization.

We used some of the money to create and pay for a brochure to be used when we walked precincts throughout the district. We spent more money on creating 4 feet by 8 feet signs to be installed in the three communities where voters would vote in this board election. We recruited volunteers to construct the signs and install them on land where we had received permission to place them. All of this took time and effort to achieve.

Other money was budgeted for placing endorsement ads in the local newspaper. We included a picture of our candidate, the policies he stood for, and appealed to voters to vote for change and return the district the high standing it once earned.

I went to the Merced County of Department of Elections and bought lists of voters in the precincts registered in this election. They were listed in alphabetical order so we had to break the lists down by cutting and pasting to assure that we had lists of voters by streets so that when we walked those precincts, we knew that the householders were registered voters, knew their name, and how many times they had voted in the last five elections.

Since the Merced Union High School District encompassed three cities our efforts had to be duplicated in each town. I attended faculty meetings in all three communities and sought out and gathered teachers to volunteer their time after school and on weekends to achieve all of our tasks.

I contacted the DTA to get approval to inform all of the teachers in the elementary school districts of our choice for trustee. Once approved, a flyer was created detailing our endorsement of our candidate and sent to every DTA representative in every elementary school and asked them to insert a copy in all the teacher's mailboxes at each campus. Thankfully, they complied so other teachers were on board with their votes.

Additionally, we contacted the school classified employees in each community and informed them of our endorsed candidate and asked for their vote. With teachers and classified employees hopefully voting for our candidate it constituted a large block of votes.

We also contacted service clubs such as Kiwanis, Rotary Club, and Lions Club to allow our candidate to speak about science, since that was what he taught at Merced College. It was a way to get his name out in the community and answer questions after his presentation about the election if anyone was interested.

We made sure our candidate was at the League of Women's Voters Candidates night to debate the incumbent whom we opposed.

We also contacted the absentee voters by mail. We checked with Merced County Board of Elections to see who took out an absentee ballot, then mailed them a letter with our endorsement.

I also created a "Get out the vote" committee. We had volunteers willing to drive people to the polls if they didn't have transportation. I advertised in the newspaper a phone number people could call if they needed a ride to the polls.

I was working seven days a week on the campaign. Often that included evenings with phone calls and meetings. My wife Donna was so supportive in that she did not complain about the amount of time I was devoting to the campaign.

I was also teaching a night class in United States History at Merced College. As it happened, my night class was scheduled the same day as the election. I went to the class not knowing the outcome. One of our teachers hosted an election night party at her house. I taught the class as planned but had a nagging tug at the back of my mind about the outcome of the election. My class ended at 10 P.M. so as soon as it ended I drove quickly to the party to learn the result.

When I walked in the door everyone cheered because our candidate won in a landslide and those who attended were appreciative that I, as chairman of the DTA political committee, had done much to organize our campaign and deliver a victory. I was re-elected to be chairman of the DTA political committee. I had learned how to campaign and actually enjoyed the work and the challenge of competing in the political arena.

Others in the three communities took notice. It was the first time the teachers had been active on a wide scale in elections. The fact that our candidate won so handily gave new credibility to our organization and I received many congratulatory comments from within the school district, from the DTA, and from the communities affected by the election.

Other trustees on our school board took notice as well. They realized that we were a force to be reckoned with and knew they were on notice to pass good policies. I made it clear to our candidate that we wanted access to him but he was to vote his conscience if he disagreed with us. We didn't want someone to rubber stamp our positions but give us a fair hearing before deciding how to vote.

I went out of my way when contacting individuals in the community to assure them that we wanted good leadership on the board and not someone who was in our pocket and who would vote only with our positions. People seemed to understand that the defeated candidate had been unfair and deserved to lose and that our candidate seemed more reasonable and level-headed.

In 1984, I was contacted by a lawyer who was running for Superior Court Judge. His campaign manager also sought me out and asked if I would help on the campaign. I liked the lawyer and thought he was the best of the many that were running for the judgeship.

Another lawyer approached me and asked me to work on his campaign. I told him that I was already committed to another candidate but said if there was a runoff, I would help him.

I met with the lawyer's election committee. They were well positioned people in the community and were well respected. They needed someone to organize precinct walking for entire county of Merced. That would include several cities and towns. I was asked to take on this duty and I accepted.

I made arrangements to buy precinct lists for every town in the county. Again, the lists were in alphabetical order and needed to be broken down so that precinct walkers would have a list of voters registered by street.

Additionally, I had to find volunteers to take the list of voters, walk street to street and contact them by knocking on doors, and leave a brochure listing the candidate's qualifications and positions on issues. The city of Merced had 27 precincts and thousands of voters. It was the biggest city in the county. I organized a group of volunteers and taught them how to breakdown the precinct lists. We met at an insurance agency that had a large conference room. We would meet in the evening, eat pizza, drink a little beer and work on our tasks.

Once that was done, I had to find volunteers in other towns to do the same thing. The next task was to find other volunteers who were willing to walk the precincts. There were several other communities. They included Atwater, Hilmar, Los Banos, Dos Palos, Gustine, Livingston, and other smaller towns.

I began working on this large job in July when I was out of school. I was able to use the insurance agent's office phone for the many long distance calls that had to be made. I was able to tap into people who had served in other campaigns and who liked my candidate.

The task was huge but I made steady progress so that by September my organization was in place and the precincts lists were ready to go. An ongoing problem was that volunteers often said they would serve but situations would change so that they were not available and therefore new people had to be found and trained to do the job.

A primary election had eliminated all but two candidates, my candidate and another lawyer in private practice. I arranged for a forum to be held in the District Teacher's Association building so that the two contenders could be introduced and present their positions on issues and answer questions from a large assembly of teachers.

As the campaign wore on, everyone on the campaign committee participated in fund raisers, campaign ads to be run in the media, community forums and solved problems as they came up. We met once a week in the evening to access the progress of the campaign.

We realized that this was going to be a close race. My candidate was strong on the west side of the county but the other lawyer had strength in Atwater and some of Merced. November came and an election eve party was scheduled at a restaurant to chart of results as they were released.

Unfortunately, my candidate lost by a small margin but he showed poise and dignity in defeat. By now we were friends and we began to socialize together. I am pleased to say that this election took place in 1984 and we are still friends today.

SABBATICAL

Educators have been encouraged to upgrade their knowledge and skills by continuing to learn so they can pass on additional information to their students. Over time, educational institutions put in place a sabbatical system. There two kinds. One allows teachers to return to college by giving released time and financial support. Teachers can enroll in courses for a semester or for a full year.

The second type of sabbatical is a travel work-study program where teachers can visit other countries, view key sites, museums, engage in local customs, tour historical places, and examine other educational institutions and its staff.

One must teach for at least seven years before you are eligible for consideration to be a candidate for a sabbatical. I had taught for over 20 years and Donna for almost 20 years. Neither of us has ever applied for a sabbatical. We had talked about applying for sabbaticals but had other responsibilities that deterred us from getting one. However, in 1986 we both thought we could improve our teaching skills by going on a sabbatical.

We applied for a half year travel work-study sabbatical. Since I taught World History and Donna French, it seemed natural that we would go to Europe and France specifically to gain additional historical information and language skills. We were both granted sabbaticals and would receive half of our pay for the spring of 1987.

We were both conscientious teachers and well respected among colleagues and the community. Since I had worked on campaigns to improve the school board, district administrators were appreciative of my efforts. I am sure that played a part in granting sabbaticals to both of us.

Once being granted our leaves we were required to pack up everything in our home and store it. We needed to find a renter for our home. We also had several rental properties and needed to select a property manager collect rent, make repairs if needed, and deposit money in our bank account. We also needed to find a way to have money sent to us while we were in Europe.

The easiest task was finding a property manager. Several were available and we settled on one who had been selected "Manager of the Year." He would take 10% of the rent for his services.

I sought out another teacher at Merced High School who was new and renting an apartment. I approached her and said I would give her a break on rent if she and her husband and child would rent our home. Since I had paid off my mortgage, I could rent our home to her for a reduced amount and therefore make it attractive for her family to rent from us. The catch however, was that we would only be gone for six months and that she would have to move upon our return. The rent was low enough to make the deal pleasing to her but it took three weeks to work out the details as she vacillated in making up her mind.

Packing everything up while still teaching was a trying task but we rented a storage unit and laid down some pallets and rodent poison. On the day we finally got everything stored we were exhausted and needed a place to stay for one night. A friend allowed us to stay at her home and was kind enough to cook us dinner. We were also invited to a party in another town 15 miles away and we decided to go. It was a good decision because it took our mind off what lay ahead and we were able to relax.

We had booked airline tickets so the next day we traveled to San Francisco and got ready to depart. It was February and in California that's usually a warm month. However, we were heading to Brussels where it was cold so we dressed in warm clothing.

We arrived in Belgium to blustery weather and had a connecting flight to Amsterdam in two hours. We had to take a bus out to the small plane that was tied down with ropes so the wind wouldn't blow it away. Once inside, the wind was so strong that we could feel the plane being moved by it. We took off and were bounced around more than in any flight I have ever been on. There were air pockets and the plane fell a hundred feet then caught an updraft that shot us up in the air faster than any elevator could. Approaching Amsterdam and the airport I was concerned that the bouncing plane would have a disastrous landing. In what can only be described as a miracle landing, the pilot greased the plane onto the runway as smoothly as silk. What a relief.

We were now in Europe and we decided to find a place in one of the surrounding countries to use as a base from which to travel to other nations. We took a train to France and then took the TGV, the bullet train that rides as smooth as silk, to southern France. From there we rented a car and traveled around until we found a city for our base. We settled on Aix-en-Provence twenty miles north of Marseilles. We dropped off the car and found a hotel and began looking for an apartment. We found one a short way from the middle of town. The owner said he would work with us in renting for short periods of time and allow us to travel. He agreed to let us store some of our baggage while we were away on our voyages.

In Aix-en-Provence there is a university and many English-speaking students attend. It also was the hometown of Paul Cezanne and his studio and home are were nearby and easy to visit. Romans called this city Aquae Sextiae and Julius Caesar's uncle Marius conquered the local tribes and a nearby mountain called Mount St. Victoire was named after the battle was won. Cezanne painted Mount St. Victoire on many of his canvases.

We found an organization called the Anglo-American Society of Provence. It provided an outlet from transplanted Americans and Englishmen. It had a library of books in English and did wine tastings, excursions, and sightseeing.

We next contacted a bank on the Cour Mirabeau, the main boulevard in Aix-en-Provence, to set up an account and have money deposited from America. I had put my niece Caroline on my checking account so she could pay bills as they came in. But more importantly, she was to send money to our bank in France so we could live. It took her some time to make all of the arrangements and some anxiety, but she managed to get everything in order.

With our lodging and money issues settled, we were now set to explore Europe. We both realized that this was an opportunity of a lifetime. We were free to go wherever we wanted and see whatever caught our eye. However, we were both committed making the most of our time in Europe to gain the most we could. We demanded of one another that we would not waste our time by laying around on a beach or lounging around in cities doing nothing. There was a wonderful world waiting for us but to truly benefit from it we had to study. We bought Michelin guides as well as other books about the great attractions of Europe. We decided to take short trips 3-4 weeks to travel to one country, then return to Aix-en-Provence to plan another trip of 3-4 weeks for another country and so on.

We began to venture out into France since we were already there. We started in Marseilles and the old port that was founded by the ancient Phoenicians. We explored the city's museums and neighborhoods. Marseilles had a large Moslem population that had come from Algeria and

Morocco. It was like stepping into northern Africa when we walked through that section of the city.

We worked our way to Avignon, Arles, Nimes, Tours, Lyon, Dijon, the Champagne region, Reims, Paris, Normandy, Strasbourg, and every major city in France. We visited every museum and historical site and had the time to go into detail at each place. We saw the Bayeux Tapistry, the hand stitched chronicle of William the Conquorer's victory over Harold of Wessex at the Battle of Hastings in 1066. The tapestry itself is 230 feet long and 20 inches tall.

We were able to visit the Normandy Beaches where D-Day took place on June 6, 1944. This was the largest amphibious landing by any army in the history of the world. It gave the allies a foothold in Europe from which to begin the destruction of the Nazi regime of Adolf Hitler. The Americans were given the most difficult part of the five beaches that were assaulted that day. There is no protection once troops left their landing craft and had to face a terrifying volley of German fire from dug in entrenchments. Casualties were high but a toehold was won so that further advances could take place to end Nazi domination of Western Europe.

Donna was such a wonderful traveler. She often said that if she couldn't carry her own luggage then she shouldn't be traveling. She was so important in buying train tickets in France because of her language skills and knowledge. She was a tremendous researcher. She found so many important sites to see, many of which I had no idea existed. She could figure out train schedules not only in France but in every country we visited. When were in Aix-en-Provence she made our little apartment a livable home. The main floor sagged so we often stayed in the small kitchen, and I mean small. From our table we could reach into the refrigerator and then check our cooking pots from a sitting position. Our bathroom had a Turkish toilet and if we wanted to shower, a painted pallet would be placed over the toilet hole to stand on so we could cleanse ourselves. She was fabulous at going to the market and cooking great meals with limited culinary equipment. I could not have had a better companion

Several highlights from our stay in Europe stand out. One was when we went to Spain. We toured Madrid and visited the Prado where Guernica was on display. This is the painting Pablo Picasso did in protest to the violence during the Spanish Civil War. Most wars prior to this one attacked military targets but this was the first time an entire village was wiped out by bombing where there was a total disregard for civilians. Picasso's cubist rendition of the destruction of Guernica, a Basque country village, depicted in black, gray, and white figures shows the agony of a gored horse, bull and flames. The dismembered figures show the anguish of the victims from the violent attack.

We also ventured out to Toledo where El Greco once had a studio. Nearby was the Alcazar, the fortress that was held by the Nationalists or Fascists during the Spanish Civil War in the 1930's. The Alcazar was surrounded by Republican forces and the commander Colonel Moscardos' 16 year old son was captured. Moscardos was informed of his son's capture by telephone and told that he would be killed unless the Alcazar surrendered in 10 minutes. The son was allowed to talk with his father on the telephone and he related that he was indeed captured and sought advice from his father as to what to do. Moscardos told his son to "turn your thoughts to God." He then asked to again talk with his son's captures. He said into the phone, "You don't have to wait 10 minutes to kill my son, the Alcazar will never surrender." The son was killed, the Alcazar was eventually relieved of the Republican siege and in time, the father and son were buried side by side in the Alcazar. We both felt the pain of the father and son who were two figures caught up in a larger conflict. I have often wondered what I would have done if I were asked to choose between surrendering a fortress and saving my son. Moscardos was a military man, so I guess the choice was easier for him.

We traveled to Granada to visit the Alhambra, the site of the Moslem occupation and toured the Generalife, the headquarters. It is an amazing building. The Koran speaks of paradise being a place where there are lush green valleys with fresh flowing water. The Generalife has luxuriant gardens and in the middle of its stairs, cutout channels reveal water continually flowing to the bottom of the stairway. The handrails similarly have ducts and water runs from the top of the stairs to the bottom.

This was the city held by Moslems for 700 years. It was a stronghold but over time, the Christians rose up in strength and during the time of Ferdinand and Isabella in 1492, the Moors were driven out of Spain. The last leader in Granada rode his horse down from the hilltop fortress into a canyon and up the other side of the hill. He stopped his horse and turned around to take one last look at the magnificent structure across the canyon. He began to cry because he had been the one leader to lose Moslem control and the loss overwhelmed him. His mother turned to him and said, "You weep like a woman for what you could not hold as a man." This was a mother that had little sympathy for her distraught son.

The year 1492 is huge in Spanish history. Everyone knows Columbus sailed the blue in 1492 but it was also the time the Moors were driven out of Spain and also so were the Jews in the same year, 1492.

Donna was amazed at what we were seeing. She had incredible knowledge of France but didn't know as much about Spanish history so these visits broadened her awareness of Spain. She had studied languages in college but she also had a genuine interest in history and gloried in the historical experiences were we sharing. She wasn't bored by the required study and the effort it took to see the sites we were visiting. In fact, she made many contributions about the places were saw.

We traveled next to Cordoba. It is an amazing place. Remains of Neanderthal men have been found. It was captured by Hamilcar Barca the Carthaginian who named it Kartuba after a Nubian commander. The Romans took over in 169 A.D. only to be conquered by the Visigoths in the late sixth century. In 711 the Moors captured it and it became part of the Caliphate of Damascus. The Mezquita-Cathedral de Cordoba is one of the most fascinating buildings we saw. It has Christian, Moslem, Gothic and Renaissance architecture. It has the red and white arches and a niche that faces east toward Mecca so Moslems could pray. We were there near Easter Sunday and there were 15 Catholic priests who performed the service, quite spectacular.

We traveled next to Saville. We were careful to watch our money both in terms of criminals and making it last for our stay in Europe. Therefore, we took a hotel that was very inexpensive and not in the best part of town. Donna was always a great traveler and would bend to the conditions we faced.

We toured the great Cathedral where Isabella of Spain and supposedly Christopher Columbus are buried alongside one another.

We were walking back from reviewing Roman ruins when I heard Donna utter a loud grunt. I quickly looked at her and saw that she had been dragged to the ground by a man who tried to steal her purse. She held on to its straps and when I saw what had happened, I charged the man who let go of the purse's strap. I was able to get close enough to him to slam him up against a wall where he bounced off and started to run. I ran after him but he had an accomplice on a motorcycle. I was close to catching him and wanted to beat the hell out of him but he was just fast enough to jump on the back of the motorcycle and the two criminals sped away. After the thieves sped away I ran back to Donna to see if she was injured.

"Are you hurt?" I asked. She was standing now after being pulled to the ground by the thief when he pulled on her purse straps. I could see that she was disturbed.

"I'm okay," she said. "Thank you for going after those guys."

"I'm just glad you're not injured and that you had the presence of mind to keep your purse from being pulled away from you."

I was so glad she had thought quickly when she was attacked and held on to her purse. All of her identification was inside including her passport. To replace all of what she had lost would have taken many days and limited what we could have done.

We walked back to our hotel and began to pack to go to Portugal the next day. Donna discovered that someone had been in her suitcase and tried to pry out some diamond-looking stones out of a brooch she had. I called the front desk and complained about the intrusion. I received no sympathy. The manager said that the hotel was not responsible for what happened in room when guests were away. It was clear to me that one of the staff was the culprit since they were the only ones who had a key to get into our room.

We stayed in that evening after what was the worst day of crime we had experienced in all of our travels. There would be others but not like this one. We traveled to Portugal by bus the next day, got on a train just in time to go to Lisbon where we had to take a ferry across the bay, then in a taxi to our hotel. It was an exhausting day and one that required that we have some drinks before bed.

Another highpoint of our stay was our trip to Egypt. To get there however, we had to book a tour that began in Madrid, Spain. That meant we had to fly from France to Spain and meet up with the tour. Once there we flew from Madrid to Cairo in Egypt. As we approached our destination, people on the plane began to stand up and rush to the windows of the plane to look at the Pyramids below.

Once we landed we departed from the plane and were told to get on an awaiting bus. A soldier was holding an automatic weapon by the bus's front door.

"Where is this bus taking us?" I demanded.

"To the terminal," the soldier said in British English.

We boarded the bus and within ten minutes we were inside the airport's building. While we had planned to get to Egypt with the tour from Spain, we had made no plans while we were there. We thought we would spend a few days in Cairo and then try to travel to the places we wanted to see.

"Welcome to Egypt," a man said to us who looked like an official. "You want to see the pyramids, Cairo, the Valley of Kings and Queens, and the Great Temple at Karnack." It was as if he had read my mind as to what we wanted to visit. I nodded in agreement.

"Go over to the money counter and buy 150 Egyptian pounds for each of you and then come back to me afterward." He instructed.

I was just about to do as he had told me but then I paused and said, "Who are you? Are you an official of the government?"

"No," he said and handed us a business card that said Green Valley Tours.

I began to quiz him as to the price he was going to charge us for seeing all of the sights.

"I will take you by motor car to a hotel where you will have a room. Tomorrow we will go to the pyramids and the Great sphinx. All transportation will be provided. Then you will have several days to see Cairo and its great museum. I will be with you the whole time."

My head was spinning. This was too good to be true. The price he quoted us was most reasonable. We had never planned a trip this way, an on-the-spot, spur of the moment adventure. I looked at Donna and she seemed to be in agreement with what was proposed and the price that was quoted.

I paid the man his fee and he directed us to follow him. He had a small bus waiting and we got in. He drove through the busy streets of Cairo and then took us down a narrow street and parked by a hotel. It was respectable but not a five star luxury hotel by any stretch of the imagination, but I didn't expect one after the amount I paid the tour guide. He went in with us and got us a room. So far, so good.

"There is a restaurant on the upper floor and nearby there are other places to eat," The man said.

We took our baggage inside the room and found it to be nice. I looked across the street and saw a garbage dump with children rummaging through parts of it to gather what they could in the way of salvage.

We had dinner on an open air rooftop and found the food good. It was March so the weather was warm in Egypt. We could hear the Muezzins calling the faithful to prayer from nearby minarets towering over mosques. The voices we heard were broadcast over loudspeakers and could be heard from blocks away.

The next morning we were promptly picked up by our guide who drove us and others in a van to the pyramids. There we were greeted by another guide named Mohammed. We were allowed to go inside the Great Pyramid at Giza whose base covers 13 acres. We had to stoop down somewhat and walk on a wooden walkway to enter the inner chamber of Khufu or as the Greeks called him, Cheops, the pharaoh who was buried inside. The room was perhaps 15 feet long and 10 feet wide. Inside this protected space was a sarcophagus with nothing inside. It had been raided centuries ago.

Napoleon who fought the British between 1798-1801 in Egypt, entered this great chamber and was so visibly shaken by the experience that he insisted that his reaction while inside was not allowed to ever be brought up again.

The pyramid itself is 4500 years old. Everyone has seen a picture of it at some time or another but when it was originally finished it had an alabaster finish that gleamed in the sunlight. A small portion of it is still attached near the top. Some of the alabaster was removed and used to build the Mohammed Ali Mosque, the burial place of the former Shah of Iran.

Nearby is the Great Sphinx with the head of a man and the body of a lion. It was carved out of a hill and is made of sandstone, a porous material that surprisingly has weathered reasonably well through thousands of years of time.

After our visit to these remarkable monuments, we were taken to an "Essence" shop where we were given cold soft drinks and of course encouraged to shop for perfumes, trinkets, and papyrus. I bargained to get an agreeable price for some papyrus. I wanted to take it back to use in my classroom. We learned how papyrus was made from the triangular shaped reed that grows along the Nile River. Strips of the material are soaked for several weeks to wash out the sugars in it. When dried it is overlapped and bonded together to form a rough feeling paper that the ancients used to write their hieroglyphics. Ancient Egyptian writing or hieroglyphs it has been learned, is a phonetic language and was deciphered by Francois Champollion from the Rosetta stone. The Rosetta stone is housed in the British Museum and has three languages carved into it, Hieroglyphic, Coptic, and Greek. Each language says the same thing so that if you know one language, you can figure out the others. Champollion did it in 1835 and has given the world a great gift because so much has been learned about Egyptian religion, its dynasties, and daily life since his discovery.

We returned to our hotel after a full day of touring but still had time to walk the streets and get our bearings. We found the Nile River nearby, the Egyptian Museum, and a number of Mosques. However, walking around Cairo brings one in contact with a multitude of street hustlers.

"Welcome to Cairo," the litany begins. A hand is thrust out for you to shake. Being polite, you take it and thank the person whom you've just met. The person however, doesn't let go of your hand but gently pulls you toward a building and says, "Come to my shop." Inside are perfumes, artifacts, and souvenirs.

This same experience happened seven times to me in an hour. Soon you pull back and avoid the handshake. It is also amazing that these street vendors size you up and know your nationality and can speak your native language. We heard French, German, and English all from the same person.

I had traveled to Mexico at a young age with my parents and learned about bargaining for items you wanted to purchase. Donna and I had a similar experience in Italy where everything sold by street vendors is transacted by negotiation. However, in Egypt things are more aggressive and in your face. Donna pulled back and didn't want any contact with vendors on the street and had me deal with them. I became annoyed at the constant intrusion by people trying to sell me something. However, I realized that if I had grown up in Egypt, I would probably be one of street sellers myself.

The next few days we had free time to explore Cairo on our own. Crossing the street is a life-threatening experience. Cars, trucks, and busses have an open season on pedestrians. Sometimes there is a policeman directing traffic which allows for safe passage across a street because he stops traffic and allows pedestrians to cross the street. However, not every intersection has a traffic controller. Timing is critical when you try to cross a street. We had to allow a lot of space between oncoming traffic. We also were astonished to witness local pedestrians crossing a lane at a time. Traffic whizzed by within inches of the courageous amblers and they seemed unconcerned about how close the vehicles were. Patiently, people waited for an opening and then would cross another lane. Since some of the heavily traveled streets had several lanes, it might take enormous amount of self-control before getting to the other side of the street. Donna and I tried to find a traffic policeman before we crossed a street. However, it wasn't always possible to find one so we were on our own in navigating street crossings.

We visited the Egyptian Museum where a great deal of ancient artifacts had been collected, including mummies. However, the museum was not well organized with detailed labeling of items on display. Chronology was lacking, incomplete descriptions left us puzzled, and proper care was not taken to preserve some of the ancient treasures.

However, the King Tutankhamun exhibit was well cared for. We had seen some of the items when it toured the United States but here there were additional items shown. King Tut was just a teenager when he died but the magnificence of the artifacts that were placed in his tomb was astounding. One can only think of what additional wonders were found in pharaohs who lived longer and were more important in Egyptian history. Most of those treasures have been stolen by grave robbers over the centuries in the past.

I am compelled to comment further on bargaining in Egypt. Almost all purchases were an occurrence of bargaining on steroids. The Mediterranean Sea area developed over the centuries of time, created a bargaining behavior when it came to pricing items. There is no set price but a negotiated one which can be different from one transaction to another for the same item. Both buyer and seller must come to an agreed price that makes both of them happy. Simply being willing to pay what is originally quoted to you is an insult to the seller so back and forth parleying must be played out until a common price is found. The Egyptians have taken bargaining to another level.

Moreover, for any service that is performed for you there is an expectation of baksheesh, or a tip. To over tip is also considered bad form. One must be wise enough to offer an amount that is in keeping for the service performed for you. To under tip is an outrage and one is confronted with a verbal assault.

After we had seen Cairo, our tour guide had us board a train destined for Luxor. It was a train that would have been modern for the 1930's in America. However, the trip allowed us to look out our window and see the bent pyramid and the step pyramid. The train followed the Nile River and green crops were on the left side of the train and sandy desert on the right side.

We arrived in Luxor and were bussed to a very modern hotel. It was new compared to the hotels in Cairo. It had a nice swimming pool and two women were topless much to the delight of the men registered in the hotel and to the workers who were constructing a wall on a new hotel next door. We dined in the restaurant in the hotel and the food was delightful.

The next day we were bussed to the Great Temple at Karnak. It was constructed over 2000 years through many different governmental regimes and dynasties. Its pillars are large around and several stories high. The site is enormous with the Hypostyle Hall being 50,000 square feet in size. Only one of the four so called precincts is open to the public, that being the precinct of Amun-Re. Even though it was March, the weather was hot and touring took the whole day.

We returned to the hotel and met a medical doctor and his girlfriend. He had left medicine and claimed to make a living playing backgammon. His girlfriend needed a shower and their lodgings had limited facilities. We allowed her to take a shower in our room but wondered if we might find some of our possessions missing because we were wary of some kind of scam. Fortunately, there was not a problem..

The next day we were bussed to the Valley of the Kings and Queens where we were greeted by a new guide named Mohammed. Most of the guides are named Mohammed. This one was knowledgeable and talkative. He was in his fifties but well versed in information about the sites we saw.

The tombs were carved into the side of a mountain and were constructed over almost 500 years and were the burial places of many different Pharaohs. Some of the most famous Pharaohs were buried there including Seti I, Tutankhamun, and Rameses II. Each tomb had side rooms off the main entryway that were long tunnel-like passages that were dug into the mountain and measured over 100 yards. These rooms it was claimed were dug without the use of torches for lighting but rather metal mirrors shown down the main entryway with other mirrors reflecting the light into the side rooms.

Howard Carter found King Tut's tomb in 1922 with the sponsorship of Lord Carnarvon who lived at Highclere

Castle, the site of the later highly successful television series titled "Downton Abbey". We were able to enter King Tut's tomb which was quite small when compared the massive tombs of other pharaohs. He died when he was only 19 years old and DNA tests show than he was disabled, had malaria, and was inbred from the royal family. Yet, in spite of his young age and size of his tomb, his golden death mask is perhaps one of the most famous artifacts still being shown from ancient Egypt.

We traveled in the afternoon to the Valley of the Queens. The most famous is Hatshepsut, the only woman pharaoh. Since all pharaohs had a beard, she had a beard made and glued it to her chin.

One of the other members of our tour was from South Korea. He was an engineer working in Egypt. He shared with us that he had been drinking heavily the night before our tour of the Valley of the Kings and Queens. It was clear that he was hungover. Instead of going through the famous tombs, he stayed in the car and slept. To come all the way from South Korea and not see these amazing sights blew my mind. Perhaps he would return another time but this visit was wasted.

Our stay at Luxor was embellished by beautiful sunsets overlooking the Nile River. The weather was mild and it was a magical time to be there.

We were provided with a return train back to Cairo and while waiting for the train to depart I looked out the window and saw an Egyptian man in the train next to ours. He was on a local train that was in bad shape. He was wearing a long garment and passively gazed out his window. He was obviously living the life that other Egyptians lived, meaning poor. He was older, tall and thin. Viewing him I thought that while were literally a few yards away from one another, we were centuries apart in time.

When our train pulled into Cairo I steeled myself for the onslaught of hucksters waiting to hustle us as we had to make our way to our hotel. Our tour was over with Green

Valley and we were on our own now. We had made hotel reservations before we left for Luxor but had to find a taxi to transport us.

We walked out of the train station with our suitcases and immediately a man grabbed my suitcase and hoisted it on top of an awaiting taxi. I told him to take it down and he did. I knew we had to bargain for a taxi fare or be gouged by locals who would take advantage of us. I began to try my hand at haggling for a fair price for a taxi. The way the system worked was that you didn't bargain with the taxi driver but rather with someone on the sidewalk who would then summon a taxi to transport you. After many tries, I finally thought I had come to a reasonable price. The man loaded our bags into the trunk of a taxi and we got in. However, we were joined by other riders so that the car was full of people.

As we drove away from the train station the driver turned to me and said. "By the way, you aren't getting to your hotel for five Egyptian pounds, it's seven."

The taxi was moving so what could I do. Traffic was so heavy and we were far enough away from any taxi stand to hail another one, so I gritted my teeth and accepted my Kismet or fate. However, the added fare wasn't oppressive so Donna and I chalked it up to a traveling experience in an exotic land.

At the hotel, I paid the driver what he demanded but felt that the locals had gotten over on us but not badly so. Inside the hotel we got our room and I needed some additional Egyptian pounds. I had been told you could get a better exchange rate from someone in the hotel. I enquired about buying more local money and was told to go to my room and someone would be up to make the deal. It had the feeling of being at Casa Blanca Ricks from the movie.

Soon there was a knock on the door and a bellman came in and we made the exchange. It was only slightly better than the official rate but I felt that we had begun to live in the local culture.

The next day we traveled to the Mohammed Ali Mosque. Another guide named Mohammed, what else, said he would take us through for a small fee. We took off our shoes and put them in a canvas shoe covering and entered the mosque. Mohammed showed us the burial site of the Shah of Iran that was covered in greenish alabaster stone. He also said that Mohammed Ali had been an Ottoman Albanian who rose in rank to Pasha and a self-declared Khedive of Egypt and Sudan and is sometimes regarded at the founder of modern Egypt due to his military, economic, and cultural reforms in the 19th century. As I mentioned earlier, alabaster was taken off of the great pyramid at Giza and attached to the Mohammed Ali Mosque.

After this tour our time was up in Egypt and we left at 4 A.M. the next morning to fly back to Madrid in Spain. Upon arrival we stayed for several days enjoying Madrid's many sights. We then flew back to Marseille. Our plane landed at 4:50 P.M. and by the time we got our bags and entered the main terminal, it was well after 5 P.M. Europe was not on the Euro at that time so every country had its own currency. I had a few French Francs but not enough to pay for train tickets back to Aix-en-Provence. I had French Francs, Spanish Pesos, and Egyptian pounds. The exchange office was closed. A nearby hotel was very expensive and we were trying to watch what we spent so we could continue to travel and enjoy the rich sites of Europe.

Donna, who was so smart, came to the rescue.

"Rent a car. You can use your credit card. We can drive to Aix and have the car the next day to travel around. When we arrive in Aix, we book a hotel. They won't demand payment until check out time the next day and by then the banks will be open and we can exchange money to pay for the hotel."

That's exactly what we did. It worked perfectly and I again was so grateful for Donna's intelligence and having her for a travel companion.

We began to study for our next trip which was to Italy. We took a train to Florence and toured the Uffizi Museum with its magnificent art. We saw the statue "David" done my Michelangelo. It is a bold young man standing tall as he awaits his famous confrontation with Goliath. We also went to the Pont de Vecchio, the oldest bridge in Florence over the Arno River. There I bought Donna a gold necklace and the price was determined by weighing the necklace. She was happy to have it and it looked great on her.

One evening when we were tired and hungry, we found a mid-priced restaurant and I ordered in my few words of Italian, spaghetti Bolognese. After finishing all of the food on the plate, I was still hungry so I called the waiter over and tried to order another plate of spaghetti Bolognese.

He spoke to me in English and said, "I order another pasta for you."

I smiled and was delighted to devour the next pasta in a white sauce.

We moved on to Venice. We stayed at a hotel three doors from the Rialto Bridge and had a breakfast on the outside patio in front and watched the morning water traffic go by. It was a wonderful moment. We toured the Doge's Palace in Piazza San Marco where great artist's works are displayed, Titian and Tintoretto to name some of them.

We found a rhythm to our touring in famous cities. We would study the night before we were to begin touring the next day. In the morning we would set out and attack museums or other sites, have lunch, then use the afternoon and evening to prepare for the next day's attractions.

We visited the Peggy Guggenheim museum and its expansive collection of modern art including Picassos, Jackson Pollocks, and Alexander Calders. Like so many sights in Venice, you have to take a water taxi to the museum.

At the Doges Palace I saw and talked to Bob McKittrick the offensive line coach for the San Francisco 49ers. I knew him when I covered the 49ers for the Merced

Sun-Star. I asked him about the team's draft picks and he was enthused about a defensive lineman named Charles Haley. His excitement was not misplaced because Haley became a Pro Football Hall of Fame inductee.

We moved on to Pisa and Lucca. Most of the Italians in Merced County came from Lucca. It is a charming medieval city with walls that protected it for centuries. Its churches are unique and the food in the restaurants stood out from other places. There is a market place that was created from a Roman Colosseum and its shape is in the form of the old arena. We spent several days in Lucca photographing. We wanted to take back pictures to Angelo Naldi whose family was from Lucca. He had never been there so we wanted to be able to show him much of what his family knew before they left to come to America.

We worked our way down to Rome and saw the Vatican and the Sistine Chapel. It was being cleaned from the soot from centuries of candle smoke and the colors were bright and vivid. While inside St. Peters Cathedral I saw a church official.

"Donna, I know that man."

"You don't know him. You're not Catholic and you don't know any priests or church officials," Donna reprimanded me.

"I do know him. I'm going to follow him and talk to him."

Donna shook her head in disbelief.

I followed the man in black robes. He stopped at many of the chapels inside St. Peters and prayed. I did not disturb him but waited for him to finish. But then he moved on to another chapel and knelt and prayed again. I waited for him to complete his journey. When an appropriate time presented itself I approached the cleric.

"Excuse me Father," I began. "Aren't you from Poland?"

He turned to me and said, "Yes."

"Aren't you Cardinal Glemp."

"Yes," he said.

"I have been following your struggle in Poland with the Communist regime and I hope you have a favorable outcome in your resistance to it."

"Thank you very much for your concern. I too am anxious for a hopeful outcome."

With that, he smiled and walked out of St. Peters.

"Donna that was Cardinal Glemp from Poland."

"I can't believe you recognized him. How did you do it?"

"I saw his picture in Newsweek Magazine last semester in Merced. He and Lech Walesa are trying to overthrow the Communists in Poland and break free from the Soviet bloc."

We saw many of the attractions of Rome, Of course we saw the Roman Colosseum, the Baths of Diocletian, the Baths of Caracalla, Circus Maximus, the Roman Forum, Trevi Fountain, and many other treasures. This took several days and we enjoyed the wonderful Italian food and the delightful service that is common in Roman restaurants.

We had been to Rome before so we retraced our steps and revisited most of the sites that make it a special place in the world. The Eternal City continues to offer travelers an entertaining visit.

We moved south to Naples. Nearby are Pompey and Herculaneum, the two cities that were buried in debris from the volcanic eruption of Mount Vesuvius. I had been to Pompey before but Donna had not. I noticed that in the twenty years since my last visit, many more buildings had been uncovered and new treasures found. Herculaneum was a smaller city but still offered us a view of life there in 79 A.D.

Our hotel was not in the best part of town but a mile or so from the train station where we could buy newspapers and magazines in English.

One evening around 9 P.M., I said to Donna, "I'm going down to the train station and buy the latest newspaper in English."

The night was warm and the walk pleasant. About half way there a side street jutted at an angle away from the main road. There was a little commotion as four young teenaged boys were surrounding a woman in her twenties. She was annoyed by their comments.

"Avanti, Avanti," I shouted to the boys and they scattered.

The young lady was pleased that I had driven the young men away. She was wearing what looked like a yellow rain slicker. She turned to me and said, "Senore?" and she opened her yellow garment to reveal that she was naked.

She was a lady of the night and was looking for business.

"No grazie, Bella." I stammered and continued my walk to the train station.

When I returned with my newspaper, I told Donna what had happened on my walk and she laughed at my experience.

The next day we toured Naples' museum. It has most of the antiquities taken from Pompey and Herculaneum. Mosaics, pictures, artifacts and many other treasures from the past are on display. It was a major find.

Bob Scarpitto a friend in Merced said he had family just south of Naples. This family had a distillery that made Amaretto and other spirits. I said I would look up his family and bring back a sample of their product.

I contacted the hotel manager and had him call the family business. I booked a train to the village and was picked up by an elderly member of the family at the train station. He took me to the distillery housed in a modest building and was greeted by a younger member of the family, a man in his late 30's. He expected me to make a deal for transporting their products back to the United States for thousands of dollars.

I said I was there to pay my respects to the family from my friend in America and wanted to buy a sample of one of their products to take back to him.

They were disappointed but gave me a bottle of bitters. I offered to pay for it but the younger man said it was a gift for coming all the way to his business and I should give the bottle to my friend and his distant relative in America.

I was taken back to the train station and returned to Naples. I made arrangements with the hotel manager to transport the bottle I had been given, back to Merced. He charged me 50,000 Lira and said he would send it by ship.

As we left the hotel the next morning intending to return to Aix in France Donna said, "He has your bottle and he has your money. Good luck getting that bottle back to Merced."

I knew she was right but trusted the man in the hotel to be honest and do what he said he would do and mail the bottle back to America. Upon our return some time later, we learned that the bottle never arrived. The man kept the bottle and our money and took advantage of gullible travelers.

Back in Aix we reconnected with the Anglo-American Organization in Provence. That included several trips to nearby cities. One of the villages we visited was Arles, the place where Vincent Van Gogh lived at one time and the hotel where he cut off one of his ears in a tormented rage. We visited the actual hotel where the event happened and had lunch. Other diners were there as well and at one table one customer complained about the wine that was served and the owner of the restaurant agreed that the wine was not up to drinkable standards and gave the table one of his best to make amends.

Once back in Aix, we attended a lecture at the university and listened to a visiting speaker Sir Harry Hinsley, a historian and cryptologist who served at Bletchley

Park during World War II where code breakers tried to unravel German messages. Hinsley was instrumental in using an Enigma Machine which the Germans used to send coded messages to its military commanders. Hinsley and the English were successful in unraveling German coded messages.

"If a spy came to England, we were able to pick him up the day of his arrival because we knew who he was by virtue of our code breaking. We would try to turn him into being a double agent.

"We knew what the German military was planning in Europe. Unfortunately, we sometimes would allow the Germans to be successful in some of their military missions because if we laid an ambush for them every time we knew they were going to attack, we would tip our hand and lose the advantage of having knowledge of bigger plans."

At the end of his talk Sir Harry concluded that having the Enigma Machine shortened the war by at least two years by his estimate. That is a significant amount of time because the Germans were working on an Atom bomb and surely would have used it on Allied military forces and other targets. That the Germans would have used the atom bomb is certain because the United States used it to end World War II and if we did it, most certainly the Germans would have too.

We visited Victor Varsarely's studio outside of Aix. He is the "grandfather" of Op Art. With dramatic colors, vivid and explosive, flat surfaces seemed to have a three dimensional quality with bulging round objects appearing to jut out to the viewer. His art is creative and varied, exciting, and enlivening. It was a morning that was well spent.

On the walk back to Aix we stopped at a field where an American football game was being played with mainly European players. However, there was a smattering of Americans on the team. What was different about the game was that between plays, music blared out of big speakers. When the team broke the huddle, the music stopped.

Nearby were girls trying to be like American cheerleaders. Their outfits were not well designed nor were their routines done well. Many were quite older and less athletic than the cheerleaders we traditionally see at football games in America.

Similarly, the quality of the play by the teams was quite different. One middle guard came to the sidelines and lit up a cigarette before he was summoned to get back into the game. The effort was good but the execution was disjointed.

We connected with a wine club and Joel, the sommelier was a delight. He could tell by tasting, where the wine was grown and even what field. That was his claim but he was exceptionally knowledgeable. Along with the wine were cheese tastings. We enjoyed the same experience we had in Paris where seven trays (the size of a round table tops) of cheeses were tasted and enjoyed. Beginning with the soft cheeses of double and triple creams and working our way up to the hard cheeses of Blue cheese and Roquefort. Wonderful French bread and wine were served along with the cheese to make for a gastronomic delight and an unforgettable memory.

Our next trip was to the British Isles. We arrived in London by plane and I was put in charge of finding a hotel. I found one that was near the Charles Dickens Museum located at 48 Doughty Street which was his house. Dickens delighted millions of readers with his amazing stories and characters. Inside the museum one can see the original manuscripts in Dickens' hand. They are under glass and the tops are covered with green velvet to prevent sunlight from blanching out the ink. It is interesting to see how he would scratch out words and add others. Today authors using computers to write their works reveals no scratch outs because corrections are made on the screen and never seen by readers. Thus readers of modern stories don't get to see how authors change their minds about plots, characters, and settings.

We visited the British Museum. It houses the Rosetta Stone, paintings, the Elgin Marble taken from the Parthenon in Greece (the Greeks want it returned), and an extensive collection of Egyptian art collected after Napoleon's defeat on the Nile in 1801.

While touring in one of the rooms, I saw a man who looked familiar. I walked nearby and recognized him. He was Andy Griffith. I approached him and introduced myself and asked if he in fact, was the famous actor, producer, and writer.

"Yes, I'm here visiting before I return to America and wanted to take in this museum."

He seemed genuine, approachable, and friendly.

Next we got tickets to several plays and enjoyed the high quality of the actors who are famous for the disciplined and rigorous training they must master. Many theatres are near the Themes River.

We toured the British War Museum, the Tower of London where the Crown Jewels are housed, Westminster Abbey, and St. Paul's Cathedral.

I decided to observe court cases in the Old Baileys courthouse. There was a case involving embezzlement. It involved issues in the U.K. and New York. The wigged barrister was calm but thorough in questioning the man charged with the crime. The facts of the case were so well documented that it was clear that accused was going to be found guilty. I was so fascinated with the case that I returned a second day to watch the proceedings.

We traveled to western England and to Bath where the remains of Roman baths are housed, hence the name of the town. They were named Aquae Sulis by the Romans. There was a caldarium of hot water coming from a hot springs under the baths, a tepidarium of warm water, and a frigidarium of cold water. One would visit all three baths for relaxation. However, it has been noted that if you had a scratch on your leg or arm, going to the baths might lead to infection since clean water was not available due to the number of bathers.

Jane Austen wrote of the Roman Baths in her novels and today the baths are in remarkably good shape with columns and buildings in a good state of repair.

One of my relatives left Bath at age 21 and traveled to Utah where she met and married George Snyder who owned a lumber mill. She was his sixth Mormon wife. They had a daughter who died at a young age and my relative asked her husband to set aside three acres for a cemetery. Today, my Evans relatives are buried there.

We moved on to Wales locating in Cardiff. The castles are the highlight of the city. Cardiff Castle, Caerphilly Castle, and Hensol Castle are must to see. Garth Hill is the mountain where the book The Englishman went up a Hill and came Down a Mountain, served as inspiration. Dyffryn Gardens provided us with a tranquil moment of rest.

Walking back to our hotel, we decided to have a beer in a tavern. As soon as we ordered our drinks, the manager came over and introduced himself and bought us another beer. I bought one back for him. We began to talk and he revealed that he was Irish not Welsh. He insisted on showing us around the establishment. That included a tour of an upstairs room that was used for banquets. He was most charming and engaging. Perhaps the novelty of Americans visiting his bar had something to do with his friendliness but he seemed genuine.

From Wales we journeyed to Scotland passing Hadrian's Wall on the way. At one time I wanted to walk the 80 mile length of the wall that was built after Hadrian's visit in 122 A.D. It marked the outer boundary of Rome's empire in Britain. Today there is a misconception that the wall marks the boundary between Britain and Scotland.

We found our way to Edinburgh. We walked the Royal Mile visiting Edinburgh Castle, Gladstone's Land, Writers' Museum, the National Library of Scotland, and St. Giles Cathedral in the next several days.

Unfortunately for me, I came down sick with the "tourista" and had to visit the chemist (read pharmacist) and seek help. The medicine I was given didn't work and so I returned the next day to seek additional help.

"Still suffering from Holiday Tummy?" The chemist asked.

I nodded in misery.

"I'm going to give you two pills. Take the first one and if it doesn't work, go to the hospital." I was instructed.

I returned to our hotel and took one of the pills. I rested the remained of the day. The next morning the pill had done its job and I was feeling better and was able to resume being a tourist again and enjoying the sights of Edinburgh.

The food in Scotland and Great Britain was less appetizing than in other countries.

"Let's go to an Italian restaurant," I pleaded with Donna. She agreed that we needed some fare that was tasty. We gorged ourselves on pasta, salad, bread, and wine. It was a pleasant respite from other dinners we had.

We bussed out to St. Andrews on Scotland's east coast. Charming shops lined the street next to the famous St. Andrews Golf Course. I had just begun to play golf and could barely break a hundred strokes. I learned that one had to have a 18 handicap or less before you would be allowed to play. I longingly looked across the road at the course and noticed that some of the greens had two flag sticks. I asked a passerby why two flags on one green.

"You play one flag on the first nine holes and the second flag on the back nine."

Mystery solved, so we had lunch and bussed back to Edinburgh.

We returned to Aix and embarked on a day of filming the fountains of Aix. There were literally dozens and each had a meaning for neighborhoods. The grand fountain La Rotonde is in the heart of the city. There is a hot water fountain called Fontaine Moussue. Another is called the Nine Cannons where cattle would drink while migrating. The Four Dolphins was where our first hotel was and had a sentimental place in our hearts. So many fountains earned the Aix the title of the City of a Thousand Fountains.

We rested and planned a trip to Germany. It would be for two weeks and we would see Berlin. Once there we sought the Brandenburg Gate, the site of so many pictures in movies and where Allied troops blew up a Swastika that had been placed there by the Nazis at the end of World War II.

Passing through the gate leads to Unter den Linden, a street under Linden trees where many of the foreign embassies are located. It is a beautiful, pleasant street highlighted with good restaurants.

The old Reichstag looks ragged and many of the surrounding areas are a little seedy. We were able to ride a bus to what was East Berlin. The Soviets built a tall spire that served as a television tower and it's over 1200 feet high.

We toured Museum Island, the Old Museum, the Pergamon, Bode Museum, and the New Museum. We enjoyed the Tiergarten a beautiful inner city park. The Charlottenburg Palace rich in Royal history, made for a pleasant visit.

One of the highlights for me was being able to see the bust of Nefertiti the famous Egyptian Queen. I had seen pictures of the statue in textbooks and had wanted to see the actual figure in person. Part of her face is cut away but what remains show that she truly was a beautiful woman.

One observation we were somewhat surprised to see was that German trains didn't run on time as they do in other parts in Europe. In France and Italy, when the clock strikes the minute the train is to leave, the train moves. Not always so in Germany.

German food is hearty, good, and tasty. Large portions are served and a varied menu makes for wonderful dining experiences. German bread is my favorite in all of Europe. French cheeses are superior and Italian creativity is amazing. While the French enjoy a croissant, the Italians infuse their croissants with sweet tasting custard.

We returned to Aix and agreed that we had more than fulfilled our obligation for our sabbaticals. We had seen the great sites of Europe and they were enthralling but we never took time for us to just relax in a leisurely way. We decided to have a vacation by the sea for a few days. We selected the small town of Le Lavandou in southeastern France. It gets its name from the lavender flowers that grow nearby. We dined leisurely and took walks and enjoyed the seashore.

Our hotel had big windows and when opened warm air blew long, white curtains into our room. Donna and I decided to take a shower together. I loved Donna for all she gave to me in our relationship. She was also beautiful and standing in the shower together, both of us naked, aroused me. Our bodies touched and predictably, I became excited. In the dizzying moments that followed, I lost my balance and fell out of the tub we were standing in and hit my head on the toilet seat and opened a large cut by my right eye. Blood spurted out on the toilet seat, the floor, and on me. I grabbed a towel and tried to press it against the wound to stop the flow of blood. The towel became red with blood and while trying to stop up the cut, we began laughing about what had just happened. Then we became concerned because the towel was so bloody that it looked like there had been a murder. We didn't know how to explain what happened to the hotel staff if they questioned us about the amount of blood on the towel, so we washed and rinsed the towel over and over trying to bleach out the blood. Eventually, we were able to make the towel look somewhat normal and our laughter returned.

After a few days, it was time to return to Aix. This time however, it was to say goodbye to our stay in Europe. We packed and journeyed to Amsterdam in preparation for our return flight. We spent time at the Anne Frank House, the site where the Frank family tried to wait out the Nazi regime but unfortunately for them, they were found out and reported to the SS and captured. The family was sent to concentration camps and Anne it is believed, died in Bergen-Belsen of typhus. However, her diary has made her famous because of her insight and humanity.

We toured the Van Gogh Museum and marveled at his paintings. His mental anguish and torment pours onto his canvasses and have become mainstays in western art. In his lifetime he never sold any of his painting for more than $5.00, yet today they bring millions from collectors.

It was July 4th and it was time to board our KLM fight back to San Francisco. We had been in Europe for six months. We had the trip of a lifetime. We had traveled to Europe before, we had been to Mexico, and Canada but this was a journey that few people ever get to take. Donna was less anxious to return to America than me. I wanted to return to our friends and family and share our experiences. We both wanted to take what we had learned and include our new knowledge into our classrooms.

OUR NEW HOUSE

We arrived back in San Francisco and Donna's Mother picked us up and took us to her home in Walnut Creek. We rested for a day and got acclimated to America again.

I called a realtor in Merced and told her that we wanted to sell our home on McKee Road. It was my home before Donna and I got married but it was our home now.

The renters we had in while we were away had moved out at the end of the school year. I had alerted the realtor while were in Europe that we would likely sell the home upon our return and she had begun to work up prices and the details for a sale.

Donna wanted to sell the home because our dog Brandi had been run over and killed on busy McKee Road. Also, it wasn't "her" home in the sense that I had bought it and it was mine. She wanted a new home or at least one that was built after 1957, the date the McKee home was built.

The realtor put the home on the market and a day later it sold for $75,000.00, three times what I paid for it in 1972. Now we needed to find another place to live. We decided to rent an apartment and look around for a home. There were only a few listings on the market so we began to look into having a home built for us.

We eventually found a home that looked good to us and contracted with the builder to buy a lot and have him begin construction. It was August, 1987. I was hoping to have it finished by Christmas and the builder seemed to think that was a reasonable time for completion.

We prepared to get back to teaching. We wrote up a report of all of the things we had seen in Europe and indicated how we were going to include our new knowledge in our lesson plans. The school district accepted our plan without a lot of fanfare. We could have written up a one page report instead of the 10 detailed pages we created.

The lot we bought for our new home was cleared with heavy machinery and lines were drawn on the ground to lay out the foundation and install the rough plumbing. As school began, I would drive to the site of our new home and check on the progress it was making. I found that things were not going as fast as expected and that errors were being made in what was done. I called the builder's representative and identified where mistakes were made and insisted that corrections were made.

In my class I brought out the papyrus I had bought in Egypt and my students marveled at its rough texture. As the school year progressed I showed pictures of each of the civilizations we studied. Donna was doing the same kinds of things in her French classes and with her French Club.

The Christmas holidays approached and the home wasn't near completion. I didn't think we would get in by January. February came and it was still not finished. I began to put pressure on the builder to finish the job. Finally, in mid-March it was ready.

We called our friends who said they would help us get our belongings from the apartment and storage unit. I rented a trailer to haul the heavy items. Everyone showed up and the move was made. Donna made thick, wholesome, and tasty sandwiches and we had a bountiful lunch. When everyone had left we were still faced with putting things away and the garage was full of boxes that needed unpacking. We decided to unpack 10 boxes a day until we finished putting everything away.

Donna decided to take a bath in her new bathtub. However, we had run some items down the garbage disposal and when Donna went to run water in her bathtub, the garbage from the kitchen sink was in her tub. We were pissed.

The next day I called the builder and explained the problem. Their workmen came out the next day and found the problem. The cable company had cut through the drainage pipe in the front yard so there was no way that garbage could run to the sewer in the front of the house.

The next day it was repaired and Donna could now take a bath in our new home instead of a neighbor's house. However, there were other problems with the house. There was cracked tile in the entry way and the bathroom, and trusses were improperly installed so that the roof on the back side of the house looked like the tiles were uneven.

I called an inspector who worked in city hall and had him come out. The builder's representative argued with the inspector saying the roof line was only a cosmetic problem and not a structural one. The inspector disagreed and ordered an engineering firm to evaluate the situation and make a recommendation. It took several days for the report to be finished but the engineer agreed with the inspector that there was a structural problem and posts had to be installed outside on the patio to prevent further sagging in the roof.

Moving into a new home means other things have to be done. Blinds need to be installed, mowing strips need to be poured, sprinklers dug in, and grass and plants have to be sown and embedded.

David Olivares put in the sprinklers and his son and I prepared the yard for sod to be installed. David who was a plumber was out of work at the time so I hired him to install our blinds. It took us until May to get everything up and working so that we could relax and enjoy our new home properly.

Since this was a new subdivision, other homes were being built and the street was a mess with heavy machinery, noise, and dirt everywhere. One of our new neighbors had five children and they were noisy. As soon as possible, he built a skate ramp and his kids were rolling up and down the noisy wooden structure into the evening causing another neighbor to take up a petition calling for limiting the skating to stop at an earlier hour.

MEASURE "A"

Merced High School's North Campus was part of a two campus high school. North Campus used to be El Capitan High School and founded in 1959. However, due to the boundaries that were established, El Capital High School had a predominately white population and the older Merced High School had most of the African and Hispanic population. In spite of the best efforts of the administrative staff, El Capitan High School was considered "better" than Merced High School and a population shift was underway where people began to locate to an area of Merced that

322

qualified to be inside the boundary for El Capitan High School so their high school aged sons and daughters would be allowed to attend. Things got out of control as parents began to lie about where they lived so their residence would qualify for El Capitan High School. Some addresses were given that were vacant lots. Racial imbalance created de facto segregation.

Something had to be done to rectify the situation. The administration came up with a unique solution. They made Merced High School a two campus high school and El Capitan High School became North campus. Freshman and sophomore students attended the old Merced High School and juniors and seniors attended North Campus or what had been El Capitan High School. Now no one could say that there was racial imbalance since all students processed through the two campuses.

However, sophomores were transferred to North Campus in the 1970's. North Campus or old El Capital High School was master planned to serve 2500 students. As the population of Merced grew so did the student population so that North Campus was bulging at the seams. Portable classrooms were brought in to house the students. However, portable classrooms don't provide for lockers, gym space, science labs, etc. so that in time students were burdened with a lack of educational facilities that other high schools didn't have.

The answer was obvious. Merced needed another high school. However, the state of California didn't have the money to fund all of the growing needs of schools throughout the state and Merced was down on the lists for new schools when compared to Los Angeles, San Diego, San Francisco, and Sacramento. Legislators coming from high population areas like Los Angeles had more political legislators and therefore more political clout when it came to winning funds from the state for new schools.

So to relieve the overcrowding issue at Merced High School the administration decided to try to pass a bond issue for a new school. The only feasible bonds came under a program called a Mello-Roos bond issue. It required a two-thirds vote in the community and every home would be assessed the same amount of money no matter the size or value of the home. These were major constraints since cheaper homes paid the same amount of taxes for a new school as luxurious homes. A two-thirds vote was almost impossible to get in the best of circumstances. However, the need was so great a Mello-Roos bond was sought.

I had done some campaigning for trustees to the Merced Union High School board and had worked on campaigns for judges and city council positions. Since I was a teacher at Merced High School, I could see firsthand just how overcrowded Merced High School was. I volunteered to serve on a committee to try to pass a bond issue. I sought prominent people with whom I had worked on other campaigns and asked them to be on a bond issue committee.

Bob Carpenter was one the most respected men in Merced and would later be named the most respected member of Merced's population. He and I had worked on a judgeship race and I asked him to chair the bond campaign.

"Bob, I will agree to be a co-chair on the campaign but I want you to be the other co-chair with me."

I was flattered to be asked to serve as co-chair by such an outstanding man.

"I would be honored to co-chair the campaign with you," I said.

We began to plan by calling in other well-known community members who agreed to serve on our committee. We calculated the number of voters in the bond area and found we needed 6000 votes to win a two-thirds vote when projecting a 20% voter turnout. We studied other elections and found the 20% turnout number to be about what other elections got.

I became a speaker to community groups and educators explaining the overcrowding issue. I got a Catholic High School endorsement and some of the teacher groups. I raised volunteers to help with campaign tasks.

The bond issue as it finally took form called for one school costing about $ 35 million and it was a turnkey school complete with lockers, desks, library, gyms, etc. Our bond also called for a second high school to be phased in as bonds were paid down and retired from tax revenues.

The greatest obstacle we faced was the local newspaper. Its educational reporter came to believe that the state of California had the money in the till to pay for a new high school. When we called the state and asked the same questions, we were told that there wasn't money available. Unfortunately, the newspaper began to print articles saying that the state did have the money for new schools and all we needed to do was ask for it.

Our committee was flabbergasted when we saw headlines in the newspaper that claimed the state had the money to fund schools. Bob Carpenter approached the editor and complained that we were getting a different story from the state and that the reporter wasn't getting the whole story.

I called the reporter and asked to have a conference call with the state regulators where he would be present as well as members of our committee and we would be free to ask any question so that we would get the same information from the state. He refused.

We began to hear rumbles in the community that people weren't happy with the bond. I went to a super market and priced out how much the daily tax would be and compared it to an item in the store. It came out that the daily tax burden would be the same cost as a can of cat food.

I wrote letters to the editor. Our committee advertised in the newspapers about the benefit of the bond and plans for new high schools. We sent members of the committee to speak at service clubs. We walked precincts. We had fund raisers. We tried to get endorsements from educational groups. I spoke to a television reporter about the need for the bond.

In spite of our best efforts, the elections results rejected "Measure A". Merced High School was going to grow and have larger class sizes, fewer facilities per student, an impacted library, a shortage of lockers for students, an overcrowded cafeteria, and more wear and tear on every part of the school. I had worked on this bond for over a year and felt defeated and dejected.

DONNA AND BASTILLE DAY

The year 1989 was the 200th anniversary of the French Revolution. Donna who taught French wanted to go to France for the celebration. I didn't think we had enough money for both of to go even though I would have enjoyed the history behind the events of the day.

"You go Donna. You actually know more about French history than I do and because of your command of the French language, you'll get more out of the experience than me."

So Donna and another French teacher flew to Paris and enjoyed three weeks in France and the activities surrounding the jubilee. I stayed in Merced and took care of the house, did more with Caroline's family, and visited Jon over in Watsonville.

When Donna returned, I picked her up at the airport in San Francisco and we stayed a night at her mother's house in Walnut Creek. The next day I took her to the wine country in Calistoga where we stayed the night. We tasted wine and dined in some of the good restaurants in the area. We came back to Merced to get ready for the school year by working up lesson plans, running off materials to pass out to the students, and putting new bulletin boards up in our rooms.

RUSSIA

I was reading the travel section of the San Francisco Chronicle and an advertisement caught my eye. It was 1993 and we getting antsy about a summer vacation. We hadn't planned anything so we were on the lookout for and interesting trip

"Donna, look at this. There's an offer to spend 17 days on a river cruise down the Volga River in Russia with stops in Moscow and St. Petersburg (formerly Leningrad) and it only costs $1700.00 per person. Would you consider going on this tour this summer?"

It was a silly question. Donna was such a great traveler and wanted to see the world. I knew she would want to go.

We had been grousing at one another part of that day and this information was a good way to transition to a more civil tone.

Donna gave an unqualified "yes" to my question.

"You know we have that bottle of Dom Perignon chilling in the refrigerator. How would you like to open it to celebrate our trip to Russia?"

"I'd like that but we don't have something to go with it in the house and it would be a shame not to have something to eat with it that was appropriate," she replied.

"I agree. Why don't you go down to the store and find something that will fit the occasion."

Donna got in the car and left for the store around 3 P.M. While she was away I got out some small plates, put out napkins, and utensils to use when she returned from the store with whatever she found. I knew that she would find something good because she was a gourmet cook.

Time passed however, and at 4 P.M. I began to worry. The store was only two miles away, and while Donna sometimes took a long time to make a decision about things, this was a long time even for her. This was in early summer of 1993 and it was hot. Did something happen to the car to make it overheat? Finally, at 4:30 P.M. she returned.

"What took so long?" I queried. "Are you all right?"

"You won't believe what happened. The power went out in the store either because of the hot weather or because a car hit a power pole and knocked out the electricity."

"Why didn't you just walk out of the store?"

The doors are powered by electricity and they wouldn't open manually so that's why I took so long to get home."

She put the grocery bag down and took out its contents. She had brought back caviar, fresh bread, fruit, and some cheese. We opened the champagne and toasted one another. The Dom Perignon was a lighter style than American champagne and tasted wonderful. Not wonderful enough however, to pay its high price on a regular basis. By the time we finished the bottle we were both in a happy mood and looking forward to signing up for the trip.

The next day, I called the number in the newspaper and made arrangements to pay for the trip. It was offered by East-West Travel and signing up was easy. Within days our travel documents arrived and we were set to leave in a month during July.

The day before we were to leave for Russia we stayed with Donna's Mother Marie in Walnut Creek. She drove us to San Francisco International Airport and we said our goodbyes. Once inside the terminal we found our gate and were in anticipation of flying Areoflot, the Russian airline. I looked out of the airport window and saw the Russian jet. It looked like the same kind of plane that Nikita Khrushchev used when he came to the United States in 1959. As we waited to board the plane other passengers arrived at the gate and it was clear that many were Russia. They were carrying bags of souvenirs to take back to their homes. We could hear Russian being spoken and some clearly had been drinking.

We boarded the plane and found our seats near the front of the plane. In the back of the plane, the Russians we had seen at the gate, were drinking and smoking foul smelling tobacco, perhaps something from Turkey.

We began to taxi toward our runway but stopped suddenly. We stayed motionless for some time. I looked out of the side window and noticed that part of the plane was in the mud. Within fifteen minutes we felt the plane moving backwards. When we finally began to taxi again on the runway I looked out the window and saw that the nose wheel had been stuck in the mud. This was not a good beginning.

Eventually, we were on the runway and taking off. The Russians in the back were passing around a bottle of vodka and talking and laughing loudly. A blue hazed smoke cloud filled the plane. Several hours later we landed in Anchorage, Alaska. We got off the plane and saw another flight crew of Russian pilots waiting to fly the next leg of the flight over the polar ice cap.

We took off in the afternoon and it wasn't long before we were flying over ice caps below. This went on for hours. If any plane went down over these ice caps, no one would bother to try to rescue those who may have survived a plane crash, if any could survive.

Food was served and unlike American airliners, the meals were abundant. Chicken Kiev, potatoes, salad, bread, wine and dessert were offered. As the plane droned on and the hours passed, and the ice caps ever our guest below us, darkness fell. The drinking and smoking in the back of the plane continued nonstop. We tried to sleep a little but found little comfort as the noise woke us several times as we dozed off.

When daylight returned we were served another huge meal and due to the time change between the United States and Russia we landed at 4 P.M. in Moscow.

We got off the plane and were curious as to how we would be greeted by the Russian officials. There were armed soldiers and policemen waiting for us. They inspected our bags and had us take everything out of our pockets. I had $400.00 in American bills, mainly in tens, fives, and ones. The Russian official looked at the wad of money I was carrying, gave his approval, and passed us through to the main terminal.

With that concern behind us, we began to look for the East-West tour guide who would take us to an awaiting hotel in Moscow. However, no one was there with an East-West sign. We walked up and down the airport but there was no sign of East-West tours. I thought we had been scammed and were on our own in an unfriendly country. However, we had been told that we would be put up in the Izmailovo Hotel in Moscow so I came to believe that there had been a huge omission by our tour group and that we had to get to the hotel and hopefully begin our tour the next day.

I looked at Donna and said in an exasperated voice, "What are we going to do?"

Again Donna came to the rescue. "Walk through the airport and ask if anyone speaks English. Someone must speak English because this is an international airport. When you find someone who can communicate with us ask if there is a way to drive us to our hotel in downtown Moscow. Hopefully, we can find out what happened when we get there and be included in the tour we booked."

I began approaching people as asking if anyone spoke English. No one did. This was an international airport but I was able to figure out that it wasn't the main airport in Moscow. I kept up my search and finally I overheard a man speaking English to another person.

"Excuse me for interrupting," I began. "May I speak to you for a few moments?"

The man said he would be able to speak to me in a few moments after he had finished talking with the woman in front of him. The conversation went on for about 10 minutes and I was encouraged that he spoke good English but I was anxious about whether he could help us.

Finally, the man turned to me and said, "What can I help you with?"

I explained that we had not been met by out tour group and wanted to be transported to our hotel in Moscow.

"I can take you there but I can't leave here until after 11P.M. I have a client that needs to board a plane at that time and I need to be with her to make sure she gets through the officials who handle foreign travel."

I felt an immediate relief because we would have a place to sleep that night but realized that we couldn't leave the airport for five hours. Moreover, I didn't want to follow him around the airport for all of that time but didn't want to lose sight of him either.

"Thank you. I'll tell my wife that you will help us. We are near the gate where foreign travelers entered the airport. Is it all right with you if I check with you between now and 11 P.M. in case your client's plane leaves early?"

"Planes never leave early but I will be in this area if you need to talk to me further."

"I would like to pay you for your service. May I ask what your fee will be?"

"It will be $30.00 American dollars because the distance is 30 kilometers (about 20 miles) and gasoline is expensive."

"That will be fine, and thank you for your willingness to help us."

I only brought $400.00 with me and I planned to bring back souvenirs for our families and for us. However, the immediate problem had to be addressed and $30.00 seemed like a bargain.

There was another American on our flight, a woman from San Francisco. We told her of our ride into Moscow and she asked if she could ride with us. We said yes of course, and she offered to pay $10.00 or one-third of the cost for the ride.

After our driver had fulfilled his obligation with his client and seen her off on her flight, he came to us and said, "Come with me, my car is outside in the parking lot."

We followed him to his small car. Because we were so far north there was still some light in the sky. We all got in the car and he started the motor. No sooner than the motor started up it sputtered and stopped.

"Oh! I know what's wrong." The driver who name was Ivan. "I have to release a lever on my gas tank. People steal fuel so I have to have this valve to allow gas to flow to the motor. I shut it off when I'm parked."

Ivan was back within a minute and pumped the gas pedal several times, then turned the ignition key. The motor came to life and we were on our way. I sat in the front seat with Ivan and Donna and the lady from San Francisco sat in the back seat. Some of our luggage had to be tied to the top of the car but everything seemed secure so that part of the ride was a relief.

"Are you a travel agent?" I asked Ivan.

"No, I'm an architect. There is very little building going on now so I make my living in travel."

I found this incredulous but continued to talk about conditions in Russia. I learned from Ivan that the average person in Russia made a dollar a day in American currency. With the breakup of the Soviet Union and a change in the economy from a collective state to more of a free market state things were is a state of flux.

"Many people are making a lot of money in oil and marketing our natural resources but most people have lost their housing subsidies and access to state-run stores. Many people want the economic subsidies to return but they like the openness of the new state. Some want the return of a Czar or the monarchy."

The ride into Moscow took almost an hour to travel the 20 miles due to traffic. When we arrived at the hotel, Ivan said he would go in with us and make sure we were registered and would have a room for the night. His Russian conversation with the person at the front registration desk took over a half an hour. We learned that there had been an error on the part of East-West tours and that the hotel had guests registered by East-West tours but we were not on the list. We were called to the front desk and presented our documents and after another half hour passed we were allowed to be registered.

By the time we got to our room it was 2 A.M.

This was the hotel that was built for the 1980 Olympics, the games that the United States boycotted because Russia invaded Afghanistan. The USA was one of 65 nations that boycotted the Olympics while 80 other countries sent teams to compete.

Inside our room were two single beds. I asked if we could get a double bed for us to sleep in. The bell hop just pushed the two single beds together and said that would be our double bed. We were so tired and relieved to at least have a room for the night, we didn't complain. However, our worries were not over because we still had to somehow contact East-West tours and find our way to the riverboat on the Volga. I was determined to get up early and go down to the lobby the next morning by six A.M. and search for an East-West representative. I didn't sleep well that night.

The next morning I was up early as planned. I was on a mission to find out what happened with East-West tours. I was in the lobby of the hotel at 6:15 A.M. I asked the hotel clerk if she spoke English. She spoke broken English, much more than my two words of Russian.

"Do you know of East-West tours?" I asked pleadingly.

"Yes, they are here this morning."

I took that to mean that a representative would be in the hotel this morning. I waited and near 7 A.M. other people began to filter into the lobby. I overheard someone speak American English. I approached the two people who were speaking.

"Are you by chance using East-West tours?"

"Yes, we are."

"Will someone from East-West tours be here this morning?"

"Yes, we are going on a tour of Moscow with East-West."

"Would you point out the person from East-West tours when he or she comes? They did not send someone to pick us up at the airport yesterday so I'm a little worried about their efficiency. How have they been for you?"

"They have been fine. They picked us up at the airport and transported us here to the hotel and have been good."

My relief must have been noticeable as my new friends reassured me that things would be okay.

At 7:45 the East-West tour guide appeared and I almost assaulted him.

"I'm Bob Evans and here are my documents from East-West tours. My wife and I were supposed to be picked up at the airport yesterday but no one came for us. Luckily we were able to get to the hotel here and get a room late last night. Do you know if someone from your agency will be here to take us to the boat on the Volga for the river cruise?"

"Yes, someone will be here to take you to the shore," the man said in reasonably good English.

"I expect to be reimbursed for the cost of transportation to the hotel that we had to pay last night."

"Yes, we will take care of that."

My spirits were lifted.

"Will you point out the person who will take us to the riverboat when he or she arrives?"

"Yes, he should be here momentarily."

Twenty minutes later I said hello to Arkady. He told me to have my luggage in the lobby within a half an hour and he would take us to the boat.

I rushed up to our room and told Donna the good news that in fact, we would be transported to the boat this morning and we would be reimbursed for Ivan's fee to take us into Moscow. We have to hurry however, because we have to be in the lobby in 20 minutes.

Donna who was always late for any engagement began to rush to meet our deadline. Thankfully, she saw the importance of being on time make connections.

Within a half an hour we were on a bus driving through the streets of Moscow. Another 45 minutes passed and we were at dockside. We gathered our luggage along with the other people on the bus and crossed a plank and onto the riverboat.

"I am the director of the cruise." A man said who was dressed in street clothes that were plain and didn't project authority. His attire looked something a janitor would wear in America.

I put down my luggage and shook his hand and introduced myself and Donna to him. He smiled to greet us but was unimpressive. Our documents told us which room on the boat was ours and we found it ourselves.

Once settled marginally in, we decided to venture out explore the boat. We found an eating area and sat down. We asked if we could order food and we told we would receive a welcome meal shortly. When it came we were a little taken aback. The meal consisted of rye bread, two slices of tomato, two slices of cucumber, a slice of salami, and a cup of tea. This was breakfast. This should have passed for a mid-morning snack instead of a breakfast.

"May I join you?" The thin man who wore glasses and looked like Laura's boyfriend Pasha, in the film Dr. Zhivago, inquired.

"Of course, join us." I said.

"My name is Boris Romanov and I will be a guide for you on this tour."

"My goodness, you have a most historical name," I offered remembering that the Royal family of the Tzar was named Romanov. He said he was not related to the royal family.

When all of the guests were on board and everything was in order, we prepared to shove off from the dock. All of a sudden inspiring, maritime song blared, the motors roared, and the riverboat was tracking to the middle of the Volga River.

Some of the other passengers were American but of Russian decent. They could speak Russian and often spoke that language instead of English. We met a couple, she from New York, and he from Atlanta Georgia. They were not married but traveled together. She was a sexual therapist as well as a counselor of alcoholics. He was a recovering alcoholic and that's how they met and became travel companions. They were in their forties. He was tall and she was short, confident, and pleasant looking

Other crew members ranged in age from early twenties to mid-thirties but all served in some capacity on the tour. One we came to nickname the "Holy Icon." She looked like a lot of the pictures of icons we saw on the tour.

One of the passengers who was from Ohio fell in love with the "Holy Icon" over the course of the trip and wanted her to come with him back to America.

A young Russian woman who had just graduated from a university fell in love with Boris Romanov. This was becoming the "Love Boat" of Russia.

The boat had security, an ex-KGB operator named Alexie. When we were underway and on the river there was little for him to do so he got drunk every day. When we had tours off the boat he would accompany us as we walked along. On one occasion, a man who was obviously drunk began to walk with the tour and tried to flirt with some ladies from Cuba who were part of our group. Alexie didn't do anything to stop the drunk but did walk between the man and our tour group. Eventually, the drunk became tired of not getting a response from our group and walked away. I was surprised how little Alexie did to stop the intrusion.

On another land tour there was a small stand much like a lemonade stand we would see in America. The man behind the stand was selling beer and small bottles of vodka. I bought a bottle of beer for myself in order to taste Russian beer and I bought a bottle of vodka to give to Alexie when we returned to the boat. When I gave him the bottle he was most appreciative and offered me a taste from his new bottle. Out of the spirit of friendship, I accepted.

The boat stopped at Yaroslavl and we disembarked to walk around the town. People were anxious to meet us and tried to sell us Russian military hats, caps, medals, and watches. With the so called "peace dividend" that came as a result of a winding down of the cold war, and the new Russian economy, people were desperate to generate money any way they could and selling old military paraphernalia was a way to get some quick money.

At another stop there was a village made up of old buildings taken from other villages to show what a Russian village would have looked like in the middle ages. It included an Old Russian Orthodox Church with a wooden dome. Russian churches have a dome in the middle of the roof and four smaller domes at the four corners. The center dome stands for Jesus and the other domes stand for the apostles Mark, Mathew, Luke, and John.

On one of the days we were told that we would be cruising on the river for a long time with no stops. I went down to the lounge and began talking with a young man perhaps in his late 20's who was from Spain and working on a doctorate in Russian history. His topic was about the Russian Revolution. Sitting nearby was a woman in her late 40's and she joined the conversation. She was a history professor at Moscow University.

I asked if we could converse in English since I didn't speak Spanish or Russian and the Russian professor didn't speak Spanish. All of us spoke English so that was the language that we all could use to communicate.

I had done research on the French, Russian, and Chinese revolutions so I was interested in what each of the other two had to say about Russia's revolution. We talked for four hours and the Spaniard had several models that he was trying to apply to his research about revolutions. He had seen models similar to what I had researched and that validated that I had been on the right track in doing my studies.

The Russian professor said her country was in transition away from the heavy communist model and toward a more open society with opportunities for private investment and profit taking. She also mentioned that since Russia had lost its satellite states the society was in an awkward situation.

"Our schools have the old Soviet books that are out of date with the new order. We have access to western television and the ideas that are run on the screens are counter to the old system. Our population is embracing more of a market economy and that is the antithesis to what's in the textbooks. We don't have enough money to write new ones so many young people around the age of 15 are rejecting what's being taught in their classrooms. They see what's happening in the west and realize that the old communist information was propaganda."

It was a great conversation and we all came away with respect for one another for our knowledge and concern for Russia.

Also on the riverboat was a group of geologists who were attending a conference on how to market Russia's many natural resources. Many, like the Spaniard and Russian professor, spoke English. I began a conversation with one of the geologists and we talked about an earlier time in our lives when we well might have stared at one another with a rifle in our hands during the cold war. We got to know one another and I suggested that in a spirit of friendship that we exchanged neckties so we could remember our experience with one another. He agreed and the switch was made and I still have the necktie today.

Another day on the boat called for a land tour that had us visit a grocery store to see how Russians shopped in the countryside. If you wanted pork, lettuce, bread, and chocolate for example, you had to visit each section of the store to see if those items were in stock and for sale, then go to a cashier and pay for the items and get a receipt. Then you would return to the section of the store where each item was located and hand your receipt to the clerk and then you would receive the goods you purchased. Moreover, the calculation for each item was done on an abacas, not a cash register. It was very inefficient. I asked about whether the Russian people would consider changing to a more modern system and was told by Boris Romanov that people in the countryside resisted any change from the old system. Russian traditions die hard. It also points to the long history of Russia in that it has been isolated geographically from a more modern Europe for centuries and its traditions similarly, avoid changes.

The captain of the boat and the tour director suggested that we Americans be part of the entertainment that was presented each night. There were musicians, singers, and a ventriloquist that put on a show every night. Donna and I as well as two other Americans agreed to participate. Ruth and John, the couple who traveled together though they were not married, agreed that they would like to participate in the show as well. We sat around the lounge and tried to figure out what to present. John suggested that we act as American tourists who made many cultural errors so the Russians could laugh at our ignorance.

That night we looked goofy and said yes in Russian (da) when we should have said no (niet) and the reverse. The audience laughed and afterward many came and complimented us on our performance. I think they were just being kind and nice to international travelers.

One woman musician approached us with a balalaika, a stringed instrument with a triangular body and a long neck with frets. She asked us if we knew the words to the American song "Oh Susanna" and we said we did. We wrote down the lyrics and gave them to her. She came back and asked to help her pronounce the words correctly. She was most thankful after we went over the song.

As our river cruise was nearing the end, it is customary for travelers to give tips to the staff. We agreed that the maid service was very good and wanted to give them a good tip. The same was true of the cooking staff even though Russian fare is less than haut cuisine their service was good. The tour guides had done a good job and deserved a good tip as well. The captain had done a good job too and earned a nice gratuity. However, the Director of the cruise ship was a cold fish and distant. The only time he showed any hospitality was when we were sitting around talking about tips. Then he blossomed and tried to be an engaging ambassador. His intent was very transparent. He was only after the tip and could care less about us otherwise. He didn't deserve much of tip and so he didn't receive much at all.

When we left the riverboat and were returned to our original hotel we would be spending some time in Moscow. We looked forward to the upcoming sites.

The inefficiency we experienced on some of the land tours was ever present in our hotel. Inside the lobby, there was a gift shop and the clerk who was paid a salary, sat there bored to death. He did nothing to try to market the items in the shop. Nearby outside of the hotel was what we would call a flea market and the people there were hustling to sell aggressively their wares. They would bargain for prices, try to package deals together, and rush up to approach you.

At each floor of the hotel there was someone who had a small stand holding soft drinks, potato chips, and trinkets. They worked on a commission and were much more engaging than the clerk in the gift shop.

In Moscow we toured the Pushkin Museum and walked around Red Square. I remembered Joseph Stalin standing on a landing of the Kremlin and overseeing military weapons and troops pass in review at the height of the Cold War. Nearby was Lenin's Tomb. I also remembered that at one time, the line to see the Russian Revolutionary leader was a mile long. We however, were able to get in line of about 20 or so people and entered the tomb within a few minutes. The short line was a testament to the fall of the Soviet Empire and Russia's move to a more open and market driven state.

Inside, Lenin was lying in state. He was dressed in a blue suit with a blue necktie with white polkadots. He died in January, 1924 but has remained looking as he did when he died because he is given new embalming fluid regularly in his veins and is bathed in embalming fluid to keep him preserved.

We next entered St. Basils Cathedral in Red Square. Inside, every inch of the walls is painted over with designs and religious motifs. It is dark inside. Outside the onion domes are painted colorfully posting a bright, optimistic spirit.

We returned to our hotel and Donna, who always wanted to use public transportation, was determined to use Moscow's metro the next day to return to Red Square. I mildly protested saying that we could not read Russian and its Cyrillic alphabet. However, Donna wouldn't relent. The next day we found a metro stop and were amazed how beautifully decorated it was inside. We tried to figure out the right car to take to Red Square. We procured some Rubles and got on. The car was crowded with people. Donna's superior analysis got us to our destination. We came out of the subway stop and were in Red Square.

We went to the large department store mall called Gums. We shopped the stores trying to learn what was available to Russians and to us. Donna bought a bag with large handles. On the outside "Paris" was printed. The colors were dark brown and gold. After we had done our tour of the area we were poised to take the metro back to our hotel. We again found our way and were pleased with our effort to navigate our way around in a foreign world.

We got back to our room and Donna looked at her new bag. To our shock, one side had been slit with a razor and someone had gotten in looking for something inside. Nothing was stored there but the fact that the bag had been the target for a criminal act put a damper on our experience.

We did other shopping near the hotel. Outside in the flea market with vendors hustling to make a deal, we sampled their wares. I bought nesting dolls for my sister and a watch for Daniel, my Grand Nephew.

The Russian food we were served in our hotel was not the best. We contacted Alexi our ex-KGB officer who was in control of our security. Others agreed with us that we would like him to find a good restaurant somewhere in Moscow that served better food. He said he would look into it. He came back that afternoon and said that we could go to a good restaurant that evening. He had arranged for a bus to take us there and he would escort us as well as the other staff who had been on the river boat.

We came down to the lobby of the hotel and Alexi was wearing a suit with a white shirt and necktie. I approached him and pretended to pat him down looking for his pistol. He smiled and put his hand behind his back and indicated that he was carrying it tucked into the back of his slacks.

We bussed to the restaurant and were seated at a long table. At each place setting there was a bottle of vodka that was half the size of a full bottle. At the end of the building there was a raised stage and soon entertainers came out playing music and dancers began to display folk dances.

The dinner was better than what we had experienced on the boat and at the hotel. The main course was rolled beef with a vegetable filling. Donna and I shared one bottle of vodka and gave the other bottle to Alexi who was only too glad to have it.

The evening and the meal was a highlight and the food was the best we had in Moscow. When we returned to the hotel, we were told that we would continue our journey the next afternoon by traveling by train to St. Petersburg built by the Neva River. The city was built by Peter the Great to have a "window on the west" meaning contact with Western Europe. The Neva River flows through the city and has canals that flow off to the side, somewhat like Venice.

When we got on the bus to take us to the train station, Alexi stood and told us to stay together because there were pickpockets who hung around the train station. Upon arrival at the train station there was a large crowd. Dirt streets led to the station and it was a gray color and drab. Once inside the train we felt better about surviving the shady characters who loitered around the station.

As I walked down the aisle of the train, Alexi motioned to me to enter his compartment.

"I have some special bacon and I want you to have some." He spoke in his high voice as he handed me a slice.

It was partially cooked and like all bacon had a salty taste. I reasoned that he was paying me back for the vodka I had bought him when we were on a land tour off the boat.

"I want to tell you that no one will touch you on the train. It will take us all night to travel to St. Petersburg and if you have to go to the bathroom down the hall on the train, I will be with you. I will stand outside the bathroom and escort you back to you compartment when you are finished."

I was a little taken aback by his warning but was reassured by his willingness to protect me.

The train sped along the tracks and we were soon traveling through a wooded area. I noticed that a man with an ax was cutting down trees and building a log cabin. It was like a scene of Abe Lincoln from the 19th century in rural America.

When we went to bed in our compartment I lay my head down with the words of Alexi in my mind. In the middle of the night I had to visit the bathroom and when I slid back the door of the compartment, Alexi heard the door open. He came out of his compartment and walked me to the restroom. When I came out he was standing outside waiting for me as he promised, and walked me back to my compartment. He pulled an "all nighter" and performed his duties as he said he would.

When we arrived in St. Petersburg, the train station was quite modern. We were bussed to a hotel that looked like one we would see in Western Europe. We were given keys to our room that looked like a credit card that was to be used by sliding it through an electronic lock. The lobby had designer furniture and was very swanky.

There was a cluster of four or five women who strolled through the lobby and were very attractive. We were told they were prostitutes who offered their services to guests. The police looked the other way and there was no indication that anyone was going to prevent these ladies from working the hotel clientele.

In the next three days we were bussed around St. Petersburg. One site was a jail where Lenin's brother was brought and executed for being part of an uprising. The loss of Lenin's brother cemented his commitment to becoming a revolutionary.

We saw a beautiful cathedral that had massive amounts of green malachite attached to the walls. It was next to the Hermitage, the winter palace of the Tzars. The

Hermitage houses some of the best art from Western Europe and Russia. It has the Malachite Room where the beautiful green stone is featured.

It was here at the Hermitage where the Russian Revolution was started. The ship Aurora threatened to shell the palace if those resisting the Bolsheviks didn't surrender power. They did and soon Lenin, Trotsky, and Stalin were creating a new communist state. Visiting this area was truly a highpoint of the St. Petersburg visit.

Inside the Hermitage, now a museum, are wonderful paintings from Western Europe and from Russian painters. Thankfully, we were on a tour. The line to get into the building was long and had we had to wait, it would have been perhaps 45 minutes to enter.

Peter the Great built St. Petersburg as his "window on the west." He wanted to westernize Russia, to make it a country that was modern in shipbuilding, engaged in commerce around the world, and culturally advanced. The city has a series of canals spinning off the Neva River. It is sometimes called the Venice of Russia. However progressive Peter the Great was, his efforts were not lasting. The well entrenched cultural habits of old Russia again surfaced and in time, resorted back to a feudal state with peasants and serfs, landed estates, an aristocracy that controlled the economy and the political system. There was no social movement between the classes and the old ways of Mother Russia returned. Things remained the same with minor reforms here and there until World War I. When Russia entered the war she was ill prepared to fight a modern industrial war. With inefficiency running rampant, supplies of food, weapons, bullets and artillery shells were in such a short supply, that some Russian soldiers were sent into battle with only a prayer and a rifle but no ammunition. The Tzar, a term that means Caesar in Russian, abdicated on March 15. 1917. Ironically, it was on the Ides of March the, date when Julius Caesar was assassinated in Rome in 44 B.C.

Alexander Kerensky, a reformer tried to keep Russia in the war and make changes at the same time. The old guard didn't like the reforms and others didn't think the reforms went far enough. His administration only lasted six months and then was replaced by the Lenin and the Bolsheviks when the ship Aurora was set to fire on the winter palace.

A communist state was created and solidified in the 1920's and remained in power. After World War II Soviet expansion swept across Eastern Europe and remained in place until 1989. Our visit in 1993 was a time when westerners could visit and not feel the oppressive, heavy-handed communist state breathing down its necks.

After our stay in St. Petersburg we returned to Moscow and within a day, were taken to the airport where we had not met by East-West Tours when we first arrived in Russia. We had to wait several hours before our flight was to depart. Part of our wait was due to an official, in his twenties, who was bored and impressed with his limited authority. He stood around as passengers lined up to clear security to enter a waiting area before boarding a plane. He combed his hair looking in a window to see his reflection. He adjusted his uniform, walked away and got a hot drink, tried to order airline staff to perform some nondescript duty. After an hour of this behavior, he started to process passengers through his station. However, he took his sweet time looking over documents that were perfectly in order by demonstrating his official position as if he was preventing a nuclear bomb attack. Finally, we got through his station, entered the waiting area and eventually got on our Aeroflot plane.

Again, the passengers smoked, drank vodka, and gobbled up two servings of meals on the long flight to Anchorage, Alaska. Once there we deplaned and waited for the second Aeroflot plane to take us to San Francisco.

Russia left me with several impressions. The people seemed very approachable and friendly, at least the ones we met on the riverboat and on the street. However, there was a distinct class separation in terms of wealth, social standing, and power. I did come away with the thought that Russia was on the brink of ending its old ways from the past and a new day under new leadership.

Russia's history was one of staid backwardness with the exception of Peter the Great, Catherine the Great, and Alexander II, who freed the serfs. Alexander II was assassinated in 1879 by a group who wanted to end governmental control by the Tzars. Once these reformer's rule ended the old ways of Russia surfaced until the Russian Revolution took place beginning in 1917.

But now in 1993 I had hope for true reforms to take place in Russia. In 1989 the Berlin wall came down and most of the Soviet Republics had broken away from Russian dominance. Even Boris Yeltsin seemed like he was breaking with the past and making progress. Yet, my hopes for Russia were dashed by events in the years to follow. Corruption returned and a new strongman surfaced in Vladimir Putin who is every bit as much a Tzar as any of the former monarchs. However, he is diabolical in that he compromises elections, confiscates wealth from others, and tries to change the outcomes of elections in other countries such as the United States and France. Russia has become a world power but is not making reforms within the country and is destabilizing in the international community.

RETIREMENT

I began the 1995-96 school year with mixed emotions. This would be my 33rd year of full time teaching. Moreover, I had taught many years in summer school and had taught 31 years at Merced College in the evening. However, I would be only 58 years old at the conclusion of the school year in June. I had attended seven years of college before I entered my career and during my teaching career. If I taught until I was 60 years old I would get full retirement. If I retired at 58 I would receive about 88% of a full retirement. Coming from a poor background, money had always been an issue. My mother and step-father had always lived in a lower middle class station and groused about money when purchases were made. They always checked bargains in the newspapers for the lowest prices at super markets, we never took a vacation, and both parents had to have jobs to get by. There were no luxuries. Therefore, as I anticipated retirement having enough money was crucial to my decision.

Donna would still be teaching and bringing her salary to our income stream and since she was younger than me, she needed to continue teaching to earn her retirement. She loved teaching and worked very hard at her profession and both in the classroom and with her French Club.

I began to look at our finances. Beginning in 1978 we bought a home and turned it into a rental. Over subsequent years we added three more homes that we made into rentals. We broke even on rent, received some tax write offs, and hoped our properties would appreciate in valuation so that when we sold them we would make a profit. In 1992, we sold three of the rentals and invested in the stock market. Luckily, we hit the market at the right time when the high tech bull market was taking off. We invested in Microsoft, Intel, as well as tax-free municipal bonds. Over time we invested $16,000 in Microsoft and because it split several times, the value of our shares was $100,000. However, Microsoft was taken to trial and our value dropped to $64,000 when we sold it. Still that was four times what we invested in the stock, so it was a profitable venture for us.

We never took any dividends out of our stock investments but put back earnings back into our stocks and bonds. Our portfolio grew so that it was something to consider when I thought about retirement.

If I left full time teaching I knew I would continue to teach at Merced College part time to have that income for our use. However, I would be too young to just sit around and play golf so I wanted to do some kind of work while receiving a retirement check.

One of my former students was an almond broker. He was a natural salesman and he approached me about working with him by going out to almond growers and trying to buy their crop for three different almond processors he represented. He had made a lot of money by being involved in the almond business. I decided to retire and work with him. In June when I began to learn the almond business there was nothing going on in terms of growers trying to sell their crops. I studied the different types of almond trees, nonpareils and other trees that were pollinators that bloomed in the spring when bee hives were brought in to actually do the pollinating. As the summer wore on, I began to talk with growers and learned that they were skeptical of an unfamiliar person trying to buy their almonds. Understandably their skepticism was well placed because that was their livelihood and having assurance in the people they were dealing with was paramount.

"Growers won't deal with you unless they know you for a decade," a grower friend told me.

As the summer wore on I obtained a list of 200 growers and began to call them trying to make a deal. Three of them agreed to talk to me about their crops. One was willing to have a serious talk but even when I brought in my boss, the grower backed away.

It was now late August and I still hadn't made a deal. I realized that this was not the business for me to be in. I contacted my boss and told him of my decision to leave almond brokering. He understood and wrote me a check for my expenses and we parted on good terms.

I still wanted some part time work so I applied to Independence High School in Merced as an instructor. I was hired immediately and trained to learn how to fill out the forms for lesson plans. This would be very different from the kind of teaching I had done my entire career. This would be one-on-one instruction in several subjects (Math, English, Science, Social Studies, and Electives). This would be a challenge but one I took to it right away. I was allowed to work two days a week which was enough to help defray some of the loss of not having a full retirement. Most of my career had been oriented to classes 35 students and my team-teaching classes were 70-80 students in size so this was really different from what I had been used to.

The part time work helped with income but also allowed me to play golf and enjoy a more relaxed way of life. It was a pleasant change.

"You're now the bread winner so get out there and bring home the bacon." I teased Donna when she had to return to her classes in the September.

She smiled and drove off to Golden Valley High School and took on the rigors of full time teaching. She worked very hard at her profession. Her French Club took additional time away from her but she gladly took it on because it generated enrollment in her French classes and made a contribution to students. The club's activities raised money which was used for trips to San Francisco to see plays in French and sample French cuisine. What was left over was given in scholarships. Donna was in education for the right reason; to make a contribution to students and widened their world view of society as well as learn the French language, and.its history, and culture.

We both worked at our jobs for the next seven years. I retired again and Donna retired from full time teaching. The year was 2003. This was an important year for Donna. Her mother Marie, had moved to Merced some years earlier to be closer to us and to undergo hip replacement surgery. She came through it amazingly well. She stayed with us during her recovery. Unfortunately, she had a car accident shortly thereafter and fractured her pelvis. She stayed with us for two more months.

Donna's mother bought a nice three bedroom home and moved in after selling her residence in Walnut Creek. She made a good profit from the sale and was able to pay cash for her new home in Merced and have money left over.

For the next few years she lived close by and remained independent.

"I cut myself on my leg," Donna's mom said into the phone.

We drove over and looked at the wound. It was a deep cut and she needed to go to the hospital. There was no room at one hospital so I called our other one and got her in. When taking her vital signs, it was learned that her kidneys were not functioning at a healthy level. A nephrologist was recommended for her to see and when I took her to her appointment her kidneys were functioning at 6%. She needed dialysis and I began to take her to her treatments.

349

Her health declined and she was admitted to the hospital in November. Her health continued to worsen as she got MRSA infection requiring us to wear a gown and rubber gloves when we visited her. Then she began to aspirate her food which caused lung infections. Her kidneys continued to fail and she was put on permanent dialysis in the hospital. We couldn't leave town because we were on call because of her poor health.

Donna retired on a Friday in June, 2003 and the next Tuesday her mother died. The joy of retiring was muted by her mother's death. Fortunately, Donna's sister Charlotte had come out two weeks before and the two of them arranged for their mother's funeral in Walnut Creek. Thankfully, they did that because of the stress of dealing with the grief that came with Marie's death wasn't compounded by having to plan a funeral. Marie had a Catholic service at her church in Walnut Creek and was buried next to her husband at a nearby cemetery.

The only job I still had was at Merced College in the evening. We were able to take short trips and longer ones in the summer.

"The Chamber of Commerce is sponsoring a trip to China," we told our friends from Livingston, California, a town 15 miles away. "Why don't we all go?

We all agreed to go on the trip because we all wanted to see China but the trip was more attractive because it was subsidized by the Chinese government so the price was very reasonable. The trip included seeing Beijing, the Forbidden City, the Great Wall, and the Summer Palace of the Dowager. Additionally, it included a trip to Xian where the terracotta soldiers of the first emperor of a united China Qin Shi Huang were created. He lived in the 200's B.C. and there were 8000 terracotta soldiers, 130 chariots with 520 horses, and 150 cavalry horses. The tour ended in Shang Hai, a city that was lit up at night with spectacular neon lights. Our trip was scheduled in the spring while I was teaching at the Merced College. I decided to take that week off and go on the trip with Donna and our friends.

We flew out of San Francisco and landed in Beijing where we were met by our guide. We arrived late at night and were taken to a modern hotel and got to bed about 2 A.M. We were up early the next day and taken to the Dowager's Summer Palace. The weather was cold with overcast skies but the sites made up for the bad weather. However, there was a commercial component to the trip. We were taken to a jade shop where we were encouraged to buy some of the goods. Over the course of the trip we were taken to silk shops, lantern shops, and ivory shops. On the street vendors tried to sell us watches that looked like Rolexes. I bought three watches for $10.00.

Another stop took us to a medical facility where I was introduced to Dr. Lee who looked at me and said I had high blood pressure and was overweight. He wanted to sell me some herbs that would correct my problem. The real problem was Dr. Lee because I did not have high blood pressure nor was I overweight. I shared that with the translator who explained my comments to Dr. Lee. I did say that I had asthma and Dr. Lee took a look at my palm and yes, he saw that I indeed had asthma.

An ophthalmologist who was with our group saw this stop for what it was, a phony herbalist with no real medical basis. The doctor was offended by what was presented to us and shared his thoughts with another man in our group.

The man said, "Really, I just bought $900.00 worth of herbs. I hope I wasn't taken to the cleaners."

The air in China was so polluted we all got sick with lung infections. I came down with the malady first, the last two days of the trip. Others got it later after we returned.

The return trip was a long, long flight and that was followed by a three hour bus trip back to Merced. No one could keep their eyes open. When we finally got home we went straight to bed in the afternoon of our return.

I finished out the semester at Merced College and considered teaching an online class but demurred partly due to Donna's prompting. I had taught for 42 years at Merced College and was second in seniority among the teaching staff. The year was 2007 and now I was finally fully retired. My total years of teaching numbered 44 years of some kind of instruction, full time, Independence Study, and college instruction. I was 69 years old and I was ready to call it a career.

SOUTH AMERICA

"Donna, have you ever wanted to go to South America?" I knew the answer before I asked it. Donna loved to travel and was a great companion on any trip.

I continued. "When I was a young man I always wanted to go to Rio de Janeiro. Christ the Redeemer high on Corcovado Mountain with his outstretched arms looking over blue water seemed like an ideal lookout for a tourist. Below Ipanema beach with bikini clad men and women was a fantasy that needed to be satisfied for a young man and that was me. I'd seen movies of beautiful hotels with beautiful people walking around in luxury overlooking fantastic vistas and those scenes made me want to go and visit and be part of those striking moments."

"You are a fantasizer," Donna said smugly.

I responded. "However, I have since had second thoughts about Rio de Janeiro because of stories about rampant crime. People come out of their hotel and are accosted when they reached the sidewalk. I'm generally not afraid of going places but those events have put me on notice. I don't want to be a victim and I don't want you to be put in danger either that is, if we ever traveled there.

"We don't have to travel there. There are lots of other places that are appealing to visit." Donna offered.

"I don't want to visit the Amazon but would consider other countries." I countered.

Donna brightened and offered, "How about Argentina or Uruguay."

"I would be willing to go to those two places."

"Done." Declared Donna.

We began to buy books about both places and decided to visit Buenos Aires, Iguazu Falls, then cross the Rio de la Plata and see Montevideo, Uruguay. We looked at our calendar and settled on a March visit. It would be their September down there and the weather would be good. We booked airline tickets and located a hotel on the internet. We would fly to Dallas, Texas and transfer to another plane that would take us to Buenos Aires.

At the date of departure neared, Donna came down with a terrible cold and felt miserable. I offered to cancel the trip but she insisted that we go as planned.

We got to Dallas and it was windy and rainy, which didn't help Donna's health. We stayed overnight in a hotel that was near a mall Donna wanted to visit. The next day we went to the mall and found an ice rink inside where people were casually skating while a few others were practicing complicated jumps and turns. It was a nice break from rushed travel. We wanted another day so Donna could try to recover her health.

The next day we were taken to the airport and flew to Argentina. We landed and got to an ATM machine to buy some pesos. A taxi driver pounced on us and said he gave the best price for a ride to our hotel. We were dumb enough to believe him. We learned later that we vastly overpaid him for our transportation. Once inside the hotel Donna went to bed. I said I would go out and try to find a restaurant nearby so we wouldn't have to go far for dinner. Luckily, there was a good restaurant a half a block away. While I was out I walked perhaps a mile and a half to a travel agent we had contracted with to obtain documents to confirm our travel plans in the big city.

I returned and helped Donna get ready to go to dinner. She was able to walk to the restaurant I found and we had dinner. Afterwards we immediately returned to the hotel and Donna went to bed.

The next day she felt a little better so we decided to take a taxi to tour the city. For about $3.00 we could see most of the city's downtown area. Taxis were everywhere and almost all of the fares were $3.00.

Buenos Aires is made up of Barios or neighborhoods and each has its own personality and sites. In Ricoleta we visited the cemetery where Evita Peron was supposedly buried. No one really knows where she is buried. When she died of cancer in her twenties, her body sat in an airport and later bounced around the city. However, at the cemetery in Ricoleta there is a large monument to her memory. She was a dominant force in Argentine politics in the

353

1950's. She climbed the social ladder of the country by her beguiling personality and offering sexual favors to important men. Once influential however, she was a champion for the underclass while indulging in personal luxury for herself.

In Retiro another neighborhood, we visited the Plaza de San Martin with beautiful public buildings and toured the area.

Over the course of several days we saw the Presidential palace, the site of protests by Mothers of Argentina who demanded to know where their sons were after disappearing when arrested by the dictatorial government. We saw the pyramid at the Plaza de Mayo, symbolic of an early 19th century revolution. The Obelisk of Buenos Aires was spectacular. The national museum was a cultural gem with many European masters highlighted as well as Argentinian painters. The Japanese Gardens offered a pleasant relief from the hectic rush of tourism. Florida Street with its many shops showed a city with cosmopolitan charm.

I bought a Bonbilla to take home to my godchild Martina. It's often made out of a gourd with a stem serving as a straw. The locals stuff the inside with mate (pronounced mah tay) or a kind of grass, then pour hot water into the gourd to make a kind of tea. In the parks, vendors offer to sell hot water from their thermos' to those who are away from a hot water source so they can have mate tea while they stroll around.

Other neighborhoods had a special charm. Palermo had the most colorful buildings. San Telmo was the place of tango dancing. La Boca favored tourists with trendy shops and was the port we used to cross the Rio de la Plate by boat to enter Uruguay.

Once in Montevideo we took a taxi to our hotel 50 yards from the beach with beautiful views and a warm marine breeze that was coaxing us to come out and walk the promenade that ran for miles. We rested and relaxed the remainder of the day.

We set out by taxi to the main part of the city. Again taxis are cheap and easy to use. We visited the Museum of Fine Arts and found a nice sampling of good art. We moved on to the Plaza Independencia to view the spectacular site of a parkway with stunning public buildings.

The next day we found our way to the port area, the site of a World War II drama involving the German heavy cruiser, Admiral

Graf Spee. Hitler unleased this ship to attack commercial ships and it was successful in sinking several. However, the commander Captain Langdorff was instructed not to engage in battle with Allied war ships. Because the Admiral Graf Spee was disrupting British shipping the French and British set out to hunt down the ship and destroy it.

In December, 1939 the British found the German ship and a battle broke out. The British ships suffered damage from the sea battle but also inflicted minor but crucial destruction to the Admiral Graf Spee. Its purification section which converted oil into diesel was out of commission as was the desalination area and the galley.

Landorff made a run for Montevideo which was a neutral port and all war ships were allowed to enter. It was determined that repairs would take two weeks but under international law, the ship could only stay in port for 72 hours.

The British positioned their ships so that when Admiral Graf Spee had to leave the port, they were ready to bombard the German cruiser and sink it. Langdorff communicated with Berlin and the naval leaders of the Third Reich and a decision was reached. Langdorff decided to scuttle the ship by taking it out to sea with explosives set to go off after the 40 crew members were taken off the ship. Once off the ship the explosions sent black smoke into the air and signaled the British that they would not claim the satisfaction of sinking the Admiral Graf Spee.

Langdorff returned to Montevideo and went to his hotel. He adorned himself in his full dress uniform and committed suicide on the flag of the Admiral Graff Spee.

I remembered seeing the television show "Victory at Sea" which did a feature program called "Get the Graf Spee," which covered the drama of this World War II event. But now Donna and I were overlooking the port where the Admiral Graf Spee had been moored and it made our visit more interesting.

On a Sunday we visited the Feria de Tristan Narvaja, a park where a large flea market sprawled on for what seemed like miles. Every kind of item was for sale, clothing, purses, jewelry, food, furniture, etc. Street performers put on a show and people were drinking from their bombillas, or gourd cups stuffed with Mata grass that had hot water poured over it to create a tea. It was a festive day.

Upon our return to Buenos Aires we flew up to Iguazu Falls in Northern Argentina. There is a walkway winding through the flowing water and it as spectacular as Niagara Falls. But because you can walk around the area for miles, you feel a part of the cascading water show that is sensational. Donna was ill when we went to Niagara Falls so this visit to Iguazu Falls partly made up for her inability to see Niagara Falls.

Throughout our stay in Argentina we enjoyed the huge beefsteaks we were served even though they were a little tougher than American beef. Additionally, we equally enjoyed the Malbec wine that is widely produced and drunk.

One afternoon we were walking near shopping center and saw a dinner-theatre that included a tango dance show. We immediately went inside and bought tickets for that night's show. We arrived about 8 P.M. and were seated at a long table. At a precise time food was delivered to all of us and we began to eat. The meal was bountiful and the wine made for a festive mood. After an hour curtains opened and dancers began to entertain us. The intricate moves of the tango dance was spectacular with men and women fluidly twirling, bending, making quick leg motions, and intertwining their legs to the lively music caused the crowd to applaud furiously at the end of each dance. The costumes were colorful and sexy with women's skirts slit up the side to reveal beautiful legs. It was a delightful event.

It was time to return to America. We taxied to the airport in late March and when we looked at the airport monitor we saw that our flight had been cancelled. It was after 8 P.M. and we felt stuck. I went to the Delta Airlines counter to inquire about when another plane would come. I was told that none could come from Dallas where the Delta sent planes to Buenos Aires because of bad weather.

"You might try to contact United Air Lines, maybe there is a flight out tonight." I was told.

I went to the United Air Line counter and saw a long line of people waiting to check in. I got in line and finally got to the desk and was told that we could fly on their plane that was scheduled to leave for Miami, Florida in an hour. I showed the person at the counter my Delta ticket and she said that there would be no charge.

"What will happen when we get to Miami?" I asked.

"We'll reroute you to Washington D.C. where you will catch another plane to Dallas where you will change planes again and fly on to San Francisco."

We did not know when another Delta plane could get out of Dallas due to the weather and fly to Buenos Aires. So we accepted United's offer and boarded the plane destined for Miami. We arrived in the early morning and boarded another flight for the flight to our Nation's Capital. It was 6 A.M. in Washington D.C. and we were told we had to catch our next flight at Reagan National Airport. However, we were in Dulles National Airport. A metro line came to our airport we learned and would take us to Reagan. Shortly after 6 A.M. we became commuters on public transportation. When we got on the metro car it was empty but within two stops, it was crowded to the point of us almost holding our suitcases in our laps.

We got to Reagan at 7:30 and would have to wait until 9:30 to fly out. We were starved so we got breakfast and waited. The rush of people entering the airport while we ate showed that we were in an urban place where political power was meted out. Men were dressed in suits and women wore swank, tailored garments and sported high heels.

We finally got to Dallas and were delighted to learn that we would be upgraded to first class. Once on the plane the flight attendant asked what we would to drink.

"What are you offering," I asked.

"Sir, what would like to drink?"

Her direct question told me she had anything I wanted whether it was wine, hard drinks, beer, soft drinks, or juice. By now it was 1 P.M. so I asked for cabernet sauvignon and soon had a glass of the red wine on my table tray.

We got to San Francisco and were exhausted but glad to be back in California in spite of having to drive home in heavy traffic.

FATE

"Hi Bob, its Art," his voice said into the phone

"Happy holidays Art, what's up?"

"I've got cancer."

"Where is it located in your body?"

"It's in my liver and I've got three to six months. It's December now so I'll be gone between February and May."

"I'm so sorry Art," I said to my brother.

"I don't want your sympathy and I want you or anyone else to come weeping down here in Bullhead City. I want you to take care of my estate. Remember when I was up in Merced last summer and I asked you to you to take care of things when I was gone?"

"Yes, and I said that I didn't want to but I'd do it for you. Do you have a will or trust?"

"No, but I'm holding you to your word now. I don't have much. I owe three thousand dollars on my credit card but I've got a guy who'll buy my guns for about that. I've got a trailer parked in Kingman that's worth a couple thousand and that's about it."

"Guns? I thought because you were incarcerated, you couldn't own guns," I said in a questioning voice.

"I didn't tell you? I got a Presidential pardon from Bill Clinton. I can own guns and I got my civil rights back. I can vote now, serve on juries, run for office, etc. I registered as a Libertarian."

"No, you didn't tell me about your new status as a citizen. You sound happy about it."

"I am, but the reason for the phone call is to have you dispose of my estate."

"If there's anything left over after your bills are taken care of, what do want me to do with it?" I was probing to find out about his estranged family.

"I don't care; you can keep it or give to my son Billy. He lives in Las Vegas and runs a craps table.

"I don't have Billy's address. Can you send it to me?"

"Yeah, I've got it around here somewhere in my stuff so I'll check it out and if I find it I'll shoot it up to you. We're not close so I don't know if his address that I have is the same place where he's living now."

"Art, is there anything more I can do for you? Do you need money? You want me to come down to see you. Do you need anything I can give you?"

"No, just take care of my things and do what you promised."

"O.K. I will. But if you need anything or if there is anything I can do to help you, call me and I mean it Art."

"Yeah, O.K. I'm signing off, bye Bob."

I hung up the phone in our kitchen and turned to my wife Donna who was listening and knew what was happening. She was withdrawn, respectful, and quietly said, "I put your bagel on the table with a glass of milk." She had met Art several times but didn't know of most of his past.

"Do you want to go down to see him?" She said. "We can drop what we're doing and drive down to Bullhead City, maybe take him out to a nice dinner and a show across the river in one of the casinos in Laughlin."

"He doesn't want that. He stubborn and independent and seems to have things in order as to what he wants done."

I took a bite of the bagel and Donna stirred the fruit in her small bowl. We were quiet for a moment. Then it hit me. The contradiction of his situation was striking.

"He'll die alone Donna. You wouldn't think so because of all of the marriages and kids he's had but the fact is he'll die alone or at most with a couple of friends. I'll try to be there if I get enough warning when he's close to dying but it's an eight hour drive from here to there and there's no airline service. He has lived such a crazy life."

"How many marriages did he have again," Donna asked.

I finished swallowing a gulp of milk. "He had four wives and six children, five boys and one girl."

"I lose track, who was his first wife?" queried Donna.

"That was Jane whom he met up in Washington State when he was in the army. He got out and became a dance instructor in one of Arthur Murray's dance studios. He got her pregnant and they had to get married. We were on our way to Alaska and picked up Art who wanted to go with us. Jane was still in high school and stayed with her parents in Tacoma to finish school. She came up in June after graduating."

"Was his first child born in Alaska?" Donna asked puzzled.

"No, we were living in Ninilchik with JoAnn, my older sister and her new born daughter, Caroline. That was the place where there was no running water and no electricity. I had to carry water in a five gallon gas can strapped to a pack Art made. We all worked in salmon fishing either on fish traps or in a cannery. Only my mom stayed home and tried to create a comfortable life cooking on a coal stove and laundering clothes on a washboard."

"Art planned to leave in time for Jane to have her baby in the states. Alaska was a territory at that time. He hoped to make enough money to pay for a flight back to Washington before winter came."

"Oh! I remember now. That's when you all left wasn't it? Donna probed.

I chewed my bagel trying to form an answer that would be accurate and still hide my embarrassment about my family's dysfunction.

"Mom wasn't happy living a life like people had in the 1700's, She knew Mel, our stepdad wanted to stay the winter and none of us wanted that so we literally stole away while he was up in Kenai and we all flew to Seattle. She left a note at the house indicating where the car was left in Homer and another note on the car explaining why we were leaving. Mom didn't think she could reason with Mel face-to-face so she believed her only option would be to leave Mel and separate from the marriage."

Donna broke in, "Where did Art and Jane end up?"

"He got a job at Boeing as a riveter and Jane gave birth to their son John. They stayed in Tacoma but when we came out of Alaska for the last time we ended up in Salt Lake City. Art and Jane decided to join us there in 1955.

"Mel came down to Arizona where Mom and I were living and sweet-talked mom into going up to Alaska again in 1954. We went back up to Alaska and fished that summer and lived with a friend Mel had made in Ninilchik. That Fall I was sent to live with a family in Homer so I could go to high school since Ninilchik didn't have a school that went beyond 8th grade. After fishing season was over Mel and mom moved to Homer and mom opened a beauty shop. I still lived on the farm until spring because I didn't like Mel but when it was decided to leave Alaska in the spring, I moved back with my parents and in May we drove out and landed in Salt Lake City, Utah.

360

Donna asked, "Why there? You had lived in Tucson. Why not go back to Arizona?"

"Mel, the ever searching vagabond looking for a quick score, wanted to explore for uranium in the four corners area of Arizona, New Mexico, Utah, and Colorado. If he found it we would be rich. Art brought his family down from Washington and got a job as a carpenter. Mel found uranium but couldn't extract it from the school site where he found it. His next venture was to go to San Francisco, catch a boat sailing for Guam where painters were making double wages painting government buildings.'

We drove to San Francisco and Art and Jane followed. Mel missed the boat but found work painting in San Francisco for union wages, which were good. Art worked on a construction crew and his marriage began to fall apart. However, over the next several years, three more boys were delivered by Jane as the marriage tottered back and forth.'

"Art, who was always a little wild, now embraced a lifestyle that was fueled by alcohol, and their marriage became stormy. They separated and Jane went back to her parent's house in Washington State and filed for divorce. Art basically abandoned his children and didn't pay child support. He followed the pattern of our real father who never visited us nor sent child support.'

"Art met a guy who was on the run from the law and hid him in his apartment. The police arrived with a search warrant was issued and the authorities found the guy hiding in a closet. Art was arrested for harboring a criminal. Art jumped bail and went to Texas and enlisted in the Air Force. In time, the authorities tracked him down and brought him back to California. He served six months in jail at Santa Rita Detention Center in Pleasanton."

Donna's mouth was wide open in shock. "I can't believe he was so uncontrollable."

"Well, believe it. I'm going to make some hot chocolate, do you want a cup?"

Donna nodded that she did. As I began to prepare two cups I said, "And, that's not all.'

"When he got out of jail, he got a job in San Francisco with an import-export store and met his second wife Jackie. She was tall, in fact all of his wives were all and hefty, but she was happy and

361

easy going, very pleasant in contrast to Jane's drama queen personality. They partied and lived from paycheck to paycheck. They moved to Reno where Art began to bartend and Jackie worked as a waitress. Art always had a temper and layered with generous amounts to alcohol, he became volcanic. They divorced."

"Where were you when all of this was going on?" Donna asked.

"Through all of Art's adventures, I graduated from high school and got into college. In fact, I was at San Jose State and needed to get access to former governor Hiram Johnson' papers at Cal Berkeley for a term paper I was researching. At that time Art was living in San Francisco so I planned to stay with him overnight and go to the Cal library the next day. Art insisted that we go out for a drink which led to many more. At some point in the evening I found myself in the back seat of a car that had no brakes. The car was parked on the side of a hill. Art was yelling at the driver to put the car in reverse and back up the hill to get where we wanted to go."

Donna sipped her chocolate and shook her head.

"I graduated from college and did a year of graduate school to get my teaching credential and got a job in Merced teaching high school World History."

"You were married to Lauri than weren't you? But what happened next in Art's life?" Donna asked as she put down her cup.

"Yes, Lauri and I had our daughter Kathy but were having our own troubles. Lauri had screwed around in San Jose before we moved to Merced. I forgave her and said we could make a new start in a new town. However, she began to screw around again in Merced so we separated and in time got a divorce.'

"The second question concerning Art? He was tending bar and drinking a good deal and being wilder than ever. I visited him one summer and his friends, who were almost as wild as he was, admired Art for some of his craziest acts."

"How much wilder could he be? After all, he was twice divorced, a bad father, and living a life that had little hope of getting better," Donna said.

"Well let me elaborate. He met and married his third wife, Alice. She had been a Catholic but was now a Buddhist. She had a teaching job, special education, I think. After I got my Master's

Degree, I went up to Reno and wanted to spend a short time with Art. Lauri and I were now completely divorced. I went to the bar where he worked and his friends told me of Alice's mother's visit. Art had been out drinking and was hung over the next morning but offered to cook Alice's mother some breakfast. He wanted to make scrambled eggs. She looked at the pan which was apparently somewhat greasy and crusty and said, 'You're not going to cook in that are you?'

"Art took offense and grabbed her by the scruff of the neck and walked her to the front of the house. The house they were renting had three steps that led up the front door. He threw her through the screen door and out on the lawn and told her to go home and not come back."

"Oh, my God!" Donna gasped. "He was a demon."

"That's not all. His buddies told of a time when Art was tending bar some months earlier, and some blue collar workers came in and got loud. Art told them to quiet down and they yelled back, 'Fuck you punk.'

Art walked from behind the bar and went out the side door. He lived only a block away and he soon came back through the same door on the side of the bar. He had a shotgun with him and he blasted an empty chair by one of the tables, then walked up to the guy who yelled at him and stuck the barrel of the shotgun under his chin and said, 'Who you calling punk?'

"What happened?" Donna blurted out.

"The guy apparently said, 'We don't want any trouble Art and began to apologize.'"

"His buddies told me of another time some construction workers came into his bar to cash checks and have a few drinks. One sat next to a small, wimpy guy and began to pick, on him. After a few minutes the big construction worker turned and slapped the little guy's face and said, 'Did you like that?' Art saw what happened and reached under the bar where he always had guns. He spun two pistols on the bar in front of the construction worker and bellowed, 'Pick up one of those guns and I'll pick up the other one and let's see who's tougher you son-of-a-bitch.' The big guy begged off. Art said, 'Buy that man you slapped a drink, apologize to him and then get the hell out.' Art's friends were in awe while they were telling these stories to me."

"He should have been arrested," Donna proclaimed and she was probably right.

"I know, but in Reno, there's a little bit of craziness among the natives."

"Did you ever meet Alice?" Donna asked.

"Yes, Art told me where he lived and said I could stay there while I was in Reno. He also told me he was running a prostitute working in a cat house. He said she was coming to town and was going to give Art some money and wanted to have a good time that night after working a month straight. He told me not to tell Alice about her. About an hour later the hooker showed up at Art's bar and it was at the end of Art's shift. We all went to a casino lounge show where a band was playing. When the band went on break the hooker tried to give the drummer $20.00 but he refused. We left and went to another bar. Art told me to dance with her when the juke box came on. I danced through two songs and she told me she wanted to go to Sacramento that night.'

"I left them at the bar and headed for Art's home. When I got there Alice asked where Art was. I said I didn't know because in truth, I didn't know. He could have still been in Reno or on his way to Sacramento. I still feel a little sheepish about not telling Alice what was going on but that's what I did and I can't change it now.

"I lay down on the couch in my clothes, taking off only my shoes. By this time it was about three in the morning. Around seven, I heard a voice chanting. I didn't know if I was dreaming or not. The voice paused shortly then I heard a little ding, ding, and then the chanting began again. Chant, ding, ding, chant, ding, ding. I looked up and saw Alice. She had a miniature Buddhist temple in front of her and she was causing the dinging sound by striking a little gong with a tiny hammer. I got up and put on my shoes and drove back to California   "Whatever happed to Alice?" Donna asked assuming I knew all of the details in my brother's life.

"I don't know but I know they got divorced because the next time I heard from Art he was married to Sonia."

"Who was she and how did they meet?"

I hoped I could remember all of the events that led to Art's fourth marriage.

"I think she was a comedienne and worked in a lounge show. I guess they met when she came into his bar after she finished her performance. I'm not exactly clear as to what happened. She was the wife that gave birth to Art's last two children, a boy first, then a girl.

"I met her once and she told me that Art would roll dice with his customers to see who would pay for playing songs on the juke box in his bar. On one occasion he won a dice roll and the loser, an African-American, asked what Art would like him to play on the Juke Box. He replied, 'how about mammies little baby loves shortnin, shortnin.' The black man said angrily, 'You must be from the south.' Art replied, 'Yeah, I'm from South Dakota.'

"It was amazing that Art didn't get shot with comments like that."

"He was a bad father, a drunk, and a racist." Commented Donna. "Did he have any good qualities?"

"Not right away. He got drunk one time and Sonia called me. Art was in the hospital. I was covering the Oakland Raiders for the San Rafael Independence Journal and also the San Francisco 49ers for the Merced Sun-Star at the time. I would cover the home games. The 49ers had a home game on Monday night and the Raiders played an away game on Sunday. I went up to Reno to be with Art and check on his health. I sat in his hospital room and tracked the Raider game on television and tried to determine whether Art should stay in the hospital or whether I needed to help him get into a detox facility. He had drunk so much alcohol he had hallucinated and was hospitalized. Surprisingly, he seemed to recover quite quickly. Be he wasn't ready to quit his destructive ways then."

"Well when I met him he seemed to be sober and in control," Donna said.

"Yes, he later went on a drunk and I guess had endured enough. He was told about a detox center up in Elko, Nevada and he took the opportunity to dry out. That's when he became a sheep herder with the Basques in northern Nevada. He did that for a couple of years and then worked in a dude ranch doing everything from repairs on the place to cooking for the guests. He got tired of the cold and moved to Bullhead City, Arizona and lived at the Alano Club. It was a club for former alcoholics and drug users. It had a bar that served water, soft drinks, snacks, and provided a place where former users could socialize.'

"Art got a job in a casino doing hard count where he and others would take the coins out of the slot machines, put the money on a cart and roll it down to the basement of the casino to be counted and stored.'

"He also began to sponsor drunks who wanted to get sober. He would keep an eye on them, help them find employment, make sure they had a place to stay, and counsel them when the urge to drink surfaced. One guy I met when I went down to visit Art shared an experience he had. His name was Sam and he said, 'Art helped me when I was so sick from booze and I was throwing up. He stayed with me. He got me a job on a radio station, got me a room here at the Alano Club, and followed me around to make sure I was sober. After about a month I said I wanted to be alone to visit my mother. Art said he thought it would be safe to let me go out alone. I couldn't wait to get to a store and buy some vodka and just as I put my hands around the bottle, Art showed up. He had followed me to the store and said to me, 'You sure you want to buy that?' I put the bottle back and it saved me from falling back into a life of drunkenness.'

So to answer your question Donna, Art did have redeeming qualities but it took him until him almost to age 50 to express them.

Donna and I finished our breakfast and with Art in the back of our minds, began to resume a modified normal life, knowing that Art's cancer would interrupt the way we lived when he became seriously ill. We prepared for Christmas, visited with relatives and friends, exchanged gifts on Christmas Day and celebrated New Year, the millennial year of 2000, at the country club. Donna resumed teaching her French classes at Golden Valley High School. I retired from full time teaching but took a part time job at Independence High School. We didn't know when the call about Art and his last days would come but knew it was in our near future. Then in the middle of February, the dreaded call came.

"Your brother Art Evans is here at the veterans' hospital in Prescott, Arizona and he said to call you," the woman's voice said over the phone. He wants you to come down here to the hospital."

I replied, "I am at least 10 hours away by car and our town doesn't have air service. I'd have to drive to Fresno and hope I can get a flight to Phoenix and then rent a car,"

"He most likely won't last that long, he's close to the end.'

"Can I talk to him?" I voiced hope because I knew it would be the last time I would ever talk to him.

"He's in a coma now and unable to talk. He's very close to dying."

"Give me your phone number and I'll call you back in an hour." The nurse did but warned me that he might not be 'with us' much longer.

I was on lunch break and at home when the call came in. I walked around our kitchen helpless. There was nothing I could do to see my brother one last time.

I had to see another student in an hour and the lesson I had prepared would take another hour. I met with the student and tried to focus on instructing him but I was emotionally distracted. After I finished the lesson I raced back home and called the phone number the nurse gave me and when she answered she said, "He's gone. He died about 20 minutes ago. There's a lady here that wants to talk to you."

I heard the phone being handed to the other person.

"Hello Bob, I'm Terri. I live at the Alano Club and Art and I are friends. I drove Art from Bullhead City to Prescott."

In a stressed voice I asked, "What can you tell me about his last hours?"

"He was very sick. He threw up in my van. He couldn't hold down the pain pills so he was in terrible agony. I drove as fast as I could but it is 180 miles from Bullhead City to Prescott. I'm sorry to have to tell you this. When we got here, he was admitted right away and given some pain killing shots. He continued to throw up but seemed to quiet down a little before he went into a coma."

"Thank you for doing all you could to help him. I'm sorry but I don't remember meeting you when I was down the last time at Bullhead City. Art asked me to handle his estate so I'll be down in the next few days and I will try to find you to thank you in person for your efforts," my words stumbled out.

"Art knew he was close to dying so he put things in order. When you come down, look me up and I will help you with settling his things. My name is Terri and she gave me her phone number again."

I thanked her, hung up the phone and waited for Donna to come home from school where she taught her French classes.

"Art died this afternoon and I've got to go down to Prescott to make arrangements at the funeral home. I called Uncle Dee in Phoenix to tell him about Art's passing but I started to cry. I'm going to leave early tomorrow morning and go to Prescott to take care of things."

Donna comforted me and we cried together. She was so supportive and such a good person. I went to bed early hoping to get some added sleep before having to get up and 5A.M. I tossed and turned and looked at the clock to make sure I didn't oversleep. When the alarm went off, I jumped out of bed and dressed quickly. Donna got up too and was making me a big breakfast to tide me over on my long journey.

"I'm going to take the Solara because it gets better mileage than the truck." I declared. Donna nodded her approval.

"I'm glad you have the day off and I hope you and your friends can go out to a nice dinner to enjoy a much needed restful day. I love you Donna."

I packed my suitcase and was on the road by 5:45. It was dark and cold but there was little traffic as I drove down U.S. 99. I got as far as Chowchilla 16 miles into my journey when the motor stopped. I pulled off to the side of the highway and tried to restart the car. I thought this was impossible because the car only had 38,000 miles on it. I looked under the hood but couldn't find the problem. I did not have a cell phone at the time. I looked around to see if there was a pay phone somewhere. About a mile away there was a gas station. I walked in the cold morning air for 20 minutes and arrived at the station. It had just opened and I went inside to buy

368

some change to call Donna. I got her on the phone and told her where I was, told her to call a tow truck, and come to get me. I walked back to the car and waited, shivering. Thank goodness Donna had a day off I mused to myself.

Forty-five minutes later Donna arrived in our pickup truck. I got in and felt the warmth inside the cab. She said a tow truck would try to be here about 8 A.M. We waited for another 40 minutes and then the tow truck arrived. Driver hooked up the Toyota Solara and loaded it onto the back of his truck. We all started back to Merced with us following in our pickup truck behind the tow truck. We arrived at Toyotech and dropped off the Solara. I paid the tow truck driver and drove Donna back to our house.

"You'll have to get a ride to and from school from Nancy (a colleague who was a German teacher). I'm going to have to take the truck and try to get down to Prescott by tonight."

It was now 9:30 and the sun was up. I again started my trip down U.S. 99. After five hours on the road, I stopped at Barstow for a quick lunch then pressed on to Arizona. I arrived in Prescott at 8 P.M. and found the Veteran's hospital. I was told that Art had been transferred to a mortuary and was given the name and address. It was after closing at the funeral home so I would have to go there in the morning. I found a motel that had a restaurant and a bar. I checked in and called Donna who seemed relieved to know I made it to Prescott safely.

I don't remember what I ate at the restaurant but after feeling full, I went to the bar.

"I'd like and scotch and soda," I told the lady bartender when I got seated. When it came I drank quickly and asked for another. There was a young couple at the bar talking lightly. They wondered why I was at the bar, a stranger to their town downing drinks so quickly. I told them my brother had died and I was there to make arrangements. The tenor of their conversation changed to being quietly respectful.

A few moments later I heard my weary voice say "I'd like another scotch," and the bartender interrupted her conversation with the couple to oblige me.

She took my empty glass and replaced it with the dark brown liquid inside a new tumbler.

"I believe in the spiritual nature of rocks," I heard the bartender say to the young couple.

I looked over at her and her expression and tone of voice showed that she was dead serious. I thought I had fallen into Sedona in the Verde Valley of Arizona where the "new age" of "Harmonic Convergence" had captured the imagination of people seeking insight into life's meaning.

I drank my last scotch and headed for my room to try to get some sleep. I again had many problems to solve and they ran through my head as I tried to get to sleep. I had entered the twilight part of unconsciousness when I heard someone outside my door trying to get in. A plastic key kept being inserted into the lock. Then I heard the person banging on the door.

"Don't come in here, I have a gun," I yelled hoping that would drive off the intruder. I didn't have a gun and I was bluffing.

"I must have the wrong room," a man's voice said back in a caught-red-handed attitude.

I got little sleep that night and awoke early. I waited at the mortuary for the door to be unlocked. The man confirmed that Art was indeed there and wanted to know what I wanted done with his remains. Art had told me he wanted to be cremated so I made arrangements to follow his wishes. The man excused himself and came back with a triangularly-folded American flag. Art had been a veteran and had served in Korean War and was entitled to have the flag. He thanked me for Art's military service. I nodded numbly.

Gathering my emotions, I drove the 150 miles to Kingman, Arizona where Art rented a space for his trailer. I found the trailer park and looked up Vic, the man Art said to contract and introduced myself.

"Art said you're the man to talk to about selling Art's trailer."

"That's right, come over to my trailer and I'll give you the key to Art's trailer."

Vic was an older man, worn by age and bad experiences. His trailer was a mess inside.

"I've got a guy in mind who said he wanted to buy that trailer," Vic said.

"What do you think its worth," I asked.
"I can get two thousand for it."

Art's trailer was seven spaces from Vic's. I unlocked the door to Art's trailer and entered. It was cold and dark. Art hadn't been inside for months. I looked around and found his Presidential Pardon that was signed by Bill Clinton. It was on the wall held by gray duct tape. I pried it from the wall and walked back to Vic's trailer.

"I found this in Art's trailer," showing Vic the pardon.

"Yeah, Art was real proud of that. He showed it to me and to all of his friends."

Vic changed the subject back to the trailer.

"Art left me the title so all I have to do is sign off after the guy pays me the money. When he does, I'll give the cash to you.

"Art had said his trailer was worth around $2000.00."

"I'll shoot for $2000.00 more or less. I'll get as much as I can. After I sell it how can I get the money to you?" Vic said to me in a direct voice and showed tired eyes.

"I'm going to try to have a memorial service in two weeks at the Alano Club for Art in Bullhead City. Would it be okay with you if I asked you to bring the money there?"

"Yeah, I liked Art so I'll be at the service and I'll bring the money from the sale of the trailer if I can get it sold by then."

"I'll call you with the date and time when I firm things up. Give me your phone number." I said. "Thanks for being willing to sell Art's trailer and handling the money. It would be a lot harder for me to do since I live up in California.

A cold wind blew hard as I walked back to my truck. I got inside and drove 35 miles to Bullhead City and the Alano Club. I asked around among the members as to what I had to do to set up a memorial service for Art. Everyone was helpful and the manager was called and he set the date in the club's calendar. It was obvious that Art was well liked and the members were willing to take care of one of their own. I was taken to see Terri, the woman who drove Art to Prescott and delivered him to the Veteran's hospital on the day he died.

"I'm glad I have the chance to meet you Terri and thank you for taking Art to Prescott." I said when I greeted her.

She said, "Good to meet you too. I've got Art's things over here in my room."

She was blond, in her 40's, about five feet five and attractive. She like Art was an alcoholic and living close to her money and just getting by. She showed me a pile of clothes and shoes. On top of the pile was a wallet thick with money.

I took out the bills and counted. There 30 $100.00 bills. It was the $3000.00 Art was paid when he sold his guns. This was the money he wanted me to use to pay off his credit card. I was astounded when I realized that this cash had been sitting in Terri's room for several days and she or others could have taken it and no one would have known. I looked at Terri with an amazed look on my face.

Just then other members came by Terri's room and looked at Art's pile. The word had gotten out that Art's brother was here and some wanted to come by and say hello. One asked if he could have Art's boots. I said to everyone, "Take what you want but don't take Art's broad-brimmed hat."

Some came forward and picked through Art's stuff. Little was taken so I said, "What you don't' take, I'll give to Goodwill." A few more items were selected and taken.

Terri told me that Art banked at a branch about a mile away.

"Thanks," I said. I looked at my watch and realized the bank was still open. I drove there and told the teller I wanted to pay off Art's credit card account. I gave her the $3000.00 in cash and made Art's financial world right.

I drove across the four miles to the Colorado River, crossed it and got a room at Harrah's in Laughlin, Nevada. I was exhausted. I called Donna and told her all that I had done in this single day. She was so sweet on the phone I wished I could have pulled her through the telephone wires and hugged her. She ended the call by saying that she loved me and I felt it. I loved her back with all of my heart.

Two weeks later Donna, JoAnn my sister, and I drove from Merced to Bullhead City for Art's Memorial service. The room was packed with Alano Club members. A table with chairs was set up in the front of the room so we could preside over the ceremony. I had called Billy, Art's son about the service and he said he would attend. I looked around but he was not in the room. I wondered what happened. Then I realized that there was a time difference between Nevada and Arizona but Billy hadn't.

I began by introducing myself, Donna and JoAnn. I thanked everyone for coming to the service. Then I expressed my opinion that Art should have been born in 1832, not 1932. He had a pioneering personality, rough and tumble, defiant of authority, and depending on himself to get by. Somewhat of a loner, he preferred a lifestyle that was more suited to the old west.

I told the audience that Art called me to describe one of his back country trips. He said he was going to trek with his burros from Reno to Elko, Nevada, a distance of almost 300 miles on foot. I told him to tell me his departure date and his intended arrival in Elko. I asked him to call me when he got there. I said that if I didn't hear from him within a reasonable amount of time after his arrival date, I would call out a search and rescue unit to find him. Within two days after he said he would be in Elko he called.

"I made it, Bob!" he exclaimed, proud of himself for successfully accomplishing his goal. "I'm in Elko."

I heard the sound of cars going by and I asked, "Where are your burros?"

"I'm in a phone booth and the burros? They're across the street grazing in the cemetery."

"Art, use some common sense and show some respect for the departed and get your burros out of there."

"All right, I'll let them graze along the roadside."

"How are you getting back to Reno and what are you going to do with the burros?"

"A friend is going to drive over and pick me up. He'll bring a trailer for the burros and we'll all go back together to Reno."

The audience laughed and nodded their heads in agreement that that was Art's personality. I wound up my eulogy and opened the floor for others to share their experiences with Art.

Terri spoke first. She said that she wondered about the great desert surrounding bullhead City, Arizona and Laughlin, Nevada. She said that others told her to contact Art. She did and he took her

373

out into the desert and showed her Native American petroglyphs or rock carvings. She realized that Art knew what he was talking about as he explained the time frame when the carvings were made and by what tribes.

Another man who called himself Bill, told of the time when Art wanted Bill to join him and backpack from Bullhead City to Barstow, a distance of over 160 miles. Bill said he declined but didn't put it past Art to attempt the trek.

Someone named Chuck stood up and told about the time Art shot a rattle snake in the head with his pistol when he was out in the desert. Art put the dead snake in a sack and brought it back to the Alano Club and cut it up, cooked it, and served it to unsuspecting diners who were told the meat chunks were cut up dove breasts. After everyone had eaten, Art told them it was rattlesnake with the expected retching that followed.

The serviced went on for an hour and near the end Billy, Art's son, showed up. I introduced him to the audience and he was welcomed to the assemblage and some commented on how much he looked like Art.

My sister was asked if she wanted to say anything.

"I can't. I'll just break down and cry."

After the service I sought out Terri and told her how appreciative I was for her driving Art to the VA hospital and attending to Art's things so that I could take care of his small estate. Her look showed me that she and Art had a bond, "even though I'm a lesbian," she declared.

Next Vic came up to me and handed me $1800.00, the proceeds from the sale of Art's trailer. I didn't care that Vic pocketed $200.00 for himself. He had helped me in a difficult time and needed the money. I took a hundred from the money he gave me and stuffed in his shirt pocket.

I found Billy and pulled him aside.

"Here's the money from the sale of your Dad's trailer. It's all he has to give you."

Billy didn't expect anything from Art and he had an awkward expression on his face when he took the money.

"Thanks, I guess," he said sheepishly.

The next day the wind was blowing 20 miles an hour and it was cold outside. I drove out into the desert by myself and found a spot near the petroglyphs that Art had shown Terri.

I said to no one but the desert, "Let this strong wind spread your ashes over the land you love."

I pried open his urn and scattered Art's ashes in the desert. The wind swirled around me and I could taste some of Art's ashes in my mouth.

Art had died with no family nearby. He had friends who served as surrogates and cared for his health and belongings. But somehow, his death had a sadness attached to it and I felt an emotional emptiness for him.

Donna, JoAnn and I headed back to Merced and I asked my sister if she would like a service like Art had. She emphatically said, "NO!" Then she went on. "I don't want any service. I want to be cremated and have my ashes put next to Emil."

Like Art, JoAnn had been married four times too and Emil was her last husband. Her first husband was Joe. He was in the Air Force stationed at Davis Monthan Air Force Base just outside of Tucson, Arizona. Joe was assigned to special services and played the clarinet in the band. He was slightly built and thin. It was a marriage between two immature people and didn't last long.

JoAnn's next husband was Robert who was also in the Air Force. He was a tall, handsome man and was assigned to the security forces at the base. He was in his thirties, seemed confident in himself, and impressed all of us when he picked up JoAnn in a white dinner jacket. They were married and Robert was reassigned to Colorado. They lived in Manitou Springs and soon JoAnn was pregnant. She applied for spousal benefits from the Air Force and was told by way of a formal letter that another woman was already receiving benefits under Robert's name. The shock of learning that her new husband was a bigamist shattered her.

She left Robert and came back to Tucson and lived with us in our small house on East Lee Street and waited for her child to be born. Her daughter Caroline was born in April and we were all delighted to have a baby in the house, even under the heavy, dark cloud of her mother's disastrous marriage.

Robert had promised to send money to JoAnn while he was getting a divorce. He made her promise that she wouldn't contract his superior officer about already being married.

The next month a check for $75.00 arrived with JoAnn's name on it and she showed it to Mel as evidence that Robert was acting in good faith. The next month saw another check came. This time is was for $50.00. The next month nothing came nor did any money come for the next four months. Mel felt validated that he was right to question the whole arrangement and JoAnn retreated into more of a shell of knowing that the relationship was over. She felt shame and a deep hurt because she had been betrayed. She applied for an annulment and it was granted.

Mel in addition to being the grand inquisitor was always a fortune seeker hoping for the quick strike. In the years following we went to Alaska and back three times and JoAnn and baby Caroline went with us on two occasions. When Mel's latest venture failed, we came back out of Alaska to Salt Lake City, Utah. Mel was seeking uranium in the four corners of Arizona, New Mexico, Colorado, and Utah hoping to find a bonanza but of course, he failed.

We moved to California with Mel hoping to catch a ship to Guam to be a painter on government building for great wages. He missed the boat s we stayed in San Francisco until my asthma got so bad. We then moved to Atherton, not the wealthy part of Atherton but near the railroad tracks.

JoAnn got a job at Hewlett Packard and moved out with Caroline into a small bungalow and happily got away from Mel's dominating personality. After several years she met another man named Joe and they married and moved across the bay to Hayward. This marriage last a fairly short time too and JoAnn moved to Palo Alto and rented a small house.

From Palo Alto JoAnn was able to take Spanish classes at Foothill Community College and became fluent in the language.

She had a talent for language and her courses provided a break from work and living on the edge financially.

Some years later she met Emil, a man considerable older than she was. He had been married before but had been divorced for several years. He had invested his money wisely and had enough of a nest egg to buy a nice home in Sunnyvale. They lived there until JoAnn was 50 years old.

Caroline a teenager disliked the new family arrangement. Caroline began to have feelings of abandonment. She graduated from Gunn High School and enrolled in nearby Foothill Community College. Caroline was working at a Veteran's Hospital and living in a halfway house earning room and board. She met a man named Pete who was something of a hippy, bearded and scruffy. They started a relationship.

The next year JoAnn and Emil moved to Mexico. He had retired as a teamster and wanted a cheaper lifestyle. JoAnn was willing to move to Mexico and use her Spanish and apply her language skills. They settled in Guadalajara, hired a maid, and began living the life of ex-patriots. Over time, they moved from place to place and eventually settled near Lake Chapala where there was an American community of USA citizens.

Caroline and Pete moved to Arizona and married. Caroline delivered her first son, Daniel. She and Pete divorced and Caroline moved to Merced where I was living and teaching. She was working in the medical field and met a young doctor. They married and had three more children. The first however, passed away soon after her birth. The two who came after, Emily and Alex were perfectly healthy.

In time Emil and JoAnn moved to Merced, then back to Mexico where Emil passed away. JoAnn moved back to Merced to be near Caroline.

JoAnn was a difficult person to deal with, being judgmental and limiting the number of people she could relate to. She and Caroline continued to have difficulty with mother-daughter issues. JoAnn thought Caroline drank too much and objected to her behavior when she was inebriated. Caroline could only accept her mother in small amounts of time because JoAnn seemed to find fault with her and expressed disdain.

JoAnn now in her seventies, suffered a setback in her health. She learned she had cancer in her cervix. Surgery was performed and she became part of a medical study at Stanford University. She drove herself over and back and experienced all of the attendant aftereffects of chemotherapy; nausea, fatigue, loss of hair, and weakness.

"JoAnn, you shouldn't have to drive yourself over to Palo Alto every time. Donna and I are willing to take you to Stanford for your treatments from time to time.'

"I would like that but I can drive myself if you're busy," JoAnn said asserting her independence.

Stanford generally processed her visits efficiently. However, on several visits the staff was insensitive to the fact that JoAnn had to drive 130 miles each way for her treatments. Her chemo infusions took three to four hours. One time there was a miscommunication between the doctor and the nurse. The doctor was paged but didn't understand the page and didn't communicate back so JoAnn's treatment was delayed two hours until the nurse finally walked down to the lower floor and sought out the doctor to get authorization to begin JoAnn's infusion.

Another time JoAnn was told she had to do a second treatment the next day. She had to stay in a motel at a considerable expense because of the high cost of things in Palo Alto. When she arrived the next day, she was told she didn't have to have another treatment. There had been a mistake.

Many of the doctors at Stanford are from other countries and there is sometimes a communication issue between staff and patients. It extracts a burden on those receiving treatment often times.

Caroline had moved to Pleasanton, some distance from Merced and her husband came up on weekends. The relationship predictably drifted apart and a divorce was begun. In addition to the stress of divorce proceedings, Caroline felt more pressure due to her Mother's health.

JoAnn was in denial that her cancer had metastasized to her breast.

"It's only a bug bite," she insisted.

When finally examined, her doctor said it was quite advanced. She underwent a mastectomy and more cancer treatments.

One day JoAnn called and said, "Bob, come over here, I think I'm having a heart attack."

I rushed over to her house but once I got there she said, "I don't want to go to the hospital. I just want to lay here for a while. I think it will pass."

I decided to act. I called 911 as she vehemently protested. The ambulance arrived and the medical people talked to her. She still didn't want to go to the hospital.

"I think it's only gas." She insisted.

I finally said, "Why don't you go to the hospital and have it checked out. If you're okay then I'll drive you back home."

With that, she finally consented. In fact, she did have a mild heart attack. The reason for not wanting to go to the hospital was a fear of having to pay for the ambulance. Weeks later she learned that her insurance paid for the emergency services and she used ambulances in the future without a protest when needs arose.

She recovered from the heart attack but her cancer continued to require treatment. She saw a general practitioner who was from Mexico. Together they spoke Spanish to one another. As JoAnn's health got worse she lost weight, lost much of her appetite, felt weak, could do little around her condo, and required more attention. Much to my surprise, her Spanish-speaking doctor came to her home and gave her injections to reduce some of the suffering from pain. This occurred several times and each time I was there to witness her medical care that was going way beyond office visits. I appreciated what her doctor was doing to help JoAnn.

JoAnn began to experience pain in her back. Her primary care physician suggested she see a back surgeon. She was the first of the four doctors I took JoAnn to see that day. Next, we visited a back surgeon. He required that she see her cardiologist who was imprecise as to whether he heart was strong enough to withstand spine surgery. After that JoAnn had to see her oncologist. We began that day at 9 A.M., saw four doctors, and visited two different pharmacies. At each doctor's office we had to wait a minimum of 45 minutes and the heart doctor was close to two hours. She had to have a nuclear stress test during which she began to vomit which weakened her frail health further. I drove JoAnn home at 6 P.M. I was in good health but was exhausted and she had to have suffered considerably more than I did.

Within the next few days her oncologist scheduled an infusion of treat her cancer in Merced. Once home, she vomited, had the dry heaves, had uncontrollable diarrhea, and further weakness. Three days later she had a scan to check on her cancer. Afterward, I took her to see her primary care doctor who confirmed that her cancer had metastasized.

After hearing the results of the scan, JoAnn looked at her doctor and said emphatically, "I want to die. I thought that chemo would help me but I'm too sick to have any more infusions and what I've taken hasn't worked."

The doctor said nothing for two minutes. The silence in the room was tense. JoAnn broke the quiet by saying to the doctor, "What are you thinking?"

The doctor finally said, "I'm sad."

Moments passed and then the doctor said, "I'll call hospice if you like. You'll need to be referred."

"Can you arrange for hospice to care for me in Manteca? That's where my daughter lives and she has agreed to let me stay with her."

"Of course, I'll call today."

I took JoAnn home and helped her pack some things to take with her to Caroline's. I called Caroline on her cell phone and told her of JoAnn's decision.

"I'm in Tahoe and won't be home until late afternoon."

"I'll take your mom to your house and call the hospice number I have been given and wait for you to come home," I said.

I went home and told my wife Donna what had happened at the doctor's office and then I began to cry. She comforted me until I regained my composure.

"I'd better go now Donna. JoAnn is waiting and she is not doing well."

Donna nodded and hugged me.

When I picked up JoAnn I told her that Caroline wouldn't be home until late afternoon.

"Will you stay with me until she comes home?"

"Yes, of course, I won't leave you alone. I'll get you registered with hospice and we'll wait for Caroline to come home."

I drove JoAnn the 50 miles to Manteca and called hospice. Within 30 minutes a young woman arrived and went through the registration procedures with JoAnn. Caroline didn't come home until near 5 P.M. I drove back to Merced weary, sad, and teary. I didn't know how long JoAnn would live but I knew she was dying.

I began to reflect about JoAnn's life. She was difficult to deal with but was always there if I needed her. I recalled our childhood together, remembered the stages of our lives, our travels, our experiences and holidays together. I was emotionally spent when I arrived home.

When I arrived home Donna approached me quietly. "Let's sit at the table because I want to tell you something. I know this is a bad time for you but I just got news today while you were gone. I have been experiencing vaginal bleeding and as you know I am well beyond menopause. Tests are underway to determine the exact cause. If I need surgery my doctor recommended a surgeon in the Bay Area and said that's who she would see if she had a problem. She seemed to indicate that I more than likely would need surgery."

I reached over and held my wife because I had a premonition that it was something serious. I had just been confronted with my sister's cancer and was distraught over her impending death and now was facing the person I loved most who was telling me she had a serious problem. Donna didn't cry. She was in much greater control than I was. No one said anything for some moments as this new information sunk in. I was at a new low. My sister would die soon and now my wife was telling me she had a serious malady.

"I want to cancel our trip to Australia," I said. I wanted to be proactive about Donna's condition.

"The doctor said it would be all right if we wanted to go on our trip." Donna counseled. "But I know your sister is now in hospice so if you want to cancel we can."

I called JoAnn and Caroline and told them the news about Donna. I wanted to hear what they thought.

JoAnn said, "I don't know when my time will come but I want you to go on your trip. We never know how many days we all have so, go and enjoy your time with Donna."

For the next several days Donna and I went back and forth as to what to do. We had already bought airline tickets and we planned to see friends in Canberra who were assigned to the American Embassy there in Australia's capital. We also had made plans for stays in Sydney and Melbourne. After considerable thought we decided to go.

We took the long flight to Sydney and began our adventure. Our next stop was Canberra and our friends were at the airport to welcome us. We had a wonderful time for the next several days. We were in a museum when my cell phone rang and it was Donna's OB GYN doctor. She said Donna's tests came back and she had endometrial cancer and it was at stage IIIA. That evening I told Donna what her doctor had said and she was insistent about not telling our hosts the news about her health.

While we were Australia, Caroline sent me a text telling me that her mother and my sister had died on April 3rd. It was a month and two days after I had enrolled her in hospice. JoAnn had made plans to be cremated and have her cremains placed next to her husband Emil in a crypt. Donna was sympathetic and understanding even though she knew that she had cancer and would be facing difficulties ahead.

I reflected about what had just happened to my sister. Like my brother Art, she died without an intimate spouse to comfort her. Her daughter Caroline and her significant other Perry had cared for JoAnn the last month of her life. It included cleaning up after bouts of diarrhea and vomiting. There was a loss of appetite, a loss of weight, weakness, a lack of energy, and the travails of wasting away in a sickened state. It was consoling to me that JoAnn was in Caroline's care but was saddened that she had no husband to provide additional comfort. As Art had experienced, there was the emptiness of dying alone without that special someone in her life.

Donna consoled me as we faced the remaining days of our vacation. We put on a happy face with our hosts in Canberra and went about touring without telling them about JoAnn's death or Donna's cancer.

We continued on to Melbourne afterwards and enjoyed as much of the trip as much could with a heavy cloud hanging over our heads. When we returned home we immediately scheduled an appointment with a surgeon in Walnut Creek and planned for Donna's surgery. We didn't know what the doctor would find and we were extremely anxious. Donna's surgery went well and she recovered reasonably quickly. We were full of anticipation for the follow up visit with her doctor.

"Your lymph nodes were clear of cancer."
I breathed a sigh of relief because I thought that her cancer had not spread.

"You'll need chemotherapy and radiation to assure that all of the cancer is gone," counseled the Walnut Creek doctor.

We found a facility in Modesto and Donna began her chemotherapy treatments. She lost her hair within a week but we had purchased a wig for her and she adjusted to it quickly and went on with life with a positive spirit. Radiation was to follow after her chemo treatments. We fired the first doctor after we learned that some of his patients had been burned with badly executed treatments. We found a wonderful radiation doctor in Merced and her treatments proceeded smoothly.

We were to see her surgeon for a follow up visit after all of Donna's treatments were completed. "You are cancer free in your reproductive organs due to surgery, chemo, and radiation treatment." Her surgeon in Walnut Creek reported.

I again felt relief.

"However, your scan showed that you have a spot on your right lung," the doctor continued. "We'll have to have the spot biopsied to see if it's malignant, that's the next step. But I'm puzzled because I have never heard of endometrial cancer moving to the lung. I'm going to refer you to another oncologist in your home town and have him examine you to get a second opinion."

The oncologist in Merced came to the same conclusion as the doctor in Walnut Creek. He couldn't believe that endometrial cancer traveled to Donna's lung. Her endometrial cancer had been removed surgically, she had undergone chemotherapy and radiation, and yet there was in fact, a spot on Donna's right lung. We didn't know what to expect next.

After our visit with the second doctor Donna declared, "If that's the case, that I now have cancer in my lung, I'm a gonner."

Donna had taken excellent care of herself throughout her life. She ate only good food, avoiding fast food like the plague. She exercised three times a week, read books and joined tow book clubs, and was a gourmet cook. Her dinners became legendarily famous. She was very conscious about her health. We were as puzzled about her cancer as her doctors were.

I took a more rational view. I was not willing to say that Donna was a "gonner." I thought that additional treatments and conferring with her doctors at Stanford would turn up some effective remedy. Yet in the back of my mind I had subliminal doubts. My mother had died from breast cancer. Both my sister and brother had died from cancer. While my relatives were not connected to Donna genetically, I was aware of what could happen to Donna.

Over the span of my life my sister and brother had provided examples of how to live both good and bad lives. Throughout my life I tried to learn from my older sibling's mistakes and avoid the things that had caused problems in their lives. Neither had graduated from high school. JoAnn had dropped out of school her senior year and Art because of failing classes and unconventional behavior, left school as a junior and had mom sign papers to allow him to join the army at age 17.

Because my second stepfather (the first one died after a year of marriage to my mother) was a fortune seeker who tried ranching, owning a bar-restaurant-dance hall, commercial fishing in Alaska, searching for uranium in the four corners of Utah, Colorado, New Mexico, and Arizona, painting houses, and betting on race horses, we moved a great deal. Such moves required that I leave school before the year was out in Arizona causing me to lose a year of credit. Despite all of the moves and attending seven high schools, I did graduate from high school but I was 19 years old when I received my diploma. I went to college, earned a Bachelor's degree, a teaching credential, and a Master's degree. I began a teaching career. I had a stable income and thankfully, met Donna who taught French at the high school where we were both under contract. We bought rental property and invested well to plan for our future. We took sabbaticals and spent six months in Europe.

Both my sister and brother had gone through four marriages and I vowed that I would never get divorced when I married. But I did. My first wife was beautiful and the mother of our two children but had psychological insecurity problems that caused her to successfully attract attention from men and having extra marital affairs. When we divorced she remarried and became an alcoholic and died of cirrhosis of the liver at age 49.

Donna and I had a good marriage and did positive things with our lives. We traveled widely going to Russia, China, Egypt, and all over Europe, Mexico, Costa Rica, Argentina and Uruguay. We visited museums, saw major sights in the United States and Canada, and read widely.

Before I met Donna I covered the Oakland Raiders for Bay Area newspaper and the San Francisco 49ers for the local newspaper in Merced. While we were married I became involved with local political campaigns for trustees on school boards, judges races, mayors, and was a co-chair for a school bond election. We had comfortable incomes, developed good friends, and had a rich social life.

Donna's mother lived to be almost 90 and was for the most part of her life in good health. So was her younger sister Charlotte. So it was not without reason that I believed that Donna would live a long and full life. Her mother earlier, in her life, had cancer in her cervix. She had surgery and recovered to live a long, productive, and active life afterward. I believed Donna would overcome her cancer in spite of the new growth in her lung.

Also, Donna was a fighter and took on her disease aggressively. She followed every instruction given to her by her doctors, to the letter. She was not afraid of chemotherapy or radiation and actively researched the best doctors, treatments, and medicines. She read books on the best diet for cancer patients.

Chemotherapy had caused all of her hair to fall out soon after her first infusion but she wore a wig when the she went out of the house and didn't feel awkward in social situations.

"You have to have the growth on your lung biopsied to determine exactly what it is," her doctor reminded us.

We scheduled an appointment with a pulmonary surgeon in Modesto who was recommended to us. He passed us on to another doctor who would actually perform the biopsy. The results came back and they were not good. Her tumor was malignant.

Another scan showed not only the growth on Donna's lung but also a growth on her right adrenal gland. We scheduled a visit with a doctor at Stanford University Medical Center.

"You have to have two surgeries. One to remove the tissue in your lung and another to take out your adrenal gland," the Stanford doctor said.

Donna was scheduled to see her first surgeon in Walnut Creek for a checkup and we shared the information with him about Stanford's recommendation.

"Why have two surgeries?" You will have to go through anesthesia twice and that will be hard on you. Why not take out both growths in one surgery?" He asked.

That's what we were thinking but the Stanford team was insistent on two surgeries," I said. "Can you remove both growths in one surgery?"

"Yes, that's what I think should happen. There will be two surgeons, one a thoracic specialist and I will take out the adrenal gland. I will have to take out the whole gland because the growth is too big but you only need one adrenal gland to function so you'll be fine afterward."

"Can we schedule the surgeries with you now?"

"Let me call a thoracic surgeon who is on the staff at John Muir Hospital with me. I'll see if she is available at a time when we both can work together to take care of Donna."

The doctor left our examination room and made a phone call. He came back within five minutes and said, "The thoracic surgeon is available in ten days and I can clear my schedule to take out the adrenal gland after she removes the growth in Donna's lung."

Donna and I agreed that this was the best way to treat her cancer. We accepted the date for surgery ten days hence and cancelled our appointment with Stanford.

We arrived in Walnut Creek at nine in the morning on the day of Donna' surgery. She was scheduled to begin her first surgery at one that afternoon. I was with Donna until she was taken into surgery. It was estimated that the two surgeries would take three hours. I waited at the hospital and at six o'clock Donna was not out of surgery. At seven the doctor who removed her adrenal gland came to see me and said both surgeries went well but the thoracic surgeon had to take out the middle lobe of her right lung, another setback suggesting that things were more serious that we had thought. Donna had been under anesthetic for over five hours. The doctor said she was being transferred to the intensive care unit.

I was not allowed to see her until the next day. When I arrived I was stunned by what I saw. She was hooked up to tubes for breathing, intravenous tubes for sugar and salt infusion, and a catheter for urine removal. Without her wig she looked like a cadaver. She was pale and unconscious. She looked very sick. I waited several hours before she opened her eyes and looked at me. Her eyes were glazed over and had no focus. I took her hand and she squeezed it to let me know that she knew I was there.

I visited her every day. I stayed at a motel at night and was at the hospital all day. I was told that the hospital staff wanted to transfer her to a regular room after two days but none was available because the hospital was so full. She therefore had to stay in ICU. Donna hated it because she was not allowed to walk. She was able to talk to me but was having trouble having a bowel movement, a condition that often happens after surgery.

Finally after five days in ICU, a room opened up in the regular hospital and she was transferred over. She now began to recover more quickly. I learned that she had two incisions, one below her right shoulder blade on her back and one on her lower abdomen. Both scars hurt and required pain medication. She was able to walk but had to roll a metal post with her that had her IV's attached that provided the medicine she needed for pain.

I was able to take her home in the middle of November. She was still weak. Thanksgiving had been our holiday to host family and friends for the last 20 plus years. At times we had over 20 guests for Thanksgiving dinner, requiring that we cook two turkeys. Donna always put on a dinner that was amazing for its quality, diversity, and beautiful presentation. Now this was not possible for this Thanksgiving. I was most grateful to have Donna's surgeries behind her and have her home.

We pared down the guest list and for the first time in our lives bought a pre-cooked Thanksgiving dinner. The whole day had a different feel to it. I wondered if we would ever have a traditional Thanksgiving dinner again.

I had been diagnosed with breast cancer earlier that summer. It is very rare in men with less than one per cent having this malady. I had a modified mastectomy in August and once recovered, began chemo therapy I October. After the first infusion the veins in my right arm were as hard as electric wire because the chemo had a damaging effect. I was told to have a port inserted to make my chemo therapy go easier on my veins. I had surgery to have my port installed. I too, had lost my hair so that Donna and I were both bald in November. This was our worst Thanksgiving.

My son Jon and his wonderful wife Diane came over from Watsonville to share our Thanksgiving dinner with us which made things a little better.

Days later we heard, "There's a drug that might help you," Donna's local oncologist offered. "It is expensive but it may be of benefit due to the results of your genetic testing."

We ordered the drug. It was $2600.00 for 28 tablets.

"We can't afford to pay for the tablets," Donna said.

"I have been thinking about that. If I have to drop out of the country club and go back to substitute teaching, we can easily pay for the drug." I stated.

"NO!" Donna emphatically shouted.

"Let me look at our finances before we reject the order for the drug." I said.

I went to our stock broker and reviewed our portfolio. We had enough money to pay for the drug and after the first month, we entered a new category for drug coverage called "Catastrophic" which lowered the price from $2600.00 a month to $700.00 for the 28 tablets.

Unfortunately for Donna, the drug did not stem the growth of the cancer in her lungs.

We didn't know what other treatments were available after this latest failure. We both began to accept the fact that she was dying. We didn't talk about it with each other but I came to realize that I would be alone without her at some point in the future. I was heartsick about Donna's condition. Here was this intelligent, educated, accomplished woman struggling to survive and there was nothing that seemed to help her. Our life together would end and when I thought about it, I would breakdown and cry. I was sorry for what Donna was going through and felt sorry for myself for the loss of the most important person in my life. I didn't cry in front of Donna because she was dealing with the seriousness of her diminishing health and didn't need to attend to my depression.

"Come over for a little Christmas cheer and an enjoyable potluck treat," Nancy our neighbor and colleague who lived a block away, happily invited us.

"What can we bring?" I asked. Nancy always had such good treats at her party that guests embellished by bringing Hors d oeuvres.

"Don't bring anything. Donna's provided me with so many dinners that were so wonderful that I would feel guilty if you brought anything. Plus you and Donna have had some serious health problems and don't need to be burdened with making something to being."

Donna and I had enjoyed Nancy's Christmas gatherings for many years and always looked forward to them. This year we hoped to just appreciate the people attending her function. The evening of the party came on Saturday December 7, 2014. We arrived and sampled some of the goodies on the potluck table. We talked with the guests, many of whom were former teachers and got caught up on their lives. Donna wore her wig and I wore a cap and together they covered our bald heads.

"I didn't sample enough food tonight. I'm still hungry. Let's get a burger." Donna said.

"I'm hungry too and a burger sounds good. " I agreed.

We went to a fast food spot and ate burgers and finally felt full. However, in the middle of the night we both had the runs and spent more time in the bathroom than in the bedroom. I vomited as well which made for a long night.

I was scheduled to have my third cycle of chemotherapy on Monday December 9th, 2014. When I arrived I was shown into an examination room and a nurse took my vitals. She then began to ask questions about my health.

"Have you had any vomiting or diarrhea in the last few days?" the nurse asked.

"No," I lied. I wanted to get my chemotherapy over with as soon as I could so I could go on with my life free of those cell-killing toxins. I only needed one more cycle after this one.

The doctor whom I saw within the next half hour gave me the green light to go forward with my next round of chemo. I sat in the chair as the injection of chemicals was infused into my port. I felt fine afterward and returned home that Monday afternoon. That night I began to have liquid stools. A black brackish fluid flowed out of me and it required me to go to the bathroom every few minutes. Next came vomiting, several bouts of it necessitating more trips to the bathroom in a frantic rush to avoid spilling bile on the floor.

The next day I couldn't hold any solid food down. The diarrhea continued as well and I was becoming dehydrated. I tried to swallow soup but most of it came back up in minutes. What little remained inside soon sent me rushing to the toilet to expel murky fluid from my bowels.

Within the next two weeks I lost 14 pounds in 14 days. I was surviving by drinking Gatorade to keep my electrolytes up and eating Activia to supply probiotics. I had no appetite. I forced myself to eat and drink. I had no energy. To walk into the garage took so much out of me that I had to pause to regain my strength. I couldn't leave the house for fear of having to rush to a toilet for an emergency stop.

Donna, who was still recovering from her major surgery, tried her best to nurse me back to health. She was the one going to the store to buy my Gatorade and Activia while recuperating. Together we were a medical mess.

The horrible effects of chemotherapy lasted for 35 days. I wasn't until the middle of January that I began to feel myself gain on my debilitated state. Slowly the chemicals started to exit my body.

"How are you feeling now?" My oncologist asked.

"Doctor, I have been back here several times and have taken injections to help me feel better but I am only now beginning to feel that I am recovering from chemotherapy."

"Well you only have one more cycle to go and then I want to give you a smaller dose once a week for eight more weeks."

"With respect sir, I am not going to take any more chemotherapy. I believe I had food poisoning before my last cycle but the chemo almost killed me. I know you think I still need chemo but I don't want to take any more."

"My job is to inform you, to educate you about your cancer and recommended therapies and let you decide what course of action you want to take."

He was being gratuitous and his demeanor suggested that I continue with chemotherapy. I had done some medical research and had two other doctors tell me that I could take Tamoxifen in place of chemotherapy.

"Doctor, I don't want to seem disrespectful but I am not going to take any more chemo. I hope you understand. I would like to take a pharmaceutical regimen instead."

"Very well, I'll prescribe Anastrozole for you. It's a hormone and hopefully it will control your cancer."

"Why not prescribe Tamoxifen?" I asked.

"You have a high content of iron in your blood and you are getting phlebotomies to reduce the chance of strokes and heart attacks so this drug will be better for you."

So I began to take his recommended pill. I was called in two months later for a checkup and another doctor would have to see me because my regular oncologist was on vacation.

"Good morning," the substitute doctor said to greet me.

"Good morning doctor, it is a pleasure to meet you."

His next comment shocked me.

"Do you still have your gonads?"

391

I looked at him puzzled. He must have misread my chart because my cancer had been in my breast.

"Doctor, my cancer was up here," pointing to my chest, "not down there" directing my finger at my groin.

"I know that you have had breast cancer but Anastrozole is a drug that competes with the hormones that your testicles produce. You should be taking Tamoxifen."

"I'd like you to write a prescription for me today so that I can begin to take Tamoxifen tomorrow. And thank you for your recommendation."

I began my new drug and Donna's hair began to grow out and she started to return to her beautiful self. Things were starting to appear better for us because we felt better and looked better. However, looming overhead was the knowledge that no chemotherapy had produced cure for Donna and we were still probing to find something that would work.

"Let's take a trip" we said to one another almost simultaneously.

We ruled out Europe due to its distance and wear and tear. I suggested the Boston area and a visit with my daughter Kathy in Pennsylvania. Donna wanted to add Martha's Vineyard. Once we agreed, Donna got on our computer and put together a plan with air transport, hotels, and a list of restaurants. I made arrangements for a car rental.

We set out in June and arrived in Boston, got our car and found our first hotel. The traffic was so congested we sometimes parked the car and took metros. We did the Freedom Trail and all of the sites in Boston, drove to Quincy and toured John Adams' and John Quincy Adams' houses. We traveled to the ferry that took us to Martha's Vineyard and spent a pleasant day.

We took to the highways to travel to Reading, Pennsylvania where Kathy my daughter lived. We had a really good visit with her and Kolton, my grandson who was doing well in high tech. We were entertained by Evie my great granddaughter, who has an irrepressible positive spirit.

We returned home and traveled to Cayucos where friends had rented a house looking over the ocean, and had invited us to join them. Donna's shortness of breath became more pronounced. Walking far distances was out of the question. We were able to take short walks on the beach and enjoy the pleasant breezes as we picked up sand dollar shells.

We knew once this visit was over Donna had to go to Stanford to meet with their head of oncology. When we arrived we were directed to a special building where the doctor worked. He was an older Asian man, tall and very confident in his abilities. He reviewed Donna's file, her scans, and her other doctor's opinions.

"You are one of only a dozen people in the world who has this rare kind of endometrial cancer, the doctor said. "We don't have enough of a sample of people who have this kind of cancer to identify a treatment that we can be sure of and will be effective. We use our traditional chemotherapy drugs not knowing whether they will help you. Honestly we are in the dark as to what will work."

"I'm going to refer you to our best chemotherapist here at Stanford and she will recommend what she thinks will be best for you."

Now Donna and I both knew she had been given a death sentence. We didn't discuss things but we both knew she would die. We survived however by trying against hope to follow her doctor's order about chemotherapy.

We met with the chemo specialist and she recommended a new regimen of chemotherapy for Donna. We returned to Merced and planned to get started with the new chemo cocktail.

However, Donna had a problem with respiration. Her pulmonologist prescribed oxygen for her and two tanks were delivered with a wheeled cart and breathing tubes. It helped her oxygen intake but she still had trouble taking deep breaths. Two weeks later things got worse.

"I can't breathe," Donna's forced words came out.

It was a Monday morning.

"Do you want to go to emergency?"

Our experiences with the emergency room in Merced in the past had been a nightmare. Hours of time with full waiting rooms of people and a slow processing staff made for terrible encounters.

Donna said she would like to wait to see if her breathing got better. By 9:30 she had not improved and wanted to go to the hospital.

We arrived at 10 A.M. and I got one of the hospital's wheel chairs and guided her in with her oxygen tank and breathing tubes. Thankfully, she was triaged and entered registration ahead of other waiting patients. She was taken to an exam room and her vitals were taken but then we sat for hours without seeing a doctor.

I got lunch for Donna at the hospital cafeteria and tried to bring it to her but was denied by a registration employee who said he couldn't find her in any room and couldn't admit me into the emergency section of the hospital unless she could be found on his computer. I was angry and frantic. I found a way to sneak in through another door and we ate lunch together.

"Mrs. Evans, I can examine you now," a woman emergency doctor stated.

It was 4 P.M., six hours after we entered. A nurse hooked up an oxygen supply tube from a valve protruding from the wall for Donna. She increased the amount of oxygen to be delivered to Donna. At 6 P.M. Donna had not received any medicine or treatment except for the oxygen. No treatments were given to her to relieve her breathing difficulty.

"Can you admit her to a hospital room doctor?" I asked.

"We have to meet a certain level of medical criteria before we can justify admitting patients." She explained.

"Surely you can see she is not getting better and that increased oxygen is not significantly improving her ability to breathe," I pleaded. "Can you please find a way to admit her so further tests can be done to try to discover what's wrong and apply a helpful treatment?"

The doctor was sympathetic and left to check a computer and look in on other patients. By 7 P.M. she came back and said she had received the approval she needed to admit Donna. We were both relieved but over the next two hours no one came to move her to a room in the upstairs hospital. The only contact came when a staff person brought Donna a small dinner.

With difficulty Donna said, "I want you to go and get some dinner then go home and feed the dog and then get some rest. At some point I will be admitted and you need to take care of yourself and the dog."

Reluctantly, I took her advice and left but I was angry that more had not been done for Donna. I was also worried about her condition. When I went to bed I fell into a deep sleep and was surprised the next morning that I had slept so well.

I got up at 6 A.M., fed the dog and toasted a half of a bagel for myself. When I got to the hospital I was told where Donna's room was and went up to see her.

"I was not admitted until 3 A.M." She said weakly.

My anger surfaced but found no outlet to direct it. It simmered in me and almost burst out when her pulmonologists came in. Before I could say anything he stated.

"We found why your breathing is so labored. You have fluid on your lung and it has to be drained. I have made arrangements for it be done today, probably this afternoon. And when it's done you will be able to breathe easier.

I was so relieved that finally some treatment was planned that would help Donna. I stayed with her until she was taken for the procedure. She came back to the room and needed to rest. I left her a note that I would come back later with a decent dinner for her to eat from a nearby restaurant. I went to an Italian restaurant and ordered take out of a nice pasta with shrimp and chicken in a curry cream sauce. When I came back to the hospital she and I enjoyed a meal together happily. Her breathing was improved but follow up tests would be needed before she could be released from the hospital. That took several days but she was finally cleared and we were both overjoyed when she was again home.

Donna's birthday was September 12th. I asked her if she wanted anything special for her 71st birthday.

She looked at me and said pleadingly, "I'm basically living in a wheelchair so the birthday present I want most is your love and devotion."

I bent down and held her close to me and said, "You will always both my love and my devotion. I love you and I will always be here for you. I will never leave you alone."

By now it was the middle of September. She still had shortness of breath and her pulmonologist prescribed increased doses of medicine for her. The medicine had a marginal effect on her. She got worse and was admitted back into the hospital in late September. Her scans indicated that her cancer in the bottom of her right lung had grown and that there was another new growth in her left lung. The prescribed medical treatment for her was radiation to reduce the size of the tumors and then consider a new round of chemotherapy. She was also provided with an oxygen machine for her to use at our home.

She came home but while in the hospital she developed bed sores that wouldn't heal so a home care nurse was assigned to deal with her problem at our house. The scores got worse and Donna had to be taken to the wound doctor for outpatient surgery. By now she could barely walk. A friend loaned us a wheelchair. It was the only way she could leave the house to see her doctors.

Her radiation treatments began in Merced's cancer center under the direction of an outstanding doctor whom everyone believed was extremely competent. Donna had trouble walking because it taxed her breathing and her legs were weak so we used the wheelchair to get her into the car and then into the radiation treatment room. Her treatments began to shrink her tumors and Donna showed some improvement. She began to walk again but slowly. We could go out to restaurants again but movies would be too difficult for her because she would have to climb stairs to find a seat and her legs were too weak for that.

My son Jon and daughter-in-law came over for a visit and we went to a restaurant together. Donna had to take deep breaths to finish a sentence.

During the next few weeks Donna's condition worsened. It was a struggle to get her in the car and go out anywhere. I was only too glad to do all of the shopping, cooking, cleaning, dog walking, yard work, etc. while Donna fought against her cancer.

"I can't get into bed," Donna admitted in somewhat of a panicked state one evening.

It was the first time during her illness that she couldn't get in bed by herself.

"I'll help you sweetie," I said. I pulled down the covers on the bed and lifted her from the wheel chair where she was sitting and sat her on the bed. I then lifted her legs into the bed and covered her. I put additional pillows behind her head to elevate her so her breathing wouldn't be so labored.

One a Saturday evening in late October, we decided to go out to a restaurant for dinner. Our plan was for me to drive to the front of the establishment and let Donna out so she wouldn't have to walk so far because walking taxed her breathing. When we arrived by the front door I stopped in the street and let Donna out. When she closed the car door I drove 30 feet to a parking lot and entered. I looked back to see how Donna was doing and I saw she had fallen in the gutter. I stopped the car, got out and ran to help her. I couldn't lift her up however. Her legs were so weak she couldn't push them up to stand. A young man came by and I asked for help. He was able to lift Donna to her feet and her legs held. People who were sitting by the window in the restaurant looked on and it was embarrassing for both of us to be the subjects of this heartbreaking scene.

Once Donna was standing I asked, "Do you still want to go inside or would you like to go home. I can make something for us to eat if you don't feel like eating here."

She paused to think about our situation. "I'd like to go inside to see if I can sit at a high table with bar chairs. If I sit down at a regular table, I won't be able to get up."

"I'll make sure we have a high table when we go inside and if we can't get one, we'll go home," I promised.

We went inside and we knew some people who were waiting for dinner. I found a high table with chairs that had a higher seat. A few minutes later, another couple came inside and joined the people whom we knew. We ordered our dinner and we noticed that the people we knew looked at us with concerned looks on their faces. They glanced away and began to talk and it was clear they were talking about Donna's fall outside by the sidewalk.

We finished our dinner and began to leave. One of the people we knew came over to ask if we needed help getting to the car. I thanked him and told him that Donna was weak from her cancer but we could manage.

When we got home I said, "I think when we go out again we'd better use the wheelchair to roll you into a restaurant.

Donna looked beaten down but grudgingly agreed that the wheelchair was the best option when we went out again. To not be able to walk meant that another part of life had been surrendered. We both felt depressed with this new reality.

The next Sunday we sent out for breakfast and used the wheelchair to get Donna into the car, from the car into the restaurant, and get her placed at a table. Things went well. We did the same thing the next Sunday and joined friends for breakfast.

But now another issue confronted Donna. She could no longer use the bathroom by herself. A friend who had worked for hospice loaned us an elevated seat for the toilet and I assisted Donna when she need to go to the bathroom, I would lift her from the wheelchair onto the seat and when she was finished, lift her back into the wheelchair.

By November 10th, 2015 I was feeling overwhelmed. Donna's mind was no longer able to process how simple tasks would be performed. I would go over things with her several times but she couldn't get a clear understanding as to what would happen. She would resist me if I tried to show her how things would work. I could no longer care for her alone. I went into the garage so she wouldn't see me, and cried. I felt I had let her down even though I had tried my very best to provide everything she needed. A week or so before Donna had offered to enter a care facility to relieve me of taking care of her. I had broken down and cried then as well. I didn't want her to be in a place where someone who loved her could not be at her side. Donna had told me earlier that she didn't want to die in a hospital and I wanted to make sure that her request was honored.

When I got my composure back, I called her primary care physician and asked him to call hospice and refer Donna so she could receive their services. It was Wednesday November 11th, 2015, Veterans Day.

On Thursday, the hospice nurse came with equipment and enrolled Donna in their program. A hospital bed was placed in our living room, a tall portable toilet was stationed next to the bed and a bath was scheduled for Donna. The bath was performed while Donna was lying down and she was washed in stages. In included a shampoo and afterward she felt better. She gave me a "thumbs up" sign instead of talking because speaking was difficult for her due to a lack of air in her lungs.

Donna still couldn't understand how I was going to lift her from the bed and onto the portable toilet. When I tried to show her, she objected and would not cooperate until she had it clear in her mind where she would be lifted out of bed and how she would be turned to be seated on the toilet.

I knew now that cancer had spread to her brain. I was patient with her and asked if she trusted me to have her best interests in mind when I cared for her. She indicated that she did. I asked if she had confidence in me to go through a trial run at getting her out of bed and sitting her on the toilet. She agreed after a half an hour of talking. I was able to easily lift her from the elevated bed and held her while her feet felt the floor and she could straighten her legs to stand. I turned her toward the toilet and gently sat her down. We repeated the process several times until she gradually gained assurance that the task could be done easily.

Because she peed the bed that night, she asked for a catheter to be inserted into her urinary tract so she would not have an accident in bed in the future. It was Saturday. Donna was constipated and that was going to be the next issue to be dealt with in the near future. The hospice nurse put in a catheter and made sure things were working properly before she left for the day. Donna was not eating much now and drank Ensure to keep her nutrients up. She seemed more at ease even though she was bed ridden and very limited as to what she could do. She was very sick now but more comfortable.

On Saturday night I held her hand and told her I loved her and that I would take good care of her. I asked if there was anything I could do for her before I went to bed.

"Make sure my oxygen machine is turned up to three."

"I'll do it right now," I said and went over to the machine that was now running 24 hours a day, and moved the dial from 2 ½ to 3. "Is that better?" I asked and she nodded affirmatively.

I went to bed around 10 P.M. and felt somewhat better because Donna seemed a little more relaxed. I woke up the next morning around 7 A.M. and came into the living room to check on Donna.

"Oxygen," she struggled to say.

I could see that her breathing was more labored so I turned up the oxygen machine to full blast and hoped it would help her have more relief. It did momentarily. I kept a close watch on her for the next hour and then called the hospice nurse who was on call that Sunday. She said she would come to our house after she checked on some of her other patients. I indicated that Donna was having trouble breathing and asked if she could come over soon.

The nurse arrived at 9:30 and looked at Donna's legs.

"If you want to say something to her you'd better say it now. She will be gone today."

"Donna, can you hear me?" I said in a raised voice.

She barely moved her head to indicate that she could.

"I love you and I will be here with you." I took her hand. It was becoming more limp. I put the oxygen monitor on her finger and the level was 76. Anything below 90 was a cause for concern. It was clear that the hospice nurse was correct and that Donna was dying.

Her breathing became more of a gasp. Her chest heaved trying to gain more air. At 10:45 the oxygen monitor read 64. Her eyes were beginning to glaze over. She could no longer hear me. At 11:10 her heart stopped.

I dropped my head in my hands and began to cry.

The hospice nurse encouraged me to inform relatives of Donna's passing. With a heavy heart I went into the computer room and began to text her sister, my son and daughter-in-law, and close friends.

The hospice nurse contacted the funeral home and within an hour the morticians arrived, covered Donna's body and took her away.

The hospice nurse tried to comfort me by giving me a hug. She said, "You did everything you could to help her."

I began to cry again as she left. I thanked her for caring for Donna. My voice was weak from grief.

I was now alone with the hospice bed and other items hospice had sent over to aid Donna. It was a grim reminder of events of the last four days. I began to reflect on Donna's life. She was so intelligent, competent, cultured, an exceptional teacher, a gourmet cook, well read, a compassionate friend, and was a wonderful companion to me and who was the most important person in my life. And now she was gone after suffering through the painful stages of an unconquerable disease. So much was taken away in her last struggling breaths. I felt empty, forlorn, and isolated. It was cold outside in the November wind but inside the house, my heart was as cold as ice.

My phone rang and it was my son who said he and Diane, his wife were on their way to be with me. Within two hours they had driven over 100 miles to be with me and provide me with supportive comfort. We ordered pizza to be delivered because I was in no shape to go out in public and certainly didn't feel like cooking. They stayed the night and left the next morning. Both work so hard at their jobs, Diane for an accountant and Jon who owns a machine shop. They had to get back to work. I appreciated that they made the effort to get me through that first night without Donna.

Several days before Donna's passing I knew she was dying so I had initiated funeral plans. They were not completed when she passed away. Donna indicated to me that she didn't want to die in a hospital and didn't want to be cremated. I was pleased that Donna had died at home and I was in the process of planning for her burial. I had selected a casket, flower arrangements, music to be played, and had provided hundreds of pictures to be posted on a story board.

Donna's sister Charlotte, whom everyone called Charlie, came out from Colorado Springs and together we finalized the remaining arrangements for Donna's funeral. I had written a eulogy in the form of a letter to Donna and asked a well-spoken lawyer friend to read it at Donna's service. I knew I would break down if I tried to present my last words to Donna. Charlie and her son Douglas wanted to speak at her service as well. After our eulogies were given many guests rose and spoke of the impact Donna had on their lives and their words were a moving tribute to Donna.

401

The service went beautifully and I know Donna would have been pleased with everything. We went to the grave site and I asked those attending to bow their heads and observe a moment of silence.

I had planned for a reception to be held at my country club and the manager made sure everything was perfectly in order. I was moved that people had come so far, some coming several hundred miles to attend Donna's service. I was doubly taken aback by my son Jon's in-laws whom I had met only a few times, yet came to Donna service.

After the service Charlie helped me find addresses for thank you cards at a time when I was unable to function well. I mailed cards out the day after Donna's funeral and Charlie helped me for the next several days by identifying items of Donna's to be given to family and friends.

In the days following Donna's service when everyone had left, our many friends offered dinners and support to help me survive the next several days. I felt truly blessed to have such wonderful people I my life.

Thanksgiving was only seven days away and I wanted to host our traditional dinner with Jon and Diane as well as Donna's friends who had attended our Thanksgiving for so many years. Donna's friends bought all of the dinner items and Jon and Diane came over from Watsonville for the meal. Traditionally, I always said a few words about Thanksgiving before we ate our dinner. At this meal I said, "This is the worst Thanksgiving in my life but I am grateful for my family and my friends," and I meant it.

What followed was a great sense of loss for me because I realized that I could no longer talk to Donna anymore. We had such great conversations. We would talk about philosophy, books, movies, history, politics, about family and friends, about problems as they came up, and plans for vacations. There was an additional void when I realized that we wouldn't be going to restaurants, movies, museums, or trips together again. Her famous dinners with good friends and family would be no more.

I felt and agony that I could no longer touch her, kiss her, hold her, or make love with her ever again. We had been married 40 years and now so much was taken away. I had been lonely at times in my life before but never like this.

There were flashes of anger, maybe lasting five seconds. I was angry at Donna for not getting regular medical checkups because perhaps her condition might have been detected sooner and something could have been done to save her life. I was angry at cancer, a disease that had taken my grandmother, aunt, mother, sister, and brother's lives and now Donna. I would regain my sanity when I realized that nothing could be done to change things and I had to face reality and try my best to go on.

What helped was the gratitude I had for the good things in my life. Donna and I had planned well for our financial future. We had no mortgage, had a nice portfolio that provided enough income, and had no car payments. I was so grateful for friends and family who stepped in with caring thoughts and actions. I was included in dinners, concerts, movies, and a genuine feeling of concern. People told me things Donna had done to make their lives better. Moreover, I was reassured that they were there if I needed anything. I will never forget the warmth of humanity that was extended to me.

There was another sense that impacted me. I had a feeling of relief that Donna's suffering was over. She was taken from me but cancer couldn't hurt her anymore.

There was an odd impression that the little things that annoy people in a relationship were now gone. Disagreements about driving directions, being on time or late to events, and Donna's pickiness about food; these petty things were now out of my life. However, I would gladly endure them again if I could have Donna back in my life.

I took solace for my role in Donna's care. As I reflected on all that had happened over the last 2 ½ years I was relieved to know that I had done everything I could for her. I had given unwavering support to her. I drove her to her doctor's appointments, to chemotherapy, to radiation treatments, procured all of her medicines from pharmacies with long lines of people waiting to be served. I cooked meals creating weekly menus and then shopped for the ingredients. I cleaned the house vacuuming, scrubbing floors, dusting, and cleaning counters. I took care of the house doing all of the little repairs that show up when they are least expected. I mowed and edged the lawn, sprayed weeds, trimmed bushes, and swept the patio. I helped her as long as I could getting her into and out of bed, helping her dress and undress, aiding her by getting her onto the toilet, buying medical equipment such as rubber sheets and medical supplies. I lived up to the matrimonial phrase, "in sickness and in health." It was expected that I provide all of the things that Donna needed but I was glad that I truly wanted to help her and didn't feel like she was a burden to me. I respected her so much and she was so deserving of everything I could give her. I only wish that she had a better outcome.

Once things settled down I wondered about my future. What will happen to me when I can no longer be able to take care of myself? Donna suggested that I sell everything and move close to Jon and Diane. Diane my daughter-in-law has been so open about taking care of me but I hate to be a liability to her and Jon. They both work and really don't have vast amounts of time to deal with me. Diane has said they would find a way to deal with things but I have my doubts. When I broke my arm the day after Christmas I wondered what would happen to me if I had a really serious injury. How would I find care and still maintain the house.

Another thought came to mind. At my age another relationship with another person is limited. Not many women want to take on the encumbrance that someone my age might have. I am in good health at the moment but I won't always be so. Donna and I never talked about either of us having a relationship after one of us was gone. A friend said that he thought that Donna would want me to have another relationship. I don't think she would object but I don't know when or if I'll want to be involved with someone else.

People often ask me how I'm doing. I usually say I'm doing reasonably well. I have some good public moments and some very lonely private moments. I put on a good public show and I think I'm doing well when I'm alone. But there are times when some little thing is said and I have to turn and walk away because I will break into tears. I can't predict when these times will come. I only know that I'm not completely free of them.

I felt sad when my brother and sister died without any intimate person to care for them during the last stages of their lives. Caroline gave great care for her mother the last month of her life but JoAnn didn't have a mate whom she loved to be at her side. I thought I had planned well to avoid the mistakes my sister and brother had made in not having an intimate person close to me. I had married a woman who was six years younger than me. As Donna and I dated I looked at her age and felt she would surely outlive me and be my caretaker when I was infirm. I didn't marry her because she was younger than me. I married her because I loved her and respected her.

I thought my planned life would make me like the person in the poem "Invictus." I was going to be the "master of my fate, the captain of my soul." I took on fate and planned to beat it. Yet, here I was in the same situation as my brother and sister, 78 years old with no one intimately in my life to share the end of my life.

At this moment, much as I have tried to defeat it, **fate has won.**

Post script

I am now 80 years old in 2018 and writing 2 1/2 years after Donna's passing. During that time I slowly emerged from the grief of losing her. Staying busy helped. I became a volunteer at the Merced County Courthouse Museum, played golf three times a week, and began to workout at a gym three days a week.

I enrolled in a yoga class and the instructor said, "You don't have to stay for the full hour." She saw I was older and hadn't been in her class before.

I took her comment as something of an affront. However, a half an hour into the class I was drenched in sweat, breathing hard, and weak. I walked out of the class to recover from the strain. I realized that I was out of shape and needed to exercise to get back to normal.

Upstairs in the gym was a 29 minute workout station. There are 13 machines that when completed, work the whole body. A person is to work at each station for 45 seconds and a timer sounds a beep to alert you when 45 seconds has expired. You then have 15 seconds to get to the next machine and get set up for another 45 seconds of exercise. I went around each station twice and with a short cool down the workout was 29 minutes. In the next few days I began the 29 minute workout and afterward got on a treadmill for another 20 minutes.

I returned to the yoga class the next week and was able to complete the one hour workout. However, I had broken my arm a month after Donna passed away and many of the moves hurt my arm so I decided to only workout on the 29 minutes machines and spend another 20 minutes on the treadmill.

I traveled to Hawaii twice to see Leslie and Art Primus. Art is in the Air Force and an officer. He was stationed at Hickam Air Base and was given a nice two story home as a housing allowance. I was still suffering emotionally but the Primus family with their two wonderful boys made for an experience that helped take my mind away from my grief. The second visit we met my son Jon and his wife Diane for dinner. Jon paid for scotches for us all after dinner and we had a good time.

In July, 2016 I visited friends in Redding, California and that helped me move forward.

I met a woman at a UC Merced function and asked her to lunch. She agreed and we hit it off immediately. She was tall, had a beautiful face, and laughed easily.

At lunch she said, "I'm separated from my husband."

"How long have you been separated?" I asked.

"Twenty-three years"

"I'm surprised that you haven't gotten divorced."

"We have assets together and we both have had other people in our lives since we separated."

A call came in from one of her daughters on her cell phone. She said she had to take the call. I understood and said, "absolutely, family first," I said.

I asked her if she would join me for a St. Patrick's dinner at my country club. She agreed. I picked her up and went to the dinner. We joined my friends, had dinner and drinks and I drove her home. She invited me in and we cuddled and kissed. I liked her and asked her out for another date. We had a couple of dinners together and I asked if she would like to go to see Kenny G who was playing in town. She said she would. She was bringing me out of my shell of grief. It had been 16 months since Donna passed away.

The performance was terrific and afterward she invited me in when I took her home. I thought things were progressing nicely and looked forward to developing a closer relationship.

"I have to go away for about a week but I'll be home after that," she shared.

"I'd like to take you to dinner when you return."

She agreed.

During her time away we phoned and texted one another and I anxiously waited for her return. I decided to get her a gift, a CD of Kenny G. She called when I in the store and asked what I was doing.

"I'm buying you a gift."

"NOOOO!" she emphatically shouted into the phone.

"Your objection is duly noted but overruled." I replied.

When I picked her up for our next date I decided to take her to a restaurant in Turlock. It was a drive of 20 miles away.

We had barely begun driving when she said, "I don't want to be a couple. I'm very independent and spent a great deal of time with my daughter and grandchildren. It's not personal. Let's just have fun."

Since we had been doing so well together her comment was something of a shock. My experience in relationships told me that if things are going well things progress. And what did she mean about having fun? Sex or just a little smooching, or none at all?

We had dinner and afterward in my parked car I said, "I know you don't want me to buy you gifts but I did and you have to open this," and I handed her the gift wrapped CD.

She opened it and immediately liked it. "It makes me want to kiss you." She did.

We continued to see one another for movies and dinners. But we weren't growing closer. She took one of her grandsons to Costa Rica, she saw her daughters in Los Angeles and in Idaho.

"I like to Meander," she said.

"How about meandering with me,"

We decided to go to Cambria and then see Hearst Castle nearby.

"You have to commit to going if I get tickets and lodging."

She said she would so we went, had a great dinner, and returned to our hotel. We slept together that night but didn't have sex. We saw Hearst Castle the next day and had another nice dinner. We had another night together with snuggling but no intimacy.

By Halloween, the relationship had run its course and I stopped calling.

I was lonely however and wanted someone to care for and for someone to care for me. I tried online dating and that was less than satisfactory. There were some amazing women but the ones that appealed to me lived in the bay area, Sacramento, or Los Angeles. They had education, culture, accomplishment, a zest for living, and had their lives together. The ladies closer to me were less educated, had baggage of one kind or another, and were less interesting.

Recently, I met a lady who has a good personality, has some baggage, but is fun for drinks and dinner with friends. I don't know where this will go but for the moment, we seem to enjoy each other's company.

REFLECTIONS

Looking back on my life I have taken account of my experiences and have ruminated about what has transpired. There have been wise decisions that I have made.

One had to do with marrying Lauri because I was able to have two children from that bonding. I love them both and I think they love me as well. Looking back, it was wise to have them in my life.

My daughter Kathy has had serious mother-daughter issues and struggled with relationships with men. She married three times and had other relationships with men that were laced with drugs, alcohol, serious arguments, and violence. Through several decades she has been plagued with men problems. However, she got some counseling and removed the last negative force in her life and has come to be at peace with living with herself and her own person.

Kathy raised her son Kolton who had a difficult time growing up in a tumultuous household. She nevertheless stuck by him and supported him in his choice to join the National Guard. There, Kolton learned computers and information technology and has carved out a good career for himself.

My son Jon also is skilled in technology. He was always interested in mechanical things as a child. When he got out of high school he went to work in a machine shop and realized that he not only could perform at a high level but wanted to own his own machine shop. He built race cars and actually drove in races. At 21 he had one machine and was in business for himself. He knew the technological part of the business but had to learn how to deal with the business side of an enterprise. He learned how to drum up business, rent shops, buy more equipment, market his products, transport his finished parts, buy insurance for his equipment and benefits for his employees, price his work, factor in tax consequences, and find a way to make a profit in a highly competitive field.

Jon married well. With little experience in dating he found a wonderful person to be his mate. She is intelligent, supportive, ethical, a hard worker in her career in an accounting office, and a great partner. Unfortunately, she had a large cyst on one of her ovaries and had one of her ovaries removed. She miscarried twice and regrettably was not able to have children.

I am blessed to have both of my children in my life.

As wise as it was to marry Lauri it was even wiser to divorce her. She cheated on me more than once. After forgiving the first affair, she continued to be unfaithful. We were young when we married and neither had much experience with the opposite sex. I wanted to get an education and provide for my family. She didn't get behind that decision and her behavior detracted from having a sound family situation. She later married George and had another child. She confessed to me that she had other affairs while married to George. Unfortunately, she became an alcoholic and died a painful death at age 49. In the last few years of her life, we were able to bury some of the hurt she had caused me and have a semblance of friendship. However, it was sad to see her not fulfill her potential as a person and die much too early.

Another wise decision I made was a determination to get an education and a career. It was difficult because of time constraints. I had to work while going to school. In graduate school I worked nights and attended classes during the day. Lauri didn't work after our daughter Kathy was born so I was the breadwinner while being a student.

I was wise to save all of the G.I. Bill educational money I was paid while in school. I came out of college with $4000.00 in the bank which I planned to use to start a life with a house and investments.

I also was prudent in selecting the career I did. Growing up poor before my second stepfather came into our lives made me aware that having little money was not a pleasant way to try to live. Often, we lived from paycheck to paycheck. I never had an allowance. My mother told me she didn't have the money for me to join the Cub Scouts. When my second stepfather arrived, he had made some money during World War II on his farm and grocery store in Wisconsin. However, he made bad choices and lost his money on a ranch in Red Rock, Arizona. He never recovered from that even though he tried several other enterprises which included the bar, restaurant, and dance hall in Wisconsin, commercial fishing in Alaska, panning for gold, searching for uranium, and owning a laundry in Los Angles. We were in the lower middle class strata socially and money was always an issue in the family.

Becoming an educator brought me financial stability. While the money was never top end I nevertheless had steady work and could count on it in planning for my future. Moreover, by teaching nights and in summer school, I could earn a little more money to pay the bills, save and invest. Also, teaching was a middle class job and I earned respect in the community because of my performance.

The most important event in my life was marrying Donna. Not only did we have two incomes now, which allowed for more investments, but she gave so much to me. She was very cultured and broadened my life considerably. She shared her knowledge about wine, good food, museums, travel, and other cultures. She was as loyal a person as Lauri was disloyal. She had her life together. She provided the kind of marriage I had always wanted. She was supportive of our goals and we built a good life together. She was reliable. She earned my respect as a teacher. She was dedicated to her profession and went into education for the right reasons. She was the most important person in my life for so many reasons.

Another good thing in my life had to do with my attitude about trying new things. My love of football led me to talk my way into covering the San Francisco 49ers and the Oakland Raiders for two different newspapers. It gave me many enjoyable experiences of travel, learning how NFL teams function, and getting to know players and coaches. I met other writers with whom I have remained friends for 50 years. I was able to cover playoff games and a Super Bowl.

This same outlook about trying new things led me to also get involved in political campaigns for school board trustees, judges, mayors, legislators, and school bond issues. I found I had a knack for performing the tasks in a campaign competently and even liked doing them. I met some interesting people along the way and further established myself within the community as a responsible person.

As mentioned before, money was an issue growing up. I never wanted to be in the position that my mother was in living close to the next paycheck. I made it a point to save money and invest. I was able to buy a house and pay it off within two years. Donna and I bought rental property and held some of our rentals for 20 years. When we sold the rentals, I was able to invest the in stock market at the right time and make wise choices which led to an expanding portfolio. When I retired and later when Donna retired, we had a nice nest egg and money was not an issue in our lives.

With Donna at my side we both traveled widely. Our experiences expanded our view of the world. Together we went to

Europe several times, visited all of western Europe, eastern Europe, Russia, China, Egypt, 49 of our 50 US states, Canada, Costa Rica, Argentina, and Uruguay. Our travel experiences were used to embellish our lesson plans in our classrooms.

When Donna died I struggled to carry on. There was such emptiness, such a void, and such a radical change in my life. The adjustment is still ongoing

As I close, I look back on my life and realize that I had to overcome a lot of obstacles early in life but fortunately I inherited enough intelligence and drive to surmount most of my difficulties. I am still lonely but reasonably comfortable. Yet the journey continues.

I am pleased that in my career in education I taught close to 10,000 students. I see many of them in their various stages of life and almost unfailingly, I get warm, welcoming, appreciative receptions from them. I like seeing them and they seem to like connecting again with me. I call it my social paycheck as often favors are granted to me, hugs given, smiles expressed, and camaraderie maintained. These exchanges happen almost daily. It is a good feeling to be valued for your life's work. I am grateful and happy for that and look forward to the next time I see one of my former students.

Thank you to all who have made my life interesting and to whom I am indebted. I believe that I have been an example of those who rise above difficulties and become an expression of the triumph of the human spirit.

Best to all, Robert Evans

Made in the USA
Las Vegas, NV
14 June 2022

50185658R00226